T0247950

THE ICON
& THE
IDEALIST

ALSO BY STEPHANIE GORTON

*Citizen Reporters: S. S. McClure, Ida Tarbell,
and the Magazine That Rewrote America*

THE ICON & THE IDEALIST

Margaret Sanger, Mary Ware Dennett,
and the Rivalry That Brought
Birth Control to America

STEPHANIE GORTON

An *Imprint* of HarperCollins*Publishers*

HarperCollins books may be purchased for educational, business,
or sales promotional use. For information, please email the Special
Markets Department at SPsales@harpercollins.com.

Ecco® and HarperCollins® are trademarks of HarperCollins Publishers.

FIRST EDITION

Designed by Patrick Barry

Library of Congress Cataloging-in-Publication Data
has been applied for.

ISBN 978-0-06-303629-1

24 25 26 27 28 LBC 5 4 3 2 1

Contents

Part III: The Wandering Path to Victory

Introduction

Great is truth, but still greater, from a practical point of
view, is silence about truth.
—Aldous Huxley, foreword to *Brave New World* (1946)

I N A BROOKLYN COURTROOM ON Tuesday, April 23, 1929, the
judge and jury heard the case of fifty-seven-year-old Mary Ware
Dennett. Peering brightly through her glasses, Dennett was determined to fight the charge leveled against her: a federal indictment
for obscenity.

An artist and activist long divorced, Dennett had written a sex
education booklet, *The Sex Side of Life*, for her two teenaged sons.
Clear and informative without being moralistic, the pamphlet was
soon sought after by friends, reprinted by the medical press, and sold
directly from Dennett's apartment via mail order.

After a puritanical upbringing whose shadow she had worked hard
to outrun, Dennett had decided the next generation should be better
equipped. Defying the law was not the point—at least, in the beginning. But a vice agent had learned what she was up to and written
to her posing as a customer, and early in 1929, Dennett was charged
with violating the statute known as the Comstock Act.

According to that law, Dennett had crossed the line of decency:
she had written frankly about sex and sent those pages through the
mail. After forty-two minutes, the all-male jury returned a guilty verdict. Reporters hustled out to file their stories: "GRANDMOTHER
FOUND GUILTY," went the headlines.

Dennett stayed steady. When her sentence was announced—a $300 fine—she stood and gave a short speech she'd prepared about how she would rather serve a lengthy prison sentence. The press swarmed around her, and the next day's headlines called the verdict "medieval," speculating the jury must be frightened of sex if they were willing to punish Dennett and try to keep the next generation trapped in the Victorian era.

Dennett herself, meanwhile, balked at the media's fixation on her gray hair. "I am not doddering yet," she told her family.[1] Her perseverance paid off. After that initial decision was reversed on appeal, Dennett's acquittal in the trial for *The Sex Side of Life* was a landmark victory for free speech.

Few history books dwell on Dennett's story, and current debates over sex education and reproductive rights rarely mention her name. But what is interesting about figures like Mary Ware Dennett—the almost-rans, the bright failures, the buried drafts of the past—is that they are liable to suddenly start speaking to us again. We can choose, if we like, to listen.

. . .

Mary Ware Dennett was an inspired and stubborn visionary who shaped today's reproductive-rights and free-speech debates. Yet she is not part of the present imagination in the same way as her contemporary Margaret Sanger, though her work continues to affect us—arguably more broadly. Today, writes Laura Weinrib, a legal scholar, *United States v. Dennett* is viewed as a case that "fundamentally redefined the way that lawyers, judges, and activists understood the category of civil liberties."[2]

Besides her work for sex education and free speech, Dennett spent grueling years in the early 1920s lobbying Congress for contraception to be struck from the federal obscenity statutes. In other words, she fought to legalize birth control. She defied gatekeeping by the federal courts, the medical establishment, and vice-suppression squads, the latter a force to be reckoned with in much of America in the years Dennett was trying to change the law.

If speech about matters of everyday human existence—anatomy, sex, and childbearing—were truly free, and knowledge liberally distributed, then justice, happiness, and peace would follow. So Dennett's thinking went, shaped by early encounters with utopian ideas about gender equality and social justice.

Margaret Sanger, today simultaneously lionized as the founding mother of Planned Parenthood and decried as a eugenicist, is the most famous figure from the birth control struggle. Sanger, seven years younger than Dennett, had a background in nursing, legendary charisma, and a willingness to break the law. She had seen her tubercular mother grow exhausted and finally die after numerous pregnancies, and had tended impoverished patients who died after attempted abortions gone wrong, shunned by doctors and desperate for knowledge.

Sanger and Dennett initially collaborated as activists, as they both became leaders in the birth control cause in 1910s New York. Quickly, however, Sanger branched off, proving adept at raising money and publicity, and becoming the movement's figurehead. Many of her arguments and achievements can be directly traced to her connection to, and her competition with, Dennett. Resurrecting their parallel feats in the birth control movement reveals much about what it takes to maneuver radical ideas from grassroots acceptance to legal affirmation.

As their campaigns progressed, two rationales for birth control emerged. Both Dennett and Sanger were initially pulled into the movement because of harrowing personal experiences. Dennett's married life had been cruelly affected by repeated accidental pregnancies and traumatic births, while Sanger, working as a visiting nurse in Manhattan's tenements, had seen desperate mothers die after going to agonizing lengths to induce abortions.

However, the humanitarian justification for birth control earned little support in congress. Once Dennett and Sanger developed an economic rationale supporting birth control—a pivot that opened the door to an alliance with the eugenics movement—birth control began to take off.

Dennett was an eccentric activist, generally shunning publicity and spending much of her time on direct lobbying instead of soliciting wealthy donors. Sanger, savvier in many ways, alternately copied and ridiculed Dennett's work, resulting in a combative relationship where one vision bloomed and another faded. Both, however, grew from the same stem, toward the same sky.

. . .

Anyone using birth control today is participating in a ritual as old as the family itself. Ancient Egyptian papyri hold recipes for vaginal contraceptives (made from honey and crocodile dung). Condoms came into use in the sixteenth century, while in eighteenth-century France, the sponge was in favor.

The historical record is packed with products and methods, though undoubtedly many never made it into an archive. White settlers in early nineteenth-century Illinois wondered at the fact that local Kickapoo families had an average of four children, while white families tended toward twice that number.[3]

Birth control access in the United States has been shaped by a range of movements and policies, not all of them benevolent. At the turn of the twentieth century, the question of fertility control had more to do with whether women had the right to decline marital sex. Then the debate shifted to whether women had the right to sex without the intent to conceive. The dichotomies of choice against fate, medical technology against nature, bodily autonomy versus submission to divine will—language used in relation to the abortion rights debate today—first entered the public arena with the movement for birth control.

Dennett's and Sanger's ambitions were based on the possibilities of a new era: a time when many women had more self-determination than their mothers had had. The belief that animated Dennett—

that fertility control is an inalienable right—struck many as daring, amoral, even unnatural. In one of the few formal surveys of attitudes toward sex in her generation, Dr. Clelia Duel Mosher's study of forty-five white women born around 1860, one respondent spoke for many when she said sex without the desire to conceive was a form of prostitution.[4] When Sanger stood trial for distributing contraceptives in 1916, the judge rapidly convicted her, stating in his ruling that women did not have "the right to copulate with a feeling of security that there will be no resulting conception."[5]

Legally, following the Comstock Act of 1873, no goods or information intended as birth control could be distributed through the US mail. Doctors were not taught about contraceptive methods in medical school, though wealthier patients were more likely to find help and sympathy in their family physician. In some states, condoms could be sold for the prevention of disease, and mail-order businesses circumvented the law by marketing syringes and uterine supporters for hygiene, menstrual regularity, and marital harmony. But birth control for its own sake was a socially taboo matter and out of reach for most women.

The 1910s and '20s saw a world war, the rise of film and radio, the startling innovations of modernist literature and art, and a growing contrast between the conservatism and censorship favored by lawmakers and irreverence in the press. That taboo began to crumble early in the twentieth century. By the time of Dennett's trial, the birth control movement had a formidable array of clergy, physicians, lawmakers, and ordinary people supporting it, who were asserting that sex was not always bound to procreation.

The debates over womanhood and bodily autonomy manifested themselves across every facet of culture, from the novels of Nella Larsen and Aldous Huxley and the films of Lois Weber to the revelations of Margaret Mead's *Coming of Age in Samoa* and the blues performers and on-screen vamps whose lives and careers rocked every orthodoxy about what a woman should be, do, and want.[6] The stretch of road from one prevailing viewpoint to the other is the spine of this book. Today, as we are in the midst of another cultural inflection point of questioning gender roles and nuclear-family dynamics, the books and films of this historically transformative period provide captivating, poignant evidence of a society trying to reckon with its oppressive past and uncertain future.

When women won the vote in 1920, they gained a powerful means of political agency. In the eyes of Dennett and Sanger, however, the suffragists shortchanged the larger women's movement by declining any association with the right to birth control. Winning the vote remedied one injustice, but Dennett and Sanger saw a far more grievous inequity in the fact that women lived and often died at the mercy of their own fertility.

Familial responsibilities, unless buffered by layers of servants, kept women out of public life, and the hovering prospect of pregnancy often muted any ambition beyond the domestic sphere. As they pursued the dream of broad (and legal) birth control access, Dennett and Sanger were compelled to bring a taboo topic into the mainstream. They did their utmost to rewrite the rules, redrafting the cultural expectations of family life as they did so.

Like the suffrage campaign, the birth control movement helped set the stage for the feminist consciousness-raising of the second half of the twentieth century. Forty years after Dennett and Sanger concluded their congressional lobbying for birth control, "The personal is political" emerged as the enduring rallying cry of late-1960s feminism. These four words argue every power dynamic is worthy of interrogation—whether in the home or in public life. No issue animates the slogan as powerfully as the question of reproductive rights.

Had Sanger and Dennett heard "The personal is political," they would have immediately connected it with their work. "We now know that there never can be a free humanity until woman is freed from ignorance, and we know, too, that woman can never call herself free until she is mistress of her own body," Sanger wrote, in her February

1918 essay "Morality and Birth Control," calling for women to claim equal freedom to men.

Dennett, meanwhile, wrote her own brief manifesto on what feminism meant to her: "Women are people. That is perhaps the shortest possible explanation of what feminism stands for. . . . Feminism is not the lining up for women against men. Feminism does not imply that women want things as women. They only want to do things, have things, and feel things as people, as half the human race, on equal terms with the other half."[7] Her work for birth control reflected her commitment to a future in which opportunities would no longer be limited on the basis of sex.

The Supreme Court's 1965 *Griswold v. Connecticut* decision affirmed all married Americans had the right to birth control, and the same right was extended to the unmarried with *Eisenstadt v. Baird* in 1972. Even now, however, many strings are still attached to birth control access. More than nineteen million lower-income people of reproductive age live an onerous distance from a clinic that could provide a range of affordable contraceptive options.[8]

That bottleneck is made worse by restrictions targeting abortion, which in practice affect full-spectrum care. Eighteen states restrict public funding, even if directed toward contraception, cancer screenings, and STI testing, from entities that either provide abortions or have an affiliation with an abortion provider.[9]

Lawmakers often struggle to understand the array of birth control methods currently available on the market, and at times they purposely embrace that lack of clarity between what distinguishes contraception from abortion. Texas already has a law denying emergency contraceptives on state healthcare plans. Proposals lurk on the horizon, in Oklahoma, for instance, to entirely ban nonbarrier forms of contraception like IUDs and Plan B, the morning-after pill.

Since the *Dobbs v. Jackson Women's Health Organization* Supreme Court decision that overruled *Roe v. Wade* in June 2022, the fragility of legislating reproductive rights through the courts has been made abundantly clear. Though Dennett and Sanger attempted to legalize birth control through legislation first, pursuing their goal in court eventually yielded a breakthrough—one that now seems vulnerable to attack. When one considers what combative institutions Dennett and Sanger faced in their work, it is equally clear they had no other option if success was to come in their lifetimes.

We can't fully understand today's passionate dialogue around reproductive rights if we don't look back at the history behind our current debates, a point at the start of the twentieth century when Dennett and Sanger launched a mass movement to help American women take control of their fertility. Their characters overlapped just enough to provoke infuriated estrangement. Over time, Dennett and Sanger defined themselves in opposition to each other.

The friction between them began with differences in temperament and extended through their diverging efforts to change the law. The historian Peter C. Engelman compares their rivalry to those of Alexander Hamilton and Aaron Burr, Joan Crawford and Bette Davis, Norman Mailer and Gore Vidal.[10] Perceived slights and insecurities thrived on both sides.

This book's title paints Sanger as an icon and Dennett as an idealist, infinitely oversimplifying them both. When I started reading their letters and diaries, I was fully prepared to write a narrative in which Dennett was the underdog hero of the birth control movement, with Sanger the overcelebrated diva. Dennett's lodestars of free speech and legislation designed to stand the test of time struck me as quintessentially American. The fact that she brought a bill to Congress again and again in pursuit of those ideals—that she was the first to try to legalize birth control nationally, and is so little known—put me in awe of her.

Through five years of reading about her and Sanger, however, all simplicity evaporated. Sanger demonstrated a kind of genius as she built her side of the birth control movement. She painstakingly amassed funds, public attention, and allies among doctors and movie stars alike, and finally gained legal validation for the cause. In the end this is as much a portrait of two crusaders failing in change-averse institutions, specifically Congress and the medical establishment, as it is a dual biography of Sanger's and Dennett's busiest activist years. Working in parallel and rarely conversing, they made the first bid for reproductive agency under the law and navigated a rocky path to success.

They shared biases and a tendency to insist on their own righteousness, too. Dennett and Sanger both expressed eugenicist views, though Sanger embraced the eugenics movement far more fervently and persistently. The rise of eugenics is inseparable from the story of the birth control movement, and we continue to grapple with restrictive definitions of "fit" and "unfit" that were in operation a century ago. As many episodes in this book reveal, Dennett and Sanger were intent on disrupting a specific form of oppression and yet were active in perpetuating another.

Both women helped widen the horizons of society's conventions and the rights of its citizens. The way their decisions played out in politics, law, and healthcare left us with choices and challenges they couldn't have foreseen. In essence, however, many of the ideas and even the language of the reproductive-rights debate have stayed the same. Bodily autonomy for women was not a common notion in Dennett and Sanger's time. They embraced it fully as a birthright too long withheld, propelling us into a future in which the idea of reproductive justice is as powerful and contentious as ever.

Part 1

Sex Education

Mamie Ware

Childhood, a mixture of rebellion and beauty-hunger.
—Mary Ware Dennett, "Curriculum Vitae"

ROM BABYHOOD, MARY COFFIN WARE was called Mamie. She was a precocious, observant child, annoyingly so. Each house where she lived had plenty of books and lively conversation, though she sometimes felt anxious and overemotional in comparison with her elders, who seemed to set an example of propriety she could never hope to match. Her family, she thought, was made of "New England granite."[1]

Mamie's birth on April 4, 1872, came during the slow Massachusetts thaw. Her arrival coincided with a climactic shift, setting off a season of transition from winter stillness to springtime momentum. On that day, the *New York Times'* front page reported that women's suffrage supporters had a hearing before the State Assembly Judiciary Committee in Albany. Railroad tracks were being cleared of snow for the season. The Bucksport, Maine, ice gorge was broken, and oyster vessels had begun navigating the Connecticut River again.[2]

The United States was about to turn ninety-four. The Civil War had ended seven years earlier, leaving Americans wary of the next great upheaval. When Mamie Ware was six months old, Susan B. Anthony illegally cast a ballot. When she was two, Alexander Graham Bell assembled his first telephone. In her eighth year, Edison patented his light bulb.

Little of this touched Mamie's early life. She was often turned inward, and she was self-conscious about her body. Like the rest of her family, she had pink-and-white skin, fair hair, average stature, and iffy eyesight. As she grew she developed breasts that, privately, she was proud of. But society seemed to expect her to keep her body hidden away, even from herself. It made a "profound impression," she wrote much later, seeing how her aunts took their baths. They did so clothed in a "long-sleeved, high-necked night gown" washing "from head to foot without once unbuttoning that stern white cotton emblem of modesty." The sight was a silent reproach that Mamie would be, as she recalled, "a very shocking and reprehensible little girl if I did not take my own bath in the same manner."[3]

Walking home from school one day with two friends, talking of the great romance that marriage must be, she was chagrined when one girl "said impressively, that if she ever married, she would simply let her husband 'have his rights.'"[4] Her own life, she decided, needed more enchantment in it than that.

In a Christmas photograph taken when she was around ten, Mamie Ware stands straight in a ruffled dress and lace collar, her hair drawn back tightly, her hands posed on the back of a glossy wooden chair. Her face is mild and serious, her eyes sober behind her glasses. There is little suggestion of the grief and striving of that year, of which there were plenty. Her seriousness and stubbornness are there, though, casting deep into the camera's eye.

She looks like she already regards life as "a mixture of rebellion and beauty-hunger"[5] —the two poles pulling her into a tumultuous future. But her rebellion was for a long time awkward and unpromising. The story she would later tell about her youth painted her as a dreamer who craved affection as much as art, music, and fun.

Her "blessedly humorous" father, George, died of cancer in 1882, the year she turned ten.[6] He had made an uncertain living as a hide and wool merchant, moving his young family from his native Worcester, Massachusetts, to San Antonio, Texas, and back again in the hopes of stabilizing their income. But illness came too soon for him, and he left his widow and their three living children, Mamie, Clara, and Willie, with little in the way of security.

Mamie's mother, Livonia—Vonie, to her family—had no time to retreat into mourning. Her decisions reflected the hopes for self-sufficiency and worldliness she had for her family. She went into business as a tutor-chaperone for young women taking grand tour–inspired trips to Europe. (On one of these journeys she was forced to delay her trip home when a student came down with appendicitis, missing the passage she had booked on the *Titanic*.)

With her mother overseas for long stretches each year, Mamie grew up independent but rarely alone. The Wares lived in Boston now, in a brownstone on Saint James Avenue, with Vonie's siblings Lucia, Clara, and Charles Ames, as well as a rotating cast of boarders and guests.

Most influential was Aunt Lucia, who tolerated the nickname "Ah Loo" from Mamie. She was a "beloved auntie" and "a wonder," who maintained a "grand outside calm" in the face of any worry.[7] She was also a nationally eminent social reformer. Nearby lived an even grander relative, Charles Carleton Coffin, who'd been a famous Civil War correspondent. Mamie loved the imposing stateliness of Coffin's four-story house on Dartmouth Street. At least once a year, he staged lantern slide shows for the children and organized Christmas parties at which his friend Louisa Alcott joined for charades.

Living with her relatives, Mamie soon learned of the tendency toward defiance woven into her lineage. Vonie's people, the Coffins, were a storied family. Levi Coffin (1798–1877) of Cincinnati smuggled more than three thousand enslaved people to freedom. Slave hunters called him the president of the Underground Railroad, and it was rumored that Harriet Beecher Stowe modeled two characters in *Uncle Tom's Cabin* on Levi and his wife.[8] Another relative, Lucretia Coffin Mott (1793–1880), was a formidable advocate for abolition and women's suffrage. With a small group of like-minded women, including her sister Martha Coffin Wright and Elizabeth Cady Stanton, she helped organize America's first formal women's rights rally, the Seneca Falls Convention of 1848.

The torchbearer of this legacy in Mamie's household was Lucia, who became head of the Massachusetts Suffrage Association in 1903 and cofounded the Women's Peace Party in 1915. As Lucia Ames, she had expected to remain single for life and was skeptical any benefit could be worth the servitude required by marriage. At forty-two, however, she married Edwin Doak Mead, the editor of the *New England Magazine* and also a world-peace activist. The pair exemplified the "socially impeccable progressive" set—devotees of Emerson and Thoreau, admirers of Tolstoy and the political economist Henry George—and they formed a companionate union that was Mamie's most lasting ideal of married life.[9]

As generous as the Meads were, Mamie sometimes felt like a dud among them. One moment very close to the time of her father's death came to form the basis of her strongest, harshest view of herself, even years later. She was outside a room and happened to overhear Edwin Mead remark, "Mary is certainly about the most uninteresting unattractive child imaginable."[10]

Mead likely spoke in a moment of tiredness or light malice—after all, he was much in the company of this clever, needy child. He came to love her dearly. But to Mamie, Mead's words "echoed right straight through my whole life and have never lost their grip," she later confessed to her children. "They all but successfully antidoted the 'I love you' from the two men who have been closest to me."[11]

But they also gave her something: expanded empathy. "It is a pretty big handicap, God knows, to be uninteresting and unattractive," she wrote, "but still it is a handicap one has in common with many others, and it surely gives a sympathy and fellow feeling that perhaps can't come any other way."[12] The wound became part of who she was.

. . .

While Mamie Ware was growing up, womanhood itself was going through a metamorphosis. It had been more than a century in coming. Since the colonial era, American women had taken issue with their absence from the nation's founding documents. In the spring of 1776, Abigail Adams asked her husband to "remember the ladies" in the new nation's "code of laws."[13] John Adams found his wife's request funny, comparing it with the irrational demands of a willful child, servant, or slave.[14] "But your Letter," he noted, "was the first Intimation that another Tribe more numerous and powerfull [sic] than all the rest were grown discontented." He knew that statement had an unkind ring to it but thought it justified, adding, "This is rather too coarse a Compliment but you are so saucy, I wont blot it out."[15]

Abigail was undaunted. "We are determined to foment a rebellion," she wrote back to him presciently, "and will not hold ourselves bound by any laws in which we have no voice or representation."[16]

Such words must have seemed near fantastical at the time. Convention and the Constitution, implicitly and explicitly, decreed there was one dominant, default type of citizen for whom rights and laws were made. For women to seek a direct voice in public life meant calling into question all the received ideas about gender that then governed society and the state. By the late nineteenth century, a vibrant movement had risen up to dismantle what had been a clear hierarchy of the sexes and reestablish it in a different pattern: a binary. In politics women were invisible; in the household, they were permitted to rule.

Science said a woman was closer to a pet than equal to a man. As an 1848 medical tract explained, "She has a head almost too small for intellect but just big enough for love."[17] Darwin himself mused about women's capacities in his journal, concluding that his ideal would be "a nice soft wife," "an object to be beloved and played with. Better than a dog anyhow."[18] (For the record, Darwin loved dogs.)

Despite Darwin himself holding this view, his studies supplied a framework suggesting inequality of the sexes was socialized, not divinely or biologically decreed. "Nowhere in all nature is the mere fact of sex . . . made a reason for fixed inequality of liberty, of subjugation, of subordination, and of determined inferiority of opportunity in education, in acquirement, in position—in a word, in freedom," wrote the feminist Helen Hamilton Gardener in 1893. "Nowhere until we reach, man!"[19] For many, Darwin's work supplanted the Christian dogma that said woman was created to be man's helpmeet.

Medically speaking, a nineteenth-century woman was an extension of her reproductive tract, though prone to glitches. A New Haven professor lecturing to a medical society in 1870 asked his listeners to imagine that "the Almighty, in creating the female sex, had taken the uterus and built up a woman around it."[20] "Woman's reproductive organs are pre-eminent," one physician wrote. "They exercise a controlling influence upon her entire system, and entail upon her many painful and dangerous diseases. They are the source of her peculiarities, the centre of her sympathies, and the seat of her diseases. Everything that is peculiar to her, springs from her sexual organization."[21] Based on this theory, the root cause of any illness could be ascribed to hysteria, all symptoms traced back to the troublesome, restless womb.

A woman's purpose in the world was driven by her fertility—or her infertility. Women who couldn't have children had their mystification and pain compounded by the conviction it was their own fault. Until the 1930s, childlessness was assumed to be the result of women's bodies and minds going awry.[22] A childless woman was *barren*, a field too marred and poisonous to nurture new growth. In Hippocrates's time, barrenness could result from a uterus that was too wet, too dry, or malformed. Later authorities theorized there were nonphysiological causes, too: a surfeit of reading, education, or mental excitement; lack of pleasure in sex; or plain old overthinking it.

Too much information or deep study was not only improper, but physically detrimental to women. In *Sex in Education*, an influential 1873 study by a Harvard professor, Dr. Edward Hammond Clarke, a parade of case studies tried to persuade readers that college education had devastating health consequences for female students. After observing that many women around him were invalids, and noting the rising trend for sending girls to college, Clarke concluded there was a causal relationship. Young women, he asserted, did not have the capacity to develop their minds and reproductive systems at the same time.[23] Unlike men, in whom the brain and heart were the primary organs, he was convinced women were dominated by their ovaries, which risked shriveling or turning cancerous if forced to share a body with an overactive brain.[24]

The book was more of a sermon than a study; Clarke had barely any statistics supporting his thesis. Despite this total disregard for scientific methodology, his book went through seventeen printings and was widely read.

For eugenics boosters, a woman was a means of production— though a fickle and confounding one. The fruits of her body perpetuated every hereditary trait: a wildly unpredictable and potentially devastating power. Eugenicists looked forward to a future when that generative power could be regulated. Entire populations and nations could be grown by design.

Part of birth control's appeal, for eugenicists, was the opportunity to suppress the reproductive freedom of Black and brown women, immigrants from southern Europe, Catholics, unwed mothers, and people with disabilities. While in theory aimed at bolstering public health, in practice eugenics put a scientific sheen on white supremacy and ableism, under the pernicious guise of "purity."

. . .

By her teenage years, Mamie had become Mary, and she wasn't sure what kind of life she wanted. But the political and cultural engagement of her mother and aunts, their insistence on carrying on intellectual lives without the usual flotation device of a family fortune, suggested a path forward.

In her adolescent writing, Mary began eviscerating the meaningless conventions she saw around her, especially when it came to matters of the body: death, for instance. She had seen her father sicken despite the efforts of physicians over the course of two years, and she had trudged through the pomp and absurdity of his funeral.

At school, she wrote an essay on death rituals that presaged how she would later poke at social hypocrisies around sex and birth. Her paper "Crematoria," written when she was in high school, focuses on the cult of burial and advocates for cremation: "Sooner or later, when the almost universal prejudice against it has been overcome, cremation will be used instead of burial. There is no really good argument against it. . . . It is simply a short way of accomplishing what Nature does by a long, horrible process."[25] For the rest of her life, she disdained false delicacy around Nature's "long, horrible" processes.

While many of her classmates headed to Smith or Vassar, and from there into genteel wifehood, Mary went on to the Boston Museum of Fine Arts School of Art and Design to train in drawing, design, and craftsmanship. She was an art school kid, with charcoal on her fingers and a portfolio under her arm.

A portrait from the early 1890s proves she had developed style and individuality. Her hair is swept back to keep her sight clear, she wears a pin at her neck, and her perceptive eyes betray skepticism and amusement at the fuss of getting a formal photograph taken. She studied hard but liked whimsy.

After graduation, she was offered a prestigious academic post as head of the Drexel Institute of Art's department of design and decoration. It was a "man's job," as she put it, with an annual salary of $1,200, and she accepted right away.[26] She moved in late October 1894, exchanging the familiar landmarks of Boston, the city that had been her home since childhood, for Philadelphia.

At twenty-two, she was rarely still. She crisscrossed Philadelphia on "my wheels," as she called her treasured bicycle, her glasses shielding her eyes from street dust, fair hair firmly pinned into place.[27] She shared an apartment with her sister, Clara; their brother, Willie, left Boston too, though he fell out of touch after moving to the Midwest.

When Mary wasn't at work, she and Clara took weekend trips, hosted suppers, and took part in local dramatics and poster contests.

Mary liked having a wide, lively group of acquaintances, but she tended to keep a few loved ones close and hold everyone else at a distance. At work, instructing students barely younger than she was, she dwelled on the modern notion of abstraction, "the beauty of an idea," which for her was the animating reason to study art.[28]

Her total absorption in the life of the mind was brief. In spite of herself, Mary cared deeply what other people thought of her. Young women of her generation, if unattached, could only briefly be seen as self-sufficient and joyful, rather than sad or unnatural. As her twenties tipped toward their midpoint, the inescapable "Shall I marry?" question hovered over her—a question that made her dodge and fume.

She was not enamored of marriage as an institution, part of her legacy from Aunt Lucia, who reminded her, "A life of single blessedness . . . is infinitely better than any marriage that is only a half marriage and leaves the heart unsatisfied."[29] But friends were starting to announce their engagements.

Her musing on marriage already centered on a particular person. William Hartley Dennett was a friend from Boston, a *Mayflower* descendant, and an MIT graduate who loved poetry.[30] They first met at a party when both were in college. Though she had been invited by another boy, Mary wrote, "presently I found myself watching— a dear shy boy with red hair—who hung about the door-way and didn't dance."[31] They were introduced and spent much of the evening talking. From then on they saw each other for tobogganing in the winter and suppers by the river in the summer. He taught her to ride her bicycle, and in return asked her to read his poems. The two fell into frequent letter-writing just after her move to Philadelphia.

Hartley was kind, dreamy, and ready to fall in love with her. Mary wrote, "The letters began to mean a great deal to me—so much that I was frightened—and didn't dare think out what might be coming."[32] Initially her letters were formal, while he disarmed her with his affection and enthusiasm. One day she tore open his latest letter on the streetcar and flinched with surprise: he had started it "Dear Mary" instead of "Miss Ware."[33] By the time she'd been at Drexel a year, in October 1895, she was addressing him as "My dear Hartley" instead of "Dear Mr. Dennett."[34]

Hartley came from money, but his mother controlled it. He was drawn to a career in architecture but didn't rush to join a firm after graduation. For a little while, he toyed with the idea of writing. His sympathies lay with the progressive trends of the 1890s, which for him ranged from socialism to homeopathy to the "simple life" evoked by the Arts and Crafts movement. Mary too found a sense of belonging in the Arts and Crafts ethos. She revered its leading figures, John Ruskin and William Morris, and connected with Morris's best-known motto: "Have nothing in your houses that you do not know to be useful, or believe to be beautiful."[35] But she felt people ought to work at *making* beauty around them, not just noticing it or writing about it. Hartley was content to dabble a bit longer.

She supplied enough drive for both of them. Encouraged and occasionally hectored by Mary, he committed to architecture, and they began to outline how they would someday live and work side by side. Their ideal was a home far from the city where they could practice their crafts—he as architect, she as designer and decorator—and build with clean, modern lines. Together they would live an authentic life, full of honest work in tranquil air, enlivened by the company of fellow craftspeople, reformers, and the love of beauty. Hartley later wrote, "Our esthetic tastes, our religious beliefs, our social theories, our interpretations of society's discourses, our political opinions, were wonderfully alike."[36]

He adored her, and told her this often; she felt deeply happy, but something gave her pause. His devotion was too mystical for her taste, and her letters from this time read as if she wanted to quell his giddiness. "Love me more and more if you can, dear," she wrote. "But don't forget that I am just plain Mary Ware and not an ideal girl at all, and whose heart is yours."[37] Another letter warned, "Don't you idealize Mary, so you will come down with a thud at Christmas."[38] She felt sure in her choice, but in stray moments worried he was living among illusions. In the summer of 1896, Mary visited Boston and she and Hartley were engaged—secretly, so she could continue to work at Drexel. She wasn't in a rush to marry, and if Hartley was, his mother demanded they wait. Annie O. Dennett, also an artist, didn't take to Mary right away.[39] It is unclear why, but in time Annie Dennett warmed toward her future daughter-in-law.

The following summer Mary traveled to Europe on her own abbreviated grand tour. In Spain she became fascinated by the tradition of *guadameciles*, large-format wrought leather, often gilded, that decorated the walls of grand homes and public buildings.[40] An ancient art with roots in Islamic culture, the *guadamecil's* heyday had been in sixteenth-century Cordoba; as far as Mary could tell, the craft was dying out.

Something about the glimmering leather and vanishing tradition held special poignancy for her. She decided to keep *guadameciles* alive, enjoying the effort it took to tool animal hides and apply metallic pigments into delicate imagery. Making her own *guadameciles*— some just to be shown to loved ones and friends, though she also had gallery shows in Boston and received commissions—sustained her creatively for the rest of her life.

She left Philadelphia in the early summer of 1897. "We have had our last deviled Crab at the Broad Street Station—now we are going home again home again," she wrote Hartley.[41] Back in Boston, she moved into a loft on Province Street, set up a studio for her *guadameciles*, and began building a new profession.[42] A long engagement gave her practice collaborating with Hartley. Together they organized the Boston-based Society of Arts and Crafts; the Harvard professor Charles Eliot Norton was its first president. They opened a cooperative handicraft shop and planned out the kinds of homes they would create.

On January 20, 1900, Mary and Hartley married at Boston's King's

Chapel. The script of their wedding ceremony omitted the word
"obey" from their vows, something their peers were doing as a vogue
for egalitarian marriage replaced the old hierarchical pattern. The
rest of 1900 unfolded in a whirl of transformations. In June the Dennetts bought a farm in Framingham, west of Boston. Mary wrote to
her mother-in-law rhapsodizing about the trees, fruit orchards, blue-
berries, and columbine, the "*magnificent* hen-yard," and the "*mean
little house*" they planned to renovate.[43] They needed her help to
finance the project.

By August, Mary and Hartley started sharing the news that she
was pregnant. "It was a very great surprise to us," she confided in
Annie Dennett, "and not at all in accordance with our plans for the
immediate future, but we are grateful now that our plans were so
nicely upset, and we can't help being very courageous and confident
that all will be well."[44] She was twenty-eight and conscious of being
an older mother.

The couple had, from their chaste beginnings, become ardent lovers since their marriage. She later wrote concerning sex, "It is the very
greatest physical pleasure to be had in all human experience, and it
helps very much to increase all other kinds of pleasure also. . . . It is
then most of all that [married couples] feel *sure* they belong to each
other."[45]

She was determined to shed the prudery of her upbringing and
seemed to have succeeded. Sexual pleasure, she decided, was "a joy
to be proudly and serenely experienced."[46] That serenity was about to
meet its foil.

A boy, Carleton Dennett, was born December 23. He came in
the middle of the afternoon, "after a very long serious time," Hartley
wrote his mother in the birth announcement.[47] For Mary and Hartley,
becoming parents was a decisive loss of innocence. Carleton's passage
into the world was nearly fatal to Mary, and the pain stayed seared
into her mind.[48]

Despite her slow recovery and breastfeeding difficulties, Carleton was a healthy, happy baby, in Mary's eyes a "remarkable show-off baby" with a "beamy smile."[49] Gradually, the puzzle of family life began to fit together. Mary hired a nanny, renovated and repainted the farmhouse, cooked, gardened, and hosted gatherings. She and Hartley attended meetings and joined leagues supporting free trade, anti-imperialism, peace, and arts and crafts.

The couple was knit close by their routine of family life and varied, side-by-side projects. A friend described their Framingham place as "one of the most beautiful homes I have ever known, perhaps the most beautiful, the relations not only of Mr. Dennett and Mrs. Dennett, but the relations towards their friends and towards the community. It was, I think, to everyone who knew them a singularly blessed spot."[50] Their newly built cement house, with its pretty red-tile roof and tower, was now finished: it held ten rooms, and it had hot water, central heat, and a walled garden. Its beamed ceilings presided over built-in shelves and Morris & Co. wallpaper, a true monument to the Arts and Crafts style, and a sleeping porch Hartley loved.

By spring 1903, despite hoping for a longer interval between children, Mary was pregnant again. Appleton was born December 11, 1903. Again, the delivery was long and difficult, but this time the newborn was unable to feed from breast or bottle. Appleton died of malnutrition when he was three weeks old. As far as relatives can recall and the record shows, Mary did not speak or write of him for the rest of her life, apart from a parenthetical line in the life story she wrote up for a close friend.[51]

A third child, Devon, came barely eighteen months later. This time labor progressed fast—too fast. Devon thrived, but Mary was severely injured, with pelvic pain and dysfunction that did not ease over time. The lingering wound, probably a fistula, hobbled her daily life for at least two years. Doctors told the Dennetts they should not risk another pregnancy.

Mary and Hartley had little knowledge of birth control. They already had the certainty, hard won, that any assumptions they'd had about fertile and infertile times of the month were inaccurate. Mary later wrote, "I was utterly ignorant of the control of conception, as was my husband also. We had never had anything like normal relations, having approximated almost complete abstinence in the endeavor to space our babies."[52] Carleton and Devon—she didn't mention Appleton—were "both wanted, but both accidental."[53] After 1905, the Dennetts never risked much of a physical relationship again.[54]

Maggie Higgins

I am the partisan of women who have nothing to laugh at.

—Margaret Sanger

M ARGARET SANGER HAS HAD AT least a dozen biographers and even more mythologists. She herself published volumes of autobiographical writing, contributing as much myth as fact. All these sources agree on one point, at least: she presented a clear and present danger to Victorian-era moral values. "The movement she started will grow to be, a hundred years from now, the most influential of all time," H. G. Wells proclaimed in 1931, comparing her to Alexander and Napoléon. "When the history of our civilization is written, it will be a biological history, and Margaret Sanger will be its heroine."[1] The creator of Wonder Woman[2] looked to Sanger as a prototype. To others, she was evil incarnate.

If Sanger and Dennett ever compared the formative events of their lives, they would have found a strange symmetry. Each had lost a parent young; had married an artist-architect and lived in a home they designed as a couple. Each endured the death of a young child; raised two sons; and lived at times in the realm of the sick, battling a chronic ailment that flared up in times of stress.

The differences between them were just as striking. Whereas Sanger grew up in real poverty, Dennett saw a more genteel insecurity. Sanger's dreams of attending college were frustrated, while Dennett got as much schooling as she wanted and traveled to Europe. These differences extended from circumstance to temperament. Later, while Sanger gladly inhabited her status as a symbol and a figurehead,

Dennett avoided the life of a celebrity, with all the glory and scrutiny that entails.

When she was in her late thirties, Sanger told a reporter, "I have been called in turn a vile female, a person with a barnyard philosophy, a God-send, the greatest woman of the century, the counterpart of Abraham Lincoln and a horrible creature."[3] In the beginning, though, she was a girl with her eyes fixed on getting out.

Born Margaret Louisa Higgins on September 14, 1879, "Maggie" was the sixth of eleven living children in a family full of affection and political talk. Much of that talk emanated from her father, a boisterous stonemason named Michael Higgins. As an adult, she acknowledged him as her greatest influence.[4] "It was not pleasant," Sanger wrote in her memoirs, "but father had taught me to think. He gave none of us much peace."[5]

Her parents, both Irish immigrants, had settled in Corning, New York, on the Chemung River. Today Corning is marketed as a jewel of the Finger Lakes, still known for manufacturing; anyone who's inherited a set of casserole dishes might find original CorningWare among them. In Maggie Higgins's day, it was a rapidly expanding factory town. The burgeoning glass industry transformed the old village into "Crystal City."

Maggie's mother, Anne, had seven miscarriages in addition to those eleven surviving Higgins babies, meaning she was pregnant or nursing for the majority of her thirty years of marriage. Her chronic tuberculosis was aggravated by each successive pregnancy. Beloved by her husband and children, she had, in Sanger's memory, a habitual cough that was sometimes so forceful she had to lean against a wall for support.

She was also Catholic, and she had Maggie baptized into the church, though Michael disapproved of organized religion. The Higginses believed babies were sent by God—at least Anne did. But while babies were seen as part of a holy mystery, the Higgins children saw nothing mysterious about how those babies were born. When Maggie was eight, she assisted at a birth for the first time, washing and wrapping her newborn sibling after her mother had had another delivery at home, Michael Higgins standing by and offering his wife a flask of whisky.[6]

Sanger recalled her childhood as "one of longing for things that were always denied."[7] It was understood that the Higgins boys would find factory work as soon as they could, and the girls would go into domestic service. Maggie occasionally caught sight of the middle-class wives and mothers of Corning, and she thirsted for the elegance and breathing room they enjoyed. "Large families were associated with poverty, toil, unemployment, drunkenness, cruelty, fighting, jails; the small ones with cleanliness, leisure, freedom, light, space, sunshine."[8]

In adulthood, drafting her autobiography, Sanger borrowed lines on this subject from a letter written by Queen Victoria: "I think, dearest Uncle," wrote the young queen, "that you cannot *really* wish me to be the 'mamma d'une nombreuse famille,' for I think you will see the great inconvenience a *large* family would be to us all . . . ; men never think, at least seldom think, what a hard task it is for us women to go through this *very often*."[9] Victoria would, in time, have nine children and an empire; Anne Higgins had eleven and knew eviction.

There was no schooling in Corning for girls after eighth grade, but Maggie, bright and outspoken, rebelled against the expectation that she would go into service or marry young. In this she found one advantage of a large family: she had allies. Her older sisters Mary and Nan combined their earnings to send her to boarding school near Hudson, New York, when Maggie was sixteen. There a transformation took place. Maggie renamed herself Margaret, which sounded more elegant. She dated, debated, studied literature, acted in amateur theater, and dreamed of a life on the stage.

But this season of sheltered fun was cut short. After two years, her sisters ran out of tuition funds, and Margaret got a job teaching school in New Jersey. Then, when Margaret was twenty and her mother fifty, Anne fell into her final illness and died. In winter 1899, Margaret returned to Corning to nurse her mother until the end and keep house for her father and three littlest brothers.[10]

Faced with a daily barrage of chores and child-raising, Margaret soon started planning her escape. This ambition led her to White Plains Hospital, where she hoped to get her nursing accreditation in two years.[11] She had contracted tuberculosis in her tonsils and lymph nodes, a version of the disease that was exhausting but not immediately life-threatening, and her diagnosis didn't stop her from moving away from home.

By 1900, Margaret had started assisting at surgeries, monitoring women in childbirth, working night shifts, and hauling sanitation supplies for the doctors on her ward. She had already seen the gamut of birth, illness, and death in her parents' household, but now these crises were part of her daily work.

Occasionally, patients asked her how to prevent another pregnancy. Nothing in her training prepared her to answer this question. She had come to love maternity work. "To see a baby born," she wrote, "is one of the greatest experiences that a human being can have."[12]

. . .

The particulars of childbirth have long been fraught with status anxiety. There is cachet attached to where, how, and under whose eyes birth takes place. The performance of a smooth transition to parenthood, or through childhood, has much to do with the signals of success in currency at that time. And, of course, with who profits from them.

Pregnancy, because it implied sex, was unsuitable for public view or discussion when Dennett and Sanger were coming of age. Teachers were routinely fired if they were visibly pregnant, due to the prevailing belief their condition was distracting and inappropriate in a childcare setting. Pregnant people were supposed to crave absorption in domesticity, away from the public gaze, and pregnancy was near invisible in popular culture and entertainment until Lucille Ball appeared pregnant on-screen in 1952.

Until the 1920s, most American babies were born at home, attended by a physician, a midwife, or a trusted acquaintance, depending on the family's means and expectations. Wealthier women increasingly preferred to give birth in a private clinic, attended by a male obstetrician armed with sterilized tools and vials of drugs. Destitute women might seek out a public or charity hospital, but these differed strikingly from the private, well-staffed wards where society matrons labored and recovered, which were more like hotels or sanitariums.

The seclusion, clinical setting, and sense of authority conferred by a male specialist created a very different birth experience from one attended by a midwife, whose quiet witnessing and encouragement applied as much to postpartum healing and feeding as to delivery. Clinic births were nonetheless alluring because they offered the reassuring stamp of science, and held the status of a luxury good.

Expectant joy for most new parents was naturally mixed with existential fear. In 1900, between six and nine out of every one thousand women died in childbirth, about a third of them from blood infection.[13] As for the babies, 10 percent of them died in the first year of life, and 20 percent died within their first five years.[14] In the words of Cotton Mather, intoned at the beginning of the eighteenth century, conception meant "your *Death* has Entered into you."[15]

That still held true in 1920, when a Chicago physician described the "pathologic process" of birth. "So frequent are these bad effects," he wrote, "that I have often wondered whether Nature did not deliberately intend women should be used up in the process of reproduction, in a manner analogous to that of salmon, which dies after spawning."[16]

Fear of pain tagged close behind fear of death. When anesthesia for labor became more widely available, the shift toward the hospital accelerated and spread from the upper crust to the middle class. This coincided with a concerted policy among physicians to claim much of the maternity business away from midwives. Physicians organized themselves into the American Medical Association (AMA) in 1847, beginning an ascendant campaign of allopathic medicine over traditional and naturopathic healing. Credentialed doctors increasingly sounded the alarm about midwives, grouping them with "irregulars," phrenologists, peddlers of nostrums and superstitions, and persuasive cranks.

"Irregulars," or eclectic healers, commanded a sizable share of the healing market and were often the main recourse for poor and rural communities and people of color. More and more, however, they found themselves in conflict with local doctors, subject to harassment from state licensing boards, and unable to advertise their services for fear of suppression. (Everyone in the healing professions, regardless of credentials, was competing for the same out-of-pocket payments; the first prepaid healthcare plans went on the market in 1929.)

A turning point for both practitioners and patients came in 1910, when the Carnegie Foundation commissioned the Flexner Report on medical education. The Flexner Report forced the closure of many medical schools, narrowed the accessibility of getting a medical education (which, for women and minorities, became far more difficult), and helped discredit the practice of alternative healing modalities. The report's authors made blanket generalizations based in prejudice, like recommending Black people be trained in "hygiene rather than surgery" and tasked with "protecting whites" from infectious diseases like tuberculosis.[17]

The standardization of medicine, while purporting to be concerned with patients' safety, brought losses for both patients and practitioners. Women's health, gynecology, and obstetrics were brief chapters in the medical-school curriculum, even after the Flexner Report; these subspecialties were beleaguered by their sheer messiness and lack of prestige. The AMA was all-male until 1915, when the proportion of female graduates from coeducational medical schools averaged about 5 percent.[18]

Patients' safety and physicians' profitability went hand in hand in shaping the AMA's priorities, and abortion represented one front in this campaign. From the 1850s, medical and municipal authorities championed anti-abortion laws; by 1880, every state in the nation had passed one. Notably, these were not generally based on the concept of personhood. In 1880, a North Carolina judge ruled, "It is not the murder of a living child which constitutes the offense, but the destruction of gestation by wicked means against nature," differentiating "gestation" from a "living child."[19] Eclectic healers were more likely to supply herbal compounds to bring on miscarriage, and naturally became targets, too.[20]

Midwives prevailed in many communities, with outcomes favorably or at least roughly comparable to those of physicians. Dr. Sara Josephine "Jo" Baker, the pioneering director of child health in New York City, found births with licensed midwives had the best outcomes, a conclusion corroborated by a Johns Hopkins professor in 1912, whose survey found midwives decisively more competent than the average American doctor.[21]

Doctors themselves reported feeling enormous pressure to "give them [women in childbirth] relief and . . . accelerate the delivery."[22] More so than midwives, they tended to become agitated in close quarters with a patient in the late stages of labor and were compelled to *do* something, anything, to bring the process to a conclusion. In up to 50 percent of cases, they employed forceps and chloroform to hurry a birth along.[23] Even today, in low-risk pregnancies, midwifery care is associated with a significantly reduced likelihood of interventions during labor, including induction and episiotomy, and a 30 to 40 percent lower chance of need for a C-section.[24]

A century ago, for most AMA-affiliated physicians, women's health was a moral as well as a medical matter, and doctors intended to hold tight to their privileged powers of judgment.

. . .

In early 1902, when she was twenty-two, Margaret Higgins met William Sanger. The story goes that Bill, an architect, attended a White Plains hospital dance at the invitation of a doctor client. He was seven years older than Margaret and a devoted Socialist like her father. He had studied at Cooper Union and worked at the illustrious architecture firm McKim, Mead & White; to Margaret, he represented a different world.

Bill was dashing and intellectual, and he adored Margaret. He pursued her with letters and visits. A few months before she finished her apprenticeship at White Plains, he insisted they get married, meaning her training would be cut short. She resented his impatience, but gave in.

Less than six months after their marriage, she was pregnant. As it had with her mother, pregnancy exacerbated Margaret's tuberculosis. She checked in to a sanitarium in the Adirondacks, returning to the city to give birth to Stuart Sanger in late November 1903. Delivery was painful and protracted. The attending doctor wrote to Margaret years later, once she was famous, asking "just what bearing my lack of knowledge of obstetrics may have had upon this profound [birth control] movement that is so essentially yours," and recalling of Stuart's birth, "It was a hard night for both of us."[25]

The Sangers began building a house in the pleasant New York suburb of Hastings-on-Hudson. From the river flats of Corning, Margaret had gotten as far as an upper-middle-class neighborhood with a big white house and a well-kept lawn, a "showplace" according to local newspapers.[26] It was the kind of neighborhood where husbands commuted into the city, wives belonged to clubs, and babies were wheeled along tree-lined streets by nursemaids.

Margaret Sanger floated along in her new, primarily domestic existence. After her duties to her house and family, she had enough time left in the day to do something creative. She joined a reading group and began writing short stories herself. Though Bill's expectations of marriage were conventional, he did more around the house than other husbands, shooing his wife away from the dishes so she could focus on her writing.[27]

She had a second son, Grant, in the summer of 1908. "I loved having a baby to tend again, and wanted at least four more as quickly as my health would permit," Sanger later wrote. In the end she had just one more child. In May 1910 a daughter, Peggy, was born, and was "so satisfactory a baby that I was not particularly disappointed when my illness cropped up again and the doctor said my family must end at this point."[28]

Enveloped by household cares, Sanger began to chafe at her life. She wasn't a natural homemaker: the work was "drab and monotonous."[29] In contrast to Dennett's declaration of "beauty-hunger," Sanger wrote of her own "world hunger."[30] She felt "this quiet withdrawal into the tame domesticity of the pretty riverside settlement seemed to be bordering on stagnation."[31] Her life had "drifted into a swamp, but we would not wait for the tide to set us free."[32] Bill sympathized. He was tired of his job, and he wanted to move to Paris and become a painter.

Before they could make much of a plan, a rupture came. An overheated stove sparked a house fire. The family was safe, but their possessions turned to ash. "My scale of suburban values had been consumed by the flames," Sanger wrote.[33] The effort of rebuilding the house cemented the Sangers' conviction they were finished with Hastings.

In late 1910, they sold up and moved to Manhattan. They took an apartment on West 135th Street with an extra bedroom, and Bill's mother moved in with them to take care of the children. Bill quit his job and set about being a full-time painter.

To maintain an income, Sanger took a job as a visiting nurse. She worked for the settlement house leader Lillian Wald on her campaign to slow the spread of tuberculosis in the Lower East Side. Sanger spent her days climbing tenement stairs, caring for patients too poor to pay a doctor. Here, at last, Sanger's depression lifted entirely. Her hands were busy, and her mind aflame.

The families Sanger saw were people like the Nolans, the fictional Irish Catholic family immortalized by Betty Smith in her semiauto-biographical 1943 novel, *A Tree Grows in Brooklyn*. The novel opens in 1912, when Francie Nolan is eleven. We learn her adored little brother, Neeley, was conceived when Francie was three months old, and that their mother, Katie, had refused an abortion. The Christmas when Francie is fourteen, her father gets drunk, sick, and dies after learning Katie is pregnant again. Sanger saw people like the Nolans every day on her rounds, families who were overwhelmed by poverty and pregnancy, and she was present for some of their most desperate moments.

Sanger recognized her own mother's exhaustion in the eyes of patients who quietly asked her for contraceptive advice. Sometimes she advised withdrawal and condoms, but these could be deployed only by men.[34] "They were of no certain avail to the wife," she later wrote, "because they placed the burden of responsibility solely upon the husband—a burden he seldom assumed. What she was seeking was self-protection she could herself use, and there was none."[35]

Middle-class women were far more likely to have a diaphragm, sponge, or douching solution on hand; tenement doctors didn't carry any of these, and anyway running water was scarce. Sanger's patients keenly felt the injustice of knowing other methods existed but were out of reach. As one told her, "It's the rich that know the tricks, while we have all the kids."[36] Instead, tenement mothers passed each other advice about how to use a knitting needle, or a cup of turpentine, or a strategic fall to end an unwanted pregnancy.

According to a story Sanger later repeated until it turned into something like a legend, the great pivotal moment of her life came "one stifling mid-July day of 1912," in a third-floor tenement on Grand Street. Sanger was summoned there by Jake Sachs, a panicked young husband.[37] He had come home to find his twenty-eight-year-old wife, Sadie Sachs, unconscious, their three children distraught. The cause of Sadie's condition was a self-induced abortion attempt. Sanger called for a doctor's help, and the patient recovered enough to ask the doctor how to prevent another pregnancy. In Sanger's memory his brief reply was, "Tell Jake to sleep on the roof."[38]

Three months later Sanger was called back to Grand Street. "Mrs. Sachs was in a coma and died within ten minutes," she wrote. Sachs had once again tried to induce an abortion. Sanger stayed to prepare the body: "I folded her still hands across her breast, remembering how they had pleaded with me, begging so humbly for the knowledge which was her right."[39]

After Sadie Sachs's death, Sanger went home to her sleeping household, where she stayed awake all night. Visions possessed her, taking the form of a movie reel: "A moving picture rolled before my eyes with photographic clearness: women writhing in travail to bring forth little babies; the babies themselves naked and hungry, wrapped in newspapers to keep them from the cold; six-year-old children with pale, wrinkled faces, old in concentrated wretchedness . . . coffins, coffins, coffins interminably passing in never-ending succession."[40]

When morning came, she wrote, "I know I could not go back merely to keeping people alive."[41] She was done following the letter of the law, and done deferring to the doctors.

"I would tell the world what was going on in the lives of these poor women. I *would* be heard," she wrote. "No matter what it should cost. I *would* be heard."[42]

Married ladies, in case of pregnancy, should consult the
directions, in regard to the properties of this remedy as we
do not intend to recommend it for mischievous purposes.
But if they wish to ascertain whether they be or be not with
child a few doses of these medicines will reveal to them
their condition; and if pregnancy exists, they will produce
distress, vomiting, and pains; which symptoms,—if these
medicines should not at once relinquished—would be followed by a quick loss of the gift of nature.

—Ad for Dr. F's Periodical Female Medicines[1]

BOTH MARY WARE DENNETT AND Margaret Sanger were born
at the beginning of a great silencing. The year Dennett turned
one, the Comstock Act of 1873, a federal statute, dealt a chilling blow
to free speech. The law was the blunt weapon and trophy legacy of
the mutton-chopped antivice crusader Anthony Comstock, US postal
inspector and secretary of the New York Society for the Suppression
of Vice, whose office was awash in the suggestive images, pamphlets,
and books he and his agents confiscated and banned from circulation.

Vice-hunting and censorship emerged as pillars of the social purity
movement, a grassroots crusade that rose up in both the United States
and England in the late nineteenth century. "Social" in this context
meant "sexual," just as "social hygiene" would come to mean "sexual
health." Reformers, gathering in organizations like the Woman's
Christian Temperance Union (WCTU), inspired by evangelical
Christianity, called for sobriety, chastity, an end to prostitution, the
eradication of pornography, and Sunday closing laws. They tied white

ribbons around babies' wrists, signaling the parents' commitment to raising their child in a home free of alcohol or any other drug.

"Evil thoughts," Comstock wrote, "like bees, go in swarms."[2] But whereas bees had wings, Comstock argued, evil thoughts were conveyed on the printed page. "I unhesitatingly declare, there is no more active agent employed by Satan in civilized communities to ruin the human family and subject the nations to himself than EVIL READING," he thundered in his book *Traps for the Young*.[3] Corrupting literature was Satan's favorite tool for conquering impressionable souls. The answer, in Comstock's eyes, was to muster soldiers against vice who would keep the printing press decent.

When Comstock came of age in the mid-nineteenth century, birth control advertising operated in an unregulated marketplace. As print advertising took off after the Civil War, papers and magazines grew replete with products promising to give "ladies' relief" and "cure irregularities"—to bring on menstruation or induce miscarriage.[4] Until Comstock's legislation went into effect a generation later, at least a third of all ads in New York City's *Sporting Times and Theatrical News* were for "French rubber goods" (condoms), "Ladies' Protectors" (usually vaginal suppositories or diaphragms), and abortifacients.[5]

The "Emerald Fountain Syringe" vied for buyers alongside the "Lady's Friend," while E. Edwards and Company sold rubber cervical caps marketed as "an absolute preventative and safeguard against a certain unpleasant feature relating to women only."[6] Another company sold a preparation called "Nonmoral."[7] Just-married couples had their own listings section in local newspapers; advertisers and sales agents often targeted them directly with contraceptive products, much as infant formula samples are routinely mailed to expectant parents today.[8]

The social purity movement was tailor-made for Comstock, a son of Connecticut, Civil War veteran, and mediocre dry-goods merchant. In the fall of 1873, when he was twenty-nine, he became the first chief agent of the newly incorporated New York Society for the Suppression of Vice.[9] Comstock installed a large photograph of himself over his office desk at 150 Nassau Street: a symbol of his constant presence and vigilance.[10]

There the array of pornography piled up: *The Lustful Turk, Peep Behind the Curtains of a Female Seminary,* and *The Gay Girls of New York.*[11] Comstock's mission to eradicate sin lasted more than fifty years.[12] He liked to boast that in the course of his career, he convicted enough people to fill a passenger train of sixty-one coaches with sixty people in each.[13] He relished the fact that New York's premier abortionist, Ann "Madame Restell" Lohman, slashed her own throat after he brought the law upon her.

Comstock saw artists and novelists, especially if they were foreigners, as probable pornographers. His vice agents confiscated the work of Zola, Flaubert, Maupassant, and Balzac, and copies of Tolstoy's *Kreutzer Sonata.*[14] They were likely to see paintings hanging in galleries as art, but photographs—even photographs of those fine-art paintings—as suspect.[15] Comstock's blunt crusade against all nudity, whether displayed on museum walls or sold in cigar shops, sparked a semiserious joke among artists that they should collect funds to send him to Europe to refine his judgment, but that never came to be.[16]

Motherhood had an elevated place in Comstock's universe, as the highest vocation for any woman. When he was ten, his mother, Polly, died of a hemorrhage after giving birth to her tenth child. "As soon as the babe is born the duty of the mother is changed," Comstock wrote. "A human soul is placed in her hands to care for, instruct, and bring up for the Master. A high and sacred duty. Fashionable society no longer should have a control over her."[17] Even constant care could fail, he knew. Comstock and his wife, Maggie, had lost six-month-old Lillie, then their only child, to illness in 1872.

Comstock was effective not for his charisma or because most people agreed with him, but because his paranoia landed at an auspicious time for politicians. His federal bill, which forbade the mailing of any "obscene, lewd, or lascivious book, pamphlet, picture, paper, print, or other publication of an indecent character, or any article or thing designed or intended for the prevention of conception or procuring of abortion," had a righteous tone Washington needed just then.[18] In September 1872, the government was fending off allegations of wholesale corruption after the Crédit Mobilier scandal. In that scheme, railroad construction costs were manipulated to yield fabulous profits to a few contractors—several with ties to sitting congressmen. When Comstock came to Washington bearing an exhibit of "abominations" (mainly condoms, dime novels, and novelty playing cards),[19] elected leaders jumped at the chance to demonstrate their moral rectitude.

A lone senator tried to tweak the law in a way that would have dramatically altered millions of lives and the birth control movement then taking shape. George F. Edmunds, Republican of Vermont, suggested that after the prohibition of "any article or medicines for the prevention of conception or for causing abortion" the line "except on a prescription of a physician in good standing, given in good faith," should be appended. But Edmunds's revision never reached debate and was quietly scratched out.[20]

The National Defense Association, an offshoot of the National Liberal League, gathered more than seventy thousand signatures on a petition to repeal the new legislation.[21] Comstock insisted many of the signatures were forgeries, the work of "long-haired men and short-haired women"[22] who sneered at men of faith like himself. He reminded his powerful friends what was at stake: the innocence of children.

Comstock saw his bill signed into law on the last day of the congressional session, March 3, 1873. Three days later, he was commissioned a special agent of the US Post Office. He now had the power to search the mail, seizing and destroying anything that met his definition of obscenity, and prosecuting the senders.[23] Comstock had aspired to this office. The US mail was, as he perceived it, *"the most powerful agent, to assist this nefarious business,* because it *goes everywhere* and is *secret*."[24] It was a dangerous conduit, foiling the separation of public and domestic spheres.

From that point onward, publications that had long advertised contraceptives and abortionists turned to other markets.[25] Newspapers sought other advertisers rather than run the risk of breaking the law. The business of producing popular literature dealing frankly with sex, advertising contraceptives for sale, or mailing any information or devices having to do with contraception or abortion carried a risk of a $5,000 penalty or five years' imprisonment for a first-time offender.[26]

Consequently, the fertility-related market became increasingly stealthy and associated with radicalism. Some advertisers got around the law by turning their pitches into warnings. "Married ladies, who have reason to believe themselves in the family way, should not use them, as, by their action on the womb, miscarriage would be the consequence," read one ad.[27] Another, for a "female regulator" branded "Cherokee Pills," cautioned "the unfailing nature of their action would infallibly prevent pregnancy."[28] These were lures posing as caution labels.

Many saw Comstock's preoccupation with sex and vice as excessive. President Grant, who signed the Comstock Act into law, eventually pardoned five out of the twelve birth control peddlers sentenced under his term.[29] Comstock's fanaticism about the reality of evil and purity of youth made him easy to caricature, even at the height of his successful career. A cartoon from *Life* magazine in 1897 shows a gallery of classical sculptures with every figure clumsily swathed in clothing, and with Comstock himself skulking in the shadow. "When Anthony Comstock Shall Have His Way," reads the caption.

Though birth control in Comstock's day was widely associated with the nineteenth-century free love movement, which was largely dedicated to remaking marriage, the connection was superficial. There was little overlap between the leading figures in these movements. Free love advocates and publishers like Ezra and Angela Heywood did not universally approve of contraceptives, but they hated censorship far more.[30] After Ezra was arrested at Comstock's behest in 1877, Angela wrote forcefully to defend her family and the rights of women generally. She disdained the "real *he* men" in Washington trying to legislate "whether woman may continue her natural right to wash, rinse, or wipe out her own vaginal body opening—as well as legislate when she may blow her nose, dry her eyes, or nurse her babe."[31]

Her husband taunted hifalutin men such as the magnate Samuel Colgate, who got "rich making and selling Vaseline for preventing conception" while serving as president of the Society for the Suppression of Vice.[32] The Heywoods began carrying ads for the Comstock Syringe for Preventing Conception in their anarchist magazine, *The Word*, earning Ezra another arrest. Selling a syringe, carried by most drugstores under the guise of hygiene, was hardly radical; it was the addition of the phrase "for Preventing Conception" that pushed the Heywoods over the line.[33]

Still, once Comstock had power over the mail, birth control was no longer a mundane mainstay of the mail-order industry. Whatever code words were used—"Male caps," "rubber goods," "uterine elevators," "married women's friends," and in one instance, "copper molds. You know. $1"—they turned the purveyor into a target.[34] The market for contraceptive devices endured. One diaphragm seller said after his arrest that "500 Brooklyn ladies were using his article."[35] But if they went through the US mail, they were breaking federal law. And Comstock was not just content with having written the law; he intended to enforce it, too.

Pushed underground, birth control information was harder to come by. Once an ordinary if little-spoken-of industry, it became bundled up with notions of equality and autonomy that were decidedly fringe.

. . .

Before Comstock, fertility advice had long circulated by word of mouth, through mail-order products and services, or, for the wealthy, sympathetic doctors. Condoms were cheap and widely available, but were closely associated with prostitution and sexually transmitted infections (STIs), so stigma kept many from walking into a drugstore and requesting them from behind the counter.

Most commonly by far, couples practiced withdrawal. This method has been so widely used across cultures and generations that it has a whole glossary of localized euphemisms; the French called it "leaving the dance before it's over," the Welsh referred to "taking the kettle off the fire before it boils over,"[36] the Scots talked about "getting off at Paisley"—the train station before central Glasgow—while American wives plainly praised their husbands for "minding their pull-backs."[37] Across race and class lines, withdrawal was "so universal it may be called a national vice," one doctor wrote, "so common that it is un-blushingly acknowledged by its perpetrators, for the commission of which the husband is even eulogized by his wife and applauded by her friends."[38]

But like condoms, withdrawal lay within the man's control. Timing, breastfeeding, douching, and herbal compounds were the only methods available to women, and those sporadically so. No method was foolproof—in 1935, one study found condoms about 83 percent effective, compared with 52 percent for douching—but until Comstock, none were forbidden from circulating in the marketplace.[39]

In almanacs and household guides, "birth preventive lotions" abounded; one mid-nineteenth-century *United States Practical Receipt Book* gave readers a cheap version, "Hannay's Preventive Lotion," which consisted of "pearlash, 1 part; water, 6 parts. Mix and filter. Keep it in closed bottles, and use it, with or without soap, immediately after connexion."[40] Other common recipes included pennyroyal, rue, hellebore, savin, aloes, and ergot.[41] Clevelanders could order "the Great French Preventive Pill" from an ad in the *Plain Dealer*.[42] In the Missouri Ozarks, a brew called "character sp'ilin' tea" could be found.[43]

Slavery was, in large part, an enterprise of slave owners brutally exploiting the fertility of people they considered to be their property. Thomas Jefferson said as much in 1820 when he told a plantation manager, "I consider a woman who brings a child every two years as more profitable than the best man on the farm."[44] Such a system made self-administered birth control and abortion into dangerous and defiant acts, gestures of refusal to add to an oppressor's wealth.

In 1849, a Georgia doctor reported enslaved women had significantly more miscarriages than his white patients, either because of their strenuous labor or because "as the planters believe, the blacks are possessed of a secret by which they destroy the fetus at an early stage of gestation."[45] In Tennessee, one white physician remarked that on a plantation he visited, "every conception was aborted by the fourth month."[46] In these and many more examples, knowledge of herbal and plant medicine, passed down by word of mouth, was powerful protection.

The political movement for birth control emerged in the 1870s, with the campaign for "voluntary motherhood."[47] That movement, however, was based on abstinence: it promoted a woman's "sovereign right to her own person," to quote Elizabeth Cady Stanton—more specifically, this meant the right of a wife to deny her husband intercourse, and to be a refining influence on marriage in tandem with the more bestial male.[48] It made no attempt to separate sex from reproduction.

In her essay "Marriage" drafted in the 1850s, Sarah Moore Grimké, an abolitionist and suffragist, wrote, "The *right* to decide this matter [when to have children] has been almost wholly denied to woman," and argued that right belonged entirely to her.[49] Unsought pregnancy, she wrote, was one of the primary causes of women's dependence and oppression.

Reformers called for a "leveling up of men," not a "leveling down of women's ideals," in the words of one social-purity advocate, Anna Garlin.[50] Like many reformers, Grimké objected to the sexual double standard between men and women, and like those of others in the voluntary motherhood movement, she argued for men to be held to the same expectations of virtue and continence as women. Only free love radicals suggested women should be able to experience sex untethered to pregnancy.

Contraception, from the perspective of voluntary motherhood, cheapened sex and removed a woman's strongest justification for saying no. Stanton, for instance, vocally supported voluntary motherhood, while opposing contraception.[51] The movement for voluntary motherhood never managed to change the law. Husbands facing a marital impasse could, and often did, cast out their wives or commit them to institutional care against their will, well into the twentieth century. Marital rape was not recognized as a crime in any American state until after 1970, and wasn't nationally criminalized until 1993.[52]

In the marketplace, meanwhile, numerous companies promised easy solutions for fertility control. Many women wrote directly to Lydia E. Pinkham, a Quaker entrepreneur, for advice. Pinkham's eponymous Vegetable Compound and Uterine Tonic was a bestselling concoction (containing, among other ingredients, black cohosh, licorice, and fenugreek), which promised to relieve cycle-related pains; it is still being produced and sold today. In her replies to customers, Pinkham freely advised suppositories made of carbolic acid or small sponges dipped in the same to prevent conception. In 1895, a company pamphlet suggested a nightly "Sanative Wash" before bed, a vaginal douche applied with a fountain syringe.[53] Technological advances supplied intriguing new options. Charles Goodyear's innovation of vulcanized rubber in 1839 fed into the condom industry. New jellies, foaming powders, and intrauterine devices were sold by mail order and in drugstores.

Then, a quiet revolution: a German gynecologist, Wilhelm Peter Mensinga, produced the first widely popular diaphragm in 1882.[54] The diaphragm was a barrier method for women, meant to be a more effective, better-fitting version of the pessary or cervical cap. Rubber pessaries, some made to be inflated to release springs after insertion, were by then being used to help treat prolapsed uterus, a relatively common postpartum condition.[55]

Their alternative use, to prevent conception, was implied in how they were advertised. One pessary was branded as "so secret that it cannot be known by the husband. . . . It cannot cause the male or female the slightest injury, or interfere in the least with the fullest sexual enjoyment."[56] A thirty-year-old mother of three in Fort Wayne, Indiana, visited a doctor for lower back pain in 1883; he discovered she had induced miscarriage three times and had since been continually wearing a pessary for more than two years.[57]

The busy trade in products, devices, and practical advice worked: families grew smaller. F. Barham Zinke, an Englishman who toured the United States starting in 1867, remarked on the smallness of the average American family: "There is no secret as to the various means resorted to for carrying out these unnatural resolutions. They are advertised in every newspaper, and there are professors of the art in abundance."[58]

There was, of course, another option deployed by women far more frequently than a douche or pessary: abortion. Today birth control and abortion are viewed as distinct from each other, but when Mary Ware Dennett and Margaret Sanger were coming of age, that distinction was far less clear. Since the American colonial era, contraceptive methods and abortifacients were advertised and sold alongside each other and widely used and accepted as a part of life, in every social class and community. Pinning the point of conception to a specific week or month was an inexact science. Before 1927, when the first reliable lab pregnancy test was developed (and even then, it was rarely used), women would have found out about their pregnancies only through lack of menstruation and other physical symptoms.[59]

In both social discourse and the law, no status akin to personhood was assigned to a pregnancy before fetal movement was felt.[60] Until that point of "quickening," pregnancy was indistinguishable from amenorrhea (late or nonmenstruation), which could have a multitude of causes—stress, nutrition, or change of environment, to name a few. Bringing on the menses, or "curing irregularities," was indistinguishable from inducing a miscarriage before quickening. Women themselves had sole authority when it came to reporting the moment quickening began—until the 1840s, when the newly invented stethoscope made possible the detection of a fetal heartbeat around the fourth month at the earliest.[61]

This stands in stark contrast to today. *Roe v. Wade* ruled against fetal personhood before viability, but since the fall of *Roe* in 2022, state laws have begun categorizing fetuses as people from the point of conception. This means that, for example, if a pregnant woman is suspected of using drugs in Alabama, Mississippi, Oklahoma, or South Carolina, child welfare agencies are involved in pursuing the case alongside the police.[62] In Ohio, in 2023, Brittany Watts miscarried a nonviable pregnancy within hours of the state's twenty-two-week point of fetal personhood. She was charged with abuse of a corpse—a felony—and the case was sent to a grand jury before the charges were dropped.

Policymakers who favor the assumption of fetal personhood argue that it's safer, and that pregnant people should accept their privacy is less important than the health of their pregnancy. However, the American College of Obstetricians and Gynecologists objects to fetal-personhood laws, saying they "are used to limit, restrict, or outright prohibit access to care for women and people seeking reproductive health care" and "have been used as the basis of surveillance and prosecution of pregnant people."[63]

They also present complications for managing fertility treatments such as in vitro fertilization (IVF). To see what this might mean in the future, one can look at Italy in the early 2000s. There, new IVF restrictions based on fetal personhood limited the number of embryos that could be made to three per cycle, and required all of them to be transferred at once. Freezing or testing embryos was forbidden. Consequences came quickly: the chance of success for older IVF patients declined by more than half, from 28 percent to 13 percent, and Italians who could afford it created a lively market for fertility-treatment tourism in other European countries.[64] Most of these Italian restrictions were lifted in 2009, and three years later the European Court of Human Rights ruled against the remaining restrictions on embryo testing, saying they violated the "respect for private and family life" guaranteed by Article 8 of the European Convention on Human Rights.[65]

In the late nineteenth and early twentieth centuries, meanwhile, the concept of fetal personhood was far outside the mainstream. "It is such a simple and comparatively safe matter . . . to interrupt an undesirable pregnancy at an early date," wrote Dr. A. L. Benedict of Buffalo, New York, "that the natural temptation is to comply with the request."[66] Certainly, abortions were sought with great frequency: the estimated rate in the 1850s and '60s was one abortion for every five or six live births.[67] Far fewer Americans received any form of dental care, by comparison.

Abortions, since they were either self-inflicted or administered illicitly, could be hazardous. In 1916, a major New York insurer reported that fully one-fourth of its claims were pregnancy related, and out of these, at least a quarter had to do with infections, disability, or death after attempted abortion.[68] In his 1888 treatise *The Ethics of Marriage*, Dr. H. S. Pomeroy of Boston noted that so many Americans were concerned with avoiding pregnancy it could simply be called "the American sin."[69]

. . .

Through the nineteenth century, the rise in effective fertility control cut the average US birth rate nearly in half. Since white, native-born, married households were counted and studied more carefully than other groups, that data pulls a sharper image into view. In 1800, the average birth rate of white married women was 7.04. "Every log cabin is swarming with half-naked children," read one chronicle of the

Illinois frontier. "Boys of 18 build huts, marry, and raise hogs and children at about the same expence."[70]

As the economy moved from agriculture to industry, large families were less of an asset. By 1900, the average number of offspring had shrunk to 3.56.[71] Among western European nations, only France had a lower ratio of births per woman of childbearing age.[72] Black women in 1900, meanwhile, gave birth more than five times on average, southern white farmers' wives closer to six, and German and Irish immigrants in the second half of the nineteenth century still averaged more than seven.[73] But those rates were on the decline, too.[74] By 1945, Black women, on average, had 2.5 children.[75] No other factor could explain this dramatic demographic shift.[76] The drop was steep enough to reflect a definite intentionality.

Pre-Comstock, while French letters and Portuguese pills crowded the mail-order market, birth control was also coming into its own in the realm of ideological debate. The first American philosopher to address contraception in positive terms, giving practical advice, was Robert Dale Owen, who saw birth control as a means of uplift for the working class. In his *Moral Physiology, or A Brief and Plain Treatise on the Population Question* (1831), he advised withdrawal, vaginal sponges, and condoms. Knowledge of how conception occurred and how to control it, he argued, would bolster rather than erode virtue. "A girl," he asserted, "is surely no whit better for believing, until her marriage night, that children are found among the cabbage-leaves in the garden."[77]

A year later, Charles Knowlton, a Massachusetts doctor and freethinker, published *Fruits of Philosophy, or The Private Companion of Young Married People.* Knowlton emphasized that knowledge of human physiology was the first and most important step toward fertility control, and that it had long been obscured by timid, inexpert, or moralistic sources: a position Dennett echoed nearly a century later. In his chapter on methods, or "checks," he repeated Owen's advice, but added formulas for spermicidal douches requiring a syringe. This last option was by no means reliable, and it was convenient only if you had running water, but it was significant that Knowlton put a measure of control squarely in women's hands.

When Owen and Knowlton were writing, there were few laws regarding abortion—and those were mostly poison-control laws, designed to shut down the sale of toxic abortifacients known to kill women rather than prohibit abortion itself.[78] Knowlton also argued a fetus had no more rights than any other part of a woman's body. "The laws in this country against abortion were never made by physiologists," he wrote, "and I should hardly think by men of humane feelings."[79] Dennett and Sanger rarely condoned abortion out loud as they campaigned for birth control, but their actions indicated views that were clearly shaped by Knowlton.

An act as elementary as diagramming anatomy in detail had the power to give people agency they didn't previously have. Frederick Hollick, a physician who wrote popular tracts for a general audience, railed against the policy of ignorance that so deeply affected people like the Dennetts. This ignorance, he wrote, was a result of collusion between timid parents and self-important doctors—a hypocritical and harmful tradition that kept people from necessary knowledge about their own bodies.[80] "Society," he wrote in 1845, "will no more allow any class to possess all scientific information, than it will allow others to possess all political power, or religious rights." The restriction of physiological and reproductive awareness to men, he continued, was "preposterous, and tyrannically unjust."[81]

Keeping women in ignorance served no discernible purpose apart from disempowerment. That same year Hollick published *The Origin of Life: A Popular Treatise on the Philosophy and Physiology of Reproduction*, which had clear drawings of male and female anatomy.[82] Five years later he published his relationship manual *The Marriage Guide*. He was brought to trial twice in Philadelphia in the 1840s for exhibiting a naked manikin onstage during his lectures, but his career represented a stinging defeat for vice-hunters; the trials brought a hung jury, multiple postponements, and finally full acquittal.[83]

For the stodgier experts on physiology and marriage, abstinence was the only acceptable form of birth control. Nonprocreative sex was, like nonheterosexual sex, a sin. This, doctors assured, was why women desired maternity but never sex. "I do not believe one bride in a hundred, of delicate, educated, sensitive women, accepts matrimony from any desire for sexual gratification," a medical school professor told his class in 1883; "when she thinks of this at all, it is with shrinking, or even with horror, rather than with desire."[84] Withdrawal was considered harmful to both parties for causing "irritation and exhaustion,"[85] and barrier methods like condoms or "womb veils"— ancestors of the diaphragm—signaled immorality. In *The Physical Life of Woman* (1872), a Philadelphia physician, George Napheys, corroborated the popular belief that withdrawal could have terrible health consequences to the nervous system, advising, "No wife who loves her husband will ask or permit him to run this danger."[86]

John Harvey Kellogg, the health reformer and breakfast-cereal developer, published his own guide, *Plain Facts about Sexual Life*, in 1877—written without direct expertise, before he married. He revised it after his honeymoon and republished it as *Plain Facts for Old and Young* just two years after the first edition.

Kellogg was a doctor as well as a devotee of plain living and restraint. He asserted that contraceptive measures like condoms and douching were "crimes against nature similar to pederasty and sodomy."[87] Kellogg advised couples to have sex about once a month at most and assumed women viewed the act as a marital obligation and a way of fulfilling their ultimate desire: to become mothers. "The majority of women, happily for them, are not very much troubled with sexual feeling of any kind," Kellogg told his readers. "She submits to her husband, but only to please him; and but for the desire of maternity."[88] Other doctors advised that contraception could provoke harmful and irreversible effects, ranging from fibroid tumors to insanity.[89] The underlying justification for much of this fearmongering was the theory that women benefited in health and vitality from direct contact with sperm.

Of all the health and marriage guides, Alice Stockham's *Tokology: A Book for Every Woman*, published in 1883, was most often passed among middle-class mothers, daughters, and neighbors of their generation and is the one Dennett most likely read. *Tokology*, named after an old word for obstetrics or midwifery, covered women's health from menarche to menopause. Stockham was close lipped on birth control, prescribing periodic abstinence to ensure "voluntary motherhood."[90] Later editions discussed withdrawal and douching, but no barrier methods.

In a more daring Toronto edition, Stockham encouraged women to track their fertility. "Believing in the rights of unborn children, and in the maternal instinct," she wrote, "I am consequently convinced that no knowledge should be withheld that will secure proper conditions for the best parenthood."[91]

A later book by Stockham, *Karezza* (1896), encouraged couples to have prolonged sex without orgasm to strengthen their bond without risking pregnancy. In terms that recalled those of the free love utopians, Stockham called for "more light—more knowledge upon hitherto forbidden topics, and the freedom guaranteed by the constitution of the United States to disseminate that knowledge." For her trouble, in 1905, when she was seventy-two, she was indicted on federal obscenity charges.[92]

Just one formal study exists that sheds some light on how women like Dennett navigated sex and pregnancy. In 1892, Dr. Clelia Duel Mosher of Stanford University collected a questionnaire on sex habits and attitudes from forty-five women, all white, married, and mostly college educated and born before 1870. Out of Mosher's respondents, more than half reported they knew nothing of sex before they were married.[93] Most were deliberately kept in ignorance; this was evidently good parenting in the 1800s. (By contrast, a study of about a thousand male college students born in the 1890s reported most received "first and striking" sex education before the age of ten; the majority described the tone and circumstances of this education as "unwholesome."[94])

Fourteen of Mosher's respondents had learned about physiology and sex from books, with a major source being *Tokology*.[95] But books had their pitfalls. As late as 1910, tracts in wide circulation described the safe period as precisely halfway between menstrual periods—the fertile period for many women.[96] Others had had "some very frank talks" with mothers, relatives, friends, and physicians; still others had observed farm animals and drawn their own conclusions.[97]

When it came to family planning, responses predictably showed withdrawal, despite its supposed risks, was a common method.[98] More than 80 percent of respondents had used a condom, cervical cap, or both.[99] About three-quarters had sex at least weekly; most had experienced orgasms; but fewer than half felt pleasure alone was a reason to have sex.[100]

As a contemporary medical journal noted, "No single cause of mental strain in married women is as widespread as sex fears and maladjustments," which the author ascribed to the deliberate policy of ignorance for young women.[101] Women commonly felt they had transgressed if they had intercourse without expressly wanting another child. "The ideal would be to have no intercourse except for reproduction," wrote one.[102] In Mosher's study, the prevailing source of reluctance to have and enjoy sex was past experience of one or more unplanned pregnancies.[103]

One respondent poignantly described the distance that she now felt in her marriage. "My husband and I . . . believe in intercourse for its own sake—we wish it for ourselves and spiritually miss it, rather than physically, when it does not occur, because it is the highest, most sacred expression of our oneness," she wrote. "On the other hand there are sometimes long periods when we are not willing to incur even a slight risk of pregnancy, and then we deny ourselves . . . feeling all the time we are losing that which keeps us closest to each other."[104]

Sometimes the loss could be reversed. Sometimes, as with Mary and Hartley Dennett, it was too late.

SOUL LOVE TRIO TOGETHER AFTER ONE
YEAR'S TEST . . . JESUS, EMERSON AND
TOLSTOY THEIR GUIDES.

MOST DARING SOCIAL EXPERIMENT OF
THE AGE PROVES SPIRITUAL LOVE A
LIVABLE REALITY

—*The World* headline on the Dennett divorce

MARY WARE DENNETT WOULD COME to identify May 1907 as a pivotal time: the month when a promising friendship ended and her battle to reclaim her marriage began.

The Dennetts had become close to a couple who lived in nearby Brookline, Margaret Chase and her husband, Dr. Lincoln Chase. Mary enjoyed Mrs. Chase's company, finding a kindred spirit in this lively young mother and longtime suffragist. She shared the Dennetts' semiutopian, back-to-nature leanings.[1] She and Mary compared notes on their toddlers and studied economics together.[2] Margaret had even given Mary a valued bit of wisdom when five-year-old Carleton asked where babies came from: she encouraged Mary not to answer "God," as her own elders had done, and instead proceed with "simple truthfulness."[3] Mary respected this approach and adopted it wholeheartedly.

Later, after things changed between them, Mary would describe Margaret Chase as "the tiger type, but intellectual in her method."[4] Since the birth of the Dennetts' last child, Devon, the Chases' home was the first architectural commission Hartley had taken on alone, without collaborating with Mary on the interior design. With Dr. Chase frequently at the office, Margaret and Hartley had long meetings, exchanged books, and found inspiration and sympathy in each other's company.

In the spring of 1907, while she was in New York having surgery for her birth injuries, Mary first sensed something had changed. "It was while I was in the hospital that I became conscious of the change in Hartley," she later wrote to her sons. "His daily letters were little charming works of art as always . . . but they had, for the first time a note of kindness. He was being good to me instead of needing me."[5] Sensing his changed tone "made me cold in every fibre."[6] She tried to dismiss her anxiety as an irrational, invasive thought.

Not long before, Hartley's relatives had teased him for his "docility" and subservience to his wife; surely that dynamic couldn't be undone in a matter of a few months.[7] But quickly Mary found herself, at thirty-five, watching her life's foundation pulled out from under her feet.

. . .

Before the mid-nineteenth century, economic incentive—survival—compelled wives to stay married at all costs. Divorce was not only difficult to obtain, but, for women, meant relinquishing their children and property. Then, starting in 1839, states began to enact legislation giving them the right to keep property in their own name after marriage, and to carry that property with them after divorce.[8] Afterward, the slim margin of married women who had a chance of making ends meet after divorce felt freer to seek it out.

Divorce was nevertheless a heavily freighted process, morally as well as logistically. Though divorce could be a means to individual autonomy and more authentic relationships, the consensus was that it was a social evil and would torpedo one's virtuous reputation. In 1910, *The Atlantic* published an article by the author Margaret Deland titled "The Change in the Feminine Ideal," in which she argued divorce should not be permitted under any circumstances—rather,

that instead, "young women must understand that men were instinc-
tively promiscuous" and "male weakness offered women splendid
opportunities for spiritual growth through suffering."[9]

And yet, despite the stigma and cost, more and more American
couples found it impossible to live yoked together. In 1880, there was
one divorce for every twenty-one marriages; by 1916, there was one
for every nine.[10]

The transformation of the family had become "one of the greatest
sociological phenomena of our time; it is a social question of the
first importance, of far greater importance than any merely political
or economic question can be," President Theodore Roosevelt proclaimed in his December 1905 Message to Congress.[11] By 1920, an
Atlantic article titled "What God Hath Not Joined" blamed higher
divorce rates on the "yeasty unrest" of the century's beginnings, alongside "enfeebled spiritual authority," shifting moral codes, expanded
roles for women, and the First World War. "The riot of divorce," the
Atlantic writer remarked, "has become almost an orgy."[12]

The rising divorce rate was disturbing enough that a leader in the
eugenics movement, Paul Popenoe, opened a clinic offering marriage counseling to white, native-born couples.[13] "I began to realize,"
he wrote, "that if we were to promote a sound population, we would
not only have to get the right kind of people married, but we would
have to keep them married."[14] With religious and economic cases for
remaining married at all costs so greatly weakened, eugenics-based
arguments rose up to try to keep heterosexual, monogamous marriage
in its idealized and privileged place.

Hollywood and novelists had other ideas. In March 1920, Mary
Pickford and Douglas Fairbanks became the most admired married
couple in America, despite the fact that they'd both been married
before. In the decade that followed, divorces in comic film and theatrical plots became commonplace. The 1920 film *Why Change Your
Wife?* earned laughs with its line "There's only one good thing about
marriage and that's alimony."[15]

In fiction, heroines with complex inner lives and little hope of fulfillment in wifehood started turning the marriage plot on its head. Kate Chopin's novel *The Awakening* was published in 1899, the year before the Dennetts' wedding. Chopin imagined Edna, a New Orleans wife and mother seeking a less stultifying life. Her real-life desires are misaligned with the role assigned to her. She fears her children will "drag her into the soul's slavery for the rest of her days."[16] She is dubious about the joys of motherhood, guards her small moments of privacy and agency from husband and lover, and, in the course of awakening to who she is and how she might live with herself, she hungrily turns to art, nature, and sisterhood.[17]

Mary Dennett had done nearly the reverse. She had turned away from art toward marriage and her children. Now, against her will, that road came to a hairpin turn.

. . .

When Mary returned from the hospital, Hartley welcomed her warmly. Relieved, she put her suspicions aside. The Dennetts moved closer to nature in the summer of 1907. They now owned a vacation camp in East Alstead, New Hampshire; they had bought the land at the height of their friendship with the Chases, and it abutted the Chases' second home. The Chases had originally come to Alstead seeking fresh air for Margaret's tubercular lungs, and they lived with their two children in a cabin with running water and electricity, while the Dennetts set up an "elaborate tenting arrangement."[18]

Even in this wooded refuge, Mary's recovery was overshadowed by worry. The newly tender relationship between Hartley and Margaret Chase became glaringly obvious: the two spent most mornings hiking together, organizing communal meals and read-aloud sessions, visibly wrapped up in each other. Dr. Chase, usually unrufflable, occasionally asked Hartley not to sit so near his wife or kiss her so publicly, to which Hartley laughed and obeyed.[19]

When she had a moment alone with Hartley, Mary confronted

him about his infatuation. That argument seemed a productive one; he vowed to do better. After asking Mary's forgiveness he set off for the Chases' house, intending to clear the air with Margaret and tell her he had recommitted to his wife. But several hours later he returned in a very different frame of mind. How, he asked, could she prioritize her own jealousy over his journey to self-realization?

In a notebook where he jotted poems and thoughts, Hartley paraphrased Thoreau: "If a man does not keep pace with his companions, it may be because he hears a different drum."[20] Mary's objections, he was certain, were the workings of a petty and conventional society. Hartley resolved to follow Thoreau's rule for seekers: "Let him step to the music that he hears, however measured or far away."

While hiking the hills around Alstead, Hartley and Margaret talked endlessly about spiritual love, resolving at last to put their ideals into practice. They already had an ally in Dr. Chase, who mostly enjoyed Hartley's company. All three were confident Mary could be persuaded to combine households, becoming a living example of radically honest and mutually tolerant love.

Mary, however, liked her monogamous marriage. She didn't think her trust in Hartley was beyond repair, or that his relationship with Margaret was even physical. In the course of their friendship, Margaret had told the Dennetts she was happily celibate and that doctors had indicated her health, like Mary's, would not withstand another child.[21] Divorce still seemed close to unthinkable; surely he would return to Mary and their boys.

After the Dennetts and Chases left Alstead in October 1907, Mary made another attempt to find common ground with her husband, but this time she found Hartley unwilling to talk. He disregarded Mary's anxiety, listened to his heart, and let it lead him again and again to the Chases' door.

He began staying there for days, and then weeks. When Mary asked Hartley to at least tell her when he planned to be away, he refused. He told Mary she was "hypocritical in doing social work to uproot social privilege, and at the same time wishing special privilege for myself in my personal life—that I represented 'monopoly'—and that no woman should expect the monopoly of her husband's affections."[22] He recast Mary's unhappiness as a "selfish," "unworthy" craving for his undivided attention, and refused to compromise his "ideals."[23]

Mary wrote to the Chases to plead her case, without success. Margaret's replies urged her to leave her old-fashioned boundaries behind: "Would you build the holy city? Come let us take our kit upon our shoulders and go out and do it now!"[24]

In February 1908, Mary and Margaret spoke directly. Margaret, who at this point had begun borrowing and wearing Hartley's clothing, did not mince words: she said if she had her "own dearest wish, she would spend the *rest of her life* with Hartley," and that she loved him as "a brother, a son, a father and a lover."[25]

Later that spring, Mary started a new notebook. In her looping handwriting, she wrote, "For my dear boys Carleton and Devon / To read when they are old enough to understand." It turned into a partial record of the disintegration of her marriage. Having few confidants, she imagined speaking to her boys once they were adults, offering them her truth. "I am writing this because I no more know what the future holds for me than I do for you," she wrote, "and one thing I want you surely to know and that is, that your father did what he thought was right—and that your mother loved him and you with all there was in her."[26] If they ever found themselves in a similar situation, she continued, "perhaps you may feel the invisible sympathetic touch of my hand upon your arm."[27]

By the year's end, Mary was resigned to a future as sole breadwinner, a terrifying prospect, and she took a position as field secretary for the Massachusetts Woman Suffrage Association.[28] Her work there was demanding and unglamorous. She spent her days producing reams of prosuffrage literature, speaking at public meetings, convening luncheons and speeches, and engaging with the press.

Many days, her job entailed boarding a train to an unfamiliar town where a meeting was to be held, leaving her bags at a drugstore, checking in with the police, and finding an opportune place to unfurl a banner and deliver a speech. Then she gave a talk, often alongside one or two others, sometimes against a chorus of jeers. She described these trips as "one long scramble from beginning to end, sleeping, eating, traveling, speaking—speaking traveling eating sleeping, with hardly a chink anywhere for so much as a fresh washing or a shampoo."[29]

In February 1909, Hartley asked Mary for a divorce by mutual consent. He suggested they each take a child to raise.[30] Mary rejected his custody proposal, but before they reached any resolution Hartley moved out for good, joining the Chase household in April. She stayed with the boys in their Framingham home and, after being granted temporary custody, arranged for them to visit their father occasionally. Though she continued to hope that Hartley would shake off his enchantment with Margaret, in the end it was Mary who filed for divorce three years later, citing desertion as the cause and requesting permanent sole custody of both boys.

In his limited hours with the boys, Hartley behaved in a way that might be familiar to anyone who has seen an acrimonious divorce involving children. He blamed Mary, building a narrative of how she had alienated him from the family. The boys returned to her shaken and tearful, their pockets crammed with toys and candy wrappers pressed on them by their father. When she asked Hartley for mercy he demurred, saying the situation was entirely due to her legal action, writing her in December, "The action you have taken puts me in a position which I regret and protest against, in which I am unable to help you in the support of yourself and the children, without violence to my conscience."[31]

In court, Mary's New England–granite family proved to be an asset. Edwin Mead took the stand with sober, convincing testimony.

Regarding custody, he asked the judge, "He is living with this woman in New Hampshire. Are they [the children] to be taken into the charge of this woman for whom he has deserted his wife?"[32]

Every indication was that Hartley was an erratic philanderer and thus, in the eyes of the judge, an immoral influence on his boys. The judge visited the boys' school, the homes of Mary's relatives, and the Chase homes in Brookline and Alstead. A Framingham neighbor, Frank Patch, a homeopathic doctor, was put on the stand to describe her "characteristics as a mother" before the judge solemnly asked about two then-essential points: "Whether or not she is a womanly woman? [Thoroughly so.] And a domestic woman? [Thoroughly so.]"[33]

Hartley's obstinacy turned the hearings into a spectacle—suggesting he knew he was beaten even before the questions began. When asked where he was living, Hartley said, "I don't know what you mean by my residence."[34] Occasionally Hartley's statements—or rather his omissions—veered into cruelty. When asked about Mary's health after Devon's birth, he took pains to say he had suffered, too: "Always the birth of each of our children was attended with a good deal of discomfort, physical discomfort and mental discomfort, for us both."[35] He was unable to remember when Appleton, their second child, who had died in infancy, had been born, or the year Devon had been born.[36]

Through the hearings, no one—except, perhaps, the Dennetts and Chases themselves—could quite believe all was platonic between Hartley and Margaret. The hearings were peculiar enough to attract tabloid reporters, and like the mass of readers following the case, the judge wanted to know exactly what they were doing together. He returned to the point again and again. Mary was asked if she had been happy in her marriage, and replied, "Absolutely . . . without any flaw anywhere."[37] Subsequently she was asked whether Hartley and Margaret were "guilty of sexual immorality" and answered "No."[38]

Later, Hartley was asked if he and Margaret had a sexual relationship, and he also answered in the negative, but still the attorneys took some time to let go of the question. When the judge interrogated Hartley about evening visits he and Margaret had had in Framingham, Hartley admitted the visits had happened, but went on to proclaim they were irrelevant, that the central issue in the divorce was "a spiritual difference between my wife and myself."[39] The judge thought it relevant to note in his records that Margaret "on repeated occasions spent the night with him when no one else was present."[40] He later clarified that "after an exhaustive investigation of all the facts, I find that they have not been guilty of adulterous relations."[41]

Mary became financially desperate as the divorce progressed, as Hartley refused to help pay any household bills. When the court eventually confiscated his Boston bank holdings—which in any case amounted to less than $100—Hartley sent the boys invitations to live with him, as well as gifts.[42] He conscripted friends to tell Carleton his father was going to prison on his mother's wishes, and Carleton, who was not yet ten, was hysterical overnight.[43]

Hartley's actions and public statements contrasted bewilderingly with a note he sent Mary on their wedding anniversary, January 20, 1911, saying, "I get up this morning with thoughts all of you and of our little children. On this day I want to send you my love and my blessing. Always, Hartley."[44] But in practice he did not soften toward her, and the gesture rang hollow.

In a spoken statement in court, Mary struck back. She was frank about the brutal experience of seeing Hartley woo the children while refusing to pay for any of the family's expenses. In Mary's words, "Naturally little children appreciate baseballs, books and candies more than they do coal and bread and clothing, and they did not know that their father was giving them the one and refusing them the other. They did not suffer, so why should they see?"[45]

Faced with her testimony, her apparent good character, and Hartley's and the Chases' defiant demeanor, the judge sided with Mary. She had temporary exclusive custody, but the wait for a decisive ruling stretched on for nearly two years. On the evening of Monday, April 28, 1913, she wrote to Carleton at boarding school with palpable relief: "Carleton dear,—At last the judge has made the final decision, and the court gives you boys into *my care* and no one can take you away from me now. You know more about what this means than Devon does, because you are older . . . how worried I have been all these months for fear that somehow the court would get tangled up and not see things straight."[46] The court required Hartley to contribute to the maintenance and education of the children, but he refused to do so and moved out of state, taking up residence in Alstead and turning to farming rather than architecture.[47]

The press exploited the final hearing, which took place in September 1913. Hartley's talk of personal freedom and plural love meant this was, after all, not a run-of-the-mill breakup. Reporters framed it as a story of traditional marriage foundering on the ideals of a free love experiment.

The Dennett divorce even had echoes on the stage. The *Boston Journal* noted the parallels between the hearings and the 1912 play *A Butterfly on the Wheel*, in which the heroine, played by the gifted actor Madge Titheradge, is put through such an ordeal on the witness stand she finally cries, "It's not the truth you want; it's me."[48] At a time when divorce held connotations of scandal, the Dennetts' split represented a titillating test case, a story for any reader chafing against conformity in their own life.

Mary was discreet around reporters. By contrast, Margaret Chase welcomed the press, and so journalists descended on her household with something like glee. Reporters visiting them at Alstead noted, "Touches of Charm and Elegance Everywhere." Margaret met one reporter at the door with a neighbor's baby in her arms, and made a point of doing farm chores during the interview. Hartley, too, was sketched sympathetically, as "so Christian-like as to be more than earthly," inspired by Jesus, Emerson, and Tolstoy.

Readers followed the story eagerly, pointing out many women

desired both "a poet and a meal ticket" and thus Margaret Chase was "to be envied. She has a double portion, and the rest of us women have, many of us, not even a half portion."[49] Of Mary, little was publicly known except one thing: "MRS. DENNETT, SUFFRAGIST, GETS DIVORCE," ran one headline. Even a year later, the national paper *The World* ran an article marveling, "SOUL LOVE TRIO TOGETHER AFTER ONE YEAR'S TEST" and mentioning all three principals "Hope to Make Wife Who Got Divorce a Member."

Mary hated being cast as a supporting role in their drama. As she wrote to her mother, "You can see what effect this sort of thing has. It makes no difference *who* you are, or what you have *really* done or left undone, you are *branded* just the same."[50]

By this time Mary had gone hundreds of miles away to start a new life. In late 1909 she moved out of the Framingham house. The carefully designed homestead was rented to her old school friend Kate Ware Smith (no relation), who also cared for the Dennett boys until they were both old enough for boarding school. Once this was settled, she left for New York, enticed by the steady salary offered by a job with the Rev. Dr. Anna Howard Shaw and the National American Woman Suffrage Association (NAWSA).

As a child, Mary had seen her widowed mother reinvent herself to make a living. Now, by necessity, she too began to fit herself to a radically revised set of ambitions. The Dennett boys, like their mother, effectively lost their father midway through childhood and witnessed their mother remaking her life to reconcile her ambitions for her children with her determination to support and educate them.

Alone, Mary Ware Dennett moved to midtown Manhattan in April 1910, mother of two live children and one ghost. On the train moving south, she would have seen very few fellow divorcees, if any at all. But she would undoubtedly have shared space with many women who, like her, had endured childbirth only to find themselves with empty arms—a silent, dispersed sorority.

The Road to 81 Singer Street

> It is not possible for the selfsame work to be broadening and beautifying if women do it, and petty and inconsequential if men do it.
>
> —Mary Ware Dennett (1916)

A S THE NINETEENTH CENTURY TURNED to the twentieth, New York City was one of the few places in America where a woman could claim a new identity within a week or two. In Manhattan, working girls filled boardinghouses, sweatshops, and dance halls, far from the enforcing authorities of home—parents and religion—whether they came from a farm, village, or shtetl.

Each passing year, girls moved away from their families of origin in greater numbers than ever before, driven by economic volatility, the Great Migration, and eventually by the mobilizations of the First World War. They took jobs as secretaries and telephone girls, in factory work and domestic service, and this public-facing labor, along with their paychecks, granted them a surer voice in their households. In Greenwich Village, freethinkers launched magazines, schools, and activist leagues that fomented rebellion against the grinding demands of a free-market capitalist economy and suffocating social conventions.

Though she was, at thirty-eight, older than most of her fellow strivers pulled to the metropolis, Dennett relished her chance at reinvention. Here, she wasn't merely a pleading wife, trying to convince others of her case; she was an independent adventurer among many others like her.

As she took up work with NAWSA's national suffrage campaign, Dennett began to inhabit a role that never would have found her in Framingham: a force to be reckoned with in the women's movement. It would be more than a decade until she returned to making art.

. . .

Her longtime New York City home was in Astoria, Queens, in an apartment with a couple of bedrooms at 81 Singer Street. For the first few years, though, Dennett kept her lodgings as modest as possible. She moved into a studio apartment in midtown Manhattan, on the fourth floor of a brand-new nine-story building, the Dearborn, at 350 West Fifty-Fifth Street.

Her studio window looked out on a large sign advertising a carpet-cleaning service.[1] An opera singer lived next door, and her voice exercises could be heard through the wall.[2] There wasn't enough space for her sons to stay: when Carleton and Devon came from Framingham, where they were cared for by friends and boarding schools, to New York, she would cross the street and book a twenty-five-cent room for them at the Mills Hotel, getting a discount if they checked out by six thirty a.m.[3]

Those visits were golden. She kept their free days busy with roller skating and picnics up the Hudson.[4] She loved that Carleton, especially, shared her intoxication with Manhattan, calling it "an imagination city" on a late-summer evening when, in her words, the skyline was "silhouetted in pale gray against a hazy rosy sunset—with the spidery bridges spun across the pearl colored view."[5] The two boys were affectionate and protective toward their mother.

Dennett had been caricatured in the Boston press as "one of the most zealous of the militant suffragists," a dowdy, overserious contrast to Hartley's more alluring soulmate.[6] Once in New York, she began to reckon with this exaggerated image and tailor it to size. She embraced some accoutrements of radical Greenwich Village: she cropped her dark-blond waves short, strung beads around her neck, and wrote a little fiction. When Aunt Lucia charitably gave her packets of her past-season dresses, Dennett refashioned them, spending many evenings "tinkering with my duds."[7] Far from downplaying her single-mother status, in 1911 she had a New Year's card made, showing herself alone against a New York cityscape, with portraits of Carleton and Devon on either side.[8]

Her work with NAWSA took her into the heart of a grinding, sometimes awe-inspiring campaign. On November 9, 1912, newspapers breathlessly described the demonstration for women's suffrage planned for Fifth Avenue that night: "The flying squadron of automobiles will hike up Broadway. . . . Five thousand yellow Chinese lanterns will be carried by the women. . . . The men will wear miners' lamps in their hats."[9] Mrs. Charles Tiffany donated four-foot gold trumpets; the trumpeting women would wear white, and the procession was set for eight sharp.[10] Despite bad weather, twenty thousand participants and half a million spectators were out that night, all marveling as Fifth Avenue glowed like a "river of fire."[11]

Dennett's title was that of corresponding secretary, which meant she coordinated the Literature Department—the propaganda desk—while writing outreach letters to grow the association's membership, coordinating events, and answering the correspondence that poured steadily into the New York office. She also supported local branch offices, which introduced her to clubwomen across the country, and advised the association's leader, the Rev. Dr. Anna Howard Shaw.

With the suffrage campaign now in its second generation of leaders, Americans were used to speculating about what would happen if women had the vote. Women's clubs, labor unions, and civic associations marshaled substantial influence, but thus far, women and their causes had acted outside of government. Besides suffrage, the best-funded sectors of the early-twentieth-century women's movement drew on the traditionally feminine concerns of temperance, education, and children's well-being.

As early as 1914, Dennett had realistic expectations of to what degree, and how quickly, NAWSA could achieve its aims. "Mrs. Mary Ware Dennett Predicts Equal Suffrage throughout the States in 1920," announced the *New York Sun,* in a special-issue announcement that also promised articles on "What to Wear When Polling" and "how a good wife and mother may leave her home to vote and yet keep the family happy."[12]

She was already starting to be disenchanted with the work, noting the racism that was not just tolerated but perpetuated by many suffragists. Just before the great suffrage parade in Washington led by Alice Paul on March 3, 1913, representatives from several Black women's organizations wrote to Paul's organization and asked to participate. Paul had become head of NAWSA's Congressional Committee in 1912. She was a young, militant leader whose tactics Dennett observed with admiration and alarm. When asked to integrate the march, Paul refused, saying she did not want to confuse the "negro problem" with the "suffrage problem."[13]

Dennett wrote Paul to protest, reminding her, "The suffrage movement stands for enfranchising every woman in the United States."[14] Several weeks later she sent another letter, saying a white-only parade "amounted to official discrimination which is distinctly contrary to instructions from National Headquarters."[15]

In the end, Shaw reluctantly wired Paul to officially grant permission for a handful of Black women to join. They walked at the back of the parade. There were tense, sinister moments through the event. One marcher reported the catcalls and harassment along the parade route on Pennsylvania Avenue drowned out any cheering. "I'd like to meet you after dark!" called one man on the sidelines; "You ought to get yourself a man!" heckled another.[16] Scuffles erupted, and marchers were hurt in the fray; 175 ambulances were called that night.

Dennett was angry enough over the attempted exclusion of Black suffragists that, with her friend and fellow NAWSA worker Jessie Ashley, a lawyer, she decided to resign. But she had no other job lined up, and Shaw and other leaders urged her to reconsider.[17]

She finally left in mid-1914, exasperated over disagreements about how money was raised and spent by the organization. In time, she bluntly accused Shaw of allowing "money influence" and "money power" to govern NAWSA, saying wealthy donors had too much authority within the group to pursue their own schemes at the expense of the group's founding priorities.[18] Where her bosses saw tact and smart fundraising, Dennett saw pandering and a loss of integrity. This particular conflict would return again and again over the course of her career.

The differences between Shaw and Paul and their respective organizations also presaged the rivalry Dennett eventually navigated in the birth control movement. NAWSA had originated with two groups: the American Woman Suffrage Association (AWSA) and National Woman Suffrage Association (NWSA). AWSA, led by Lucy Stone and cofounded by Frances Ellen Watkins Harper, who was Black, emphasized nonmilitant strategies and a single goal: votes for all American women. NWSA, founded by Elizabeth Cady Stanton and Susan B. Anthony, was all-white and encompassed other women's rights issues, including divorce reform and equal pay for women. The Fifteenth Amendment, which in 1870 granted Black men the right to vote, was seen by AWSA as progress and by NWSA as an outrage aimed at further oppressing women. In 1890, the two groups combined to form NAWSA. Under Shaw, NAWSA leaned toward carrying on Stanton's and Anthony's legacies: it was predominantly white and focused on changing state laws first.

Alice Paul shook things up to some extent, announcing a new scope of ambition and militancy for American suffragists. In 1913, Paul and Lucy Burns formed the league that gave rise to the National Woman's Party. While NAWSA pursued a strategy of legalizing women's suffrage on the state level first, Paul and Burns pushed hard for a constitutional amendment that would give all American women the right to vote. They saw themselves as Stateside soldiers in the campaign heroically waged by British suffragists, who kept up continual pressure via direct action. National Woman's Party activists picketed the White House for years, were regularly arrested, and went on hunger strikes while imprisoned. Paul and Burns publicly broke from NAWSA in 1914, shortly before Dennett left her post there.

While suffrage work steeped Dennett in the intellectual arguments for equal rights, it also threw into relief the injustices stubbornly over-looked by numerous white women in the suffrage campaign. As she grew to know more of the causes and activists around her in New York, Dennett was increasingly drawn to arguments for the right of women to know and control their own bodies. But that notion of autonomy—whether brought about via sex education, birth control, abortion, a radical reimagining of marriage and the family, or all of the above—was not a plank in the suffrage platform.

Under the directorship of Dr. Shaw, herself a former leader in the Woman's Christian Temperance Union, NAWSA was relatively con-servative. It didn't dispute the commonly accepted idea that feminine ignorance and sexual abstinence were not just tolerable, but right.

Dennett knew differently. Her experiences of childbearing made her acutely aware of the gulf between what women endured and the capacity of men to grasp it. This gap profoundly hindered the medi-cal profession, male dominated as it was. Her pain was invalidated by doctors as a matter of course. When she learned some women had the privilege of blocking their labor pains from memory through a miraculous new drug, Twilight Sleep, she was shaken to think of how different her passage into parenthood might have been.

Two documents Dennett collected during her suffrage years reveal interests she did not yet publicly pursue. The first is a memo printed by the International Neo-Malthusian Bureau of Correspondence and Defence, commenting on the prosecution of an American named Margaret Sanger for her advocacy of birth control and for her pamphlet *Family Limitation*. Signed by a group of English and Dutch birth control supporters, the memo criticized the Comstock Act and boosted birth control as a eugenic measure.[19] The group was inspired by Thomas Robert Malthus, the English author of *An Essay on the Principle of Population* (1798), who warned that the expanding human population would exhaust the earth's resources unless checked. Calling themselves Neo-Malthusians, these late-nineteenth-century social reformers shared Malthus's dark warnings about a coming population crisis, but while Malthus thought abstinence the only virtuous solution, this newer generation championed birth control.

The second souvenir from that time is the transcript of a public discussion in 1911 between Emmeline Pethick-Lawrence and Charlotte Perkins Gilman with the opening question "Does a Man Support His Wife?"[20] The debate was an updated take on the argument Gilman made in *Women and Economics* (1898), in which she dissected the power dynamics inherent in traditional marriage. For a wife to be economically dependent on her husband was problematic, Gilman wrote. Housekeeping, cooking, and childcare should be collectivized whenever possible, and wives should pursue remunerative work in order to strip financial dependence from the marriage bond. Writing in 1929, in *A Room of One's Own*, Virginia Woolf used a version of this argument to justify why women needed to distance themselves from motherhood in order to write. A large family, in Woolf's view, was an insurmountable obstacle to women's potential for creative work and ability to build wealth.

The same year as that debate, Gilman had published her first utopian novel, *Moving the Mountain*. The protagonist, Robertson, lost in time for thirty years, is brought home to New York in 1940. He is confused to find that his sister Nellie is a college president; now women have the same types of careers as men. Men, however, seem much changed: none of them drink, smoke, or hunt. "You women are trying to make men over to suit yourselves," he accuses Nellie. "Yes," she replies. "Why not? Didn't you make women to suit yourselves for several thousand years? You bred and trained us to suit your tastes; you liked us small, you liked us weak, you liked us timid, you liked us ignorant, you liked us pretty—what you called pretty—and you eliminated the kinds you did not like."[21]

Dennett began to think and write about her own philosophies around marriage and parenthood. Homemaking and caregiving were sacred, holy, all-important duties, according to traditionalists. The labor involved went beyond the realm of dollars and cents; it was unpaid not because it wasn't important but because it was deeply influential and never-ending. Yet as a rule husbands and fathers seemed to think domestic work was peripheral to their own lives.

As early as April 1912, Dennett formulated her theory that three elements were necessary for a fair society: economic independence for women, the end of every type of privilege, and safe, reliable contraception.[22] In a May 1915 article in *The Century* titled "The Right of a Child to Two Parents," she described her ideal of family life. Starting with an image of a "padonna and child"—a father tenderly holding a baby—she emphasized the importance of parenthood as a shared project. "It is not possible," she wrote, "for the selfsame work to be broadening and beautifying if women do it, and petty and inconsequential if men do it."[23]

· · ·

Dennett's new ideas emerged through conversations with new friends. When she wasn't at work for NAWSA, Dennett liked to go downtown. She joined a lively, irreverent club called Heterodoxy.

Heterodoxy was founded in 1912 by a writer, Marie Jenney Howe, who envisioned a woman-only salon with a feminist, literary slant.[24] Howe wanted club members to have a space where they could socialize and debate, free of the hampering presence of men. "We're sick of being specialized to sex," Howe asserted. "We intend simply to be ourselves, not just our little female selves, but our whole, big, human selves."[25]

Within Heterodoxy, which was nominally integrated though only one member was Black, about a quarter of members were queer and a third were divorced.[26] If they had husbands, their marriages abided by new and unusual rules. One member, the novelist Fannie Hurst, maintained her own household after her marriage, giving the name "Fannie Hurst marriages" to the separate-but-together living arrangement.[27] Nearly all were at one time members of NAWSA or had marched for suffrage.[28]

Heterodites, as club members called themselves, were described by one member as "a little band of willful women, the most unruly and individualistic females you ever fell among."[29] The club's central aim was to define the boundaries of "individual psychic freedom."[30] Mabel Dodge Luhan, a famous salon hostess of the 1910s, saw the club as being "for unorthodox women, that is to say, women who did things and did them openly."[31]

For Dennett, this was a bold progression from her Society of Arts and Crafts and Anti-Imperialist League back in Framingham. A pursuit of "psychic freedom" was more ambitious, and more individualistic, too. Sigmund Freud's beliefs about the hazards of repression were resoundingly popular after *The Interpretation of Dreams* was published in English in 1913. His ideas helped inaugurate the age of the individual, granting childhood development and parent-child bonds an overwhelming influence, and valuing catharsis and self-realization over conformity and repression.

Freudian theories gave Americans a framework in which to analyze the subconscious, talk about sexuality under the guise of the healing sciences, and cast a new perspective on self-realization and middle-class propriety. As the Greenwich Village playwright (and Heterodite) Susan Glaspell remarked, "You couldn't go out to buy a bun without hearing of someone's complex."[32]

At Heterodoxy, Dennett was pulled into an overlapping group, the Feminist Alliance, run by Henrietta Rodman. They rallied for causes like maternity leave, cooperative nurseries, and shared guardianship of children. "Feminism has nothing to do with suffrage," Dennett told a reporter in May 1914. "It is the rebellion against being ticketed and treated as somebody's female relative."[33] A newspaper clipping about Heterodites from 1914 announced: "FEMINISTS 'BREAK INTO HUMAN RACE.'"[34]

With a few fellow Heterodites, Dennett wrote and played a role in a short film, "Votes for Women," released in September 1912. At its New York debut in the Hammerstein Theatre, the activist-actor (and politician's daughter) Fola La Follette lectured on feminism to a crowd of about a hundred. "All the female would-be-voters wore white dresses," *Variety* reported. "It's some stunt, this, getting nice women who think they are brainy because they are nervy, to exhibit themselves before people who pay for the privilege of looking at them." The critic concluded by calling the film "some 'freak act,' without a shadow of a doubt."[35] Dennett was dismayed by how she looked on screen but enjoyed the novelty of performing with her friends.

"Feminist" came into common use in the 1910s, and implied a specific strain of rebellion. Feminists tended to be white, urban, and educated. They prioritized issues like suffrage, social purity, and marriage reform over issues like structural racism, unsafe labor conditions, and inhumane working hours. "The revolt of white women against [their] preordained destiny," wrote W. E. B. Du Bois, had "reached splendid proportions, but it is the revolt of an aristocracy."[36]

In her quippy, witty 1915 book, *Are Women People?*, Alice Duer Miller pitched women's suffrage, and feminism generally, as a long-overdue corrective:

> *Father, what is a Legislature?*
> *A representative body elected by the people of the state.*
> *Are women people?*
> *No, my son, criminals, lunatics and women are not people.*[38]

No one yet knew how long women's civic influence would be kept constrained to clubs and leagues, or when this half of the population would be unleashed upon the ballot box. Feminist editorials vied with antisuffrage screeds. The influence of women as voters had yet to be seen, and hovered like a promise or a bad joke.

. . .

Dennett likely first saw Margaret Sanger at a Heterodoxy meeting.[39] She had taken a seat in Polly's Restaurant on MacDougal Street in Greenwich Village—a self-consciously anarchist bistro where management sometimes addressed patrons as "bourgeois pigs." There, one Saturday in 1914, Sanger delivered a lecture on birth control.

Sanger was thirty-four or thirty-five, Dennett seven years older. At the Heterodoxy lecture, Dennett would have seen a narrow, straight-backed figure, with warm auburn hair and greenish hazel eyes, who talked about birth control in a commonsense tone, with an occasional smile and constantly gesticulating hands.[40]

Yet the lecture fell flat. Sanger complained she'd "struck no responsive chord" with the crowd.[41] She was profoundly irritated afterward, sensing a lack of enthusiasm.[42] She never joined Heterodoxy herself: its feminism focused on "trying to inspire women in this country to have a deeper meaning in their lives," in Sanger's description.[43]

The likes of Charlotte Perkins Gilman, Crystal Eastman, and Henrietta Rodman were inscrutable and misguided to Sanger. "It seemed unbelievable they could be serious in occupying themselves with what I regarded as trivialities when mothers within a stone's throw of their meetings were dying shocking deaths."[44] Sanger had no appetite for watching such a concentration of intelligence, energy, and money channeled toward debating whether women should keep their maiden names or maintain a second, separate property just for themselves after marriage.

"Hundreds of thousands of laundresses, cloak-makers, scrub women, servants, telephone girls, shop workers would gladly have changed places with the Feminists in return for the right to have leisure, to be lazy a little now and then," Sanger wrote, her desire to grab their shoulders and shake them palpable.[45] "When I suggested that the basis of Feminism might be the right to be a mother regardless of church or state, their inherited prejudices were instantly aroused."[46] She held out little hope of inspiring them to direct action beyond fundraising balls.

Despite the apparent indifference of the crowd that day, Dennett was rapt. Sanger talked about sex as if it were normal and, even more surprising, as if it were natural for women to like it. In Mabel Dodge Luhan's memory, "[Sanger] was the first person I ever knew who was openly an ardent propagandist for the joys of the flesh. This, in those days, was radical indeed when the sense of sin was still so indubitably mixed with the sense of pleasure."[47] Sanger's insistence that birth control was paramount to women achieving equal rights resonated with ideas Dennett had just started putting into words herself.

After the meeting, Dennett invited Sanger to her apartment for lunch. They exchanged stories about their lives, talking long into the afternoon. Here was Dennett, a highly educated divorcée without much money but with an insider's knowledge of the loudest feminist crusade of the day. Not a classic privileged clubwoman, but conversant with their ways. Sanger grouped her with the abstract-intellectual bunch at Heterodoxy, but unlike much of that set, Dennett saw the urgency and promise of Sanger's work. Out of that meeting a promising collaboration began to take shape.

The one unpardonable sin on the part of a mother is to let her children learn the truth elsewhere than from her own lips.

—Margaret Sanger (December 1911)

S ANGER WROTE THAT WHEN SHE began her career in New York, the nation was in "one of the most interesting phases of life the United States has ever seen."[1] What made it especially interesting to her was the sense of a revolution about to break out. "Radicalism in manners, art, industry, morals, politics was effervescing, and the lid was about to blow off in the Great War," Sanger wrote.[2]

The 1910s are often compared to the 1960s for the intensity of the protest movements simmering and periodically boiling over throughout both decades.[3] A sense of shifting norms was everywhere, driven by technological innovations, urbanization, and widespread skepticism about the previous generation's moral codes.

Sanger joined Branch 5 of the Socialist Party of New York, as did Bill, who was now otherwise focused on painting. Politically, the Socialist Party had real traction now. Eugene V. Debs won nearly 6 percent of the vote in the 1912 general election as a Socialist candidate;[4] Socialists were elected mayors, aldermen, and school trustees throughout the United States. Sanger's father and husband both passionately supported Debs, but soon her political awakening made theirs seem like just a lot of talk.

Sanger began to host anticapitalist and labor-justice meetings, supporting the platform of the Wobblies, as members of the International

Workers of the World (IWW) called themselves. She was watchful at these meetings, more likely to busy herself serving mugs of cocoa than to join the discussion. Whenever she had an idea at a meeting, she recalled, her habit was to whisper it in Bill's ear. Her husband would then raise his hand and say, "Have you heard Margaret? Margaret has something to say."[5] Only then would she speak.

Her timidity quickly ran its course. In March 1911, just a few months after the Sangers moved to New York, the Triangle shirtwaist fire killed 146 workers, most of them Jewish women. Afterward, a crowd of at least 80,000 marched down Fifth Avenue to honor them and protest the dangers they faced just by going to work. Sanger described feeling "absolute rapture" at a 1911 laundry workers' strike in New York, while listening to Elizabeth Gurley Flynn, called "Rebel Girl" by the tabloids, who soon afterward visited Sanger to talk strategy as they bathed baby Peggy in the sink.[6]

In the early months of 1912, Sanger joined her comrades in supporting the textile workers striking in Lawrence, Massachusetts. State laws had recently been passed cutting working hours for women and children, and mill owners reacted by cutting hours and salaries across the board. The average lifespan of Lawrence mill workers at that time was under forty years, and around a third died within a decade of taking their jobs. One fourteen-year-old girl recounted how a mill accident had torn off her scalp.[7]

Cornered and desperate, workers took action. Tens of thousands joined the strike, and some even took arms against the means of production. Workers brought in knives to cut machine belts; they dismantled equipment, threw bricks through windows, and stolidly resisted policemen armed with billy clubs and militiamen with rifles and bayonets.[8] Sanger helped get 119 children on trains from Lawrence to Manhattan, to stay with relatives or sympathizers until the strike's conclusion.

Quickly, she became the political driving force in her household, getting Bill to lectures, amassing articles and books, making friends with other committed Socialists, attending her tenement patients with new, politically motivated zeal. "Gone forever was the conservative Irish girl I had married," Bill wrote; "a new woman, forceful, intelligent, hungry for facts, tireless, ambitious and cool, had miraculously come into being."[9]

. . .

Sanger found herself part of a conclave of activists far removed from the Eliot-and-Browning-reading ladies of Hastings. Crucially, in her new life, one imposing figure offered a kind of apprenticeship: Emma Goldman.

Born ten years before Sanger in present-day Lithuania, Goldman emigrated to the United States in 1885. Over the course of two decades, she became a heroic and notorious figure in the American social justice struggle. An accredited midwife, she had, like Sanger, worked as a visiting nurse in slum neighborhoods and was deeply marked by seeing so many women forced to give birth at near-yearly intervals and resorting to desperate measures to end pregnancies.[10] "It was incredible," she wrote, "what fantastic methods despair could invent; jumping off tables, rolling on the floor, and using blunt instruments."[11]

Goldman's memoir, *Living My Life*, claims she wove birth control into her speeches as early as 1900. Reluctant to risk a long prison term, she never described actual contraceptive methods in her lectures. Instead, she promoted birth control in general, as an important plank in the class struggle. Her 1915 pamphlet "Why and How the Poor Should Not Have Many Children" got into the nuts and bolts of it, advocating pessaries made of cotton balls soaked in borated Vaseline and a dubious version of the rhythm method.[12]

In her lectures she also argued against the stigma surrounding illegitimacy, which still wielded a terrible power to brand mother and child throughout their lives. Foundling asylums, a common feature of European cities, were established in New York, Baltimore, San

Francisco, and other American cities in the 1850s and '60s. They
were needed to house children abandoned by mothers who couldn't
care for them or whose social circumstances forbade having a child;
these were nearly always unmarried women. New York's first foundling asylum took in 123 infants in its first three months of operation:
an average of one to two babies left wrapped on the doorstep every
night.[13]

Besides the social stigma attached to children born out of wedlock, unmarried mothers were routinely rejected by landlords. They
were denied pensions available to widows and deserted wives who
could prove their status. Goldman wanted to tear down this prejudice;
she viewed marriage itself on the same terms as "that other paternal
arrangement—capitalism," an alienating institution that enlightened
people should not tolerate.[14]

Goldman drew from literature and art to argue for expanded rights
for women. Reflecting on Nora's abandonment of her children in
Henrik Ibsen's 1879 play, A Doll's House, she argued that "woman . . .
must become free and strong to choose the father of her child and
to decide the number of children she is to bring into the world and
under what conditions. That is the only kind of motherhood which
can endure."[15]

Taking after Goldman, Sanger began reporting her nursing experiences in lectures and the Socialist paper, the New York Call. Her
stories were a kind of verbal continuation of Jacob Riis's photojournal-
istic How the Other Half Lives. They dwelled on the day-to-day lives
of impoverished families on and around the Bowery. In a September
1911 article, she described one home: "Everything is thrown out of
the windows . . . where the toilets are in use by the many families
on the same floor, the mother allows the children to use paper as
toilet receptacles and it too is thrown out of the windows. . . . And
the vermin . . . kitchens swarming with, not thousands but millions
of roaches. . . . Bed bugs are everywhere . . . thousands of mothers
leave their little children in the care of the older boy and girl (usually

not over nine years old) and go to work early in the morning in the factories or work shop to return at night to do the work of the family."[16]

Sanger's 1911 series for *The Call*, "What Every Mother Should Know," made a plea for early, honest sex education. In 1912, she began publishing the series "What Every Girl Should Know," and there she was markedly bolder. Arguing that no one could understand what was happening to them in puberty without thorough knowledge of physiology, she described the female reproductive organs, menstruation and menopause, and the emotional tumult of adolescence.

The series held hints of a style Sanger was beginning to burnish as her own, though it had much in common with Goldman's. Both combined a no-nonsense nurse's perspective with that of a missionary from the future bent on correcting Victorian repression. Controversially, Sanger separated sex from reproduction, writing, "The creative instinct does not need to be expended entirely for the propagation of the race."[17]

The *New York Times* suggested Sanger was "an enemy of the young"[18] for her frank talk. Readers, however, felt they'd found an ally. One letter exclaimed, "I am a woman of most 66 years and I have learned more from them [the articles] than from any books or even from my own life, and I am the mother of eight children!"[19]

By the print date of the final article, Comstock's post office censors had cottoned on to Sanger, and her column was declared unmailable. The final installment in the series was startling to readers' eyes, as Sanger had replaced her text with a spare white box containing a few biting words: "What Every Girl Should Know: NOTHING! By Order of the Post Office Department."[20]

. . .

Despite the force of her determination after witnessing Sadie Sachs's death, Sanger had trouble getting people behind birth control. Even erstwhile allies urged her to keep quiet. "Wait until we get the vote. Then we'll take care of that," was how she heard the response from suffragists.[21]

The patriarchal slant of the Socialist Party provoked her deeply. In one of her articles in *The Call*, she noted, "Most radicals are stirred by the Socialist call to the workers to revolt from wage-slavery, but they are unmoved by the Socialist call to women to revolt from sex slavery. They are still too oversexed, too tainted with the sins of their fathers, to be able to look upon women's claims as their own."[22] She resigned herself to the fact that, among her Socialist comrades, the importance of birth control might never be understood.

The Sangers' marriage was tested by Margaret's new vocation and the general ferment of the 1910s. The couple were increasingly at odds, with Margaret feeding her new ambitions with writing and new lovers, while Bill would have preferred them to be monogamous. In the summer of 1912, around the time she met Sadie Sachs, Margaret had met and begun an affair with John Rompapas, a Greek-born anarchist. She was not so much betraying Bill as adhering to her new professed code of ethics, the law of Greenwich Village: "Free love in the Village," wrote one historian, Judith Schwarz, "was not illicit self-indulgence, but instead was a serious ethical undertaking . . . the only sin was in living with someone you no longer loved. That was seen as almost a form of prostitution."[23]

The Sangers were also consumed with concern for Peggy, their youngest. She had contracted polio as an infant, and though she had long recovered and was an energetic child, one of her legs required a brace. Margaret resisted using it, despite Peggy's pronounced limp and difficulty using the leg. It became a point of contention with Bill, who could not understand why Margaret wanted to keep up the facade of pretending Peggy was typical in every way.

When the summer heat came to the city the Sangers took their children to Provincetown, at the end of Cape Cod, a haven for New York artists and writers. They blended into the background, for the most part. The writer Hutchins Hapgood described them as a "sweet gentle painter who lacked ego and ambition" and his "pretty wife . . . [who] seemed to grant [him] little value."[24]

Margaret played along with the Greenwich Village summer scene, but she was unable to pause work for more than a week or two at a time. Throughout the summer, Margaret left the children with her sister Ethel Byrne, also a nurse, while she researched sex and psychology at the Boston Public Library. "It was a period of gestation," she said of that summer. "Just as you give birth to a child, so you can give birth to an idea."[25]

In September 1913, the Sangers decamped for Europe. Margaret had a pretext: a commission to write about Glasgow's public housing for *The Call*. It was her first time outside the United States, and she relished the prospect. Ahead of the trip she and Bill finalized the sale of their Hastings property. "Although we did not realize it at the time," Sanger later wrote, "our gestures indicated a clean sweep of the past."[26]

At first, the long-dreamed-of trip was a fiasco. They were plagued with seasickness. In Glasgow she was appalled by the ubiquitous drunkenness she saw.[27] Traveling with their children proved burdensome. When they finally landed in Paris, their temporary home was a cold, fourth-floor walk-up apartment near the Luxembourg Gardens.

Birth control was a discreet but common practice in Catholic France. There, over the course of the nineteenth century, the average number of children per woman declined from 5.0 to 3.2.[28] (In 1920, reeling from the losses of the First World War and uncertain of its future as a nation, France would pass a restrictive law on birth control information and supplies, not repealed until 1967.)[29] It was a French zoologist, Félix-Archimède Pouchet, who first connected ovulation and menstruation in the early 1840s, though his resulting theory of an infertile or "safe" period starting just before menstruation and lasting for eighteen days after its onset was inaccurate for most bodies.

Sanger must have been a gifted interviewer, for her new acquaintances spoke openly with her. They shared their trusted contraceptive methods, "special recipes" for spermicidal potions passed down through families like *"pot au feu,"* according to Sanger.[30] The Frenchwomen she met told her family limitation was viewed as a practical matter, a form of home economics, as was the occasional discreet abortion.

After three hard but illuminating months, Margaret decided to return to New York. "Bill was happy in his studio," she wrote, "but I could find no peace. Each day I stayed, each person I met, made it worse. . . . I could not contain my ideas. I wanted to get on with what I had to do in the world."[31] On New Year's Eve, she and the children boarded the ocean liner *New York*.

"Bill and I said good-by," she wrote, "unaware the parting was to be final."[32]

It is hard to give this full credence, given how efficiently she then shed the trappings of married life. She found an apartment of her own, on the northern end of Manhattan in Inwood, and in a letter, she asked Bill to be "physically and spiritually" released from their vows.[33] He tried to plead his case, but his possessiveness combined with his financial instability repelled her. "I shall never forget the expression in your face when I threw the last kiss . . . I feel now that nobody can take you away from me," he wrote in his first letter after their parting.[34] It was painful to realize how completely mistaken he had been.

She had outgrown marriage, at least with someone who expected her to take on all the homemaking and put his interests first. "I could not live with a human being," Sanger wrote, "conscious that my necessities were thwarting or dwarfing his progress."[35] This line appears in her autobiography, but it seems to describe the central problem in reverse: Bill's needs were thwarting *her* progress, not the other way around.

Bill blamed their separation on Greenwich Village itself, calling it a "hellhole of free love, promiscuity and prostitution masquerading under the mantle of revolution."[36] He had never embraced polyamory as easily as Margaret had. Separately, he admitted, "If Revolution means promiscuity, they can call me a conservative and make the most of it."[37]

As for Margaret, her world-hunger was still strong. Their divorce would take seven years to finalize, but from 1914 she counted herself free.

. . .

It began as a dream Sanger had on the ship home from France: a magazine. In March 1914, she launched an eight-page "monthly paper of militant thought" called *The Woman Rebel*.[38] She called it her "little sass box,"[39] and she worked "day and night to make it as red and flaming as possible."[40]

Magazines proliferated in Greenwich Village: Socialists had *The Masses* and anarchists had Goldman's *Mother Earth*. In the first issue of her own magazine, Sanger printed a piece by Emma Goldman critiquing marriage and an article titled "The Prevention of Conception." She also stated her provocative aims. "Why the Woman Rebel?" asked the last page, and in response, among other points, Sanger wrote:

> Because I believe that deep down in woman's nature lies slumbering the spirit of revolt.
> Because I believe that woman is enslaved by the world machine, by sex conventions, by motherhood and its present necessary child-rearing, by wage-slavery, by middle-class morality, by customs, laws and superstitions.[41]

In the July 1914 issue, Sanger set out her manifesto: "A woman's body belongs to herself alone. It does not belong to the United States of America or to any other government on the face of the earth. . . . Enforced motherhood is the most complete denial of a woman's right to life and liberty." It sounds like the corollary to a much later feminist rallying cry for reproductive rights, the Manifesto of the 343 (1971), in which Simone de Beauvoir wrote, "I will have a child if I want one, and no moral pressure, institution or economic imperative will compel me to do so." Nearly sixty years before Beauvoir, Sanger had the same certainty.

"It was a marvelous time to say what we wished," Sanger remembered. "All America was a Hyde Park corner as far as criticism and challenging thought were concerned."[42] Six months after starting publication, Sanger reported receiving more than ten thousand letters asking for birth control information.[43]

But this was the age of Comstock, and the *Woman Rebel* brought on a crackdown from vice agents almost immediately. Of the seven issues eventually printed, six were suppressed by the US Post Office.[44] A postal employee, Bertram Wolfe, recalled that in April 1914, he'd been tasked with holding up to the light all second- and third-class mail, periodicals, and any piece of mail that might hold Sanger's handiwork.[45]

In August, Sanger received a visit from two post office inspectors who gave her an earnest reprimand about what she called her "impropoganda."[46] She wrote Upton Sinclair the following month that she'd been warned to avoid a few specific topics: "Dear Comrade Sinclair. . . . Following are the articles on which I am indicted. 'Prevention of Conception' (March). 'Open Discussion,' 'Can you Afford to have a Large family'? [sic] 'Abortion in U.S.' (May)."[47] Then the agents went further: they arrested her on four counts of violating the Comstock Act, a crime that could potentially earn her forty years' imprisonment.[48]

The Woman Rebel and Sanger's ensuing arrest vaulted her into a new echelon of activist fame. She began exchanging letters with a set she called the "leading Feminists of Europe" (and beyond): Ellen Key in Sweden, Olive Schreiner in South Africa, Emmeline Pankhurst in England, and Rosa Luxemburg in Berlin.[49] They helped embolden her to an even more hazardous act.

In the six weeks before her trial, Sanger produced a sixteen-page pamphlet she called *Family Limitation*.[50] Fulfilling the promise of *The Woman Rebel*, Sanger at last laid out her birth control knowledge:

a combination of what she had learned as nurse, researcher, and freethinker. She described douching, condoms, pessaries, sponges, and vaginal suppositories made of cocoa butter, recipe style. She cautioned against trusting any theory about a safe period, said withdrawal had an "evil effect upon the woman's nervous system," and approved of condoms and Lysol (creosote, distilled from wood and coal) douches, but her strongest recommendation was a "well fitted pessary"—a cervical cap or diaphragm.[51] It was best for a doctor or nurse to do the initial fitting, but "then women can teach each other."[52]

She dismissed the whisper-giggle tone of most existing sources associated with sex and birth. "Birth control must not be set back by the false cry of obscenity," she wrote; "women must learn to know their own bodies."[53]

Sanger poured her savings into printing a staggering one hundred thousand copies, which she sold at her lectures and asked friends to do the same.[54] Because of its practical wisdom and the volume of copies in circulation, *Family Limitation* was her first culture-changing contribution to the birth control movement.

In early versions of *Family Limitation*, Sanger wove in a spirit of political radicalism—"The working class can use direct action by refusing . . . to populate the earth with slaves," she wrote—as well as sensitivity to how readers might perceive her methods. "It seems inartistic and sordid to insert a pessary or a suppository in anticipation of the sexual act," she wrote. "But it is far more sordid to find yourself several years later burdened down with half a dozen unwished for children, helpless, starved, shoddily clothed, dragging at your skirt, yourself a dragged out shadow of the woman you once were."[55]

Later revisions to *Family Limitation* reflect the gradual and deliberate separation between Sanger and her early Socialist and radical associations, as well as her determination to put birth control in a separate ethical framework from abortion. In the first edition Sanger advised taking quinine if a woman's period was late and she suspected conception might have taken place. By 1921, for the eleventh edition, this section was removed, and Sanger would never again print any indication that she condoned abortion under any circumstance.[56] Though she did occasionally refer women for abortions, in her writing she had to publicly pit herself against abortion to maintain her credibility with donors, doctors, and most of all with politicians. While abortion had the same legal status as birth control in many states, it was seen as the greater moral crime.

Family Limitation taught generations of women about the mechanics of conception and offered details of methods they had never heard of before and could access relatively cheaply. It quickly became a how-to that women quietly slipped into one another's pockets or passed over the fence.

One reader, however, felt scooped. Caroline Nelson, a Danish American Socialist, had grown close with Sanger over the months preceding the pamphlet's publication. Nelson had published an article, "The Control of Childbearing," in October 1913 and received hundreds of letters in response; "I found that I had accidentally put my finger on a vital spot,"she marveled.[57] When Sanger asked Nelson what else she knew of contraception, Nelson passed her some translations she had done from French and Swedish sources. A few days later Sanger returned them, claiming she had shown them to a doctor who pronounced them "no good."

"Fancy then my surprise," Nelson reminisced years later, in a letter to Dennett, when she was sent a bundle of *Family Limitation*s and read through to find "the identical 'no good' information"replicated, her research published under Sanger's name.[58]

. . .

In the same few months in which Sanger produced *The Woman Rebel* and *Family Limitation*, the term "birth control" was born. Sanger wrote that "finally it came to me out of the blue—'Birth Control!'"[59] In fact, "birth control" came out of a collaborative process and several rough drafts. It was chosen from a carousel of options that included "constructive generation," "prevenception," and "race control."[60]

The exact origin story remains blurry, but either the writer Robert Allerton Parker, a playwright and yoga devotee, or Sanger's friend Otto Bobsien finally landed on "birth control." The term felt scientific and authoritative, but easy to pronounce. A senator would be able to say it without blushing; an illiterate grandmother would understand it.

In another five years' time, Dennett would carefully consider the options before naming her organization the Voluntary Parenthood League. That name that called to mind more old-fashioned notions, emphasizing parenthood—not birth, and not population control—as the core idea.

Sanger's trial for *The Woman Rebel* came up in October 1914. She pleaded for a month's postponement and was denied. Drafting letters to the judge and prosecuting attorney explaining that she needed time to ready her case, Sanger enclosed copies of *Family Limitation* for both and sent them off. Then, she fled the country.

Mary Ware in 1892.

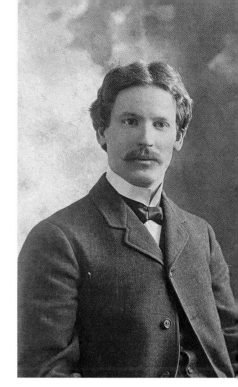

Hartley Dennett in 1897.
He was engaged to Mary, who
wrote him, "Love me more and
more if you can, dear. But don't
forget that I am just plain Mary
Ware and not an ideal girl at all,
and whose heart is yours."

Margaret Higgins in 1892 or 1893.
She later wrote of her childhood as
"one of longing for things that were
always denied."

Bill Sanger, n.d. In the early 1910s, when the couple attended labor-justice meetings together, he encouraged her to speak up, calling to the crowd, "Have you heard Margaret? Margaret has something to say."

Margaret Sanger Papers, Sophia Smith Collection, SSC-MS-00108, Smith College Special Collections, Northampton, Massachusetts. Published with the permission of Alexander Sanger.

Margaret Chase with her children in 1903 or 1904, close to the time the Dennetts and Chases first met. Dennett called her "the tiger type, but intellectual in her method."

Margaret Chase Perry

Dennett with her youngest son, Devon, in 1905. Her children were, she wrote, "both wanted, but both accidental."

Sharon Spaulding / Dennett Family Archives

The Dennetts in 1906 or 1907. In spring 1907, Mary later wrote to her sons, "I became conscious of the change in Hartley." *Sharon Spaulding / Dennett Family Archives*

The first American birth control clinic, which Sanger opened at 46 Amboy Street in Brooklyn. This photograph captures an instant in October 1916, during the nine days the clinic operated before being raided by the police. *New York World-Telegram and the Sun Newspaper Photograph Collection, Library of Congress Prints and Photographs Division*

Peggy Sanger in 1912. Her death in 1915, aged five, convinced her mother that "the joy in the fullness of life went out of it."

Margaret Sanger Papers, Sophia Smith Collection, SSC-MS-00108, Smith College Special Collections, Northampton, Massachusetts. Published with the permission of Alexander Sanger.

Sanger, aged thirty-seven, with her sons Stuart and Grant in 1916. In later life, she grew to "envy mothers who had leisure to grow along with their children or, at least, to watch them develop."

Margaret Sanger Papers, Sophia Smith Collection, SSC-MS-00108, Smith College Special Collections, Northampton, Massachusetts. Published with the permission of Alexander Sanger.

Dennett's New Year's card for 1920. "I have no faith in authority, but only in the unquenchable aspiration of the human soul," she wrote that year.

Sharon Spaulding / Dennett Family Archives

Sanger labeled this 1915 portrait "In Exile." While she missed her family during her year overseas, she recognized her time away presented an opportunity to "get acquainted with myself, to reflect, meditate and dream."

Margaret Sanger Papers, Sophia Smith Collection, SSC-MS-00108, Smith College Special Collections, Northampton, Massachusetts. Published with the permission of Alexander Sanger.

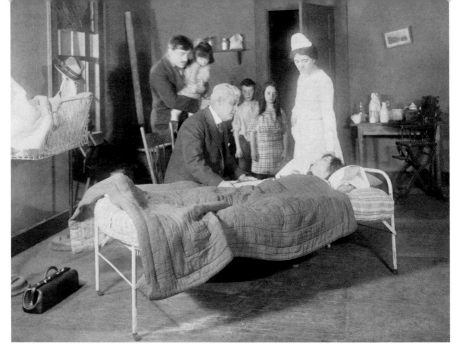

A still from the film *Birth Control*, written by Sanger, starring Sanger, and released in 1917 but since lost. This scene re-creates her encounter with patient Sadie Sachs. *Margaret Sanger Papers, Sophia Smith Collection, SSC-MS-00108, Smith College Special Collections, Northampton, Massachusetts. Published with the permission of Alexander Sanger.*

Morris Leopold Ernst. He overcame bans on Dennett's *The Sex Side of Life*, James Joyce's *Ulysses*, and Radclyffe Hall's *The Well of Loneliness*, and represented Sanger too. "I'm a ham. I like publicity," he liked to say.

Morris Leopold Ernst Photography Collection Literary File, 984:0010:0023, Harry Ransom Center, The University of Texas at Austin.

Marie Stopes, c. 1921, the year Dennett invited her to New York and the year of Sanger's First American Birth Control Conference.

Underwood & Underwood, photographer. Library of Congress Prints and Photographs Division.

Sanger at a congressional hearing in 1932. Bureaucracy, hostility, and moments of desperate hope characterized Sanger's lobbying campaign, just as they had Dennett's—though Sanger was better staffed, better funded, and commanded greater press attention. *Margaret Sanger Papers, Sophia Smith Collection, SSC-MS-00108, Smith College Special Collections, Northampton, Massachusetts. Published with the permission of Alexander Sanger.*

A publicity photo of Dennett taken for the *New York Journal-American* around the time of her obscenity trial. "It is the government which is disgraced, not I," she wrote in her book *Who's Obscene?* after being found guilty.

New York Journal-American Photographic Morgue, Harry Ransom Center, The University of Texas at Austin

A Mizpah cervical cap. Sanger favored this brand of diaphragm, which had a thick rubber rim and replaceable dome. In this specimen, the dome has decayed and fallen open.

Science Museum Group

Twilight Sleep

> If the male ever had to endure this suffering, I think he would resort very precipitously to something that would relieve the unavoidable, so-called psychological pain.
>
> —Dr. James Harrar, *Transactions of the American Association of Obstetricians and Gynecologists* (1914)

IN THE UNIVERSITY TOWN OF Freiburg, Germany, on the mountainous border of the Black Forest, two doctors, Bernhardt Krönig and Karl Gauss, spent the earliest years of the twentieth century inducing amnesia in birthing women.

Their drug compound, called Dämmerschlaf, or Twilight Sleep, was not all that far removed from the herbalist's mixing table. Opium, extracted from the poppy, was combined with scopolamine, derived from a deadly nightshade. It is thought that scopolamine was consumed recreationally in ancient Greece, and that it was the drug used to poison Hamlet's father.

For Dennett, Twilight Sleep signaled the dress rehearsal for what would become the central cause of her career. Her future sex education and birth control work drew from passions and convictions she developed years before she even heard of the birth control movement.

Her devotion to the aesthetic movement was one of these; suffrage was another. Her public commitment to Twilight Sleep brought her into her first tussles with a hostile medical establishment, standing in defense of women convinced of their right to birth in the way they chose.

The Twilight Sleep movement—for under Dennett's guidance it bloomed briefly into a national campaign—went deeper than the desire for pain control. Mothers-to-be demanded that their pain be seen as real, first of all, and worthy of a state-of-the-art remedy. As middle-class women increasingly pursued "scientific" births, they demanded every anesthetic modern science could offer.

Today, Twilight Sleep is shorthand for a historical episode with a brutal cast. It conjures women infantilized by doctors offering erasure rather than relief, kept in padded, enclosed beds and sometimes straitjacketed. Photographs taken of patients under the influence of the drug, restrained and blindfolded, are indeed chilling. Many of those who experienced it, however, remembered no pain; they were rapturous.

. . .

From the earliest evidence of poppy cultivation, in Mesopotamia around 3400 BC, archival references to pain remedies taken during birth are plentiful. In Western culture these remedies were associated with midwifery, herbalism, and, occasionally, the dark arts. In 1591, among the allegations against Agnes Sampson, a midwife burned for witchcraft in Scotland, was that she had offered Euphemia Maclean pain relief during childbirth, in the form of "an unspecified powdered substance, a bored stone to be laid under her pillow and some 'Inchantit mwildis' (the finger, toe and knee joints of disinterred corpses)."[1]

Today, the availability of pain relief for childbirth is taken for granted, even if unmedicated birth is often valued as more natural or authentic. During Dennett's and Sanger's childbearing years, the more common question was not how to evade pain, but how to live with it. Theirs was an age when, as William James said, people "looked upon pain as an eternal ingredient of the world's order, and both caused and suffered it as a matter-of-course portion of their day's work."[2]

For physicians who knew that infection, hemorrhage, and permanent injury to mother or child were very real possibilities, the screaming was the least of their troubles. Most doctors dismissed the possibility that birth pains could be traumatic, too. "I've never observed that the painfulness of the first labour kept a woman from having a second," declared one obstetrician, and his colleague rejoined with, "Yes, a woman with plenty of grit would always rather carry it through without anaesthesia."[3] One theory posited that screaming in labor served as "the aeration of the blood by pain."[4]

Then there were the spiritual implications of disrupting labor pains. American doctors tended to be observant Christian men. For them, easing the pain of a normal labor was not just medically superfluous, but theologically problematic. Women shared Eve's punishment for eating of the Tree of Knowledge. It was bad for the soul—both the mother's and the doctor's—to interfere.

It took a powerful influencer to banish the sense of sin around pain relief for birth. The ultimate aristocrat and model of propriety, Queen Victoria, was dosed with chloroform during childbirth and pronounced it "delightful beyond measure."[5] Even then, many doctors were haunted by the suspicion that labor pains were biblically ordained.

But if any desire is strong enough to defy divinity, nature, and convention, it is probably the yearning for a manageable, even dignified birth: a way to leapfrog from the first serious contractions to a Madonna and Child tableau. In her essay "Marriage," written in the 1850s, the abolitionist and suffragist Sarah Moore Grimké echoed something she'd heard a physician say: that if wives and husbands could alternate who gave birth, "no family would ever have more than three, the husband bearing one and the wife two."[6]

In the nineteenth century, anesthesia began preceding surgery for matters large and small. In the 1840s, an American physician had success removing cysts from patients who inhaled ether, and thereafter promoted the use of ether in birth.[7] Months later, in Edinburgh,

Dr. James Young Simpson introduced the use of chloroform in birth; in the same period an American dentist began using nitrous oxide, which also made its way to obstetrics.

Excepting Simpson's work with chloroform, these methods were developed for other complaints—minor surgeries, war wounds—and passed along to laboring women afterward. Today's most frequently used obstetric pain relief, the epidural, was pioneered in the early 1920s by a Spanish military surgeon, and not popularized for labor until the 1940s. The fact that Twilight Sleep was developed specially for birth was significant. It implied labor pain was as deserving of treatment as a soldier's ordeal.

It's uncertain where Dennett first heard about Twilight Sleep, but it likely would have been either a journal article or word of mouth. In a 1914 series of articles in *McClure's*, for instance, two journalists went to Freiburg with a pregnant patient, Mary Sumner Boyd. The writers marveled, "No article ever published in *McClure's* attracted more attention than 'Painless Childbirth,' in the June issue."[8]

By then Dennett was already involved. In a headline in the *World* on February 1, 1913, a reporter offered an update on the reconfigured Dennett-Chase family. "MRS. DENNETT WILL NOT JOIN 'GOLDEN RULE TRIANGLE': Wife Who Divorced Mrs. Chase's Soul Mate Deeply Interested in Suffrage and Twilight Sleep," read a subhead.[9] Twilight Sleep was covered in *The Ladies' World* and the *Woman's Home Companion*; one editor noted in 1915, "There can be no doubt that it was the most widely known and most generally talked about medical achievement of last year."[10]

The fad of having a "Freiburg baby" started with a few bold and wealthy souls and grew into a groundswell that was ultimately disrupted only by the First World War. Charlotte Carmody, an adventurous Brooklynite, wrote up a description of a Twilight Sleep birth that became gospel for women seeking it out. She reported that when her contractions began, she was given the first shot, and emerged more than twelve hours later feeling as if she'd had a brief nap. "Perhaps the baby will come tomorrow," she thought, but then realized, "I felt lighter, and sat up easily, and my figure had changed." A nurse brought her a baby boy, whom she named Charlemagne.[11]

Dennett was seized with imagining the course her own life might have taken if she'd been able to give birth the Freiburg way. What if American doctors carried it in their black bags, and knew how to use it? It would save mothers incalculable trauma and pain; it might even save marriages. On January 22, 1915, the *Washington Herald* reported: "'Twilight sleep' babies from Lebanon, Gouverneur, and Long Island Hospitals will be an interesting exhibit at the Twilight Sleep Association meeting in the ball-room of the Hotel McAlpin [New York City]."[12]

Dennett, alongside Fola La Follette and several Freiburg mothers, had organized the meeting with the aim of giving "authentic information to American women about this wonderful boon to womankind," in the words of the *Herald*.[13] It was a glossy, festive affair. "Pretty Women Combine to Spread the Gospel of 'Twilight Sleep,'" ran the *Washington Post* caption under a full-page image of Mrs. Astor.[14]

As a culmination to the meeting, Dennett announced the formation of the National Twilight Sleep Association. It was her first foray into running a national organization; she was forty-three. It was also her first time trying to cajole the medical establishment to listen to women, and to change.

A stream of letters flowed into the New York office, showing an "intense interest in every part of the country among women of all classes but particularly among the poor and those of moderate means— the great childbearers of the world," noted the association's young secretary, Marie Virginia Smith.[15] The Twilight Sleepers agitated for the right to gain control by losing consciousness, brought together by the determination to "relieve one-half of humanity from its antique burden of a suffering which the other half of humanity has never understood."[16]

American doctors were skeptical. Twilight Sleep was foreign, there was little medical literature in English about it, and patients asking for it seemed possessed by the desire to participate in a trend concocted by magazines and hearsay.

In fact, a Harvard professor had attempted morphine-scopolamine anesthesia in 1906, but abandoned it because his results were unpromising.[17] Now the Freiburg method struck many as "quackish hocus-pocus advocated by our notoriety seeking German contemporaries," as one doctor put it.[18] "Doubtless many others have shared our recent experience in being the recipients of inquiries on account of recent sensational articles in the lay press on 'painless childbirth,'" wrote Dr. Ross McPherson of the Lying-in Hospital of New York. "The first attitude was naturally to ridicule the whole matter as preposterous."

Medical schools rejected proposals to include it. Obstetrical training, according to one 1904 graduate, "consisted in reading my textbooks, listening to lectures dealing chiefly with abnormalities, delivery of a manikin . . . and the witnessing from the amphitheater of the delivery of a few cases."[19]

Dennett arranged for Smith to make personal calls on ten leading New York obstetricians, to find out how they could best be persuaded to study painless childbirth. "The answers," noted Smith, "without exception amounted to 'No, thank you, we will proceed in the ancient way . . . because (a) we never will forgive the laity for having caught us napping; (b) the method is too much work *for us*—good for the mothers, oh yes, but it does not expedite our work."[20]

It *was* a lot of work. Doctors had to individualize the dose and frequency for each patient.[21] Even hospital architecture would be up for revision, since patients undergoing Twilight Sleep needed rooms without interfering stimuli and the norm, even in many expensive clinics, was a shared ward. Media buzz about the treatment and a rising number of requests for it only made the doctors' resistance calcify into antagonism. They refused to be "stampeded by these misguided ladies."[22]

Given this recalcitrance, the Twilight Sleepers floated the idea of a new hospital, a standalone teaching institution where Twilight Sleep could be perfected. Then, as objections from doctors' groups mounted, they added another goal: the creation of a blacklist of obstetricians who did not offer Twilight Sleep.

Since the popular press and direct inquiry had not made the doctors budge, expectant mothers exerted another source of pressure: their pocketbooks.[23] A doctor writing in *Scientific American* in 1914 noted he and his peers had started offering Twilight Sleep not "because we think the patient needs the narcotic, but because she will promptly go to another doctor if we refuse."[24] The practice began to expand. In November 1914, the *St. Louis Post* printed an article marveling that the "Jewish Maternity Hospital in New York reports 250 cases [of Twilight Sleep] without a single fatality to mother or child."[25]

In New York and other cities, "Freiburg mothers" invited women to their homes and to department-store demonstrations, setting up between the suits and tablecloths to spread the gospel of Twilight Sleep, to show off their healthy, alert "scopolamin babies," and to resolve together to lobby doctors to learn the method.[26]

Dennett wanted to take these meetings nationwide, and she helped organize a lecture tour through the Midwest. This plan, however, imploded on impact. The tour "met with interference by local medical societies everywhere," her secretary wrote in a bulletin.[27] The tour was abandoned, but by then many more women had found out about painless childbirth because of the controversy and wrote to her, clamoring to know more.

Very gradually, Dennett formed ties with doctors, via a mostly anonymous advisory board of physicians, whom she hoped would help establish Twilight Sleep's credibility. But they frequently dropped out without explaining themselves, or made excuses about how their professional standing was at stake and they couldn't afford to be connected with Twilight Sleep, after all.[28]

Besides the doctors, Dennett had a personal problem. Marie Virginia Smith, the association's secretary, developed an intense attachment to Dennett, a one-sided and passionate emotional onslaught. In a letter, Smith described their relationship in marriage-like terms: "Mary—to me—you are bone of my bone + flesh of my flesh—there is no other way to put it. . . . I do not wish to secede from the best and most beautiful thing I know because it has a few ugly + painful aspects. I want to see it through."[29] Dennett's replies have not been preserved, but in other notes she referred to Smith's "idiotic emotionalism about me" and it is clear she distanced herself.[30]

The movement sustained another blow when Charlotte Carmody, the Brooklyn mother who had evangelized for Twilight Sleep, died in childbirth. The cause was a hemorrhage unrelated to the drug, but the negative publicity around the tragedy held many times the weight of each positive report.[31] The day after Carmody's passing, the *New York Times* called Twilight Sleep "a dead issue."[32]

Eugenics turned out to be a boon for Twilight Sleep. In the two years Dennett led the Twilight Sleep Association, "race suicide" preoccupied some of the most prominent men in Washington, who panicked over white, Anglo-Saxon Protestants being outnumbered in the population by everyone else. Twilight Sleep promised that women would want larger families if they didn't have pain memories attached to their births—a valuable proposition at a time when the faltering WASP birth rate was a focus of near hysteria.

A decade after harping on the changing face of the American family in 1905 and 1906 speeches to Congress, former president Theodore Roosevelt was still speaking on the topic, voicing the prejudice that eventually underpinned American eugenics: "If the average family in which there are children contained but two children the nation as a whole would decrease in population so rapidly that in two or three generations it would very deservedly be on the point of extinction," he told a meeting of the Mothers' Congress in 1914.[33] He encouraged couples to have at least four children. He himself had six, though his first wife died two days after the birth of their first child, stricken with Bright's disease, a kidney condition often aggravated by childbearing.

If Twilight Sleep could persuade upper-class gadabouts to have one or two more children than planned, its less convenient aspects might be excused.

Some doctors warmed to it for other reasons, too. Not only did Twilight Sleep take some of the fear out of birth for the mother, but it was unexpectedly empowering for attending obstetricians. The patient's amnesia meant there was no chance for her to make critical observations of her doctor's skill or lack thereof. "I catch up on my reading and writing," reported one physician; "I am never harassed by relatives who want me to tell them things."[34]

These arguments centered the concerns of doctor and nation rather than those of the birthing person. For a brief moment before it was co-opted, however, Twilight Sleep affirmed, for the women who could afford it, that their unconscious bodies had a kind of wisdom. "I had wakened from a ten-hour labour believing that I had been caught napping and the labour was still before me," wrote Mary Sumner Boyd, the subject of the *McClure's* series on Twilight Sleep. "While my brain was sleeping, my muscles and nerves had been working and I had brought forth the baby from beginning to end of labour by my own efforts."[35] The drug encouraged women to believe their bodies had untapped reservoirs of strength and ability, not a message commonly promoted in a culture that valued feminine delicacy.

Twilight Sleep allowed women the illusion that birth could be seemly, controlled, even peaceful. Mothers were still executing a biological function, usually one that involved screams and secretions, but their memory of that aspect was wiped clean, the baby's arrival nearly as neat as if it had happened by stork.

· · ·

Dennett resigned from the Twilight Sleep campaign in late 1915, after the money diminished, disagreements erupted within the group, and she was consumed by antiwar work. After the First World War broke out, her money and energy were quickly siphoned into the campaign for peace.

Despite the war and Dennett's withdrawal from the cause, Twilight Sleep persisted in American hospitals through the early 1960s and was a powerful factor in moving births from home to clinic. Its fall from favor was hastened by other options for pain relief and exposures of malpractice connected to it. The procedure remained medically risky, since dosages could not be standardized.

In 1958, the *Ladies' Home Journal* published "Cruelty in Maternity Wards," an investigation that featured accounts of laboring women left alone and restrained for hours, writhing in agony, drugged against their will and churned through hospitals that felt more akin to chicken-processing factories.

In *The Bell Jar* (1963), Sylvia Plath's protagonist, Esther Greenwood, thinks, "I thought it sounded just like the sort of drug a man would invent. Here was a woman in terrible pain, obviously feeling every bit of it or she wouldn't groan like that, and she would go straight home and start another baby, because the drug would make her forget how bad the pain had been, when all the time, in some secret part of her, that long, blind, doorless and windowless corridor of pain was waiting to open up and shut her in again."[36]

With the rise of the epidural in the 1970s and '80s, the reliance of Twilight Sleep on amnesia began to seem outlandish.[37] The method has by now become a symbol of disempowerment, a sideshow from our oppressive past.[38] But it has left a legacy: it is a rare medical practitioner today who doesn't offer as a matter of course an array of pain-relief measures during childbirth.

Dennett had a different connection to this cause than to world peace or the single tax. Propelled by the visceral memories of her own experiences, she sought to change widespread expectations and policies around an intensely intimate event.

Throughout her midlife years, Dennett continued to consult doctors and undergo procedures to deal with her lingering birth injuries.

As she campaigned for Twilight Sleep, she was pushed to articulate why women should have the right to individualized care, and why their choices should matter. For the first time, she saw the growing popularity of eugenics work in her favor. Most of all, she learned firsthand just how much misperception and fear she would need to dismantle to take the movement even a few inches forward.

Jeanie, Jeanie full of hopes
Read a book by Marie Stopes
But to judge by her condition,
She must have read the wrong edition.

—1920s schoolgirl chant

IN LATE OCTOBER 1914, MARGARET Sanger took a train to Montreal and boarded a steamer to Liverpool, before finally landing in London. As she had explained in her letter to the judge, she needed more time to prepare for her trial than he had allowed.

Once she decided self-imposed exile was her best option, friends helped her secure travel papers under the assumed identity of Bertha Watson, and, with her children at boarding schools, she left furtively and alone. It must have been a solitary, anxious trip, to a country riveted on the war.

And yet, once in London, Sanger instantly felt she had found "a second home."[1] She met the physician and birth control advocate Alice Vickery, who introduced her to Havelock Ellis. Sanger first visited Ellis just before Christmas 1914, when she was still intensely homesick. She was thirty-five, he a white-bearded fifty-six, seen through her eyes as a "tall, lovely simple man with the most wonderful head and face and smile."[2] He welcomed her in his high, thin voice, and they fell into easy conversation.

They rapidly grew close. Early in the new year he was addressing her in letters as "My darling woman," "You wicked woman," or "Dear twin."[3] In her own letters she called him "The King." They seem to have been lovers, though Ellis suffered from impotence, causing his friends to quip he'd managed to become an expert on sex without having any. His main gift to Sanger was spending generous time with her at the British Museum's reading room, lining up books she needed to read about human sexuality.

Sanger reflected that in the United States she had often felt like an outlier, a target for allies and enemies alike "heaping criticism and fears upon me," whereas England was full of kindred spirits.[4] She was sometimes heartsick for her children, especially craving the touch of four-year-old Peggy's "soft chubby hands."[5] Simultaneously, Sanger realized this flight from justice and motherhood presented an opportunity. She told herself to shake off the blues, to "get acquainted with myself, to reflect, meditate and dream."[6]

Two months into this congenial exile, she learned of a drama unfolding at home. On December 19, 1914, Bill Sanger answered a knock at his studio door at 10 East Fifteenth Street. He opened it to a man who introduced himself as Mr. Heller, a friend of Margaret's, who wanted to buy a copy of *Family Limitation* to translate and distribute among the immigrant poor.[7] Bill walked over to where Margaret's things were stored, found a copy, gave it to Heller, and waved him off when the man tried to pay. Their meeting was swiftly concluded. The next month, Comstock placed Bill under arrest. Heller, it transpired, had really been a vice-hunter named Bamberger.

Comstock himself presided over Bill Sanger's arraignment.[8] The trial was repeatedly postponed, and the constant homework of following the case via letters and news reports became a source of exasperation for Margaret. Over the course of Bill's ordeal she fell in love with Lorenzo Portet, a Spanish anarchist. They embarked on an affair, and she spent the spring of 1915 with him in Spain, growing enamored of French vermouth and anchovy-stuffed olives.[9]

Knowing Bill was suffering and that she had something to do with the cause was a profound irritant. She wrote to one of her sisters from Barcelona saying that "Bill had to get mixed upon my work after all & of course make it harder for me & and [sic] all of us!"[10]

From Spain, she went north. Dr. Aletta Jacobs in Amsterdam had founded the first recorded birth control clinic in 1882, and Dr. Johannes Rutgers ran a clinic in The Hague to help married women space their pregnancies. Sanger arrived for a two-month stay in the Netherlands but was flummoxed when Jacobs snubbed her. Contraception, the doctor insisted, was a matter for physicians alone. Sanger's nursing experience didn't count.

But Dr. Rutgers welcomed her, and even allowed her to fit patients with diaphragms at his clinic.[11] Sanger returned to London impressed with the clinics and determined to open her own. "I had a new goal, but how difficult and how distant its attainment was to be I never dreamed."[12]

On July 5, 1915, she gave a speech to London's Fabian Society, originally a Socialist society that had more recently helped to organize the Labour Party. A great awakening was on its way, Sanger told her audience. Once women took control of their fertility, economic and traditional hierarchies would rapidly fall. "Produce your own slaves, keep your religion, your ethics and your morality for yourselves," she told the audience. "I'll have none of it and we refuse to be longer enslaved by it, for we are creating our own and are building up a New Society through which we are creating our own morality and individuality."[13]

Just after this talk, Marie Stopes approached the stage and invited Sanger to visit her in Hampstead, mentioning she was writing a book about sex that was likely to "electrify England."[14] "Over the teacups I found her to have an open, frank manner that quite won me," Sanger later remembered.[15] Stopes's confidence and warmth enraptured Sanger. "I felt," Sanger wrote to Stopes after their first "jolly talk," "that there was after all a real human being in England."[16] She promised to send Stopes a copy of "the Naughty pamphlet" (*Family Limitation*).[17]

Dr. Marie Carmichael Stopes never worked as a physician or nurse. She came to the study of sexuality after getting a PhD in paleobotany. The precipitating event that drove her to study sex, she confided to Sanger, had been her first marriage. Though Stopes's mother was active in the British suffrage movement, Stopes herself found strident feminism and radical socialism distasteful.

She and her first husband, a Canadian geneticist, married when she was thirty and he was two years younger. They never managed a mutually satisfying sexual experience. When Stopes sought divorce in fall 1913, her lawyers told her divorce could be achieved only via an Act of Parliament, with adultery as the only justifiable cause.

The problem, as she had to explain to her lawyers—one senses they were far more embarrassed than she was—was her own sexual dissatisfaction. Her husband was satisfied with hours of foreplay but could not maintain an erection for penetrative intercourse.[18] After much press coverage, she finally succeeded in having the marriage annulled.

Before Sanger left London, Stopes handed over a copy of her manuscript for *Married Love*.[19] It thoroughly debunked the long-accepted theory that women did not feel sexual desire and barely, if any, sexual pleasure. (It also pushed back against the widely held theory that infertility was always due to some fault on the part of the woman.) "In my own life, comparatively short and therefore lacking in experience though it be," Stopes wrote toward the end, "I have known both personally and vicariously so much anguish that might have been prevented by timely knowledge."[20]

Stopes's signature theory in *Married Love* was the "Periodicity of Recurrence of Desire," in which she mapped the crests and ebbs of female sexual desire. Traditional ideas of marriage, Stopes wrote, assumed a husband "has the right to approach his wife whenever he wishes, and that she has no wishes and no fundamental needs in the matter at all."[21] She claimed women's bodies were governed by "rhythmic tides," which she illustrated with charts.

Stopes prescribed freer, more intimate knowledge and communication between women and men, and also between individuals and their own bodies. Far from being a free love advocate, however, she had traditional ideas about coupledom. Women needed to learn to recognize and communicate their needs, not toward the goal of seizing power from their husbands or living more individualistic lives, but because doing so would benefit their marriages.

Married Love was a startling work, especially from a writer without medical training. But Stopes's freshness to the subject matter was an asset in one way: she hadn't internalized any of the received wisdom, much of it spurious, from medical experts. In 1916, interviewing a prominent London gynecologist, she was aghast when he "looked me blandly in the eyes and assured me that normal women do not have orgasms, even in coitus."[22]

That view was so widespread that after publication, she received grateful letters from couples relieved they didn't have some kind of sex-induced sickness. One Cambridge man wrote, "When my wife had [orgasms] which she did freely when aroused, I was frightened and thought it was some sort of fit."[23]

The book also put the physiology of reproduction in plain terms, which many appreciated. One *Married Love* reader, a twenty-two-year-old wife, admitted that before reading Stopes during her engagement, "she had always thought that children were secured as the result of prayers offered at the marriage ceremony."[24]

Stopes finished her manuscript in the fall of 1917. No publisher would touch it. Then a patron materialized: Humphrey Verdon Roe of Manchester, aircraft manufacturer, a firm believer in birth control. *Married Love* was published in 1918. Thereafter Stopes was hyper-prolific, producing pamphlets, textbooks, plays, poetry, and even a collection of fairy tales.[25] Roe and Stopes married. Within the year she had a stillborn son, and had to return to the clinic weeks later to have surgery for a birth injury.[26] A second son, Harry, was born in spring 1924, and this time the child lived.

As Sanger's name became synonymous with fertility control in the United States, Stopes became the parallel figurehead in Britain. In *Married Love* Stopes was circumspect about birth control, advising barrier methods or spermicidal douching rather than withdrawal, and concluding rather abruptly, "The knowledge is easily obtainable."[27] Birth control was, however, the central focus of Stopes's later book *Wise Parenthood* and the main offering at her clinics.

Stopes's books lifted the shroud of silence that had for generations made sex mysterious and terrifying. Virginia Woolf wrote in a 1923 letter, "I've been talking to the younger generation all afternoon. They are like crude hard green apples: no halo, mildew, or blight. Seduced at 15, life has no holes or corners for them. I admire, but deplore. Such an old maid, they make me feel. 'And how do you manage not- not- not to have children?' I ask. 'Oh, we read Mary Stopes [*sic*] of course!' Figure to yourself my dear Molly—before taking their virginity, the young men of our time produce marked copies of Stopes!"[28]

Sanger confided in Stopes about her yearning to return to New York, speculating on what might await her there. Prison time, perhaps—and publicity, for certain. After nearly a year, Sanger felt she was reaching the limits of what she could do in exile. She had read the books Ellis prescribed, toured Continental clinics, and reached a level of prominence in liberal London society, but she could not meaningfully pursue her real work in America from an ocean away. In mid-September she wrote to Stopes, mentioning Bill's trial: "No matter the results I expect to leave the 18th from Bordeaux. . . . If I am out on bail Im [*sic*] going to organize the whole intellectual & Scientific country in my case—if possible. *I just can't fail! & I won't.*"[29]

Stopes was a stalwart friend, with a flair for dramatic monologues. She wrote a petition in support of Sanger and got it signed by H. G. Wells, Arnold Bennett, and other writers and scholars she thought likely to be known in America. To this she added a letter of her own, which she sent to President Wilson in September 1915: "Have you, sir, visualised what it means to be a woman whose very fibre, whose every muscle, and blood-capillary is subtly poisoned by the secret, over-growing horror, more penetrating, more long-drawn than any night-mare, of an unwanted embryo developing beneath your heart?"[30]

At this point, there was a noticeable ideological divide between Sanger and Stopes, though it would soon narrow and all but disappear. Stopes wholeheartedly considered birth control a form of practical eugenics. Sanger's passion for birth control was still closely bound to her night with Sadie Sachs; it was, for now, a humanitarian, social-justice cause.

Stopes, maybe because of her background in academia, was more at home in theoretical frameworks focused on what a population ought to look like generations down the road. And she was firmly convinced it should be as white and nondisabled as possible. In her early alliance with Stopes, Sanger saw a version of what she would later create herself in the United States, as she sought to move away from the radicalism of her younger years: a birth control campaign inextricably linked to the eugenics movement.

The eugenics movement originated in England, with Francis Galton and his 1883 book, *Inquiries into Human Faculty and Its Development*. Galton invented the term "eugenics," tying together the Greek words for "well" and "born."[31] Galton believed primarily in "positive eugenics," or promoting marriages (and thus procreation) among individuals with "superior" traits.

John Harvey Kellogg, a eugenics enthusiast, compared his hoped-for "Race of Human Thoroughbreds" to "wonderful new races of horses, cows, and pigs."[32] The Carnegie Institute became an essential funder of the movement, supporting the Station for Experimental Evolution at Cold Spring Harbor, New York, which opened in 1904, as well as the Eugenics Records Office, which launched in 1910 and counted Alexander Graham Bell as an early chairman.[33]

Proposed measures to strengthen American stock included blood tests before marriage for the "fit," mainly to detect syphilis, and sterilization for the "unfit." A pamphlet titled *A Eugenics Catechism* was distributed by the American Eugenics Society to schools and churches nationally, and it listed the reasons for sterilizing the "unfit": "To rid the race of those likely to transmit the dysgenic tendencies to which they are subject. To decrease the need for charity of a certain form. To reduce taxes. To help alleviate misery and suffering. To do what Nature would do under natural conditions, but more humanely. Sterilization is not a punitive measure. It is strictly protective."[34] In state laws and in the press, compulsory sterilization was discussed in the same light as state-sponsored vaccination.[35]

In 1915, Victor Robinson, the pro–birth control editor of the *Medical Review of Reviews,* pulled a publicity stunt that demonstrated how eugenics was seen as a strong argument for surveilling and controlling people's fertility. Robinson hired a group of down-and-out-looking men, hung placards around their necks, and had them occupy a stretch of New York City sidewalk. A sample of the placards' texts read: "I am a burden to myself and the State. Should I be allowed to propagate?" "I cannot read this sign. By what right have I children?" "I must drink alcohol to sustain life. Shall I transfer the craving to others?"[36]

Harry Laughlin, when he was the assistant director of the Eugenics Record Office, summarized the point Robinson was trying to make: "Approximately 10 percent of our population, primarily through inherent defect and weakness, are an economic and moral burden on the 90 percent and a constant danger to the national and racial life."[37]

The race-suicide alarmists sounded a panicked outcry about WASP culture being "submerged" by immigration and migration. Between 1880 and 1920, around twenty-eight million people immigrated to the United States; within that time, more than 1.2 million Black southerners moved north.[38] And in all this talk about "fitness," social burdens, and preservation of "the race," the birth control movement began to see an opportunity.

. . .

On September 10, 1915, Bill Sanger stood trial before three judges for distributing *Family Limitation*. It was a crackerjack day for reporters. Around a hundred Sanger supporters filed in, making things raucous in court. The *New York Times* noted that the case had captured the imaginations of "sober-minded persons who believe that there should be a wide discussion of birth control" as well as "Socialists and anarchists," represented in the courtroom by Elizabeth Gurley Flynn, Carlo Tresca, and Alexander Berkman, who had, a generation earlier, attempted to assassinate Henry Clay Frick during the Homestead steel strike.[39]

Bill had dismissed legal representation in favor of reading a prepared statement. The *New York Times* printed as much as would fit: In it Bill accused Comstock of "incurable sexphobia" and lacking "the intelligence to distinguish between pornography and scientific information."[40] He argued that the pamphlet was in no way obscene; that he wanted the case put before a jury; and that Comstock's conduct in orchestrating the entrapment and then offering Sanger a suspended sentence if he pleaded guilty was reprehensible.[41]

Bill read, "I deny the right of the State to compel the poor and disinherited to rear large families, driving their offspring into child labor when they should be at school and at play. I most certainly deny the right of the State to arm a prudish censorship with the right of search and confiscation to pass judgment on our art and literature."[42]

Comstock stood to make a direct rebuttal. He called Bill a perjurer, denied offering a suspended sentence, and concluded with the querulous claim that he himself was only pressing charges out of the strength of his convictions. He had, he told the court, been threatened with assassination for prosecuting the case.[43]

In the tense courtroom, Chief Justice James J. McInerny seemed to hear both arguments as mere noise. He was more concerned with what the verdict would mean for family values than with appeasing Comstock or responding to Sanger's ideas. McInerny's opinion hardly touched on the notion of whether the pamphlet was obscene. Instead, he dwelled on the question of whether women had the right to choose a role apart from motherhood. "Some women are so selfish that they do not want to be bothered with them [children]," pronounced the judge. "If some persons would go around and urge Christian women to bear children, instead of wasting their time on woman suffrage, this city and society would be better off."[44] He found Bill guilty as charged.

Given the choice between a $150 fine or thirty days in prison, Bill chose the latter. The courtroom erupted with shouts and claps as Sanger's supporters stood on benches and waved hats and handkerchiefs. Reporters noted McInerny pounding his gavel continuously, "which only marked time for the din in the room."[45]

The anarchists were herded outside, and the *Times'* article concluded by announcing Margaret Sanger was expected soon to return. It was excellent publicity for the Sangers, *Family Limitation*, and the birth control debate. The media made hay of the spectacle provided by the Sanger-Comstock face-off; the *New Republic* noted that coverage of Comstock's efforts to suppress *Family Limitation* "accelerated the spread of the doctrine to which they were opposed."[46]

It is said that Anthony Comstock caught a cold in the crowded courtroom that day. He died of pneumonia ten days after Bill Sanger's trial, on September 21, 1915. In his later years, Comstock's vice-hunting had been depicted in the press more as a relic of Victorian values than a force for good. In 1914, he had confiscated nude female drawings in a pamphlet of the Art Students League in New York City, an action that led to much protest but no legal consequences.[47] In the same month as the Sanger trial, *The Masses* ran a cartoon by Robert Minor, who had been present in the courtroom, that featured the vice-hunter blustering before a judge and accusing a harried woman, "Your honor, this woman gave birth to a naked child!"[48]

The Comstock Act still wielded a terrible power to judge and to silence, but it could not emerge unscathed from a world war. The body—entrenched or at home, nude or clothed, shell-shocked or syphilitic or dancing—was about to come unveiled.

Sex does not stand alone in our lives, but is tied up with many other things. If you try to understand it by itself you are sure to misunderstand it.

—Mary Ware Dennett, *Youth in the Life of Today*

"I WILL MAIL YOUR SEX BOOK in a day or two," Dennett wrote her son Carleton just after the winter school vacation, in January 1915.[1] Fourteen-year-old Carleton had stayed with her on West Fifty-Fifth Street, bringing with him a sex education book he'd gotten hold of at school. Dennett had studied it closely, then decided to write her own.

Monthslong periods of separation from her sons meant every time they came to stay, Dennett was struck by how they'd changed. Carleton, now in the throes of puberty, had a "new bass voice," "still childish awkwardness," and "utter helplessness before a feeling of any description," she noted.[2] Unable to mother them at close range, she kept a close eye on what they read.

After reading the sex education book Carleton had found at school, she was galvanized—and indignant. The author was a full-throated Victorian, prudish and patriarchal, not the kind of influence she wanted over her sons. "He talks as if women were made to be *taken care of*, and not as if they were the *partners* in life with men," she wrote. And another thing: he talked "as if the sex relation was *in itself* a *wrong* thing—to be suppressed or ashamed of. It *isn't*." Lastly, she wondered why "he does not explain carefully enough *just what* the sex act is. He takes it for granted that people know what it is and how it should be done but they don't." She urged Carleton to "save all your questions and ask me. I will tell you *everything.*"[3]

She didn't wait for Carleton to ask; she couldn't hold still. Here was a way she could help—not only to reward his curiosity, but to benefit other young people, too. As she saw it, her sons' personal fulfillment was at stake, and that of a generation that could find greater happiness if sex weren't tarnished with ignorance and dread.

Sex education in the classroom was not a feature of the schools Dennett or her boys attended, but there were already glimmers that this would change. In Chicago's public schools in 1913, Superintendent Ella Flagg Young had planned a purity-oriented lecture course on anatomy and sexuality. One physician would lecture boys on topics like "problems of sex instincts" and "personal purity," while a woman physician gave a separate talk to girls.[4] Students objected to the lack of "plain facts."[5] Parents and clergy, on the other hand, protested so vociferously that the sex ed curriculum was withdrawn after a year.[6]

Afterward, if teachers addressed sex in school it was mostly via punitive measures. A teacher survey from 1928 admitted "heterosexual activity" had long been the most disruptive problem behavior among students, followed by stealing, masturbation, and "obscene notes and pictures."[7]

Gradually, moral and medical arguments for sex ed in schools accumulated credibility. In his 1904 book, *Social Diseases and Marriage,* Prince Morrow, MD, described the dangers of ignoring sex education during adolescence to an intended readership of fellow doctors.[8] STIs had long been characterized as the righteous consequence of prostitution. Syphilis, since it had visible symptoms, was seen as a curse on moral lawbreakers. Morrow argued it was time for a reassessment. There were too many innocent victims to ignore.

Of all the women who came to New York Hospital for syphilis treatment, he wrote, 70 percent were married and had been unknowingly infected by their husbands.[9] "The male factor," Morrow punned, "is the chief malefactor."[10]

As Morrow saw it, adolescence presented a uniquely malleable phase, one in which sex education—or the lack thereof—had lifelong consequences. Teens needed to be taught about sex so they would do it right, which meant within a heterosexual marriage. This instruction should ideally happen at home, but Morrow wrote that "the majority of parents were not qualified to give it, and that the duty therefore devolved upon teachers, and should be an integral part of the course of study in all normal schools."[11]

There was little that was scandalous or revolutionary about Prince Morrow, a dermatologist and married father of six. In 1905, he founded the Society of Sanitary and Moral Prophylaxis, which earned support from the Woman's Christian Temperance Union and the YMCA, and would eventually evolve into the American Social Hygiene Association (ASHA). These groups were aligned with Morrow's driving aim, to merge public health with the purity movement in order to help young people survive the modern world with their morals intact.[12]

In his effort to rally physicians and educators around sex education as an important preventative measure, Morrow almost single-handedly normalized the idea of teaching the physiology of sex and STI prevention by experts, using a predetermined curriculum. He envisioned sex education as "constructive and positive . . . and not critical and negative. . . . It should say do and not don't."[13]

Physicians and policymakers began trying to reconcile the movement for classroom sex ed with the moral anxieties that were dusty and old-fashioned if you believed the press, but alive and well among many American parents. Direct talk about sex, it was thought, would annihilate teens' self-control and make them sex obsessed. But some parents and teachers made the opposing argument: that keeping children in ignorance would only breed misinformation and a hysterical attitude toward the topic.

Charles W. Eliot, president emeritus of Harvard, noted the "remarkable change in public opinion" on sex education. In the past, he told an audience at the Congress of School Hygiene in Buffalo, "the policy of silence was almost universal." In 1913, however, "fathers and mothers feel a new duty toward their children."[14]

Dennett's working hours were still consumed with the suffrage and single tax campaigns, with a dash of Twilight Sleep, "on the jump with work every day and all day."[15] But her evenings and weekends that year were surprisingly productive—and seditious. She decided her sex education pamphlet would be more than a basic summary: it would be authoritative, carefully illustrated, and—hopefully—able to counteract the moralizing and vagueness of the tracts her boys were finding at school.

Her pretext, she told her family, was a $1,000 prize, advertised in a contest sponsored by ASHA and the Metropolitan Life Insurance Company. When asked, she played down her ambitions, but it was a reward grand enough to justify the effort she was putting into the project. Although she had little time or money to spare, she gave herself an entirely new kind of education.

First, she absorbed the entire canon of sex education literature. Dennett trawled libraries and ASHA's reference shelves, reading more than sixty pamphlets and books aimed at school-age readers and parents.[16] What she found was a grave injustice to children, as she outlined in her "Introduction for Elders," the preamble to her work in progress. From a physiological perspective, few authors gave young readers the complete picture. The science was handled "with sentimentality," she wrote, with frequent reliance on analogies to plant and flower reproduction.[17]

Parents still sought out scripts that used metaphor instead of anatomical terms, many of them having received instruction that way from their own parents. One popular example came from *Good Housekeeping* in 1911: "When God wants to send a little child into a home, he fits up just beneath the mother's heart a snug nest not unlike the nests birds live in. Then out of two tiny eggs the father and mother bring together in the nest, a little child is hatched just like a little bird."[18]

The journal *Social Hygiene* reported in 1915 a story about a parent answering her kindergartener's question in "an allegorical way about the flowers, and the pollen, and the bees . . . 'How did she take it?' the neighbor asked. 'She seemed interested and asked if babies came from bees.'"[19] When it came to informing and preparing young people, comparisons to botany and agriculture were decidedly unhelpful.

By August 1915, Dennett had produced and mailed Carleton *The Sex Side of Life: An Explanation for Young People,* a pamphlet for readers aged twelve to sixteen. With a straightforward tone and line-drawn illustrations she'd done herself, it was a corrective to the older generation of sex-ed books. Sex was "a vivifying joy . . . a vital art," Dennett wrote.[20] The female and male orgasms were given equal focus. Her intention was to convey facts clearly, in an unembarrassed way, and in this she succeeded.

With its assumptions of heterosexuality and an eventual monogamous marriage, Dennett's pamphlet still had plenty in common with its ancestors, due to a combination of her own principles and her ambition to win the ASHA-Metropolitan contest. It pinned most of the blame for STIs on prostitution, for instance. But it was sex positive to a degree that was rare and new outside the free love set. "We have contented ourselves by assuming that marriage makes sex relations respectable," she wrote; "We have not yet said that it is only beautiful sex relations that can make marriage lovely."[21]

One section hints at her lingering postpartum bewilderment. "The birth process is called labor, and it is indeed labor, for it usually means much pain and struggle for the mother, although the baby's journey from the uterus to the world is only a few inches," she wrote. She predicted that in another generation childbirth would be "practically painless for most women," linking that idea to the "time people will more generally understand how to have babies only when they want them and can afford them."

The section ends with a curt reminder that "at present, unfortunately, it is against the law to give people information as to how to manage their sex relations so that no baby will be created unless the father and mother are ready and glad to have it happen."[22] But she held on, at least on the page, to the ideal of a future when all birth would be tranquil and all pregnancies welcome.

She didn't win the prize, but Carleton, at least, approved. On a visit to her apartment, he stuck his head out from the shower to yell to her that it was "all right," which Dennett recognized as high praise from a teenaged boy. "I would far rather have had those few words from him," she later wrote, "than all the thousand-dollar prizes in the world, or the approval of any sex-hygiene jurors, no matter how academically distinguished."[23]

She began to send it out. Some readers were startled by Dennett's frankness, but it earned praise from Havelock Ellis himself. One friend's letter told her the pamphlet was better suited to newlyweds than teenagers;[24] but Ellis, in May 1916, wrote that she had produced an admirably concise yet comprehensive text, and that it deserved a very wide circulation.[25] His letter bolstered her resolve to publish it one day.

The Sex Side of Life marked a heady time in Dennett's life. As she was researching literature of sex ed, two events turned the tide of her career and overpowered her emotional guardedness: she put herself at the center of the birth control movement, and she fell in love.

. . .

In the spring of 1915, birth control waltzed cheerfully through the pages of popular magazines. The *New Republic*, all of one year old, printed a supportive editorial, proclaiming, "We are done with the irresponsible stork. We are done with the taboo which forbids discussion of the subject. We are done with the theory that babies, like sunshine and rain, are the gifts and visitations of God, to be accepted submissively and with a grateful heart."[26]

A few weeks later, *Harper's Weekly* printed the first of more than a dozen articles on the topic it would run in 1915, stating "the subject insists on coming up, as many Americans are not willing to be kept in tutelage on a matter so freely treated in Europe,"[27] and remarking, "A woman's right to exist is no longer considered to lie wholly in her fertility."[28] In 1914 there were three *New York Times* articles on birth control; in 1915, there were fourteen; in the two years that followed, there were ninety.[29]

In March 1915, Dennett and Jessie Ashley, a feminist lawyer and close friend, gathered a salon full of birth control supporters at the home of Clara Gruening Stillman, at which Dennett gave a well-received speech. The National Birth Control League (NBCL) was formed at that meeting. *The Survey* magazine printed a complete list of those who signed the call for the league's formation: Dennett, Ashley, and Stillman were joined by their fellow agitators Martha Gruening, Bolton Hall, Otto Bobsien, Charles T. Hallinan, Paul Kennaday, Helen Marot, James F. Morton, Lucy Sprague Mitchell, and Lincoln Steffens.[30] They were Socialists, suffragists, lawyers, settlement house workers, and educators, and most of them were journalists or writers, too. They were friends of Margaret Sanger, who was still in exile.

The new league aimed to repeal the New York State Comstock laws and eventually the federal ones as well. For some, birth control was also the spark igniting a larger revolution: abolishing the nuclear family unit. Jessie Ashley wrote Dennett that while the nuclear family "*has been* necessary" and she didn't exactly "regard it as a disease," it was on par with "private property and the rest. . . . I think as our economic system changes, the family will inevitably disappear too and personally, I think that is desirable."[31]

A decade Dennett's senior, with pale, patrician features and the assuredness of one born into financial security, Ashley admitted she had never liked children or the "present method of caring for them."[32]

But for most birth control advocates, the goal was to change what went on inside the home rather than tearing it down.

Busy with multiple campaigns, including her work at NAWSA and long-distance mothering, Dennett had a healthy sense of self-preservation but a hard time listening to it. "I'm crazy to get in and help actively," she wrote her mother. "I think it is the biggest single help that can come to women," she wrote, "but I can't do that. I can't afford the time, nor the chance that my name would again get tangled in awful newspaper tales." Never again would she face the press as she had during the divorce, she was sure. "A leddy 'with a past' is awfully handicapped!" she concluded.[33]

Dennett's birth control work was animated by the same principle that compelled her to dive into sex education: she saw a taboo causing needless damage to individuals and relationships, she bore the scars of that damage herself, and she was adamant about banishing that taboo before it could harm her sons' generation.

Quickly, birth control became the cause closest to her heart. If she had been able to space her pregnancies, she would have been able to heal between births. She wouldn't have had to renounce sex with Hartley. She wouldn't have needed the surgery that had required her to leave Hartley to Margaret Chase's influence over the summer of 1907. Living at the mercy of her fertility and labors had shuttled her into this new life, far from her children, financially stressed, and regularly dogged by physical pain.

Dennett's speech at that first NBCL meeting hinted at how even civic life could be transformed by the absence of anxiety around pregnancy, a rare moment in her birth control work when she championed agency and social life for their own sake. "We do not have an annual baby. It would be anything but ideal to do so," she told the group. "But instead . . . we find creative scope in the whole side field of science art and community life."[34]

She was already claiming a leading role within the new league, one with the voice of a commonsense New Englander ready to identify and sweep away petty hypocrisies. Just about everyone who made the laws practiced some form of family planning, she pointed out; congressmen nearly all had small families. They just had to be persuaded it was decent to discuss birth control in public. It "is no more indecent to discuss the anatomy, physiology and hygiene of reproduction in a scientific spirit," Dennett and her colleagues wrote in their founding documents, "than it is to discuss the functions of the brains, the heart or the lungs."[35]

The new league's founding documents claimed birth control would remove "temptation to criminal abortion," stem the "birth of the unfit (from which class our prisons, reformatories and insane asylums are largely filled)," combat illegitimacy, improve women's health, keep poor people off government relief, and encourage earlier marriage, thereby reducing "the evils of prostitution."[36] Their reasoning was eugenic and budget-driven, not overtly feminist or Socialist.

Regardless, to the purity brigade, this was intolerable. By April 28, the new league was already sparring with Comstock. The vice-hunter wrote to Stillman, secretary of the weeks-old NBCL, to puncture the legal basis for the league and to warn of the struggle to come. He pointed out that anyone with legitimate medical reasons for contraception could simply consult a physician; in New York, doctors could indeed legally fit diaphragms for the cure or prevention of disease, though not all of them were aware of it.

Then, between the lines of his letter, Comstock issued a threat. "You cannot safeguard the children on the public streets by turning loose mad dogs," he wrote.[37] In May, a *Harper's Weekly* reporter interviewed him and confessed she was "somewhat confused at first that Mr. Comstock should class contraceptives with pornographic objects which debauch children's fancies, for I knew that the European scientists who advocate their use have no desire at all to debauch children." To this he said impatiently, "If you open the door to anything, the filth will all pour in and the degradation of youth will follow."[38]

Comstock had the NBCL in his sights, but he died before he could take further action.

With birth control central to its name and mission, the league attracted pleas for help from across the country, mostly from women asking for practical information. A form letter was designed to answer them, likely written by Dennett herself: "Your request for specific information about birth control methods, can not be complied with by the League, much as it would like to do so, until the laws forbidding such information are repealed," it read. "Help us maintain the work of the League so we can repeal the law. *Then we can and will help you with the information.*"[39]

Thus far, the new league was making mischief in Margaret Sanger's absence. With Sanger's imminent return and given her history of defying the censors, some friction was perhaps inevitable. For the time being, however, Dennett felt sure of herself. She had found where she belonged.

Oh, let me live on Broadway, where the lights are all a-glow,
Where ev'ryone seems happy in the crowds that come and go,
Thus speaks the foolish dreamer, and he prays his dream come true
But he'd never leave the village if he knew.

> —Howard Johnson, "There's a Broken Heart
> for Every Light on Broadway" (1915)

O N A RARE COOL DAY in August 1914, while at work on the suffrage campaign, Dennett met Charles Thomas Hallinan. The year that followed—the year they spent in love—coincided with Dennett's creative and energetic renaissance. At forty-two, she helped launch the National Birth Control League and wrote *The Sex Side of Life*. She was used to working hard, but Hallinan's admiration accelerated her productivity even further. He gave her a belief in her own ideas and an appetite for defying old rules.

He was eight years her junior and married, and their relationship made her recognize the mutability of her own values, at least when it came to what love and sex could mean. "I was at least two different people . . . it was confusing and baffling beyond anything I'd ever experienced before," she later wrote.[1] Her feelings for him broke down any idealization of monogamy that had remained in her.

Hallinan was, in her memory "the one and only *man*" employed by NAWSA, a Chicago journalist who was helping the suffragists with press and promotional films.[2] After crossing paths at the office and chatting about a film project, he and Dennett headed to lunch. "Seemed like a regulation thing," in Dennett's memory, a matter of a couple of colleagues grabbing a bite.[3]

Sitting across from Hallinan at the Craftsman restaurant, on the top floor of a new, Arts-and-Crafts-inspired building in midtown Manhattan, Dennett felt "instantly companionable" with him.[4] She liked his delicate features, his restrained manner—though he would turn out to be a much freer spirit than she first assumed. She knew early on that he was married. At the end of their first lunch together he mentioned he had a wife, then walked Dennett to her office door and was gone.

Once he was home in Chicago, he kept her in his thoughts and made sure she was thinking of him, too. He sent her books; his letters engaged her in conversations about art in a manner that, in Dennett's words, "I had deliberately put out of my thoughts when Hartley went out of my life."[5] When Hallinan came to New York, he and Dennett went together to the theater and the symphony. By the fall of 1914, Hallinan would spend the evening out on the town with Dennett, return to his room at the Plaza, and immediately write her a letter.

"Emotions came thick and fast," Dennett confided in her notebook.[6] She dedicated a pigeonhole in her desk to his notes, and was torn between relishing his interest and sternly talking sense to herself, dismissing his interest in her as a consequence of the tensions in his marriage.[7] Then she wondered—was she acting as Margaret Chase had? She was determined "to play fair," she wrote. "My play mustn't hurt anyone else, you know," she wrote him.[8] It almost sounded like the reverse echo of something Margaret Chase had written to Hartley in 1909: "Let us play that we are free, and Let us play to win."[9]

Hallinan moved his family to New York and Dennett befriended his wife and daughter, whom she found charming. The family called on her around Christmastime and met her boys. She felt less guilty now that she could safely say there was nothing clandestine about her friendship with Hallinan. With her conscience thus satisfied, she began inviting him alone for lunches at her apartment—meetings that weren't entirely proper, she knew, but his wife and daughter were frequently sick, and anyway times were changing. His interest and conversation were ballast when she badly needed it.

The new year started with a humiliating surprise. On the fifteenth anniversary of their wedding, January 20, 1915, Dennett sent Hartley a note. In it she wrote of her present happiness in New York. "Life never before seemed so full of stirring thoughts and doings and feelings. . . . There is a splendid throbbing urge in the seething conglomerate life of this great city that is vastly stimulating," she wrote, and after wishing him well, she signed herself "Sincerely your friend."[10] It was a milestone: at last, she had the ability to write Hartley from a place of sincerity and benevolence instead of wounded betrayal.

A few days later she answered the phone, heard a warm, masculine voice, and assumed it was Hallinan. Instead it was a reporter from the New York *World*. He had just spoken with Hartley and the Chases at Alstead. They were reextending an invitation for Dennett to come live with them, he said. The reporter asked, "What is your answer going to be?" Dennett answered, "I have nothing to say at all."[11] She didn't know if her letter to Hartley had directly provoked this, or why his and Margaret's invitation was reaching her via a reporter, and was immobilized with confusion and regret. "That was a hideous day," she recalled. "I sat here hours, paralyzed and numb with misery."

In the following weeks there were feature-length updates on the Dennett-Chase situation in the *World*, the *Boston Globe*, and other papers. Dennett didn't know it, but Hartley's mother was nearly equally appalled at the press. "Why can't you keep your affairs private & out of the newspapers?" Annie O. Dennett wrote her son, adding she wasn't alone in wishing he would "change your name & spare us."[12]

Tabloids ran front-page features on Hartley, the Chases, and Margaret's sense of style. "Clad in velvet bloomers and a white shirtwaist whose low-cut V-neck was loosely knotted with a flowing tie," ran one story, "Mrs. Margaret Chase sauntered one day into the village of East Alstead, her soul-mate on one arm, her faithful husband on the other!"

A subheadline further down the column read "World Astonished," and surmised what the cast-off wife must be living through: "Though there is joy within the Golden Rule Triangle, there is a saddened, broken home in New York, where dwells Mrs. Mary Ware Dennett."[13]

Dennett came close to crumbling. As she wondered how she would "face life alone and earn bread for the boys and keep a smiling front," the Hallinans were there to listen and feed her dinner.[14]

After Bill Sanger's arrest for distributing *Family Limitation*, Dennett and Hallinan went to a solidarity meeting at Mabel Dodge Luhan's studio. She thought what the Sangers were doing was important, and she helped raise funds for their defense whenever she had the chance.

"I had been immensely interested in Margaret Sanger's heroic effort to defy the atrocious laws that made it a crime to give information about the prevention of conception," Dennett wrote in her memoir of this time. "My own experience [of motherhood] and Sister Clara's, and my recent observation of other women's lives had prepared me for a very vigorous interest in the subject."[15]

On the bus going to the meeting, she and Hallinan talked about the case and birth control generally. She marveled at their modern friendship—or whatever it was. Just a decade earlier, she wrote, it would have been "just about impossible" for men and women to discuss birth control outside the bedroom, and then to plan public action about it.[16]

Over the following weeks, Hallinan gave her poetry by Wallace Stevens and Rupert Brooke, and she sent him "the loveliest short poem there is"—"To an Oriole" by Edgar Fawcett, which Hartley used to recite for her:

> How falls it, oriole, thou hast come to fly
> In tropical splendor through our Northern sky?
>
> At some glad moment was it nature's choice
> To dower a scrap of sunset with a voice?

Or did some orange tulip, flaked with black,
In some forgotten garden, ages back,

Yearning toward heaven until its wish was heard,
Desire unspeakably to be a bird?[17]

In the spring of 1915, they went together to the inaugural meeting of the NBCL, where she was to give a talk on the rationale for birth control. She walked to the meeting with Hallinan, his wife, and two friends, keenly aware that her emotional life and her work had gotten tangled. "I was conscious that my ideas were becoming more or less revolutionized," she wrote, "and for me, the occasion involved a much more searching survey of the whole question of sex relations than was evident in what I said."[18]

Alongside Dennett and Jessie Ashley, Hallinan joined the NBCL's literature committee, creating another opportunity for them to spend evenings together. At committee conclaves, usually held at Ashley's apartment, he would instigate Victrola-playing and dancing after their tasks were done.

Dennett's friends enjoyed seeing her have a crush. A few told her "that I was so inflexible . . . in some ways that I needed a good shaking up."[19] She knew she could be "dogmatic and intolerant," that she had "a certain unyielding quality," and in Hallinan her friends saw someone who brought levity and mischief into her life.[20]

When he visited her apartment they had a routine of sitting on her couch, each taking off their glasses, and talking for hours. One night he confessed he was coming down with a cold. After dosing him with a homeopathic remedy, she decided it was time to act. "I closed his lips for him with my fingers and kissed him squarely, leaving him the most surprised man in town."[21] Then they walked together along Madison Avenue, one of his fingers tucked into her glove.

"My mind protested faintly that something queer was happening to me," Dennett wrote. She spent hours in her apartment "dazed and inert, I who had been an indefatigable hustler from dawn till dark, for years and years. It was amazing—inexcusable—ridiculous!"[22] No matter how often he told her she was lovely, she saw only the remnants of a "painfully homely" girlhood, the chronic dark circles under her eyes, and her unfashionable curves.[23] The only appealing thing she recognized about herself was her voice, which she'd often been told was beautiful. She was dimly conscious she might be acting ridiculous. It also felt ridiculous to stop.

Their shared disdain for the racism in the mainstream suffrage movement helped bring them together. Hallinan threw a dinner party for Dennett and W. E. B. Du Bois, with whom he was friendly. She thought Du Bois "just about the most graceful man—socially speaking—that I ever met," as she wrote to her sons. "How he has ever managed to witness as much hatred and prejudice as he has had to, and keep his manner free from bitter tenseness, I don't see."[24]

She must have been somewhat relieved to share that evening with him, and to observe that grace. Four years earlier, in October 1911, she had been charged with delivering bitter news to his door. At the NAWSA convention in Louisville, Kentucky, leadership had dismissed a resolution calling for NAWSA's "sympathy to black men and women who are fighting the same battle," arguing that taking such a resolution seriously would offend their southern hosts.[25] One of the resolution's authors, possibly Martha Gruening, asked her to tell Du Bois what had happened; in her letter Dennett sounded anguished, signing off with the hope that another chance would come, and that "those of us who care about the subject can have the privilege of doing our best to put it through."[26]

In early May she and Hallinan went together to a suffrage luncheon. Two Black suffragists had reserved tickets, throwing the entirely white organizing committee into a tailspin. Could the organizers create a "colored table" without invoking Jim Crow? (No, they could not.) Would the rest of the suffragists tolerate sitting with them? Who would they be offending by letting in these newcomers? This incident was emblematic of Dennett's frustration with the group. Dennett, Hallinan, Ashley, and Henrietta Rodman finally moved their own place cards to the Black suffragists' table, but conversation was stilted. Dennett left the party dispirited. It was a clear illustration of the dissonance between the suffrage movement's purported egalitarian ideals and the racist pandering with which it actually operated.

The difficulty of making conversation with her Black suffrage associates is another telling detail gleaned from Dennett's notebook. While Dennett included and defended Black suffragists as a matter of principle, the record suggests it was much rarer for her to connect with people of color in real life. One notable exception was Emmanuel Brown, a sharecropper's son who, inspired by Booker T. Washington, attended Harvard before returning to the South to set up a school modeled on the Tuskegee Institute in the early 1900s. Dennett became one of his conduits for fundraising appeals, and she sent him donations and reading material as best she could. Edwin and Lucia Ames Mead and Dennett's sister, Clara Hill, helped too, all of them staying in touch as Brown built and ran the Street Manual Training School in Minter, Alabama. It was characteristic of Dennett to admire Du Bois's sweeping vision for a more just America, while feeling closer and more comfortable to the incremental, education-focused, law-abiding path modeled by Washington and Brown.

As Dennett's romance with Hallinan was intensifying, Clara wrote with heartrending news. She was pregnant, with fragile health and finances, and determined to have an abortion. Clara's first two children had been welcome surprises; the next two were met with a spirit of forbearance; and the fifth pregnancy, Clara admitted, brought despair. She'd tried periodic abstinence, but her guesses as to a safe period had proved inaccurate. Dennett mailed her Sanger's *Family Limitation*, which helped for a time, until a sixth pregnancy announced itself. Clara resolved that her husband would never even know of it: "This is my affair. George has enough to bear . . . I don't care about laws or customs or so-called morals or anything. Nothing could be more of a crime than to let a sixth child come into this family, now," Clara wrote her sister.[27]

With Dennett's help, Clara was installed in a private hospital where a doctor terminated the pregnancy. Afterward, Dennett went to Boston to be with her mother, Vonie, and the boys for a few weeks. She drove out to look at the Framingham house, which she had sold at a steep loss, and was in a bittersweet mood when she boarded the Fall River Line steamer back to Manhattan. Disembarking, she walked past Hallinan, who had tried to surprise her by meeting her off the boat. He caught up with her at home instead, and took her out to dinner.

Until then, Dennett and Hallinan had had only long, intellectual conversations about whether or not they would ever become lovers. Now Dennett decided: yes. When he asked what had made up her mind, she said it was a day trip to the sea, with "the simple bigness of the ocean and the sky" that made her feel she was "shedding my New Englandism."[28]

She wanted one night with him, or possibly two, and it had to be somewhere besides her studio. An ongoing affair, and the prospect of being the other woman long term, of keeping his clothes and laying claim to his everyday attention, of having to face the neighbors—of truly becoming a Margaret Chase—was intolerable.

She arranged with Jessie Ashley to swap apartments over the long July 4 weekend. The night before, self-conscious and laughing at herself for campaigning for birth control without any experience of it, she asked him to "look after some safe-guard—you see I really don't know anything about it—that is, practically."[29] Then, for two days, they retreated together. When not in bed, they listened to Gilbert and Sullivan and Bach, read Chekhov, and went out to dinner.[30] When it was time for Hallinan to go home to his family, Dennett returned to her studio and was horrified to find herself convulsed by sobs. Then, characteristically: "I pulled myself together, made some black coffee, dressed" and went out to preside at a meeting.[31]

Despite their resolution to remain friends and comrades, she and Hallinan were never close again. Their efforts to remain friends fell flat, foiled by his decision to tell his wife he had fallen in love with Dennett and his subsequent promise to recommit to his marriage. Aching, isolated days descended. "My very soul feels tired," she wrote her sons, a phrase she used more than once over the years. "The old temptation to shut my shell tight is overwhelming."[32]

She didn't share her distress with Carleton and Devon right away. The affair went unspoken of after its conclusion. It settled into her memory like a "coast journey in northern Italy where you plunge in and out of tunnels for hours on end, and emerge tired and smoky, realizing that you have had gorgeous views mixed in with much discomfort."[33] In September 1915, Dennett wrote up an account of it in a notebook titled "For My Sons after My Death," her main confessional outlet for that year.

She also wrote a piece of fiction, "The Winner," speculating about the interior life of Hallinan's wife, which helped her process the end of the affair. It was published in *The Century* a couple of years later.[34] In the story she called herself the "other woman," describing an unlikely heroine, whom, she wrote, "had learned somewhat about doing a hard thing like that [being alone] when she had pulled away from the wreck of her own marriage a few years before. . . . As she put it: 'A heartbroken woman is of no particular use to herself or the world; so why be one?'"[35]

Despite the rancor she felt for her ex-husband, she still occasionally wrote to Hartley, especially in times of stress and ill health. In July 1916, she sent him a letter that began, "It is possible that I shall not live much longer."[36] It's not clear whether she was sick at the time, or wanted to make her wishes clear as a matter of due diligence, or wanted to make a bid for connection and wasn't sure how.

What followed was a record of her plans for the boys' future and a chronicle of Dennett's maternal anxieties. She outlined how she wanted Hartley to support the boys in her absence, asking him to send money for their education. She told him bluntly that she preferred that he didn't try to form a closer relationship with them until they were finished with their education.

In his reply Hartley had little mercy for her. "You ask me to contribute to a plan of which the cornerstone is the elimination of me from the lives of my own children," he wrote.[37] He had already told her of his conviction that they lived in different worlds, with different truths: "Your North Star and mine are in different quarters of the sky."[38] She became deeply averse to ever seeing him face-to-face. When she eventually traveled to Alstead again, she would sink down in her seat in the car rather than risk catching sight of him.[39]

Yet as Dennett reflected on her year with Hallinan, the words she chose echoed Hartley's just before their divorce. "Exclusive sex connections are just plain tyranny," she wrote. "Indeed I am strongly inclined to think that even those life long unions would be freshened . . . if now and then contrasted with another relation of a temporary or supplementary sort."[40] She cautioned her boys against a "narrow traditional view" of love and marriage, though her idea of parental responsibility, she told them pointedly, was serious and steadfast.[41]

Dennett never had a steady romantic relationship again, though over the next three years she struck up a close correspondence with one other man, a meeting of the minds she described as an "amazing lovely—I don't know what to call it—all the accepted names are so horrid—I almost said liaison."[42] Edward Krehbiel was a fellow peace activist and a Stanford history professor, and married. After meeting in Washington they exchanged articles, political opinions, and joking terms of endearment until their correspondence went quiet in 1918.

Her ideal of coupledom—of what she wanted for herself—resettled into a new pattern. She remained single, with only a little ambivalence about it. She quoted a fellow Heterodite: "I have always thought Frances Bjorkman's phrases, 'a visiting husband,' and 'a weekend husband,' suggested very comfortable possibilities."[43]

Facing the Inexorable

At last a voice that knew not how to lie,
A call articulate above the throng
Of those who whispered of a secret wrong
And longed for liberty and passed it by.

> —from "The Woman Rebel: Margaret Sanger"
> by Walter Adolphe Roberts (1914)

O N AN OVERCAST DAY IN the fall of 1915, Margaret Sanger disembarked her steamer at the West Fourteenth Street wharf and hailed a cab. A newsstand caught her eye, specifically the cover of the popular *Pictorial Review*. The magazine carried the headline "What Shall We Do about Birth Control?"[1]

Startled, she pulled over to buy a copy, and carried on to the Hotel Rutledge, on Thirtieth Street and Lexington Avenue. She had just a few minutes to scan it before she got to hold her children again.

Although she had fled the United States the previous year to buy time before standing trial for the charges relating to *The Woman Rebel*, Sanger eventually came to see that same trial as a reason to return. Vice agents had muzzled her by driving her out of the country just as well as they would have by putting her into prison. While abroad, she couldn't make a start on pursuing her dream of an American birth control clinic, she couldn't effectively lead an American birth control league, and she was separated from her children. A return, a trial, and even imprisonment promised far greater opportunity for professional advancement and public sympathy.

As she awaited her *Woman Rebel* hearing, Sanger's first concern was to raise enough money and publicity to do it right. Naturally, she turned to the NBCL. She knew the league had been growing in her absence, thanks in large part to Dennett's efforts, and it would have been reasonable for Sanger to assume there would be a ready-made place for her there.

Sanger remembered Dennett as a friendly and unthreatening comrade. She hoped—even expected—the NBCL would embrace her. In her autobiography, she wrote of how she asked the group "what moral support I could expect," and a few days later she received an invitation from Clara Stillman to come talk it over.[2] Eagerly, Sanger rang at the appointed hour. In a fit of hopefulness, she was "totally unprepared for the actual answer."[3]

Before her sat Dennett, Stillman, and Anita Block, one of the founders of *The Call*. Dennett spoke, in Sanger's memory, saying the league "disagreed with my methods, my tactics, with everything I had done. Such an organization as theirs, the function of which was primarily to change the laws in an orderly and proper manner, could not logically sanction anyone who had broken those laws."[4]

Then Dennett walked a silent Sanger to the door. Just before they parted, Dennett asked if Sanger would help the league by passing along the names and addresses of any prominent Europeans who might be interested in their work. "Heartsick as I was over my reception," Sanger wrote, "I was also amused at her shrewdness."[5]

Dennett's response came more from a desire for due process than a sense of direct competition. She followed Sanger's work with interest, had attended rallies in support of Bill Sanger, and certainly had no desire to take over the mantle of lawbreaking crusader for birth control herself. But she suspected that tying her league's aims and finances too closely to Sanger could jeopardize her efforts to gain credence with lawmakers.

This meeting was an inflection point for Sanger and Dennett's alliance, such that it was, and it warped their previously cordial relationship. When she insisted that operating within the law was the best and most effective path, Dennett implied Sanger had acted otherwise for her own glorification, or at least that personal ambition played into it.

Sanger must have felt betrayed; she had spent a year in exile, trusting her supporters would stand by her upon her return, and instead she was given a lecture and no promise of financial help. Dennett, meanwhile, was doing what seemed logical. She and her colleagues had been working carefully to build a league that could stand up to Comstock's agents, that could legitimately lobby for birth control at the state and—someday—the federal level, no doubt partly modeled on what she'd seen and done in her suffrage work. She couldn't trust Sanger to share that vision.

Dennett no doubt felt protective over the new league, but it was a bold and unsympathetic choice to shut Sanger out so decisively. The rift that started in Clara Stillman's parlor would last for decades.

A month after that meeting, Sanger's dismay was dwarfed by grief. Five-year-old Peggy Sanger was admitted to Mount Sinai Hospital with pneumonia. Sanger and her sister Ethel nursed her there; the boys stayed at their boarding school. But the sickness had gone too far. Peggy, the baby of the family whose "dominating" nature had won her Sanger's adoration, whose "chubby hands" Sanger had pined for while in Europe, died November 6, 1915. At that moment, Sanger, at just thirty-six, felt "the joy in the fullness of life went out of it then and . . . never quite returned."[6]

She was more devastated than surprised, she later wrote. She felt she'd half known what was coming. Before Peggy's death, she'd had a series of oppressive dreams about losing her daughter. Some of them had dwelled on the number six; she recorded them in her diary.[7] For the rest of Sanger's life, November 6 would be one of the most difficult days of the year.

Her life suddenly seemed devoid of the intimacy and affection she craved. In January 1916, she began an affair with a Jamaican-born writer and editor, Walter Adolphe Roberts, which would continue intermittently for two or three years. "I love being swayed by emotions by romances," she wrote in her diary, "just like a tree is rocked to and fro by various breezes—but stands firmly by its roots."[8] She was living downtown now, in a studio apartment on East Fourteenth Street, near her sister Ethel Byrne.

Grief sharpened her. Emma Goldman bustled back into Sanger's life, and got the brunt of that new spikiness. A month after Peggy's death, Goldman sent Sanger forty dollars she had collected after a lecture along with a letter essentially telling her to pull herself together. After expressing sympathy, Goldman wrote, "You owe it to yourself and the work you have before you to collect your strength . . . unless you will take hold of yourself you will lose whatever little you have, and yet not change the inexorable."[9]

Sanger decided the time had come to leave her old mentor behind. In her memoir, she wrote of her growing distaste for Goldman, dwelling much on her appearance. She was "short, stocky, even stout." Constantly aware of her own diminutive figure, Sanger seemed to marvel that Goldman, who was ten years her senior, didn't try to fit herself to conventional beauty standards.[10]

The press tended to characterize Goldman in masculine terms. Sanger, in contrast, used her own appearance to disarm: she was "young," "feminine," and "mild-looking" to reporters' eyes, surprisingly modest and soft spoken.[11] She wrote with evident pride that at events, people seeking her out "invariably approached the biggest woman and addressed her, 'How do you do, Mrs. Sanger?'"[12] She hoped to put behind her any association with Goldman, with her thick body and abrasive tongue.

During Sanger's year abroad, Goldman's cross-country lecture tour had again focused heavily on birth control. After Bill's arrest and Margaret's exile, Goldman also used her lectures to collect money for the Sangers. For a while, Goldman went about her work without interference from law enforcement.

But in 1916, vice agents began to pay closer attention. In January

1916, Goldman's partner Ben Reitman stood trial in Cleveland and was found guilty of distributing obscene material. He was sentenced to six months in the workhouse and fined. Then Goldman was arrested in New York City on February 11, despite having delivered her birth control lecture there eight times previously. The papers were consumed with stories on war in Europe, but the *New York Times* found space to recount Goldman's arrest. It sounded like a circus: "Some 500 followed, cheered Miss Goldman, and scoffed at the police."[13]

Publicly, Sanger called for readers to unite behind Goldman and birth control. They must forge ahead "without quibbling," she wrote in an editorial for Goldman's *Mother Earth*.[14] Yet she was noticeably absent from rallies in support of Goldman. Privately, she began making a case that Goldman's birth control work was a lot of hot air.

This change of loyalties was permanent. In a 1929 letter to a friend, Sanger wrote that Goldman "had never been an advocate of Birth Control until after 1914 when I issued my first statement on the subject."[15] In her autobiography, Sanger further dismissed Goldman's commitment to birth control as more of a whim than anything else: "Earlier she had made me feel she considered it unimportant in the class struggle. Suddenly, when in 1916 it had demonstrated the fact that it was important, she delivered a lecture on the subject, was arrested, and sentenced to ten days."[16]

Goldman realized Sanger didn't want her—or anyone—as a co-leader. "From numerous places friends wrote me that Mrs. Sanger had given the impression that she considered the issue as her own private concern," Goldman wrote.[17] Dennett and the NBCL had pushed Sanger out, had pointed out the pitfalls to her actions without recognizing the good she had done and might still do in the future. Now Sanger began to inflict a similar treatment on Goldman.

After her American citizenship was revoked and her subsequent deportation from the United States in late 1919, Goldman called on influential friends to help her reinstate her American citizenship in

1934. Sanger refused, explaining, "She never liked me personally and has belittled my work in her book. . . . One can get slapped just once too often, and I am through."[18]

. . .

On the eve of Sanger's trial, January 17, 1916, about two hundred sympathizers gathered at the stately Brevoort Hotel. Sanger addressed them, urging them to see birth control as a giver of life. Dennett spoke in her support, as did a prominent pediatrician, Abraham Jacobi.

The following day Sanger walked to her hearing at the head of a phalanx that included Jessie Ashley, Fola La Follette, and Elizabeth Gurley Flynn. Sanger wrote, "The stage had been set for an exciting drama," with reporters and photographers assembled in a thick scrum by the federal court building, which was overflowing with Sanger's supporters.[19]

That the trial was postponed, then postponed again, hardly mattered. The birth controllers had executed a perfect spectacle.[20] The publicity, combined with public knowledge of Peggy's death, turned Sanger into a kind of martyr in the press. Individual donations poured in, amounting to more money than she had dared to hope for, with heartfelt letters and tokens from other mothers who had lost children.[21] As a result, the government decided to drop the charges against her.

Though on the surface the decision seemed a mercy, it must have stung. Sanger's exile in Europe, for the sole purpose of avoiding the *Woman Rebel* trial, had meant missing the last year of her daughter's life. In the years that followed, Sanger defied the law again and again, but instead of evading the consequences, she stayed to fight.

Part II   *Fighting for Control*

The Lawbreaker

One thing's sure and nothing's surer
The rich get richer and the poor get—children.

—Popular variation on the song
"Ain't We Got Fun," 1920

O N A FALL MORNING, WELL over a hundred women lined up around the block near the new birth control clinic at 46 Amboy Street in Brooklyn. Many of them held hands with young children or jostled baby carriages.[1] Forty or so men stood in line too, most of them with their wives. Some of the women, it would turn out, were pregnant already and seeking abortions.

It had taken three enterprising minds and quiet but generous patronage to make the clinic a reality. Sanger had recruited her sister Ethel Byrne, younger by four years and a trained nurse, and Fania Mindell, an artist and activist from Minsk who, usefully, spoke Yiddish. They'd found a cheap commercial space in Brownsville, a poor and heavily immigrant neighborhood. Sanger called the setting "dismal . . . particularly dingy and squalid."[2] The first month's rent of $50 was covered by Kate Crane Gartz, a birth control supporter from Los Angeles.[3]

Printed notices promoting the clinic called out, "MOTHERS! Can you afford to have a large family? Do you want any more children? If not, why do you have them? DO NOT KILL, DO NOT TAKE LIFE, BUT PREVENT."[4] Signs in English, Italian, and Yiddish advertised "Safe, Harmless Information" to prevent pregnancy.

The clinic's purpose was primarily to help the women in that line by dispensing diaphragms. There was a second goal, though, and in

Sanger's mind it was just as essential. Antagonism from law enforcement was foreseen from the start, and the inevitable police raid would
be her means to provoke a test case about the legality of birth control.

Sanger had tried fruitlessly to find a doctor to oversee the clinic.
The presence of a licensed physician would have bolstered her case,
since in New York doctors had the right to prescribe contraceptives for
the cure or prevention of disease. But it proved impossible, and finally,
doctor-less, the clinic opened its doors on October 16, 1916.

Sanger, Byrne, and Mindell took each patient in turn to a private
examination area, gathered their vital information and health concerns, gave advice, and fitted diaphragms. They charged a ten-cent
fee for most consultations. All day long, they demonstrated the use
of the Mizpah cervical pessary, a device Sanger had seen in Dutch
clinics. The Mizpah was made of corrugated rubber with a string for
easy removal, and it could be used for up to two years. Crucially, it
was already stocked in many American drugstores, ostensibly to help
treat pelvic organ prolapse.

For many patients, repeated unwanted childbearing was the nexus
of a paralyzing web of health and economic struggles. "One Jewish
wife," Sanger later wrote, "after bringing eight children to birth, had
had two abortions and heaven knows how many miscarriages. Worn
out, beaten down, not only by toiling in her own kitchen, but by taking in extra work from a sweatshop making hats, she was now at the
end of her strength, nervous beyond words, and in a state of morbid
excitement. 'If you don't help me, I'm going to chop up a glass and
swallow it tonight.'"[5]

Reporters eagerly worked the long line outside 46 Amboy. One
of them asked a "little Catholic woman" whether she would tell the
priest about her visit to the clinic, and she snapped in reply, "It's none
of his business. . . . We have enough children."[6] The friend next to
her, age thirty-six but "who looked like sixty" to the reporter, added
that her own priest had encouraged her to have a large family. "I had
fifteen," she said. "Six are living. Nine funerals in our house."[7]

Sanger and her staff ran the clinic for nine full days, receiving 464 women in total.[8] On the tenth day, a stolid patient entered, wearing a well-cut suit with an old shawl around her shoulders. She claimed to be the mother of two children and wanted to know how to prevent future pregnancies. After she paid for a copy of *What Every Girl Should Know* with a two-dollar bill instead of a handful of scraped-together coins, Mindell had a clear suspicion of who she was, and she pinned that bill to the wall with a note flagging it as police department money. The next day, this patient returned and arrested Sanger and her staff. She was actually Mrs. Margaret Whitehurst, a plainclothes member of the vice squad.

The police detail blocked the clinic doors, terrifying everyone inside. They confiscated case histories, Mizpah pessaries, and copies of *What Every Girl Should Know.* As they tried to bundle Sanger into the patrol wagon, they met vocal resistance. According to the *Brooklyn Daily Eagle* for the afternoon of October 26, Sanger balked, hissing at Whitehurst, "You're not a woman! You're a dog!"[9]

Sanger insisted on walking the mile-long route to jail, thus making herself available to reporters. She later remembered how one wild-eyed patient screamed after her: "Come back! Come back and save me!" before the woman's friends took her arms and led her, weeping, away from the crowd.[10]

Sanger opted to plead not guilty and paid $500 in bail with help from friends. She became absorbed in strategizing her defense with the young attorney handing her defense, Jonah J. Goldstein, and the two fell into an affair. Awaiting her trial, Sanger reopened the clinic on November 13, 1916. She was rearrested the following day, and from then on police guarded the clinic's door to keep it shut. The barred door became a temporary monument to Comstock's power and to Sanger's defiance.

At the December preliminary hearing, Goldstein argued the law denied women "free exercise of conscience and pursuit of happiness" because it denied them "absolute right of enjoyment of intercourse."[11]

The judge, James J. McInerny, rejected Goldstein's reasoning, asserting instead what he considered common wisdom, that women had no right to a sexual life without fear of becoming pregnant—indeed, the entire purpose of women's sexuality was childbearing.

He was already disenchanted with the Sanger name; Judge McInerny had presided over Bill Sanger's trial the year before. When Margaret's hearing came along he applied to be taken off the case and instigated two months' worth of postponements.[12]

The trial finally took place January 29, 1917, in a "bare, smoky, upstairs Brooklyn court," as Sanger recalled.[13] About thirty Brownsville clinic patients were subpoenaed, but "about fifty arrived—some equipped with fruit, bread, pacifiers, and extra diapers, others distressed at having had to spend carfare."[14] She was quickly found guilty.

The court was loud with indignant women who'd been compelled to have too many children. One woman told a reporter, "This [the clinic] is the kind of place we have been waiting for all the time. I have seven children, two are dead, and my husband is a sick man. Do you know how I got bread for them? By getting down on my knees and scrubbing floors for the baker, that's what I did when we couldn't pay the bill. Seven children . . . that's enough for any woman."[15] Byrne and Mindell were tried separately, and Mindell was eventually released.

Byrne's case, or rather, her burgeoning fame, soon became bothersome to Sanger. After being sentenced to thirty days at the workhouse on Blackwell's Island, Byrne hatched the plan of going on a hunger strike, inspired by stories of British suffragists who were force-fed in prison and gained publicity and sympathy as a result.

The hunger strike began with a final turkey dinner and Byrne's vow to "die, if need be, for my sex," quickly reprinted in the papers. After that theatrical launch and nearly a week without food, Byrne began to be force-fed through a tube, the first time such a thing had happened in the American carceral system.[16]

Sanger was flummoxed to find herself briefly replaced as birth control's martyr figure. Byrne and birth control claimed front-page stories in the *New York Times* four days in January 1917. The public wonderment over Byrne's one hundred and three hours without food, followed by her tube-feeding of milk, brandy, and eggs, irked Sanger.[17] "The cause did not mean to Ethel what it did to me," she wrote. Though Sanger had initially agreed to Byrne's plan, she quickly soured on it.[18]

While the hunger strike was ongoing, however, Sanger kept up a supportive front. When three thousand pro–birth control New Yorkers gathered at Carnegie Hall in the middle of Byrne's hunger strike, raising $1,000 to support the cause and clamoring for justice, Sanger delivered a stirring speech. "I come to you from a crowded courtroom, from a vortex of persecution," she began. "I come not from the stake of Salem where women were tried for blasphemy, but from the shadow of Blackwell's Island where women are tortured for obscenity."[19]

She wondered aloud why Colonel Roosevelt could go "all about the country telling people to have large families and he is neither arrested nor molested," while she had opened sixty-three letters in one recent week from Roosevelt's hometown of Oyster Bay, all from women seeking birth control information.[20] "No woman can call herself free until she can choose the time she will become a mother," she concluded.[21] A group of Brownsville mothers stood behind her onstage. One audience member, who had also agitated for abolition, said the same spirit from that struggle was present when Sanger spoke.[22]

The driving force behind that Carnegie Hall rally was a group of moneyed women calling themselves the Committee of 100. Formed in early 1917, the Committee of 100 sustained both the NBCL and Sanger, led by influential philanthropists like Gertrude Minturn Pinchot and Juliet Barrett Rublee, whose inherited wealth kept the birth control movement together.

Their official credo proclaimed: "We maintain that it is no more indecent to discuss sexual anatomy, physiology and hygiene in a scientific spirit than it is to discuss the functions of the stomach, the heart and the liver. We believe that the question as to whether or not, and when, a woman should have a child, is not a question for the doctor to decide, except in cases where the woman's life is endangered, or for the state legislators to decide, but a question for the woman herself to decide."[23]

Dennett was a member from the start, and that credo clearly drew from her inaugural speech to the NBCL (in which she compared discussion of "anatomy, physiology and hygiene of reproduction in a scientific spirit" to discussion of "the functions of the brains, the heart or the lungs").[24] Several on the committee, however, notably Rublee, soon came to see Sanger as the lone heroic figure of birth control. For the moment, however, Byrne was getting all the press.

Byrne's hunger strike was front-page news for ten days. New York's governor, Charles S. Whitman, offered Byrne a pardon, so long as she promised to stop agitating about birth control; though Sanger didn't want to concede this point, Byrne accepted the governor's pardon and was released February 2.[25] The commissioner tried to force her to walk out of prison, for the sake of photographers, but she had to be carried out on a stretcher instead.[26] It took a year of convalescence, according to Sanger, until Byrne got back to her old self. It took years more for the sisters' friendship to return to its former closeness. An editorial in the New York Tribune speculated, "It will be hard to make the youth of 1967 believe that in 1917 a woman was imprisoned for doing what Mrs. Byrne did."[27]

At her own sentencing on February 5, Sanger listened passively at first. That changed when Goldstein made the concession that Sanger promised not to violate the law again. The court had offered leniency if she would commit to be law-abiding henceforth. At this point Sanger, echoing Bill's courtroom demeanor more than she might have admitted, spoke up: "I am today and have always been more concerned with changing the law regardless of what I have to undergo to have it done."[28]

Pending an appeal, she would not break the law, but wouldn't commit to anything beyond that point. "I can't respect the law as it stands today," she told the court.[29] Given the options of a $5,000 fine or imprisonment, she picked thirty days in the workhouse, this time the Queens County Penitentiary. Blackwell's Island had seen enough trouble from the Higgins sisters.

In prison, Sanger didn't replicate what her sister had done. She ate the food, read whatever newspapers she could find, and periodically met with Goldstein. All the while, however, she was at work on her appeal, a new magazine, and a new league. Compared with the sensation of her younger sister's hunger strike, Sanger's work while imprisoned would have far more lasting consequences.

. . .

Sanger had embarked on her first real lecture tour in the spring of 1916.[30] She practiced her standard birth control talk again and again, memorizing her script and training her voice to carry. For her audiences she outlined seven justifications for birth control: disease or insanity in the parents; if pregnancy endangered the woman's health; if the parents had already had "subnormal children"; if the parents were younger than their early twenties; if they couldn't afford another child; if pregnancy happened at a shorter interval than two to three years; and if the couple had been married less than two years.[31]

A few respectable political scientists had begun to talk about birth control, though they didn't warm to Sanger, whom they thought too radical. Warner Fite, a Princeton philosopher, published an article titled "Birth-Control and Biological Ethics" in the October 1916 issue of *Ethics*, touching on Malthus, Darwin, and the Hegelian idea of "being for others" versus "being for self."[32] He noted anesthesia in childbirth was now widely accepted and that opposition to birth control was "a survival of this discarded point of view," and he that argued superior technology, not greater manpower, was what defined a strong modern nation. Birth control was a feature of rational social organization, as opposed to "primitive superstition, fortified by a biological view of life."[33]

In 1916, a small but vocal fraternity of doctors favored it, too. Dr. S. Adolphus Knopf, a prominent TB specialist, endorsed it in an address to the American Public Health Association; Dr. William Josephus Robinson published *Birth Control, or The Limitation of Offspring by Prevenception*; and a book by the British reformer Charles V. Drysdale, *The Small Family System: Is It Injurious or Immoral?*, was released in America to generous coverage in the *New York Times*.[34] The majority of physicians still considered contraception "absurd, frequently dangerous, filthy and usually unsatisfactory" and a threat to "personal morality and national strength,"[35] but a few progressive voices stood out.

Robinson was one of the most committed to the cause, and the most convinced of his own preeminence within it.[36] A urologist by training, he was determined to make birth control—which he called "rational prevenception"—part of routine medical care. Between 1912 and the 1930s, he produced more than thirty books, nearly all of them concerned with sexuality, the case for birth control, or eugenics. "There will come a time—and it is not far off," he wrote, "when the prevention of undesired pregnancy will be as proper, as respectable and as much the function of the medical practitioner as is now the prevention of typhoid, diphtheria or tuberculosis."[37] Robinson considered it "criminal" for a physician *not* to prescribe birth control to any woman presenting with not just the typical list of conditions—disease, disability, deformity—but also high anxiety about pregnancy.[38] His sons Victor and Frederic eventually joined the movement, too.

Robert Latou Dickinson, a Brooklyn obstetrician-gynecologist, wanted the movement to be brought in from the fringe. He addressed a physicians' group in Chicago, urging them "not [to] let it [birth control] go to the radicals."[39] Dickinson set about designing his own research surveys and clinical services, launching the Committee on

Maternal Health in 1923. In time he became president of the New York Obstetrical Society, the Euthanasia Society of America, and the American Gynecological Society, and his work was deeply influential to later twentieth-century sex researchers such as the Kinseys and Masters and Johnson.

Doctors tended to seize on birth control either for eugenic reasons or because they were alarmed that feminist agitators were claiming too much authority within the movement. There were comparatively few physicians who supported birth control purely from a human-rights standpoint. Dr. Antoinette Konikow, an active Socialist who practiced in Boston and published *Voluntary Motherhood* in 1923, was an intriguing exception. "Woman can never obtain real independence unless her functions of procreation are under her own control," Konikow wrote.[40] Average Americans, in her estimation, were "surprisingly ignorant of the functions of their own bodies, especially their sexual organs."[41]

Her patients spent very little time unclothed. To bathe, many took sponge baths in long underclothes, as Dennett had seen her aunts do. Few had ever fully disrobed for sex. They were entirely unprepared for Konikow's assertion that "the normal vagina is as clean as the mouth."[42]

While New York state laws said physicians could provide contraception for the cure or prevention of disease, the lawyers and doctors Sanger interviewed about this tended to say this referred only to sexually transmitted infections.[43] Only a few physicians had an interest in changing this interpretation. Robinson was an exception, and he also spoke out against the medical monopoly on birth control: he thought it would make birth control less accessible and affordable.[44]

Sanger took note of these first signals of approval from the medical establishment. For her, the time had come to take action again—first in a clinic of her own, then in court, and finally through persistent, organized resistance.

. . .

March 6, 1917, marked "Margaret's Coming-Out Party." The metal doors of the Queens County Penitentiary opened and Sanger, who'd just completed her thirty-day sentence, stepped into "a bitter, stinging morning . . . the tingling air beat against my face. No other experience in my life has been like that."[45] Friends and supporters greeted her singing the "Marseillaise." It was bracing, jarring even, to go from the restrictive penitentiary to freedom.

Sanger had channeled her prison time into two big endeavors, a magazine and a new birth control league. She launched the *Birth Control Review* in February, while she was still incarcerated. The production and finances were handled by a group of allies, including Jessie Ashley and Agnes Smedley. Its tone was less profane than *The Woman Rebel*, but still defiant. "Shall We Break the Law?" read the title of Sanger's first editorial.

It read like a manifesto. "Throughout all the ages, the beacon lights of human progress have been lit by the lawbreaker," Sanger wrote from her cell. "To-day legality has become so encumbered with lifeless relics of the past that the courts no longer express living social standards and the ideal of Justice, but merely the dead weight of legal precedents and obsolete decisions, hoary with age."[46] There was a statement of support from Helen Keller, articles by Havelock Ellis and H. G. Wells, and Goldstein's first-person account of the Byrne and Sanger trials.

As with *The Woman Rebel*, readers of the *Review* sent disgruntled letters because no practical contraceptive instruction could be found in its pages. Sanger had a secretary answer most of these with a form letter explaining it was illegal to print what they were seeking, but she sometimes went further. "Some of the appeals, particularly from women who lived on lonely, remote farms, were so heart-rending that I simply had to furnish them copies of *Family Limitation*," she wrote.[47] The post office periodically called her in for a reprimand.

The *Review* grew into one of Sanger's most far-reaching and long-lasting platforms. While *The Woman Rebel* had had a circulation of about 2,000, the *Review* reached between 15,000 and 30,000 readers per month through the course of its life until its final issue in 1940; letters from readers flooded in along with subscriptions.[48] Each issue printed contact information and updates from state and international birth control leagues, lending a sense of cohesion to the movement.

Its fiction pages became an important venue for writing that evoked the raw reality of forced pregnancy, with contributors including Theodore Dreiser, W. E. B. Du Bois, Upton Sinclair, and Angelina Weld Grimké.

In Rita Wellman's story "On the Dump," published in the *Review* in 1918, the protagonist takes stock of how her own body has been obliterated by overwhelming demands. It is an indelible description of dissociation: "There was always another [child] growing within her body, the body that must care for the living child, the body that must clean and cook for those running around, the body that must always be at the disposal of her husband."[49]

Publishing the *Review* took a leap of faith, for it was, suddenly, a dangerous time for the free exchange of ideas. In 1917, antiradical feeling in government bloomed. News of the 1917 Bolshevik Revolution stoked paranoia of the working classes roused to violent revenge. The government's reaction brought the 1917 Espionage Act, amplified the following year into the Sedition Act, and the 1918 Immigration Act. Fear of Bolshevism Stateside brought on a climate of suspicion marked by peaks of hysteria.

Historians have called this period a "free speech catastrophe" because of the scale of dissident repression.[50] Propaganda, censorship, and ideological cleansing were all deemed necessary and patriotic. College students accused professors of radicalism and got those professors fired. *The Masses* was shut down; in December 1919, Emma Goldman was deported to Soviet Russia.

The Espionage Act gave the Post Office Department expanded powers to halt and investigate the mailing of any morally suspect periodicals or pamphlets. In response to World War I–era laws restricting civil liberties, lawyers and activists convened the National Civil Liberties Bureau in 1920; it evolved into the American Civil Liberties Union (ACLU), which would later play an important role for Dennett and Sanger.

Besides the magazine, Sanger now had a new advocacy organization. In December 1916, before her imprisonment, she had laid the groundwork for the New York Birth Control League (NYBCL). This new league announced three primary goals: It would support Sanger's legal defense as necessary—just what Dennett and the NBCL had refused to do. It would also lobby for the amendment of state and federal laws, and promote birth control knowledge in order to safeguard maternal and infant health. The new league soon began holding public events: the first one, a week after Sanger's release, was a ticketed luncheon to honor her and Byrne at the Plaza Hotel.[51]

Among the several leagues Sanger led through her life, this one stands out for one particular and important detail. In her announcement of the NYBCL, Sanger expressed her intention to make doctors the gatekeepers of birth control. The NBCL, in a newsletter to its members in January 1917, noted that Sanger's new league had the "avowed object of so modifying the present law that only physicians and nurses will be permitted to give birth control information." Someone with a tone much like Dennett's then reminded readers, "The National Birth Control League is unalterably opposed to this compromise."[52]

The "doctors and nurses" idea, soon revised to "doctors only," surprised Sanger's allies as well as Dennett. Even the Committee of 100, which had come together just weeks earlier to help fund and publicize Sanger's work, had made a point of arguing that contraceptive information shouldn't be restricted to doctors. But now, with growing numbers of physicians warming to birth control and the experience of her clinic being shut down fresh in her mind, Sanger had changed strategy. It is at this moment, with the announcement of this new league, that she seems to have decided her best chance at achieving success would be to follow the "doctors only" compromise. Being shut out by Dennett and the NBCL at least had this advantage, of freeing her up to be as pragmatic as she chose.

This kerfuffle among birth control groups was a signal of things to come. Sanger announced her willingness to give physicians and nurses a privileged role, keeping birth control part of the domain of organized medicine. In doing so she made one thing eminently clear: she intended to ally herself with doctors, to amass credibility, and to build a persuasive case for changing the law.

She gave herself a scope that, as many saw it, had a better chance of success than the more radical proposal of freeing birth control information from the Comstock Act. It was a departure from her early ideas, inherited from Emma Goldman, but the great tactical advantage of this compromise was that Sanger now had a fighting chance of success among lawmakers and doctors: the realm of men.

Now thirty-seven, she had only scraps of time for family life. Motherhood, as Sanger experienced it, differed starkly from the *Ladies' Home Journal* ideal of constant tender ministry. "Inevitably," she wrote, "I have been constantly torn between my compulsion to do this work and a haunting feeling that I was robbing my children of time to which they were entitled."[53] She keenly felt Peggy's absence. But unlike Dennett, who worked toward social justice full-time because she was forced to live apart from her children, Sanger deliberately arranged her family life so she could prioritize changing the world.

She bought a small house in Truro, on Cape Cod. It was to be her summer base, where Sanger, her father, her siblings, and her sons could gather. A photograph taken near there shows four of the Higgins sisters standing arms-round-shoulders in the surf, with their slight, surprised-looking father pointing up to the sky. Margaret and Ethel are bright faced; Anna and Mary more hesitant to smile. Another fire ended their idyll there. "This house was eventually to burn," Sanger remarked in her memoir, just like their home in Hastings; "fate seemed to decree I should not be tempted to slip back into peaceful domesticity."[54]

. . .

A month after her release from the penitentiary, Sanger reshuffled her inner circle. She had grown close to Juliet Barrett Rublee, the heiress to a Chicago roofing and tar fortune, who became one of Sanger's longest-standing correspondents and financial backers. Their intimacy came easily, to the point that Sanger speculated in a letter to Rublee, "Perhaps we were goddesses in the past or sisters or something."[55] Rublee helped create a parent company for the *Review*, the New York Women's Publishing Company. Dennett sat on the board of that parent company until her conflicts with Sanger made that impossible a couple of years later.

Influenced by Rublee, the Committee of 100 essentially became a pro-Sanger propaganda machine. They printed a booklet, *The Birth Control Movement*, describing Sanger as "the first woman who has had the imagination and freedom of spirit to realize that the quickest way to change these laws, which have been covertly broken for generations by the privileged few, was to come out and by taking a striking stand, draw public attention to the subject."[56] They also produced a collection of letters to Sanger, all from married people seeking birth control advice, carefully selected so as not to feed arguments that legalizing birth control would benefit only vamps and prostitutes.[57]

The letters tell of excruciating circumstances. A Minnesota mother wrote: "Dear Madam:—I am coming to you for information. I am a young woman not yet thirty years old, and am the mother of six children. I dread and fear child birth. . . . One doctor says it was best I had no more children but that is all he says, and I don't like to go to a man for such information, even he be a doctor [*sic*]. . . . Is there any sure relief? Hoping to hear from you, and thanking you in advance"[58]

Then, from Boston: "I am twenty-four years old, and have had six children, four of which are living. My husband earns thirteen dollars weekly. The fear of having more children has caused me to lose interest in life and almost everything else."[59] Husbands wrote of their low salaries, unfriendly doctors, and wives in such constant pain they seemed like ghosts of themselves.

All the while, Goldstein was pursuing Sanger's appeal. The decision came at the start of 1918, and it proved to be the signal legacy from the brief life of the Brownsville clinic as well as a linchpin that made possible much of what followed.

At the appeal's ruling on January 8, 1918, Judge Frederick Crane upheld Sanger's conviction under the state's obscenity law. Then he did something remarkable. Crane asserted licensed physicians in New York did indeed have the right to give contraceptive advice and supplies to married people for the prevention or cure of disease, and argued pregnancy *itself* could be classified as a disease.

Crane's decision was based on the 1909 *Webster's New International Dictionary* definition of "disease," a general definition not aimed at genital or obstetric conditions. Pregnancy, Judge Crane remarked, was a condition that produced "an alteration in the state of the body, or of some of its organs, interrupting or disturbing the vital functions, and causing or threatening pain and sickness."[60] It could be life-threatening and incapacitating; at its very mildest, it qualified as an alteration.

The overall effect of Crane's decision was to clarify how pregnancy and doctors' rights were viewed in the eyes of the law. If *sickness* applied to pregnancy itself, not only an STI or tuberculosis, then physicians had much broader rights than they had previously thought, if they had thought about it at all.

Sanger and Goldstein petitioned for Crane's decision to be expanded to nurses, to no avail. After a series of postponements the court refused to take the matter further. On the face of it very little had happened, but the ruling created a gleam of nuance in the indifferent blockade of the Comstock Act. Sanger seized on it. It would be enough, at least for the time being, if doctors could be persuaded to lead the way.

A few weeks before Crane ruled in *People v. Sanger*, Americans were thrust into a reality that made league scuffles seem like the concerns of a more innocent age. On December 7, 1917, the United States declared war on Austria-Hungary.

Be fruitful, and multiply, and replenish the earth,
and subdue it.   —Genesis 1:28

Desire not a multitude of unprofitable children.
—Ecclesiasticus 16:1

FOR MARY WARE DENNETT, PACIFISM was as close to her
heart as feminism, and the two were closely intertwined. On
April 22, 1914, she told a reporter she'd "searched [her] vocabulary
for words hot enough to express her detestation of war. . . . I have no
patience with the cheap, spread-eagle patriotism that would plunge
the country into war over a so-called 'insult.'"[1]

The archduke hadn't even been shot—that came in June—but
Dennett was fixated on the tensions brewing in Europe. Once the
war began, she shuddered to see roundups of draft dodgers and was
more furious than ever that she had no right to vote.[2]

Dennett had closely tracked the fallout from the raid on Sanger's
clinic and the announcement of the NYBCL, but her own birth control work slowed down as the United States grew closer to entering the
war. She withdrew from the American Union against Militarism and
joined the Women's Committee to Re-Elect Wilson in 1916, before
the United States was officially involved, on the understanding that a
vote for Wilson was a vote for peace.

When Wilson altered course and entered the war the following
year, Dennett signaled her sense of betrayal by resigning immediately.[3]
Afterward, she became a cofounder of the pro-peace, anti-Wilson

People's Council and a board member of the Women's Peace Party in 1918.[4]

She liked the work, though it "has not put any much needed pennies in my pocket," as she wrote Devon.[5] At times it seemed she hardly slept because of her wholehearted commitment to peace work. The NBCL, after years of painstaking fundraising and promotion work by Dennett and an initial mission to Albany, started to languish.[6]

Besides the war, the 1918–1920 influenza pandemic jammed the cogs of everyday life. "The radicals were convulsed and their own ranks torn in two by the opposition to conscription," Sanger wrote in her memoir. "Influenza swept over the world and in its passage took off many of our old companions."[7] Around twenty million Americans (out of a population of just over one hundred million) caught the flu, and about half a million of them didn't survive it.

Put through this crucible, the birth control movement went through a metamorphosis. In the brief twenty-seven months when Americans were at war and then demobilizing, reproduction itself seemed to come up for reappraisal. Matthew Connelly, a historian, has summed up the question that shifted both birth control and war into a different light: "What are people for?"[8]

Was population growth meant to feed a military machine, justify territorial expansion, and keep workers keen and hungry—or, if there was some other purpose, what was it? The daily casualty list, a fixture of the newspapers, brought home this question every morning.

Many pinned the underlying cause for the war on Germany's rising population. On this basis, a Chicago surgeon interviewed in the *Medical Review of Reviews* in 1919 suggested birth control had the power to avert wars in the future: "If Germany had not been overcrowded, she would not have yearned for 'expansion.' Possibly 'twere better to have no 'beginning' at all than to die in the filthy trench."[9]

Writers and artists questioned old ideas about the blessedness of family life. In Virginia Woolf's *Mrs. Dalloway*, the shell-shocked veteran Septimus Smith decides, "One cannot bring children into a world like this."[10] Amid a climate of violence and privation, forced pregnancy presented an especially cruel sight. In his paintings and etchings, the German expressionist Otto Dix documented some of what he saw, making a visual case against the criminalization of abortion. One 1922 image, *Schwangerschaft* ("Pregnancy") shows a bony pregnant figure standing beside rubble and a corpse.[11]

Käthe Kollwitz's *Pregnant Woman Contemplating Suicide* (1926), is eerily similar: a charcoal-sketched pregnant woman, wrapped in a shawl, looks down a flight of stairs, a hand covering her face. Bertolt Brecht wrote a heartrending portrait of an impoverished woman crushed against Germany's anti-abortion law in "The Ballade of Paragraph 218." The merciless doctor tells her, "You'll make a simply splendid little mummy/Producing cannon fodder from your tummy."[12]

Young people, regardless of political leaning, lashed out at their forebears for leaving them a ruined world. The proximity and frequency of death, specifically the slaughter of just-grown boys, threw a new spotlight on the question of what citizens owed society, and vice versa. "They give us this thing, knocked to pieces, leaky, red-hot, threatening to blow up," wrote a self-proclaimed "wild" youth named John F. Carter in *The Atlantic* of September 1920, "and then they are surprised that we don't accept it with the same attitude of pretty, decorous enthusiasm with which they received it, way back in the 'eighties."[13]

The war also exposed a silent epidemic of sexually transmitted infections. It is estimated that 116,516 American men died in the war, a modest number compared with that of other combatant nations (France lost nearly ten times as many). Disease caused more American deaths than direct action.

The 1910s were an age of deadly disease transmission, especially around Dennett and Sanger in New York City. "It is three times as safe to be a soldier in the trenches as to be an American baby in a cradle," wrote Dr. Jo Baker, head of the Department of Child Hygiene in New York City (and another Heterodite).[14] Just before the Spanish flu, as the postwar influenza epidemic was known, an outbreak of poliomyelitis in 1916 closed not just indoor public gatherings but play-grounds and schools too, with eight weeks' isolation recommended for all positive cases.

Now STIs were ravaging Americans of all classes. In 1917 and 1918, when Americans were active in the war, the military recorded 3.5 mil-lion outpatient and hospital encounters; 11 percent of those were for sexually transmitted infections, mainly syphilis and gonorrhea.[15] For every thousand men admitted to clinical care, 181.5 were there for STI treatment, compared with 27.1 for measles, 2 for dysentery, and 1 for malaria.[16] A final damning statistic: roughly five out of every six men with gonorrhea or syphilis had been infected before entering the military.[17]

The American policy had been to reject draftees with STIs. Then it was found that in some regions, infection rates for syphilis and gonorrhea were as high as 25 percent. In the interest of rais-ing enough manpower, the rule was repealed and the government rapidly implemented sex education and STI-prevention programs.

The military was at the forefront of tackling a public health catastrophe that had already spread like a mycelium through every community in the nation. By the end of the war, syphilis and gonorrhea had cost the army more than $50 million in treatment expenses and around seven million days of lost labor.[18]

Physicians realized a major proportion of the infertility cases they were seeing were caused by men infecting their wives with gonorrhea, which in women presented ambiguous symptoms or none at all while the infection spread through the uterus and Fallopian tubes.

But what kind of response could deal with the scourge and keep future generations safe from it? The government's strategy, like Prince Morrow's a decade earlier, turned out to be a burgeoning sex education movement aimed at one powerful demographic: teenagers.

. . .

Despite the beginnings of sex education in schools, most young people learned the facts of life via "unreliable gossip . . . quack doctors and . . . lurid motion pictures," according to a US Public Health Service study in 1917.[19] Most parents neglected to have "the talk" or they put it in such vague or forbidding terms that the mechanics of pregnancy and STI transmission remained entirely mysterious. In 1918, the Public Health Service's message to parents was that "it is no longer possible for you to choose whether your child will learn about sex or not": the government was taking charge.[20]

The crusade against STIs prompted an enormous propaganda effort, from pulpits to movie screens. The explicit goal of government sex education programs was "a life of continence before marriage."[21] An exhibition titled *Keeping Fit*, with fifty slides or posters demonstrating how physical fitness could ensure moral and sexual health, circulated nationally.

The messaging of *Keeping Fit* exhorted boys to channel their energies into physical activities like "chopping wood, mowing lawns, shoveling snow and gardening."[22] The Health Service worked with church leaders to inaugurate Social Hygiene Day on Sunday, February 2, 1919, with sermons focused on abstinence. More pragmatically, it also added a chemical prophylaxis program.

By the end of the First World War, sex ed moved decisively from a private family matter to a civic one. The Public Health Service targeted high schools: in the 1910s, adolescent boys were more likely to be working than in school, but by the 1920s the balance had shifted and they were in the classroom, ready for indoctrination.[23]

Other sexual-health efforts were less benign, like the policy called, with bizarre vagueness, the American Plan. Beginning in 1918, the federal government supplied states with a model law, and within three years every state had adopted a version of it. Under this measure, "any person reasonably suspected by the health officer of being infected with any of the said [venereal] diseases" could be detained, put through a gynecological examination, and incarcerated until deemed no longer infectious.[24]

Though the law was meant to apply to everybody, the majority of its targets were women. The Chamberlin-Kahn Act, signed into law in July 1918, put bricks-and-mortar infrastructure in place to serve this new policy: $427,000 in federal funds were disbursed to build twenty-seven new institutions and expand sixteen others, solely for the purpose of incarcerating anyone suspected of carrying an STI.[25] Under the guise of preserving public health, the government criminalized tens of thousands of women (at a conservative estimate) between the 1910s and the 1960s.

The law's implementation ran wildly beyond its original scope. Known prostitutes were quarantined, but *possibly* wayward females— waitresses, salesgirls, even unchaperoned pedestrians—were caught up in the operation, too, especially if they were Black. In his chronicle of the American Plan, Scott W. Stern, a historian, describes how officials "enthusiastically warned that nonwhite women were less moral, intent on infecting soldiers and that blacks were a 'syphilis soaked race.'"[26]

Once arrested, suspects were taken to physicians who administered pelvic exams. If they tested negative for syphilis and gonorrhea, they were released. If there was any shred of doubt, they were imprisoned and dosed with mercury- and arsenic-derived medications that often did more harm than good; penicillin wasn't used to treat STIs until 1943.

If the goal of the American Plan was to throw barriers between uninfected and infected citizens, there were surely less harmful methods, starting with the humble condom. American soldiers were those of the only nation sent to war without an allocation of condoms. (The French, justly concerned, offered to share their supply; the Americans declined.) As the extent of the STI epidemic was revealed, condoms were exempted from Comstock restriction so long as the packet was stamped "for the prevention of disease," but they weren't adopted as part of the Public Health Service's plan.

Furtively, buyers purchased Trojans, Ramses, and Sheiks at drugstores and barbershops, from five-and-dimes, and from traveling salesmen. In Baltimore, condom sales rose from 3 million to 6.25 million between 1914 and 1928.[27]

Once latex was invented in 1920, condom production became less hazardous and the products themselves were thereafter thinner and more reliable.[28] However, they were forbidden from mail distribution by Comstock laws and weren't regulated or tested, and, since they were sold from behind the counter, druggists could drastically mark up the price.[29]

In this climate newly friendly to sex ed and sexual responsibility, Dennett's *The Sex Side of Life* took off. In February 1918, it was a main feature of the *Medical Review of Reviews*. Its editor, Victor Robinson, praised it as a welcome corrective: "Instead of the familiar notes of fear and pretense, we were surprised to hear the clarion call of truth."[30] Physicians expressed their hope it would be reprinted as a pamphlet and distributed generously among the public, calling it a "splendid contribution."[31]

The following year, Dennett revised it for a reprint, updating her opinion on masturbation. Instead of cautioning against it, now she wrote that "the chief harm has come from the worry caused by doing it, when one believed it to be wrong."[32] (Kellogg, by contrast, had advised parents to bandage their children's genitals and tie their hands if necessary; other guidebooks had dire warnings about letting them slide down bannisters or ride bicycles, since masturbation was widely believed to be a risk factor for syphilis, epilepsy, insanity, and a life of crime.)[33]

Dennett began to hear from a new band of readers. One young man wrote her that he'd been given the text by his father; previously, he'd thought babies came from prayer. "We had often heard of sexual intercourse—under another and simpler name—but did not know its real purpose, thinking it merely for some sort of low pleasure; and we were at first shocked to think of its being connected with birth," he wrote. He admitted that, over a past summer when a camp pal asked him how babies were born, he had answered "through the breasts."[34]

Outside of the $1,000 prize, direct and meaningful impact on young Americans was exactly what Dennett had wanted. But for much of 1918, she struggled, and not just because the war made her angry and helpless. She worried about Devon when he caught whooping cough in the summer. A measles outbreak followed, and he lost a dramatic amount of weight before recovering.[35] The specter of the influenza pandemic haunted her.

Professionally, she faced hostile circumstances and sensed a transition on the horizon. She took a second trip to Albany to lobby for the NBCL, but found no traction. "It is an awful job," she wrote Carleton. "These legislators are mostly a rather low minded lot, who tend to a *smutty* consideration of the subject to hide their ignorance and embarrassment."[36]

A few assemblymen asked her the same question: "Why do you come up here asking to consider a bill of this sort when our National laws set us the example they do on this subject?"[37] Dennett had no solid rejoinder. And that, to one who relishes debate and the moral high ground, was intolerable. Life was "just *full* of stress," she wrote her sons. "I wonder if *your* lives will be, too."[38]

The bright spot that year was the prospect of peace. On November 11, 1918, in the wee hours of the morning, the armistice was broadcast from the State Department to reporters. *Harper's* editor Frederick Lewis Allen described how "people had poured out of offices and shops and paraded the streets singing and shouting, ringing bells, blowing tin horns, smashing one another's hats, cheering soldiers in uniform, draping themselves in American flags, gathering in closely packed crowds before the newspaper bulletin boards, making a wild and hilarious holiday. In New York, Fifth Avenue had been closed to traffic and packed solid with surging men and women, while down from the windows of the city fluttered 155 tons of ticker tape and torn paper."[39] Girls kissed soldiers; Barnard students "snake danced" in the street.

The war and the ravages of syphilis and gonorrhea it uncovered had forced the government to take on an active role in sex ed and safe sex. Though feminists had had little influence in these campaigns, some of them detected an opportunity in Washington's new openness to these topics. As soon as her peace work was put to bed, Dennett began plotting to take the birth control movement national.

I for one
Think the country would be better run,
If Mary Ware Dennett
Explained things to the Senate.
                                   —Ogden Nash

A T FORTY-SIX, DENNETT WAS, WITHOUT knowing it, on the
verge of the most promising and disillusioning phase of her career. In January 1919, she checked in to a hotel near the Capitol and
visited some old NAWSA colleagues. She shared their dinners and
took notes on their lobbying methods.

"I have had an unexpectedly good time. There are some very jolly
women here, and the meal times have been quite delightful," she
wrote her boys.[1] "They are lobbying in a most systematic way. They
each have a list of senators and Congressmen to see every day—and
off they go right after breakfast, then after dinner at night they meet
and report the successes and failures and plan out their next day's
work."[2] Each day's efforts revolved around two unwieldy projects:
winning over individual legislators and building public support across
the country.

Between 1919 and early 1925, Dennett tried to bridge two worlds—
the norms of popular culture and the marketplace, and the bombastic illusions of Congress. Books and movies were fixated on sex and
scandal, and some even treated them with humor. The Public Health
Service was printing its own sex ed resources, and condom sales were
rising exponentially by the year.

Congress, meanwhile, remained in the age of Comstock. Elected leaders, regardless of what they practiced in private, hectored Dennett for being an agent of corruption. In each day's lobbying notes, she recorded what they'd said, noting how many of them lived in an imagined world they feared or simply refused to change or leave, since it had granted them power.

On March 5, 1919, Dennett wrote to NBCL members announcing her readiness, with five former league leaders, to organize a new group. The Voluntary Parenthood League (VPL) had bigger ambitions than changing state laws; it was dedicated to passing a federal law removing Comstock's prohibition on birth control.[3] The League's subordinate goals were bold, too; one was "equal legal and social rights for illegitimate children, and justice for the unmarried mother."[4]

She saw the new league as an all-embracing humanist group, with aspirations to break out of the Greenwich Village feminist circle now rallied around Sanger. She deliberately chose to emphasize the word "parenthood" in launching her new league, on the principle that birth control concerned both sexes and that parenthood was too great a responsibility to be left up to nature.[5]

The Voluntary Parenthood League would be more focused and nimble than the NBCL, with a greater measure of control apportioned to Dennett. The old league seemed to have run low on energy, especially since Jessie Ashley's death from pneumonia in January 1919, a loss Dennett felt keenly. She grew frustrated by her own limited leeway to work on changing the federal law, since not all NBCL leaders shared her conviction to put that goal first. Even if it meant sacrificing a steady source of philanthropic funding, Dennett decided to make a break with her old comrades.

. . .

Dennett lived and worked through an age of committees. The excesses and inequities of the Gilded Age energized the workers and dreamers who defined the Progressive Era, and who coalesced around unions and associations galore. In the mid-1910s, national organizations sprang up for members of long-underpaid occupations such as nurses, policewomen, and educators; the National Association of Colored Women was founded in 1896, the NAACP in 1909. The Women's Trade Union League, which Jessie Ashley had helped form in 1903, grouped together middle- and upper-class activists with working-class women, a model that Dennett's and Sanger's own leagues would try to emulate.

The mechanics of these leagues, made up of well-intentioned individuals clustered around a goal that was meant to unite them, were rarely smooth, and the reality of the group dynamics within them rarely lived up to their lofty founding ideals. Dr. Jo Baker, who had belonged to twenty-six committees, wrote, "In some curious way, these committees seemed always to be made up of much the same people," a combination of settlement-house reformers and wealthy philanthropists who took long summers off.[6] Nearly always, league meetings "took a great deal of time out of life, were usually tiresome, only occasionally helpful, but they gave the members a sense of importance that made them cooperative and so they seemed to be worth while."[7]

Dennett shared Baker's cynicism; she was ambivalent about the whole business of committees, votes, and power struggles submerged in scuffles over process. She once wrote that she felt a "general kick against anything and everything that tends to *institutionalize* one's mind" and "a distaste for organizations as such," but she recognized that only a well-organized, well-funded group had a hope of achieving change on a national scale.[8]

Funding was naturally central to the movement's operations, and it was a fickle business. The nascent birth control movement depended on large infusions of cash from a few regular benefactors. Katharine Dexter McCormick, the MIT-educated philanthropist who had married an heir to the International Harvester fortune, was one. Julius Rosenwald of Sears, Roebuck was another.

Juliet Barrett Rublee was Sanger's financial angel, underwriting clinic expenses, mailings, and public events through the 1920s, until her reserves were eaten up during the Depression.[9] Gertrude Minturn Pinchot's donations enabled the NBCL to rent office space; she also sent Bill Sanger subsistence checks while he was awaiting trial and paid for *Family Limitation* to be translated into Polish and Lithuanian.[10]

Dennett had gotten her fundraising training while at NAWSA, and she now tried to balance soliciting donations with keeping the leadership of the Voluntary Parenthood League streamlined. She was wary, given the financial disagreements that had led to her resignation from NAWSA, of giving undue influence to a small clutch of donors, but at the same time league work burned through cash quickly.

Middle- and working-class donors gave when they could; as one of them put in a note attached to his $5 check, "I hope this trivial donation will help to save at least one mother from the same tragic end of my dear Mother who gave birth to twelve children, had one miscarriage and passed away at the age of 35."[11]

Once someone signed on as a league member, they committed to paying monthly or annual dues, though these arrived sporadically. In an accounting of donors to Sanger's American Birth Control League in 1925, only fifty-four had given more than $100.[12] Primarily, activists like Dennett and Sanger needed the great philanthropists—themselves benefiting from Gilded Age fortunes—to pay rent on league offices, run clinics, hold events, print and circulate literature, and allocate themselves a salary.

Though the new league struggled financially almost from the start, the VPL became Dennett's home for the next five years. Its crest was a circle, and within it a line drawing of a wide-eyed child surrounded by the slogan, "The first right of the child is the right to be wanted."

The group's primary aim was changing the federal law. Dennett sent her supporters promotional copy and urged them to advertise locally: "ATTENTION! EVERY MAN AND WOMAN IN THIS

TOWN! Which sort of family is the biggest asset for the country in time of war, or peace, the one in which an annual baby is born to deplete the mother's health, the father's earnings, the other children's food and care; or the one in which the babies are intelligently 'spaced' like the vegetables in the war gardens, so that the health and money of that family can be used to the utmost advantage for its own strength and that of the nation?"[13]

"Spacing" children had benefits for maternal health, but Dennett's slogan also relied on an unscientific opposition between quality and quantity of children. As with the NBCL's founding document, it harked at the eugenic idea of a specific type of family being "an asset," with the clear implication that other types are not.

Dennett hoped Sanger would view this as a chance to turn the page on the tensions between the NBCL and Sanger's newer NYBCL. Prospects looked good for two birth control groups to work alongside one another: Dennett assumed she would lead the attack on the Comstock Act in Washington, while Sanger would focus on state laws, clinics, and propaganda. Dennett even asked Sanger to join the VPL's executive committee, underestimating the hard feelings that remained; Sanger refused.[14]

Dennett did her best to shake this off. She had persuaded most of the NBCL to migrate to the VPL, and the old league soon folded.[15] She rented an apartment in Washington and moved there nearly full-time. Then she began trawling for congressmen willing to talk about birth control.

On July 22, Dennett sent a confidential report to the VPL's national council, full of optimism. "After two days and a half of preliminary skirmish in Washington," she wrote, "the outlook seems decidedly good."[16] She felt close to ebullient, despite being so close to broke she had to ask the boys' school for tuition relief.[17] Dennett had, a few years previously, read a self-help book about willpower that had made her "sure the impossible was possible."[18] Taking birth control to the Capitol put this certainty to the test.

The legislative process requires a bill to have sponsors in both the House and the Senate. In both houses, the bill must be introduced and referred to a subcommittee, where it might be approved, revised, or killed. If approved, the bill goes through the same process within a full committee. It is during these committee sessions that bills can be the topic of hearings, during which experts, advocates, and opponents testify. If once again the bill passes through, it is reported to the floor of the House and Senate and scheduled for consideration. Once both houses have given their approval, and the House and Senate versions have been aligned, it reaches the president's desk.

Somehow, Dennett marveled, Comstock had succeeded in navigating all of this. Now the suffragists were in their final months of doing the same, and the birth control movement was just entering the ring.

Dennett's petite, unglamorous demeanor served her well in Washington. She kept her blondish-gray waves tucked under a practical hat, her eyes beaming out her conviction behind her spectacles. She pitched what she called a "clean repeal" or "unlimited" bill, simply deleting "prevention of conception" from the Comstock Act. It was, she hoped, an elegant and uncontroversial strategy.

Reluctant as they were to be publicly connected with birth control, in private some congressmen expressed relief that at least she wasn't a radical.[19] She assured them they wouldn't need to make any public statement in favor of birth control, that the campaign was not seeking newspaper publicity, and that the bill was "a dignified piece of work for public welfare." Her suspicion was "the Congressmen will doubtless behave better, if the subject is presented as an obvious piece of welfare legislation than as part of 'the revolution.'"[20] She knew she didn't impress anyone as a firebrand, given her age and Boston-intellectual accent.

Campaign days were laborious and inefficient. Appointments were "practically impossible," at least for Dennett. Senators and representatives were rarely in their offices, and buildings were organized so that she had to walk enormous distances every day. If she couldn't get through a congressman's door, she presented her bill to his secretary. If she found no one, she went back to the office, searched to see if any VPL supporters lived in the relevant constituency, and asked them to send their elected leaders a letter. "One tramps miles in pursuit of a member,—only to find he is at the Capitol. Another tramp then,—to discover he is not in the House. An interminable game of hide-and-seek."[21] *This* was democracy in action?

The Midwinter 1919–1920 issue of the *Pictorial Review* published a feature on birth control—"Keeping the Stork in His Place"—that was useful ammunition.[22] Eleanor Kinsella McDonnell wrote the article as a paean to Dr. Aletta Jacobs, birth control pioneer of the Netherlands. Though McDonnell concluded the piece by mentioning Sanger as birth control's American torchbearer, Dennett thought the article achieved something rare: it justified birth control without drawing primarily on eugenics- or free-love-inspired justifications.

The Netherlands was portrayed as Richard Scarry–like, with adorable houses and industrious people "who saw the light while the world was still wallowing in Mid-Victorian sentimentalism."[23] Dennett made copies to send around to members of Congress, with a covering note explaining she only wanted the United States to be "as wholesome as Holland."[24] She frequently mentioned the Netherlands in her arguments, since it was a place where birth control was legal, public health was measurably better than in the United States, prostitution less common, and, as a quasi-eugenic bonus, "the average stature of the Dutch has increased over four inches in fifty years."[25]

Once Dennett successfully got in the door to do some actual lobbying, she faced bluster and indignation. Representative William Boies, Republican of Iowa, whose downturned mouth did not signal a warm welcome, was aghast at her talk of birth control. He scolded Dennett out of his office, saying women should "have children instead of poodles." ("A tough customer! Took to my bed after the interview!" Dennett noted.)[26] Some insisted that they needed to read more about it, that they were still recovering from the flu, that though they were themselves amenable, Congress was simply not ready for such a revolutionary step.

Hostility to birth control transcended party lines, though Dennett had better luck among Republicans than Democrats. The three congressmen who eventually agreed to sponsor her bill all belonged to the Republican Party. Many legislators went blank faced as Dennett presented data on maternal and infant death, reacting only to ask if she was married and a mother herself before shaking their heads and showing her out.[27]

A few meetings turned into what she called "opera bouffe"—the stuff of satire. Most extreme among these was Senator Knute Nelson, Republican of Minnesota, whom Dennett vented about in her diary as "cranky and in a class by himself," and who was "[so] bad as to be a grotesque scream . . . an utter ignoramus. Scolded, denounced, interrupted [me] constantly, undertook to tell me what I *thought* regardless of what I *said*, then denounced me for it."[28]

Nelson had close-set eyes under a suspicious brow. He favored bow ties and sported a wiry beard that enlarged his narrow, jutting profile, and was chairman of the Judiciary Committee at that time. It was rumored Nelson's wife had been several months pregnant with their daughter at the time of their marriage. They now had five children. The mention of birth control provoked in Nelson "a tirade which went on with increasing violence for over an hour," Dennett noted in her diary.

Though incensed, she maintained "a bland and tolerant manner" as he dismissed the birth control movement as "lazy stuck-up wives who never had children, and if they did, it was only a few dudes."[29] Dennett herself had clearly gone wrong, he said, but not irretrievably so. "You *look* like a *nice* woman," he told her sorrowfully.[30] In several meetings, Dennett clarified the difference between contraception and abortion for men who had studied medicine yet considered them one and the same.

The medical establishment still had little consensus on whether birth control was a matter of interest. In March 1919, the main feature in the *Medical Review of Reviews* was "A Symposium on Birth Control," conducted by Dennett and Frederic Robinson. The foreword declared, "Birth control is one of the most insistent of all the unsettled social questions."[31] The editors surveyed forty-seven physicians and found twenty-one believed in birth control. Most supporters had come around to approving of birth control for economic reasons, as a measure to alleviate poverty and hunger.

Only one respondent, G. Frank Lydston, a surgeon of Chicago, raised the question of "whether the woman—with whom the wear and tear of child-bearing and rearing is a very important consideration and whose health should be most carefully conserved by society—should not have a voice in the matter of both control."[32] Lydston echoed others when he suggested that reliable, freely accessible contraception would increase sexual license, but unlike others, he didn't see enormous danger in it—in fact, he suggested that if premarital sex were normalized, illegitimacy might carry less of a stigma.

Dr. Howard Kelly of Johns Hopkins University, a staunch opponent, told the *Review of Reviews*, "I know of nothing more destructive to a sense of national decency and honor, and I look with disgust and horror on any such propaganda, which is properly forbidden by law."[33] Birth control was "meddling," in his opinion, and "total abstinence" the only decent way of controlling fertility.[34]

Respondents within the US government chimed in. "The crying need of the world is children, then children and then more children," wrote Harvey Wiley of the Department of Agriculture. "A legalized system that produces one childless family is a horror a thousand times worse than a dozen families of many children struggling for the needs of life. Out of the first family nothing can come. Out of the second, a LINCOLN may come."[35] The same year, a joint pastoral letter from a majority of American bishops condemned family planning by artificial means.

Then Sanger spoke up. If Dennett had hoped for her support or even merely a lack of direct opposition, her illusions were swept away when, in the *Birth Control Review* of July 1919, Sanger publicly criticized Dennett's campaign. "Personally, I object to the so-called 'unlimited bill,'" she wrote. "My objection, however, is not the usual one, that it would increase immorality."[36]

Instead, she put forth three arguments: first, that doctors and nurses were trained professionals, unlike the irregulars who often peddled contraceptives; second, requiring examinations would allow healthcare professionals to give individualized information, unlike what women could get anonymously through the mail; third, the doctors- and nurses-only approach would allow records and statistics to be collected. "I do not believe it to be more advisable to have an amateur instructor in contraceptives than to rely upon an amateur dentist or surgeon," Sanger finished, tartly.[37]

Sanger's article affirmed both her commitment to the doctors-only strategy and her willingness to cast Dennett out of the movement, if she could. It was a reality check. Dennett and Sanger were not, as Dennett had optimistically envisioned, leading two complementary efforts to make birth control legal and accessible. They were not two arms of the same movement.

Instead, they were leading ideologically incompatible campaigns, in isolation from each other. Sanger's hostility toward Dennett left over from that fateful meeting four years earlier, which Dennett seems to have thought would pass quickly, had intensified instead.

Dennett's meetings went on, day after day, to dispiriting effect. She was relieved that, at least, Sanger was not yet trying to change the federal laws. But being the only birth control lobbyist in Washington was demoralizing, both in terms of her emotional resilience and her close view of how bills passed through the legislature. Highly apt was a comment from Wisconsin senator Robert La Follette to her that senators were all "rabbits sitting on their haunches with one ear cocked toward the public, and one toward self-interest."[38]

Occasionally she had a good hour. Senator Thomas Sterling of South Dakota was one of her favorites. "Exceedingly gentlemanly and with a wholesome mind," she wrote; he asked to take some pamphlets home to give to his wife and sister.[39] Senator Joseph France of Maryland, a physician, was sympathetic. He actually compared mainstream acceptance of birth control to "the way the sun comes out of the fog."

For now Dennett kept up her campaign, eyes fixed on the dream of a breakthrough, willing the fog to vanish.

You are a nasty, nervy, immodest bunch of fanatics, and I
do not want to be bothered with you anymore.

—Rep. Joe Eagle, Democrat of Texas
(September 1920)

FOR HER 1920 NEW YEAR card, Dennett sent out a photograph
of herself between her sons. They stood with their shoulders
touching, Carleton with his hands clasped behind his back. The
printed message read, "From the Dennetts, big and little, Greeting!"[1]
The boys now stood head and shoulders taller than their mother.

Though the trio were close, each had their own stresses. Carleton
was getting ready to attend Haverford College in the fall. Devon, still
at boarding school, became the target of bullying.[2] Dennett herself
had constant money worries. The "financial incubus," with her unpaid wages now amounting to $2,000, was relentless.[3]

Just before the New Year, she asked the boys to write to Hartley to
ask for help paying their tuition; she'd already taken out a loan from
Vonie to reprint *The Sex Side of Life* and had nowhere else to turn.
Hartley declined the appeal, again blaming Dennett for her problems
and for the fact that, as he put it, he was unable to perform his duties
as a parent.[4]

The 1920s are often eulogized as a roaring, jazzy chapter in the
nation's history, but the bopping soundtrack accompanied cultural
changes that were disturbing for many. In his rollicking history of
the '20s—*Only Yesterday*, written in 1931—*Harper's* editor Frederick
Lewis Allen describes the decade between the end of World War I

and the crash of 1929 as singularly transformative. Sex, the radio, risqué dancing, shorter dresses for women, the proliferation of automobiles, and the Problem of the Younger Generation preoccupied magazines and the chattering classes.

For some, preserving the old ways was vitally important, and for a little while legislating female flesh out of sight seemed like a viable way to make that happen. Allen wrote,

> The New York American reported in 1921 that a bill was pending in Utah providing fine and imprisonment for those who wore on the streets "skirts higher than three inches above the ankle." A bill was laid before the Virginia legislature which would forbid any woman from wearing shirtwaists or evening gowns which displayed "more than three inches of her throat." In Ohio the proposed limit of decolletage was two inches; the bill introduced in the Ohio legislature aimed also to prevent the sale of any "garment which unduly displays or accentuates the lines of the female figure," and to prohibit any "female over fourteen years of age" from wearing "a skirt which does not reach to that part of the foot known as the instep."[5]

In light of the fact that Prohibition was ratified in January 1920, maybe it didn't seem so ridiculous to set tight rules over daily habits and dress.

Comstock's legacy was fading fast now, overlaid with a new cultural norm more averse to repression than passion. Divorce rates rose steadily, and to be divorced in the 1920s was far less shocking than it had been when the Dennetts did it. Indeed, Allen wrote, "there was often about the divorced person just enough of an air of unconventionality, just enough of a touch of scarlet, to be considered rather dashing and desirable."[6]

New York theaters advertised the play *Strange Interlude*, "in which a wife who found there was insanity in her husband's family but wanted to give him a child decided to have the child by an attractive young doctor, instead of by her husband."[7] The top-grossing film of 1920 was *Way Down East*, and the runner-up was *Over the Hill to the Poorhouse*. Both films indirectly touched on birth control, portraying illegitimacy and the plight of a woman with more children than she can manage, respectively. A year later, *The Sheik* mesmerized moviegoers with its depiction of barely contained sexual violence turning to true love.

In literature, a glimmer of a future battle came in February 1921, when the editors of the *Little Review*, Margaret Anderson and Jane Heap, were tried for obscenity for publishing the "Nausicaa" episode of James Joyce's *Ulysses*. This part of the novel dips into the consciousness of Gerty MacDowell, who mentions her habit of taking Widow Welch's Female Pills. These were a real product, believed to have abortifacient properties to help women avoid "calendar worries." Because they'd violated the Comstock Act by publishing a work that mentioned such a thing, Anderson and Heap were fined and forbidden from ever printing any part of *Ulysses* again.

Dennett reasoned to herself there was no way Congress could reject birth control much longer, especially when, at last, the final certification of the Nineteenth Amendment on August 26, 1920, brought American women in every state the right to vote. "Now that the suffrage ratification is clinched," Dennett speculated, "the opinions of all these club women will count doubly in Washington."[8] She reasoned politicians' self-interest would begin to work in her favor, as surely they'd want to pander to their masses of first-time woman voters.

Yet what was supposed to be a triumphal campaign turned grim.

The men of Washington were unaltered from a year earlier. Sanger needled her too, not always directly. Dennett felt as much when she picked up the January 1920 issue of the *Birth Control Review.*

On the *Review*'s front page, Sanger surveyed instances of starvation, disease, and unrest around the world. "What shall we women, as citizens of the nations, and of the world, do in this crisis? . . . Shall we bring children into a world that is bankrupt and starving?"[9] Her response was a passionate no: "All of our mother instincts, all of our humane feelings, all of our common sense must cry out against such a course." Governments had failed to consider the reality of family life at such a tumultuous moment in history. Only by uniting in action could women begin to take charge of remaking the patriarchal political structures that had failed them.

She called for a global birth strike. "In this hour of crisis and peril," Sanger emphasized, "women alone can save the world. They can save it by refusing for five years to bring a child into being. And there is no other way."[10]

Dennett thought Sanger's birth strike idea did the movement a gross disservice and that Sanger's fiery rhetoric hampered what Dennett was trying to get done in Washington. In response to Sanger's editorial, Dennett resigned from the board of the New York Woman's Publishing Company, the parent organization of the *Birth Control Review.*[11] The editorial "inject[ed] into the situation a militantly feministic policy or the terminology of the labor struggle," Dennett wrote in her resignation letter. "It is obvious that the majority of Congressmen are not warm hearted toward the strike idea in general," she noted with some acidity, "and neither are they moved by feminism. On the contrary, they are antagonized by both."[12] Public health, child welfare, the economy, eugenics—any of these were stronger grounds for getting a bill passed.

Dennett's protest against the birth strike idea invigorated the bitterness between them that had been made obvious a year earlier when Sanger criticized Dennett's bill in the *Review.* Now, as if echoing her criticisms of Sanger's lawbreaking tactics back in 1915, Dennett called out her rival for being too stridently feminist and for clumsily alienating congressmen.

Dennett tried to believe, and to make her readers believe, that her campaign had the potential to win in Washington, but that potential was still far from reality. In March 1920, Senator Lewis Ball, Republican of Delaware, agreed to sponsor the clean repeal. He was the fifth member Dennett had asked, and seemed in no rush to get it to a vote, which made it hard to tell whether it would pass or die.[13] For months, Ball made excuses until time ran out.[14] In June Congress adjourned. Dennett reported herself "CAST DOWN BUT NOT DESTROYED!" in a memo to supporters.[15]

Not just politicians, but fellow feminists were turning traitorous. The women's movement had become a target of cynicism lately, as conveyed in a report in *The Nation* from the mid-February 1921 National Woman's Party convention in Washington, DC. "At a convention human intelligence reaches its lowest ebb," a "disheartened delegate" told the reporter, Freda Kirchwey.[16]

Crystal Eastman commented that "all doubtful subjects, like birth control and the rights of Negro women, were hushed up, ruled out, or postponed."[17] Attendees concerned with these topics were met with an "amiable contempt" from leadership. Black delegates were included only grudgingly at the convention, their contributions treated as interruptions, and were barred from riding elevators at the convention hotel until they protested.

At first Alice Paul, who had the final word on convention events, wanted to exclude birth control, but after intensive correspondence with the VPL and ABCL, Dennett and Sanger both spoke. Still, no resolution on birth control was formally raised at the gathering. There was a touch of irony in Paul's position on this point. She had previously been far more militant than Anna Howard Shaw, leading White House pickets and hunger strikes for suffrage.

Dennett had had friction with Paul the preceding June, at the biennial convention of the General Federation of Women's Clubs, in Des Moines. It had been a battle just to get there, and to be heard. After being asked to attend, Dennett was uninvited. She protested, of course, and finally traveled all the way to Des Moines to talk for roughly five minutes, to a mostly empty room. Just beforehand, she was accosted by Paul, who "quite lost her temper, manners and poise," in Dennett's words, and "demanded that I withdraw."[18] Dennett "sat tight," to Paul's "great disgust."[19] Paul's influence, she wrote, had something in common with Sanger's—it "seems to me to verge on the hypnotic."[20]

The medical establishment, meanwhile, began to see Dennett as a troublemaker. Ever hopeful, she had sent the New York Academy of Medicine a copy of the VPL's draft bill, seeking their endorsement. After hearing through the grapevine that an academy officeholder had commented that the Comstock Act ought to be revised, specifically to be more lenient regarding birth control, she assumed the academy was about to take action and endorse her work publicly. Without waiting for any further information or encouragement, she excitedly told all VPL contributors and began generally spreading the news that her draft bill was about to receive the academy's support.[21] This represented—or would have, had it been true—a significant breakthrough for the cause.

Dennett hadn't considered that doctors could be even more leery of publicity than politicians. On April 6, 1920, the academy notified her that the VPL's draft bill was unanimously deemed undesirable. They would never endorse it. When she tried to convene physicians for a discussion about her bill at the Colony Club, no one showed up. Never adept when it came to managing optics, she could not let go of the conviction that they had let their ideals fold under social pressure.

The mistake reflected badly on her leadership, and the rest of her league demanded an explanation. To her credit—or maybe testament to her guilelessness—Dennett simply shared some of her correspondence with irate physicians. The doctors clearly supported a "medical monopoly" on contraceptive knowledge, she wrote, "and are nervous accordingly."[22] Idealistically, she was sure that once her colleagues had the facts, they would support her again. But at that moment it mattered less who was right, and more who stood together.

. . .

The afternoon of December 16, 1920, Dennett took a seat at the Woman's Party tea gathering. Sanger was the featured speaker. It was the first time since their clash over the birth strike editorial that Dennett considered Sanger's ideas, and seriously assessed what other advantages Sanger might have that she herself lacked. "She was a charming vision in a reddish gown—and she surely is a genuine spellbinder," Dennett admitted. "But oh, her English, and her facts that aren't facts, and her logic that isn't logic, and her amazing faculty for being the whole 'moomunt'!"[23]

Sanger brought out Dennett's persnickety academic side. It was as though she craved a chance to take an editorial pencil to Sanger's very self. But as repelled as she was by Sanger's emotive public utterances and jealous ownership over the birth control movement, Dennett could see her overwhelming charisma, too.

With her own bill languishing, Dennett also took great interest in watching Congress debate a bill she saw as closely related, the Sheppard-Towner Maternity and Infancy Protection Act. It gave her a clearer sense of what she was up against—and of what it might look like to win.

Sheppard-Towner was "the real test of women's power" in Dennett's view.[24] Drafted by Julia Lathrop of the US Children's Bureau and sponsored by Representative Jeannette Rankin, Republican of Montana, the bill offered states $1 million annually in matching federal funds for prenatal and infant-care education.

The bill faced multilateral opposition. The AMA never favored it, in part because it was administered by Lathrop, a nonphysician.[25] Others pointed to the expense or saw it as communism sneaking in the front door. Dennett heard protests identical to ones levied at her regarding birth control. One senator asserted that "the heavy maternity mortality is normal—so why worry," and "as women grew civilized the dangers of maternity increased," and ultimately, "it couldn't be helped anyway, and why waste the country's money!"[26]

When Dr. Jo Baker testified regarding the bill, she was overruled by a doctor who said, "We oppose this bill because, if you are going to save the lives of all these women and children at public expense, what inducement will there be for young men to study medicine?" Senator Sheppard, in Baker's memory, "stiffened" before asking, "Perhaps I didn't understand you correctly. You surely don't mean that you want women and children to die unnecessarily or live in constant danger of sickness so there will be something for young doctors to do?"[27]

"Why not?" asked the doctor. "That's the will of God, isn't it?"[28] Sheppard-Towner passed, but it never had enthusiastic backing from physicians or from Congress. It would expire in 1929 and never be renewed.

Dennett returned to hunting down congressmen, who continued to scorn her and treat her bill like a hot potato. To one senator after another, she wrote hefty letters, enclosed press packets, listed economic statistics. "It's going so maddeningly slow," Dennett wrote in her campaign diary on December 16, 1920. "Yet I must not be so impatient as to do the wrong thing for the sake of getting on."[29]

Barreling forward too fast had, after all, been her great mistake with the doctors. Even friends, like Lathrop of the Children's Bureau, would not agree to be publicly connected with the cause because of the precarious status of her own office. Donors like Mrs. Julius Rosenwald gave $1,000 at most, when Dennett knew their deep pockets would have allowed for larger grants if the VPL's work were seen as more promising.

Her patience had been stretched thin as she tried again and again to persuade congressmen birth control did not belong in the obscenity statutes. Convincing them it was even an acceptable topic of conversation was a daunting hurdle in itself.

. . .

As the '20s dawned, Dennett came close to losing another child. The summer of 1920 was horribly punctuated by fifteen-year-old Devon falling into a depression and attempting suicide.[30] He had, just previously, appealed to his father for a loan, with interest, to help pay for his schooling. Hartley refused, but offered to help on the condition that Dennett would bend on the custody arrangement.[31] She declined, writing of Hartley's relationship with the boys, "The possibilities of friendship are perhaps very rich. The prospect for parenthood looks arid. Why not follow the *open* road?"[32]

Devon was deeply anguished by his parents' emotional and financial deadlock. A week after getting Hartley's reply, he swallowed a lead-based poison, lost consciousness, and had to be rushed to the hospital, where he recovered.[33]

A new friendship born that year helped carry Dennett through, and became one of the longest alliances of her life. Vine Colby Mc-Casland of Saint Louis was a writer who had once been part of the Potters, a group of artists and poets, several of whom were lesbian or bisexual. Then, in 1912, she married a man from Springfield, Massachusetts, and moved there with him, eventually returning to Saint Louis and finally settling in Pasadena, California.

Eight years after her marriage, she wrote to Dennett, McCasland found herself "almost a complete bankrupt in health and courage, exhausted, sleepless, hypersensitive to noises and living in a very Bedlam of noises"—and she was pregnant.[34] She had a copy of *Family Limitation* and had used a contraceptive successfully thus far, but now it had failed.

Dennett replied immediately, asking if McCasland had considered an abortion. "I know that ten years ago I should not have dreamed that I ever could feel that there was sufficient warrant for interfering with pregnancy after it was once started," she wrote, "but I have been close to so many gripping cases of need in the years that have followed that I have very considerably changed by mind."[35]

McCasland confessed she was even more afraid of abortion than maternity. Though the two rarely met, they kept writing about matters large and small. They witnessed each other's lives through every hard campaign and sick child.

Dennett's other unexpected ally was Dr. Walter Franklin Robie, a sex therapist. She had read and admired his book *Rational Sex Ethics* (1916), and they became warm correspondents. Dennett confided in him her own history with Hartley and recommended his expertise to others whose marriages she knew could use some realignment around sex—including, awkwardly, Aunt Lucia and Uncle Ned. After Devon's suicide attempt, Robie, because he could get to Devon's boarding school quickly, had taken charge of the situation until Dennett arrived.[36]

Occasionally, Dennett spilled her innermost thoughts and questions not to her friends but to a beloved old critic, Aunt Lucia, now sixty-three. Lucia questioned her niece's work, citing concerns about sin, promiscuity, and "moral law," which made chastity the only acceptable birth control.

In a fiery letter, Dennett rebutted each point in turn. The letter is revealing because Dennett was pushed to articulate her rationale to an antagonist she loved and respected, one whose approval meant a great deal to her. "You just *assume* that chastity is a part of the 'moral law,'" Dennett wrote; "Well, what *is* moral law? Who made it? Where did it get its authority? Is it not subject to evolution like other phases of human development?"[37]

In her view, Dennett wrote, "*God is in the making yet*, rather than that he sits above somewhere holding a rigid standard toward which he encourages us to struggle." Fear and enforced ignorance would never improve human society—that would come only with education and the free exchange of ideas.

"I have no faith in authority, but only in the unquenchable aspiration of the human soul," she wrote. "The most worth while happiness is ahead in the realm of freedom rather than behind in any of the static conventions of the past."[38] She held tight to the idea of making a new, freer world.

No woman can call herself free until she can choose
consciously whether she will or will not be a mother.

—Margaret Sanger (1920)

N H. G. WELLS'S 1922 novel, *The Secret Places of the Heart*, the
protagonist is captivated by a "finely-featured, frank-minded but
soft-spoken" American, Miss Grammont, who is dedicated to birth
control. Miss Grammont proclaims, "In the New Age all lovers will
have to be accustomed to meeting and parting. We women will not
be tied very much by domestic needs. Unless we see fit to have children. We shall be coming and going about our business like men. . . .
It will be a world full of lovers' meetings."[1]

Miss Grammont was clearly based on Sanger, and Wells's novel
was a kind of love letter to her.[2] Two years earlier, Sanger had simultaneously begun an affair with Wells and solidified her friendship
with his wife, Amy Catherine "Jane" Wells, who was well aware of
her husband's belief in free love. Sanger wrote of Wells, "There was
no aloofness or coldness in approaching him, no barriers to break
down as with most Englishmen; his twinkling eyes were like those of
a mischievous boy."[3]

She enjoyed staying with him and Jane at their home in Essex,
Easton Glebe. For several years their affair would pick up again every
time she saw him, though they never spent extended periods together,
and their correspondence lasted until his death in 1946.

Sanger was glad to be back in England without the shadow of a
trial hanging over her, and with the war over. In 1920, as Dennett

trawled the corridors of Washington, Sanger traveled, wrote her first book, and laid the groundwork for a glittering summit that would further cement her position as the unrivaled avatar of the birth control movement: the First American Birth Control Conference of 1921.

At just past forty, Sanger redrew the parameters of her social world, too. Though she had a way of seeming vulnerable and submissive—an attitude she seemed able to switch on and off at will—she navigated her time in Europe like a cool diplomat assigned a tricky set of international relationships. Some people she drew closer, ensuring steadfast loyalty and the free exchange of intelligence. Others, she began to freeze out.

In the same season as she became involved with Wells, she enjoyed a romantic interlude with the novelist Hugh de Selincourt, one of Havelock Ellis's circle. Selincourt brought her into yet another world: Wantley, his four-centuries-old estate in Sussex once owned by Percy Bysshe Shelley's father. He encouraged her to think and write, in the company of his wife, Janet, and their daughter, as well as Janet's lover, the literary critic Harold Child—who, in time, became Sanger's lover, too.[4] Together they made up the kernel of the Wantley Circle, intellectual and irreverent, dedicated to honoring love and sexual pleasure, surrounded by the beauty of the past and dreaming of a future full of possibilities.

Sanger also spent a weekend at Marie Stopes's country house, where she found friction of a chillier kind. With some ambivalence she saw her friend succeeding as the architect of the British birth control movement. *Married Love* had circulated widely in England since its 1918 publication. Stopes spoke often of her plans to open a birth control clinic in London, "as a memorial to [her] marriage" to Humphrey Roe.[5]

To Sanger's mind, Stopes didn't grant due credit or appreciation to Sanger's pioneering achievement with the Brownsville clinic. Stopes, meanwhile, was taken aback by Sanger's suggestion that she, an American, could possibly open a London clinic before her, a dream

Sanger had unwisely shared with Stopes. She was also dismissive of Sanger's preferred birth control method, the Mizpah pessary, instead advocating a "French cap" she considered simpler.[6] Eventually Stopes designed and manufactured her own cervical cap, which she, a passionate eugenicist, dubbed the Pro-Race pessary.

Stopes's Mothers' Clinic opened on March 17, 1921, at 61 Marlborough Road in the London district of Holloway. Like Sanger's Brownsville clinic, the Mothers' Clinic was located deep in a working-class community, clearly serving a different clientele from the pampered, childless-by-choice types demonized by politicians. Staffed by nurses who examined patients and dispensed advice and diaphragms, aided by visiting doctors, Stopes's clinic was the first in what would become a network. Sanger congratulated her in a letter but was privately appalled at how Stopes had co-opted and realized her own plans while apparently facing a fraction of the obstacles.[7]

From England, Sanger visited Berlin to pursue a rumor Ellis had heard about a chemical contraceptive being manufactured there. She landed in a starving postwar nation where birth control advocacy vied with a movement to legalize abortion. Sanger noted a statistic she'd heard and couldn't put out of her mind, that in a single year since the war, more than half the known pregnancies in the city had been terminated.[8] Many Berliners still struggled to feed themselves and their families.

Sanger didn't come home with a chemical contraceptive, but she was struck once more by the urgent importance of her work, of the inhumane demands of pregnancy and hunger together. She recovered from that trip by stealing an August week in Ireland with Ellis, writing Juliet Rublee that she had "talked" to Peggy via a local medium.[9]

Her book-length manifesto, *Woman and the New Race*, was published in 1920. Sanger opened the main text with an incendiary line: "The most far-reaching social development of modern times is the revolt of woman against sex servitude. The most important force in the remaking of the world is a free motherhood."[10] Suffrage, regulated working hours, equal property rights—all these were well and good, but none of them "affected directly the most vital factors of her existence"—sexuality, parenthood, and economic independence.[11]

In the book, Sanger positioned birth control in opposition to "primitive" and "sordid" population-control practices like infanticide and abortion, which, in her telling, were sanctioned in the distant past but were no longer tolerated.[12] Birth control, in contrast, was a civilized, scientific salve for many threats to a thriving society: overpopulation, hunger, poverty, child labor, prostitution, "mental defects," STIs, and tuberculosis.[13]

Sanger's focus on tuberculosis is interesting, considering her mother's acute case—the book is dedicated to Anne Higgins—and her own struggle with the disease. She doubtless speculated about how her mother's life would have been different had she been able to put her energy toward recovering from the disease instead of relentless childbearing.

For herself, she sought medical attention and managed to avoid the chronic version of the disease that had killed her mother, but the fear of flare-ups, especially at moments of stress, preoccupied her. When fatigue or illness overwhelmed her, her idea of rest was to find a warm, dry climate and write a book. In February 1919 she had done just that, renting a place in Coronado, California, where over a few months she produced much of *Woman and the New Race*.

She was no longer writing as a Socialist provocateur. With this book, aided by Ellis's glowing preface, she had become a philosopher, crusader, and self-made authority. After she returned to New York, Sanger continued assembling the materials she needed to put the movement, with herself at its helm, in the headlines: followers, donors, events, arrests, and editorials.

Sanger was in a phase of divesting herself from troublesome appendages. Her tubercular tonsils came out in September; then her divorce decree from Bill arrived in October. She no longer had much interest in maintaining her ambivalent ties to Stopes and Dennett.[14] While Sanger had reason to feel slighted, her mode of retaliation would prove severe. Very soon Sanger started to act, Dennett confided to Carleton, "like the devil."[15]

. . .

In April 1921, Dennett wrote to her sons of being moved by springtime. Though she'd collapsed again early in the year, her energies had since returned.[16] "I, who sort of thought I was blasé and could not again be stirred by spring," she wrote, "found myself quite intoxicated with 'spring fever',—and feeling all *alive* once more."[17]

A puzzling situation was just then developing with Sanger.[18] In March, Dennett sent Sanger an editorial she was hoping would be published in the *Birth Control Review*. It was likely a rebuttal to an article by Sanger in the March issue, which was critical of Dennett's work in Washington, saying it aimed "to open the United States mails to the distribution of birth control knowledge by amateurs."[19]

Furthermore, Sanger had written, Dennett's vision of free speech around birth control was a product of her privilege: offering a pamphlet "to a woman who cannot read or is too tired or weary to understand its direction," she wrote, "is like offering a printed bill-of-fare to a starving man."[20]

In her answering article draft, Dennett implied Sanger, while certainly a good talker, was not the one doing the real work. The VPL, she wrote, was the "only national birth-control organization in the country" and it was making progress "steadily and practically for nearly two years on the Federal campaign."[21] Then Dennett's piece turned to an impassioned critique of the Comstock Act and boosted the VPL's effort in Washington—her own present work—as "the greatest single return for time, effort and money expended by those interested to end the need for a birth-control movement."[22]

Dennett wrote as if she was determined to establish her primacy and institutional authority, money and fame be damned. Sanger had published her own, gloves-off critique of the VPL; now Dennett aimed to answer along similar lines.

Unsurprisingly, Sanger declined to publish it in the *Review*. To do so, she explained in a short, stiff reply, would be to muddle the public's perception of the purpose and tactics of the birth control movement. Dennett rejected the rejection, a futile and highly characteristic move. "I have carefully reread my letter and see nothing [in] it which would make its publication inappropriate from the point of view expressed in your letter," she wrote.[23]

Then Dennett, having raised some funds on a midwestern speaking tour, landed on the idea of inviting Marie Stopes to come to New York for a public meeting. Though Dennett had never met Stopes, she had read and shared her works widely, and in 1919 they began a cordial correspondence.

Figuring she had nothing to lose, Dennett invited her new friend to be the featured speaker at the VPL's upcoming rally, slated for October 27, 1921. She had no idea that Stopes and Sanger had recently had an uneasy reunion in England. After stipulating that she required first-class accommodations, a porter for her things, and assurance that the venue was "the biggest and best reputation hall or theatre in New York," Stopes agreed.[24] By June, it was all arranged.[25]

If Sanger was wounded to hear about the new chumminess between Dennett and Stopes, she soon struck back. Weeks later, Sanger announced plans to launch yet another new league and to hold a birth control conference in November in New York. All too soon, the VPL would have a rival group, set to be the center of much publicity. And there would be a marquee event, to which neither Dennett nor Stopes was immediately invited. Sanger intended to go beyond just writing what she thought of her rivals; she was ready now to show her power.

For months, Sanger had been working to rally feminists, physicians, eugenicists, and philanthropists around her new league. Among many renowned figures, she had courted the suffrage champion Carrie Chapman Catt, who hedged. In a friendly note to Sanger, she explained she couldn't endorse birth control: "Civilization is not produced by a single movement. It is rather a fabric woven of many threads, each of which is necessary to its perfection. I do not feel that I want to pull on every thread. . . . I am no apponent [sic], even though I do not stand by your side."[26] When she spoke publicly as founder of the League of Women Voters, Catt was markedly more negative, possibly anxious that Catholic members of her audience would leave otherwise.

Sanger's interest in recruiting luminaries was evidence of a shift that had started during her stint in the penitentiary. In a letter to her sister, she wrote, "It is true that the fashionable seem far removed from the cause, and its necessity—but we cannot doubt that they and they alone dominate when they get an interest in a thing. So little can be done without them."[27] She had overcome, for now, her contempt for the genteel-progressive set.

In July, Dennett wrote Sanger an earnest letter, taking a very different tone from their recent spat concerning the *Review*. "Dear Margaret, I was mighty sorry to hear that you had again been seriously ill," she wrote.[28] Then the letter shifted from neighborly to heartfelt. She admitted she had felt slighted by Sanger's dismissal of her work thus far.

This culminated in a proposal: "The time is ripe now," Dennett wrote, "for a careful survey of the field and a great joining of forces instead of further splitting them by forming still another organization." She asked Sanger "whole heartedly" to "discard all prejudice" and come to the table to discuss merging her plans with those of the VPL.[29] It wasn't a wholly admiring letter, but it was full of goodwill.

New disappointments in Washington—partly due to her own blunt methods—had inspired Dennett to propose this merger. In August she met with Postmaster General Will Hays, who liked her practical talk about "spacing babies." (Hays would later become the architect of the Hays Code that governed movie-screen morals between 1934 and 1968.) If Hays championed the bill, it would go to Congress at the behest of a cabinet officer instead of a congressional sponsor— a neat way of leapfrogging through the typical process.

Hays and Dennett got as far as outlining a bill that would delete "prevention of conception" from the obscenity clause, define pornographic literature more clearly, create a separate section about abortion—differentiating therapeutic from criminal abortion—and finally block from circulation any birth control literature not approved by a physician.

Excitedly, Dennett wrote to the entire VPL subscription list about this new development and urged them to write Hays in support of it.[30] But after being deluged with VPL mail praising him as a valiant champion for birth control, Hays backtracked and declined to take any leadership in changing the penal code after all.[31]

When Dennett tried other post office authorities, she quickly reached a dead end. Dr. Hubert Work, assistant postmaster general, admitted to having "fixed ideas which could be stated in one sentence, namely, 'sterilize all the boys and girls who are unfit to become parents, and then let nature take its course unhindered.'"[32]

Shut out by the post office, and stymied in Congress, Dennett turned back to preparing for the two big events of the fall: the VPL-Stopes meeting, and Sanger's conference. This took some tact, for before Stopes arrived in New York to find a divided field in the birth control movement, Dennett felt she had to come clean about the coldness between herself and Sanger. She gave a brief explanation of the situation, confessing she was excited to host Stopes partly because Sanger's upcoming conference was likely to exclude the VPL. "Unfortunately Mrs. Sanger is antagonistic toward our campaign for the change in federal law," Dennett wrote. "We are all very sorry indeed that Mrs. Sanger has swung so far away from the disinterested generous service she gave to the movement when she first started."[33]

Sanger never replied to Dennett's letter asking to join forces. Far from softening her opposition, it infuriated her. Learning of the VPL-Stopes meeting further stoked her rancor. Hearing that her two adversaries had formed an alliance, no matter how incidental, burned any vestige of civility between herself and Dennett and soured Sanger's remaining sense of true friendship with Stopes.

She notified her staff that Stopes was absolutely not to be invited to the conference.[34] To Rublee, she wrote, "I understand M.W.D. is trying in every way to shortstop the effect of our conference. I am quite decided that I have been too Christian-like with her. . . . I have decided to *ignore* her absolutely."[35] Rublee, and soon the rest of Sanger's coterie, understood: Dennett was to be frozen out.

At the same time, she painted Stopes as out of touch and slightly nutty. Regarding Stopes's ambitions to someday open a clinic in America, Sanger wrote they were "positively humorous! . . . Of course she is such a climber she believes all that Mrs D—— tells her."[36] She hadn't let go of the betrayal she'd felt when Dennett hadn't offered the support of the NBCL during Sanger's legal troubles in 1916. "We have kept D—— alive by our agitation & education & silence about her duplicity," Sanger mused to Rublee; "she accepts *all* our principles after she fights them a while & finds people are with our ideas."[37]

Sanger decided to weave a little intrigue, if she could. In a friendly tone, she wrote Stopes a warning letter. Sanger insisted Stopes's reputation would be sunk if she associated publicly with the VPL. "The League in question has been . . . repudiated by the medical profession," Sanger wrote, and Dennett herself was "outside the pale of honesty + decency."[38]

Stopes replied a week later; the tone of the separation between Sanger and Dennett felt decidedly weird to her. She pleaded for a full explanation and wouldn't commit to severing her ties with Dennett. But Sanger's replies were vague, focused on Dennett's bad reputation among physicians. She stalled on inviting Stopes to the upcoming conference. Stopes, meanwhile, carefully filed her letters from both of her American counterparts.

Unaware of the letters about her being traded across the Atlantic, Dennett worried about Sanger's upcoming conference; she would not take her exclusion quietly. She waited until September, hoping for a place on the conference's speaking program. Finally, she wrote directly to the organizers to request an invitation. Returning from travel, Sanger wrote a rushed, vague note inviting Dennett to contribute a report of her work in Washington. In other words, Dennett should share "the exact data of your aims, how you wish to change the law, et cetera and the results."[39] This was information that had, thus far, been sent only to VPL members.

Dennett recoiled; the request felt invasive. She told Sanger she would share such information only if she were invited to present it herself at the conference.[40] Sanger went silent again. Conference committee stationery continued to drift impersonally into Dennett's mailbox, reinviting her to submit a report and asking for an ever-greater range of details.

This circular conversation left Dennett on high alert. Sanger herself was on the road for much of the year, lecturing. Her demanding schedule and carefully instructed secretaries gave ample cover for Dennett to be effectively ghosted for months. It wouldn't, Sanger knew, be advantageous for Dennett to reveal the division within the birth control movement by complaining or editorializing about the situation. She had so recently expressed the desire to work together. But faced with deliberate exclusion, Dennett changed course. She *would* be heard.

. . .

On October 27, 1921, birth controllers gathered at the newly built, McKim, Mead & White–designed Town Hall on West Forty-Third Street. The hall had been laid out with social justice in mind: there were no box seats, so no one in the stalls could have their view obscured by bigger spenders. This redbrick, arch-bedecked building, today given over to the performing arts, became the gathering place for the birth control movement. On that particular night, it was finally the hour of the VPL-Stopes meeting.

To Dennett's joy and mystification, it was "lovely in atmosphere, quality-of-audience. . . . No gain financially."[41] In her speech Stopes dwelled on eugenics. She had, two months previously, founded her own birth control league that made the link with eugenics explicit in its name, the Society for Constructive Birth Control and Racial Progress. Without birth control, society wasted its dollars on "jail keepers," "reformatory masters," and "protectors of the feeble-minded."[42] She boosted Dennett and the VPL by saying "though I am sympathetic to all birth control movements, I think that this is the one most valuable movement in your country, and the one which wants every bit of help and support."[43]

The VPL-Stopes meeting took place just a month after the Second International Eugenics Congress, held at the American Museum of Natural History. At that gathering, where Herbert Hoover and Alexander Graham Bell were featured speakers, more than three hundred delegates were steeped in eugenics research while surrounded by displays showing the superiority of Nordic man.[44] The *New York Times* gave daily updates on that conference with pull quotes about "Tainted Aliens" and "Deterioration of Race."[45]

One day before the VPL-Stopes meeting, President Warren G. Harding gave a speech in Birmingham, Alabama, warning that racial segregation was essential to prevent "amalgamation" and emphasizing that equality was a fruitless dream for Black Americans.[46] Social planning, which had become a matter of urgency to the president as he sought to maintain segregation, was a short leap from the eugenicist vision of population planning via controlled fertility.

Two other shadows marred the VPL-Stopes event. First, Dennett was exasperated that she'd offered Sanger prime seats at the meeting, and received the reply that the invitation was too short notice. And as it turned out, Sanger quietly attended despite sending her regrets— she had taken a seat in the balcony, Dennett later heard. "Lawd! Isn't a shame that being a heroine and martyr so often spoils people completely!" Dennett wrote Carleton.[47]

Second, Dennett had expected, even hoped, that she would be arrested and the meeting shut down by the police. She was finally willing to become once again the focus of controversy and publicity, with Stopes by her side, if it would help her campaign. Instead, the meeting passed peaceably, without much fuss at all. Drafting a memo to VPL members, Dennett seemed aggrieved that police didn't view her as a valuable target. Archbishop Hayes eventually said the VPL-Stopes meeting made a "mockery" of the law "by clear evasion," and that Stopes "disclosed to me illegal information that I never had before."[48] But the vice squad kept clear, and Dennett was nettled.

The shift in Stopes's esteem from Sanger to Dennett was now complete. While Stopes had hoped to see Sanger one on one during her three days in New York, she was disappointed. "Have you forgotten and wiped out 1915 in England and all that followed?" Stopes asked Sanger in a letter, a day before she went back to England.[49] To Rublee, the same day, Stopes sent a similar note with a plea at the end: "You in so many ways are in a stronger position than Margaret Sanger. Do help her to be true to her best self."[50]

Then, in a move that stirred tensions with impressive efficiency, Stopes shared parts of Sanger's "warning" letters with Dennett. Dennett was scandalized—but also sensed an opportunity to clear the air. "Dear Margaret Sanger," Dennett wrote on Halloween 1921. "It is well for you to know that Dr. Stopes read to me the salient portions of the two letters you wrote to her."

She pointed out she had grounds to take legal action for libel and slander; in the next line she expressed hope Sanger would "'come back' to the generous-hearted, disinterested service which characterized your earlier work."[51] She let her hurt and anger flow.

Sanger never replied.

> Visions and dreams of a happy healthy humanity are
> always inspiring; but too often they act as opiates which
> close our eyes to the cruel facts of life. . . . In our intoxication
> we are apt to place all our faith in some "political or
> legislative magic lamp" which we need merely to rub to
> effect a glorious transformation.
>
> —*Birth Control Review* editorial (March 1921)

DENNETT TOOK HER SEAT FOR the International Birth Control
Conference as it opened on Friday, November 11, 1921, determined to contain her consternation. The splendor of the Plaza Hotel
surrounded her, yet she barely took in the novelty of an exhibition
hall devoted to birth control: the charts illustrating maternal and
infant mortality, excerpts from letters from mothers, analysis of the
birth rates in rich and poor quarters of four European cities.

Speeches washed over her: Sanger gave a pointedly eugenics-
angled speech, saying, "Now the time has come when we must all
join together in stopping at its source misery, ignorance, delinquency
and crime."[1] Then she announced the launch of a new organization,
the American Birth Control League (ABCL): a national advocacy
group to rival the VPL, and clearly intent on outshining it.

For weeks, Dennett had been drafting a statement to read at
the conference. She took pains to characterize her own Voluntary Parenthood League as the organic center of the birth control
cause, committed to the clean repeal: "The League stands for laws
which will require *medical endorsement* of contraceptive methods,

but not for *medical monopoly* in the giving of information as to methods."[2]

She wrote up a brief, sunny summary of her Washington work, and included her vision of a future where birth control clinics were a normal feature of the landscape: "Just as the kindergarten was introduced into the educational system by separate demonstration kindergartens, privately financed, so birth control clinics may be introduced into the existing health machinery of the country."[3] Finally, in a presumptuous conclusion, Dennett expressed her enthusiastic hope that this new American Birth Control League, Sanger's ambitious-sounding organization, would be fully focused on clinics and promotion, as opposed to legislation.

She waited eagerly for her turn to speak, half listening to the other sessions. The conference featured a wide range of topics. A gynecologist, Dr. Edward W. Lee, gave a presentation advocating vasectomy as a simple and safe family-planning method, but he received scant attention.[4]

There were eugenicists, as well as eugenics skeptics. (Dr. Abraham Myerson dismissed anti-immigration sentiment, saying, "I thought the Indian was the only native stock.")[5] The state of medical education was reviewed by Dr. Antoinette Konikow of Boston. A few Harvard students had told her they intended to "demand from their professors some information about Birth Control. . . . [When] a woman comes to them for information, they cannot give it to her because they don't know anything about it."[6] Abortion was debated, as was Prohibition, now nearly in its second year.

The complexion of the conference was very white. The birth control movement used terms that called up slavery to describe the plight of women forced to bear many children, but integration of the movement itself was not seen as a priority. To quote one of their Black contemporaries, the activist and writer Anna Julia Cooper, most of the reformers present were "oblivious to any other race or class who have been crushed under the iron heel of Anglo Saxon power," and the conference reflected as much.[7]

Dennett grew agitated as the days wore on. She had been promised fifteen minutes to speak at the conference, but still her name was not called. She scribbled a note and passed it to Sanger, asking whether or not her report had been excluded.[8] At one point a resolution was introduced on whether to support the work of the VPL in changing the federal law. Dennett bitterly remembered, "A 'doctors only' proponent, speaking from the floor against allowing a vote on this resolution to be taken by the Conference said, 'If we could have the Federal bill passed to-day, we would not want it.'"[9] Attendees debated how to approach legislative change, and ended the conference unresolved.

In the end Dennett wasn't called to speak at all, with limited time and space given as the reasons.[10] Sanger did her best to avoid Dennett entirely. There were, however, moments when Sanger seemed to speak directly to her rival, justifying her position. She stood at the end of each day to sum up the proceedings, to reflect on what had brought her there, and to defend her sometimes-theatrical style.

"Whenever anybody says 'emotional' in Birth Control, I know they mean me," she said.[11] She intended to "agitate, educate, organize, and legislate" until family planning moved from theory to reality. "When a house is on fire," she told the group, "you don't criticize the voice that calls your attention to it. It may not be ladylike, and just the tone and quality of voice we would like to hear, nevertheless we are glad that the voice has aroused our attention to the fact that the house is on fire."[12]

. . .

Outside the Plaza, tensions erupted in a chaotic physical assault. A centerpiece of Sanger's conference was a meeting at Manhattan's Town Hall, where Stopes had headlined without incident just days earlier. Sanger's rally was called "Birth Control, Is It Moral?"

The hall was swarming before it started, Sanger wrote, with police trying to block the doors. She squeezed through a crowd that was chanting, "Defy them! Defy them!"[13] and was "seized and literally tossed" onto the stage by Lothrop Stoddard, the author of the eugenicist polemic *The Rising Tide of Color against White World-Supremacy.* (In *The Great Gatsby,* this book, ascribed to an author named "Goddard," is praised by ur-WASP Tom Buchanan, effectively branding it as being as bombastic and entitled as Buchanan himself.)

Sanger raised her voice to proclaim, "We're going to hold the meeting," only to be confronted by a man—he was Monsignor Dineen, secretary to Archbishop Patrick Joseph Hayes—approaching and calling, "An indecent, immoral subject is to be discussed," followed by police who stopped each speaker from proceeding.[14] Sanger was arrested and led to the police station.

"It was bedlam," in Sanger's memory.[15] She and Rublee walked up Broadway to the station at West Forty-Seventh Street, flanked by police and followed by a crowd. "Newspaper men were scribbling stories," she wrote, and the onlookers quickly turned into protesters.[16] Someone gave Sanger a bouquet of long-stemmed red roses as the crowd heckled the police.[17] Many reporters doorstepped Dineen, who made a statement: he had attended on behalf of the archbishop, seen children in the audience, and acted according to his moral compass. The supposed victims turned out to be four Barnard sociology students, whose bobbed hairstyles and slim necks he had glimpsed from behind and mistaken for children.[18]

The archbishop and Sanger had a war of words in the newspapers, with Hayes addressing the topic in public in his Christmas Pastoral. Unusually for his time and place, the archbishop denounced contraception as a worse crime than abortion. It was, he wrote, not just criminal but deeply evil. "Children troop down from Heaven because God wills it," he wrote; "to take life after its inception is a horrible crime; but to prevent human life that the Creator is about to bring into being is satanic."[19]

In the *New York Times* two days later, Sanger advised the archbishop to stay in his lane. "There is no objection to the Catholic

Church inculcating its doctrines to its own people," she wrote, "but when it attempts to make these ideas legislative acts and enforce its opinions and code of morals upon the Protestant members of this country, then I do consider its attempt an interference with the principles of this democracy, and I have a right to protest."[20]

In flagging a threat to Protestants—itself a dog whistle designed to outrage WASP supremacists like Stoddard and his followers—Sanger knew exactly what she was doing. Doubling down on this line of attack, the *Birth Control Review* of December 1921 mocked the "dictatorship of celibates" who "cannot have any basis of experience" to rule on matters of sex and birth.[21]

Dennett was moved to express solidarity with Sanger. Her animus against Comstock was stronger than her hurt feelings. After the breakup of Sanger's meeting, she went to the police station to plead for Sanger's release, feeling "very weary and half ill" but duty bound.[22] "I can be counted upon for the most complete and wholehearted moral support in defending the right of free speech for the birth control movement," Dennett wrote Sanger.[23] Her loyalty lay with the cause rather than with Sanger herself, a point she made painfully clear, but regardless, she showed up.

Dennett got to the station to find a mass of reporters gathered and Sanger's supporters in a state of high emotion. Sanger herself, after being discharged for lack of evidence, was speaking to the press. Once Sanger finished, Dennett, who was standing just behind Juliet Rublee, began to give an interview to one of the papers. Rublee, in Dennett's memory, "turned and *struck* me, with a backward swing of her arm, saying, 'This is *our* affair, we don't want you in it.'"[24] The blow was hard enough it would have knocked her down, she noted, but for the density of the crowd.

In shock, Dennett took herself home. Undoubtedly she tried to find comfort, maybe with her habitual hot bath and strong black coffee. Then she took to her desk and began to fire off letters. Writing to Rublee, Dennett speculated about what had provoked the assault.

Rublee was known as a generous hostess, with an unusual sense of style that matched her assertive personality—"The only woman I ever knew who dared to wear bright greens, reds, yellows, all together," in Sanger's description,[25] with the "gall of a brass monkey" to quote Rublee's own nephew.[26] But for Dennett, Rublee's uncontrolled behavior betrayed a vein of desperation. Rublee's "adoption of the police method of using physical violence to express resentment," Dennett wrote, must be attributed to her acting "under emotional stress, in ways in which otherwise would be unthinkable."[27] Rublee never replied.

It was an inexcusable breach, and Dennett decided to strike back. Three days later she sent a memo to VPL supporters addressing the issue of why two separate groups were needed for the birth control movement, titled "Why are not the V. P. L. and Mrs. Sanger working together?" It was a question Dennett fielded more frequently than she could bear anymore.

Dennett wrote that she had invited Sanger to join committees as part of the NBCL in 1915 and VPL in 1919, and Sanger had declined in both cases, focusing instead on *Family Limitation* and the *Birth Control Review*. Second, the VPL was for federal legislation first, while Sanger claimed she wanted to prioritize state legislation, a strategy Dennett described as "a slow and expensive progress somewhat analogous to winning suffrage a state at a time instead of by federal action." Their one point of agreement was that both factions intended to someday establish birth control clinics.[28]

Then Dennett got more provocative. She summarized "libelous personal aspersions" Sanger had written to Stopes, when trying to warn her off coming to New York under the auspices of Dennett and the VPL.[29] She appended some correspondence exchanged ahead of the conference. Finally, she threw in her own irritation at having heard Sanger privilege "direct action" over the "bourgeois . . . pink tea . . . lady-like" legislative work.[30] It was a package of unvarnished grievances.

With Dennett's vengeful memo circulating through the movement, Sanger got a copy of it in less than a month. Within weeks, Sanger was openly telling people Dennett was insane and possibly dangerous. Her public support after the Town Hall meeting was not worth mentioning; "the more I see the acts of the person in question," Sanger wrote to Henry Gibbons, a lawyer and birth control supporter, "the more I am inclined to believe that a sanitarium is the proper place for her."[31] Sanger was unaware Gibbons, who was married, had tried to pursue Dennett romantically and had been kindly but firmly turned down earlier that year.

For the November 1921 issue of the *Birth Control Review*, Sanger wrote an editorial titled "Unity!" She noted every progressive movement in history had the tendency to "grow 'wings'—left wing, right wing, and centre . . . it begins to exhibit something closely approaching the phenomenon of cell-division in biology."[32]

Then, using the third person to refer to herself, Sanger publicly separated her own work from any association with Dennett, also mentioned in veiled terms. "[The] editor decided, due to the need for a strict economy of time and space, to refrain from editorial participation in the exchange of personal opinion or discussion with agitated adherents of the same cause or leaders of subsidiary agencies," she wrote.[33]

She wished Dennett luck, after a fashion—"We welcome difference and differentiation in idea and policy, as the finest and surest sign of health and growth."[34] At the same time she rejected any notion that the organizations were on an equal footing or that the VPL was anything other than a rogue element. A more sincere title would have been not "Unity!" but "Begone!"

. . .

On the evening of January 3, 1922, seventeen VPL activists held a war council to decide what to do. Should they sue Sanger for libeling Dennett? Or should they reorganize themselves, in light of their near-empty bank account and the fact that physicians were offended by them? Just before midnight, the meeting adjourned with the decision to build whatever bridges they could; the league should meet directly with Sanger and hope for a joining of forces, or at least a truce, at last.[35]

When members of the two groups convened, however, Sanger no longer spoke of the richness of diverse opinions. Instead she intended to censor them. The VPL, she mandated, was blocked from coverage in the *Birth Control Review*.[36]

From the start, Sanger and the ABCL wielded more clout than Dennett's league. They had raised enough cash and had enough staff to create a heavyweight birth control propaganda machine. In the year after its founding, the ABCL produced and gave out around 75,000 pamphlets and more than 300,000 letters. At its highest point of circulation, it printed 15,000 to 30,000 copies of the *Birth Control Review*.[37]

Soon, Sanger established a dedicated Motherhood Department to respond to the tens of thousands of letters from women pleading for help with family planning, STI symptoms, infertility, and other personal problems, referring them to pro–birth control doctors where possible. Her international reach was growing too; in the spring of 1922 she left for a lecture tour in Japan.

The contrast between the lively ABCL and faltering VPL was all too clear. Dennett, having started the VPL and charted its course into financial precarity, was unwilling to adjust her goals for the sake of unification. In February, Jean Burnet Tompkins, a lawyer and VPL member, attempted a kind of intervention. Tompkins urged Dennett to admit a "radical re-organization" was necessary. Since Dennett had alienated physicians and fallen out with Sanger, the league was "discredited. We may as well face that fact to start with. No amount of 'intensive promotion' can save it."[38]

Indirectly, Tompkins was asking Dennett to abdicate her directorship of the VPL. The scuffle with the New York Academy of Medicine and the rancor between Dennett and Sanger had demoralized the league. "Last year I had a more embarrassing time than you can ever know, trying to defend you against criticisms, which I knew to be more or less justified," Tompkins wrote.[39] It must have left Dennett feeling flayed.

She grieved for what she had thought was a solid, loyal, and honest organization. Why, she wondered, did she feel so alone? Why was the rest of her league so quiescent in the face of gossip and criticism?[40] She quickly embarked on a "promotion" phase. If people knew the facts, Dennett was convinced, they would see she was right. Her biggest misstep had been losing control of the narrative.

Dennett stated her case in a substantial *New York Times* article, on February 26, 1922. The piece gave her a chance to set out her chronicle of the birth control movement for a wide audience. First came the absurd and unenforceable Comstock Act; then sporadic protests for thirty years, "while information, despite the law, was more and more circulated among the sophisticated and well-to-do."[41] She continued, "Then, in 1914, Margaret Sanger made her meteoric appearance, with her vivid demand that the poor who most need instruction as to family limitation should receive it, and with her challenging slogan that a bad law is better broken than kept."[42] Dennett mentioned the Brownsville clinic, Sanger's jail time, and the work of the NBCL; from this rose the Voluntary Parenthood League, "based on the 'eventually, why not now' idea"—prioritizing changing federal law, because "the Federal bill is the key to the situation, the master stroke for the birth control movement."[43]

Dennett contrasted Sanger's short-lived clinic, lecturing career, and undeniable fame against her own "do it, not talk about it" ethos.[44] But telling her version of the story did little, in the end, to mend the crisis in her league. Being the sole face of the movement was not appealing or natural to her. During the months that followed she saw her efforts blocked while her debts grew.

. . .

Summers in New York before air-conditioning brought a kind of mental hibernation. The heat drove out thoughts that didn't concern the heat. "Hot!" Dennett wrote her boys, typing her letter in just her chemise. "I am thumping my Corona in my shimmy, and feeling very moist and sticky at that."[45]

Horse-drawn ice wagons meandered along the avenues, inviting overheated kids to steal a few manure-scented chips. Families pulled mattresses out onto fire escapes or stretched out on the grass in Central Park. With the only breeze coming from the river or a moving elevated car, the fug of human sweat was everywhere.[46] Anyone who could get away to the shore, or to somewhere up north, left town.

Dennett, now fifty, craved a fresh start. Back in late March, she had pushed out to the press an open letter to President Harding asking him to support the birth control cause and repeal the obstructing law.[47] She wasn't sure where to direct her hopes; the outlook had grown no brighter.

After Postmaster Hays handed his office to Dr. Hubert Work, Work sent out a bulletin to be hung in every post office reading "IT IS A CRIMINAL OFFENSE / To send or receive obscene or indecent matter by mail or express" and reminding customers of the punishment: a $5,000 fine, five years' imprisonment, or both.[48]

By August 1, Dennett told Carleton, "There is not money enough in my bank to cover my own rent, nor money enough in the League bank to pay *its* rent! Ta da—ta-da!!"[49] She made up her mind to quit, all the while on fire with curiosity to know where Sanger's money was coming from.

Dennett resigned from the directorship of the VPL in September 1922. The committee was "startled," she told the boys, especially when they learned the league owed Dennett about $2,400 and that she could not get by anymore.

She was bereft, while recognizing all that had been achieved. "It is most unlikely that any other executive will have to live through just such disasters, broken promises, personal attacks, and financially arid summer as I have," she wrote in a draft of her resignation letter.[50] "Such experiences belong to the early history of many fundamental causes."[51] Later on, she hoped "there comes less fear, more team-work . . . more popular support from the public and then the whole program rolls along to its finale in comparative ease."[52]

This fantasy of Dennett's raises the question of what exactly might be required for a movement to "roll along" to success. Dennett had made inroads in Congress so far as creating a birth control lobby, embattled and joked-about as it was. She had laid a foundation. Meanwhile, Sanger was writing books and editorials, holding conferences to promote the cause, and testing and pushing the parameters of the law.

Unwilling as they were to work together, they were each assembling necessary components for a movement that had momentum—a movement that could persuade a meaningful mass of people who wielded cultural and political clout, and who could carry birth control out of the muffled darkness of a taboo into legality and legitimacy.

It had been seven years since Dennett had given that stirring speech at the NBCL's first meeting, long enough to get the itch for something new. To Stopes, she wrote, "You see I am done for, at least so far as the B.C. cause is concerned."[53] In fact, she was about to reenter the fray.

The Turbot told it at the Crab's,
She had it from the Sole—
The very latest thing in thought
To-day, is birth control.

Oh, think, Sardine, what this will mean
To such poor fish as we,
Who give to Commerce, without stint,
Our countless progeny!

—"Birth Control of the Seas,"
Life magazine (1923)

I N SEPTEMBER 1922, SANGER MARRIED James Noah Henry Slee, an oil magnate twenty-three years her senior. Rublee had first introduced them to each other at a dinner party in 1921. Sanger nearly refused to marry him; she wrote Rublee a year previously, "Don't you worry your blessed dear head a minute about me & Mr S. . . . He could not inspire me to love. . . . Freedom is too lovely & I want to enjoy it for a time."[1]

Likely the prospect of financial security proved too alluring to reject. For years she had joked with those close to her about wanting to "go west and find a widower with money and settle down for life."[2] After meeting Slee, she sometimes referred to him in letters as "the millionaire."[3]

Even though Slee seemed tailor made to fulfill this dream of Sanger's, a lot of tension and paperwork preceded their union. Initially,

Sanger wanted the marriage kept secret.[4] Slee needed to divorce his wife, and Sanger needed to finalize her divorce from Bill. But Slee was certain she was the woman for him, and he followed her on tour through Asia, Egypt, and Europe in early 1922. On September 18, just after her forty-third birthday, the couple married in London. In November Sanger began to share the news with friends, and three months later the press discovered it.[5]

Sanger's friends collectively raised their eyebrows. "He seems a nice man," Havelock Ellis wrote her, "and deserves a more suitable wife."[6]

Despite the couple's surface incompatibility, Slee clung to his roving spouse. For a time they were content enough, while often apart. "Our American husbands are everything but lovers. It seems to be a lost sense in the American male," Sanger would write Selincourt after a decade of marriage to Slee.[7]

Lover or not, he gave generously to Sanger's endeavors, despite his conservatism. Slee supplied the money that made the ABCL the nation's preeminent birth control advocacy group. In the five years after they met, Slee donated tens of thousands of dollars to the league. He also agreed to smuggle diaphragms from Europe to the United States in empty oil drums he was importing for his business.[8]

As she had with Bill, Sanger and Slee started building a house— "A simple one, something like Shelley's in Sussex," in her imagining— but near Fishkill, New York. "Domesticity, which I had once so scorned, had its charms after all."[9] That domesticity wasn't overly intimate, however: the couple not only maintained separate quarters in their new Fishkill house, which they named Willowlake, but also had adjoining apartments at 18 Gramercy Park. Sanger ensured this would continue, asking Slee to sign a contract to this effect when they married.[10] Their love would be that much stronger, she explained to her husband, with a healthy dose of separation.

· · ·

Dennett spent much of 1922 ensconced in her apartment at 81 Singer Street, which became 24-34-30 Twenty-Ninth Street when the streets were renamed later in the 1920s, in the neighborhood she affectionately called "Astoria-by-the-dump."[11]

In fact she grew deeply attached to the place. She was up two flights of stairs in apartment 3A, in a stately development called the Crystal Garden Apartments, surrounded by a neighborhood full of Irish, Italian, and Jewish families. She especially loved the view from her back window, which looked out onto an old willow tree.[12] A Bohemian beer hall had recently gone up around the corner (it's still thriving). Around another corner was the Elevated, which took her easily into midtown Manhattan and returned her to her leafy, ivy-framed refuge at the end of the day.

On pause from lobbying, low on funds, and out of favor with her league, she set up a magazine for the VPL, the *Birth Control Herald*. She had been shut out of Sanger's *Review*; in the *Herald*, despite its relatively small circulation, at least she had a platform for her work.

The main purpose of the *Herald* was to report on the progress of the VPL's campaign, and the league paid her just enough to keep it going. In July, before a hiatus of several months coinciding with Dennett's retreat from Washington, she used it to tear into the Comstock Act in a spiky editorial.

She wasn't expecting a direct retaliation, but weeks later it came. On September 2, 1922, she received a letter from E. M. Morgan, Postmaster, warning her that *The Sex Side of Life* had been found in the mails and declared unmailable.[13] When she asked the department to send edits or any guidance at all for how to make her pamphlet decent, they fobbed her off.

This was alarming—and exciting. Now *The Sex Side of Life* was officially banned, "like your 'Married Love,'"[14] she wrote Stopes with a note of pride. Dennett had had a hard year. "Still I think on the whole I am game," she concluded her letter.[15] If the post office wanted a fight, she'd bring one.

In the meantime, she let herself be drawn into difficult discussions with VPL committee members who wanted to rehire her, on the condition she agree not to contradict or antagonize Sanger again.[16] "As for me, my upper lip is not so stiff as it might be," she told the boys. "I can't even get mad. I get sad instead, and then I'm no good for thinking out the next step."[17] It was a blue end to 1922, spent waiting and trying to clear her mind.

Then, suddenly, she was packed and on the train to Washington. An anonymous donor had stepped in and offered to fund the VPL through the end of the current congressional session, March 4, 1923, on the condition that Dennett remain director.[18] Once again she was hiking around the Capitol with her bag of pamphlets, confronting "hard-boiled, pompous" congressmen and sparring again with Senator Nelson.[19]

The new campaign seemed to have the wind at its back. The league splurged on an assistant for Dennett, hiring an experienced lobbyist, Edwin Potter, a friendly soul. After their meeting with Albert B. Cummins, Republican of Iowa, on January 5, 1923, Cummins agreed to sponsor the bill.

This was a coup: Cummins was president pro tempore of the Senate, third in line to the presidency. He had already had a storied career, serving as Iowa's governor and twice pursuing the Republican nomination for president, without success. His wife, Ida, was a suffragist and child labor law proponent. He heard Dennett with unusual open-mindedness, and decided it was just possible the time for birth control had come. Representative John Kissel, Republican of New York, agreed to be the House sponsor. What had previously taken Dennett months, stretched over two congressional sessions, had this time been the work of a couple of weeks.

Riding high on this success, she extended to Sanger a gauntlet and an olive branch combined in a *Birth Control Herald* editorial. At this point Dennett had little reason to think Sanger's animosity would have waned since the demoralizing (for Dennett) skirmishes between

the rival birth control leagues the year before. "The VPL is not working against Mrs. Sanger . . . there is room in the field for more than
one group, but . . . we believe our program to be the broader and the
quicker and therefore the one that should be achieved first."[20] There
was no direct response.

Incredibly, Dennett's good meetings kept adding up. A few congressmen changed their minds about birth control after she spoke with
them. Senator Royal S. Copeland, Democrat of New York, who had
previously been hostile, now planted the idea that the repeal might
get passed if a stipulation were in place requiring five licensed physicians to approve any contraceptive information in general circulation.

Dennett was open to it. She envisioned a review structure akin
to the Food and Drug Administration's approval process. "There are
bad, even fatal, results from harmful contraceptives," she would later
write. "So also are there sickness and death from harmful foods, but
we try to correct that situation by widespread education on diet, and
by such protective measures as the food and drug acts. These can
perfectly well be made to apply to contraceptives also."[21]

Knute Nelson continued to dish out blustering opposition. When
Dennett and Potter met with him to push the bill along in February,
he "fairly yelled, with his bald head getting very pink in his rage . . .
that he was sick of the whole matter, that no one wanted to have
anything to do with it, that all the men laughed at it."[22] Now that she
had support from other quarters, she could afford to laugh it off.

A common objection to birth control was that it would deprive
society of genius. If Abraham Lincoln's parents had waited until they
could afford a proper house, they may never have had children at
all.[23] If Benjamin Franklin's mother had used birth control, she never
would have had him—the tenth son in a family of seventeen children.
Other geniuses Dennett heard mentioned, who were born fifth or
later to their families, included Voltaire, Darwin, Jane Austen, and
J. S. Bach.[24] She had to rebut this argument again and again. Sanger
had her own pet line, designed to ruffle those who'd decided she was

a compulsive blasphemer: she liked to point out Jesus Christ was "said to be an only child."[25]

The bill didn't get to its first vote by early March 1923, but Dennett held out hope the summer session would bring success. It was "*all but achieved*," she reported to her league.[26] Cummins had sincerely tried to raise the bill at the end of another amendment vote, but the room emptied fast. "They simply don't *want* to vote on it. I don't know a single man who is *really* interested," Cummins concluded. He told Dennett they needed one more try.[27]

Kissel, meanwhile, proved vulnerable to mockery. He withdrew from sponsoring the bill in the House after hearing a colleague heckle him as "birth-control Kissel."[28] Dennett found a new House sponsor, William N. Vaile, Republican of Colorado, shortly afterward.

Dennett dreamed so intensely of her bill being voted into law she wrote her visions of it into her notebook. She imagined one day confronting her detractors, as Anna Howard Shaw had done after suffrage passed in Kansas: "She hunted in vain for any of the 40,000 men who voted against it. Everywhere she went, they crowded up at her in meetings to shake hands and tell with pride how they had 'always believed in it.' When our Cummins Bill is passed the country will be full of people who 'always believed in it.'"[29]

With that vision before her, Dennett reached out to Sanger. If this was truly Dennett's final season in Washington, she felt duty bound to pull every string she could. Sanger's endorsement would, she knew, further bolster the VPL's standing and clarify its role. Despite all that had happened, despite the evidence Sanger preferred to ignore her entirely, she decided she had nothing to lose. In May 1923, she wrote to Sanger's ABCL, opening her note "Dear Friends." She asked the organization to endorse the Cummins bill.[30]

A month of silence passed—not a promising sign. Then Dennett heard from Anne Kennedy, Sanger's longtime lieutenant. Kennedy now put Dennett in her place, or tried to. "My dear Mrs. Dennett," Kennedy began, acidly: "It is with great surprise that we received this request." She reminded Dennett of the late-1921 tensions, including Dennett's "unwarranted, malicious, and untruthful attack upon the president of this organization." Though Sanger would benefit financially and in reputation from an amended Comstock law, Kennedy continued, she would never endorse Dennett's bill.[31] Sanger was instead fully committed to "the scientific dissemination of contraceptive information by the medical profession"—the doctors-only path.[32]

Then Kennedy followed through with more active opposition. She went to Washington, interviewed both Cummins and Vaile, and did her best to persuade them a clean repeal would be irresponsible.[33] She sent a memo to everyone she knew connected to the VPL, enclosing a proposed amendment with doctors-only language, which, Kennedy told the VPL, Cummins and Vaile both believed had a better chance of passing than Dennett's clean repeal.[34] She even, in the same memo, called for VPL members to send her "assistance both moral and financial."[35]

These interventions signaled that Sanger and her allies were ready to go further in opposing Dennett than just exerting the silent treatment. Sanger was no longer just belittling Dennett's work, or shutting out her attempts at communication; she was trying to reroute what support Dennett had mustered, and to pass her own version of a birth control bill in its place.

Thanks to Kennedy's visit, Sanger's ideas began to trickle through the Capitol, derailing Dennett's progress. Some members expressed anxiety about the free use of contraceptive information; others wondered if "the question of abortion should be included, that there were many arguments for that as well as contraception," fully aware that any close and positive association with abortion would be fatal to birth control legislation.[36] Why, Dennett wondered, was it so necessary for Sanger not only to ignore her efforts, but to torpedo them too?

. . .

In 1923, a new clinic opened its doors in a former dentist's premises at 317 East Tenth Street. The primary purpose of this clinic, Sanger wrote, was not only to help married women space their babies, but also to collect data. She named it the Birth Control Clinical Research Bureau (CRB). "It was to be in effect a laboratory dealing in human beings instead of mice," she wrote. "I was going to suggest to women that in the Twentieth Century they give themselves to science as they had in the past given their lives to religion."[37]

This time a physician was in charge. After a false start with Dr. Dorothy Bocker, Sanger hired Dr. Hannah Mayer Stone, "a fine young woman from the Lying-In Hospital."[38] Stone was brilliant and stalwart. She helped Sanger formalize the medical indications for contraceptive advice, a wide-ranging list of physical and mental factors, including cardiac and renal disease, anxiety, and already having a disabled child.[39] Pushing the liberal interpretation of preventing or curing disease, Stone added child spacing to the list. This meant any mother with a baby younger than nine months automatically qualified for contraceptives, a point that drew objections from an investigating committee visiting from the New York Academy of Medicine.[40] When a patient confessed her reasons for seeking birth control were solely financial, she was told New York law required a health reason. "I told her I had no health reason I could think of," the patient continued. "She said that the doctor would examine me and that she might possibly find something that would allow her to give me the information."[41] There was no base fee at the CRB; women were asked to pay only what they could.[42]

Maintaining a stock of contraceptive supplies was a constant headache. In addition to using empty oil drums from Slee's business, Sanger and her staff made a habit of smuggling diaphragms back into the country whenever they went abroad, using pleasure trips to British Columbia and Europe to squirrel handfuls of pessaries into their soiled clothing.[43] Two years later, this problem spurred Sanger to get involved in the birth control supply market, too. She helped organize the Holland-Rantos Company in 1925, developing contraceptive jelly and diaphragms. (After the turn of the millennium, Holland-Rantos became HR Pharmaceuticals, which still supplies ultrasound gel to clinics.) Finally, instead of risking interception and confiscation by customs officials, she had a local manufacturer.

The CRB is probably most famous today for its cameo appearance in Mary McCarthy's novel of the mid-1960s, *The Group*, centered on eight Vassar graduates of the class of 1933 making their way in New York City. In the following scene, Dottie gets fitted for a diaphragm:

> The doctor's femininity was a reassuring part of her professional aspect, like her white coat. . . . Her skill astonished Dottie, who sat with wondering eyes, anesthetized by the doctor's personality, while a series of questions, like a delicately maneuvering forceps, extracted information that ought to have hurt but didn't.[44]

In the clinic, the diaphragm was billed as a ticket to security. And for some, it did feel that way. Other writers who went through the ordeal of getting fitted for a diaphragm wove its peculiar significance into their work. When Esther Greenwood climbs onto the examining table in Plath's *The Bell Jar*, she thinks, "I am climbing to freedom, freedom from fear, freedom from marrying the wrong person, like Buddy Willard, just because of sex, freedom from the Florence Crittenden Homes [for unwed mothers] where all the poor girls go who should have been fitted out like me, because what they did, they would do anyway, regardless. . . . I had done well by my shopping privileges. I was my own woman."[45]

But in McCarthy's version of this rite of passage, Dottie is quickly disillusioned. While the fitting is happening, the diaphragm shoots across the room, a foreshadowing of the larger-scale loss of control that awaits. She realizes her boyfriend, Dick, who urged her to visit the clinic in the first place, will assume she consents to anything and everything once she has a diaphragm. Contraception is a false friend, a tool enabling him to possess her. She abandons her hard-won rubber device under a park bench.

While the CRB served married New Yorkers (or those who faked the part, as Dottie had), Sanger's *Family Limitation* had become a kind of canonical work, in the canon of life-changing works read with furtive desperation. Five years after its first printing, it was already being handed between generations. A reader in Tindall, Idaho, wrote Sanger a letter of thanks, saying she had just gotten a copy of *Family Limitation* from her mother. "We have been married six years this June and I really havent [sic] had breathing spells between 'Lambings' as we call it out west," she wrote.[46]

Women got word of it even if they couldn't find it, and wrote asking Sanger for a copy. "I am a girl fifteen years old married and have two children my fother [sic] left my mother with ten children three sets of twins," read another.[47] Some readers wrote to Sanger with painful confessions. Birth control knowledge had come too late for them; they had grown to hate sex because of the risk entailed. "To me intercourse is so very, very repulsive," one woman wrote in 1924. "Before my first baby came, I did enjoy it. Six months before the second baby was born I began to grow nervous and irritable. I grew continuously worse. . . . When the penis touches me I felt as if I'd have to scream."[48]

The CRB's opening prompted competing research into birth control methods and practices. In early 1923, Robert Latou Dickinson embarked on clinical research into birth control and had solicited the backing of the New York Obstetrical Society. "We all know that contraceptives are generally used," he said. "The question is, are they harmful? Are they harmless? Do you know? I don't know." He pointed out that if a respectable physician didn't take an interest, "some Sanger group" would become the authority instead.[49] Wouldn't it better—for the public, and for physicians' profits—if doctors stepped in instead?

Dennett took heart from the news of the CRB. She continued to hope Sanger would focus on clinical work, and leave legislation to the VPL—stubbornly ignoring signs that Sanger had no intention of abiding by this division of labor.

Dennett herself spent the summer of 1923 trying to heal.[50] She had surgery in August for her persistent pelvic pain.[51] Washington, she saw now, was a purgatory. Her occasional pessimism, which she'd mostly ignored during the heady success early in the session, had proved accurate.

In November, Cummins withdrew as the sponsor. He was sorry, he said, but he had some close relatives who were "hopelessly shocked" by his association with it.[52] Dennett urged him to think of the millions who would suffer if the bill did not pass, and he admitted to acting out of fear and a deep-seated feeling of distaste about birth control. Dennett made an unusual admission: "Told him how I understood the aversion, had it myself as a young woman."[53]

He remained a helpful conduit, relaying Senate conversations on birth control back to Dennett. Before they parted he added that he thought the doctors-only version would stand a better chance.[54] She managed to calmly, crisply disagree. Even if Sanger hadn't arrived in Congress herself, her vision had already taken up residence.

MILDRED. In her family there is insanity, alcoholism, mental deficiency, and epilepsy. MARRIAGE DOES NOT MERELY UNITE TWO INDIVIDUALS BUT IT UNITES TWO FAMILY LINES, as the offspring generally prove.

—Caption in *The ABC of Human Conservation*
(c. 1940)

AT THE 1926 PHILADELPHIA WORLD'S Fair, the American Eugenics Society's display featured a series of flashing lights: "a high grade person" was born every seven and a half minutes, while a mentally deficient one was born every forty-eight seconds.[1] "How long," asked a sign, "are we Americans to be so careful for the pedigree of our pigs and chickens and cattle—and then leave the *ancestry of our children* to chance or blind sentiment?"[2]

It was clear early on that the eugenics movement was intent on Aryanizing the population. State fairs featured Fitter Family contests through the 1910s and '20s, in which families submitted to medical exams and intelligence tests, and presented their family trees. All winners on record had ancestry that originated in England, northern Europe, or Canada.[3] A few scientists criticized the sloppy, bias-prone methods of eugenics researchers from the start, but enough politicians signed on that the movement's delineation between "fit" and "unfit" people proved highly influential.

By the mid-1920s, eugenics was a dominant theme in the birth control movement. Equality of the sexes was not a plank on the eugenics agenda, so bodily-autonomy arguments for birth control had to be sanded down to make an alliance make sense.

Though their interest in "racial progress" never equaled Stopes's, both Dennett and Sanger sincerely believed in some of the basic tenets of eugenics. Dennett insisted birth control would bring higher-quality offspring. However, she was decidedly less keen than Sanger was to meld her birth control activism with the eugenics movement, and she never embraced "negative eugenics" as Sanger did when she repeatedly argued the "unfit" should not be permitted to reproduce.

The definition of "unfit" was a moving target, but regularly included physical and intellectual disabilities, epilepsy, tuberculosis, STIs, illiteracy, and addiction. It disproportionately meant Black people, who were overdiagnosed as feebleminded, pathologically promiscuous, or having criminal tendencies. When several states outlawed mixed-race marriage, it was in service of a eugenics-driven march toward a whiter nation in which a strict racial hierarchy was recognized and preserved.

Eugenics had changed drastically since its beginnings in the 1880s, when it was associated more with utopian thinking than on-the-ground population-control efforts. Now the movement was represented by men like Charles Davenport, the director of the Cold Spring Harbor Station for Experimental Evolution. Davenport's work focused on increasing fertility from the "right" genetic stock.

The buzzword for the fundamental unit of life was "protoplasm," signifying the contents of each cell—a term Sanger thought somewhat absurd. Davenport, she recalled, "used to lift his eyes reverently and, with his hands upraised as though in supplication, quiver emotionally as he breathed, 'Protoplasm. We want more protoplasm.'"[4]

Finely calibrated protoplasm was also the fixation of powerful eugenicists like Madison Grant and Lothrop Stoddard, who for a time sat on the ABCL's board of directors. "Nordic" protoplasm was idealized as the strongest, finest, and best for the national interest. Grant, a zoologist by training who was nearly as concerned about saving the bison as he was about Nordic protoplasm, admitted, "It would be in a democracy, a virtual impossibility to limit by law the right to breed to a privileged and chosen few."[5] Under the guise of public health and "preserving the race," however, eugenicists were determined to try.

Eugenicists tended to distance themselves from any feminist campaign. Women were, after all, the main culprit behind "mongrelization"; left to their own devices, Nordic women consistently chose the "wrong" mates, argued Madison Grant, while nonwhites were likely not intelligent enough to use birth control effectively.[6]

Sanger sought him out anyway, looking to build an alliance. After a succession of meetings between 1921 and 1929, Davenport decided Sanger was "a charming woman," but dismissed the birth control movement as "a quagmire, of which eugenics should steer clear."[7]

Immigration restriction had a smooth ride politically, compared with birth control. After Harry Laughlin, a leading eugenicist, provided "expert testimony" to the House Committee on Immigration and Naturalization, the 1921 Emergency Quota Act and 1924 Johnson-Reed Immigration Act succeeded in putting quotas on foreign-born immigrants to the United States.[8] Defending the latter piece of legislation, the House committee proposing Johnson-Reed baldly characterized it as "an effort to preserve, as nearly as possible, the racial status quo in the United States."[9]

The 1924 law set annual quotas—2 percent of the total number of people of each nation of origin, according to the 1890 census, and the total exclusion of immigrants from Asia.[10] "America of the Melting Pot Comes to End," announced a 1924 headline in the *New York Times*.[11]

The medical establishment was particularly friendly to eugenic ideas and helped bridge the distance between eugenicists and birth controllers. Among Sanger's closest pro-eugenics allies was Dr. Lydia Allen DeVilbiss, a clinician in Florida. DeVilbiss ran her own studies to develop cheap, effective contraceptive foams, sponges, and pessaries.[12] She also, after assessing patients for mental impairment, began referring selected patients to hospitals for surgical sterilization. In letters to Sanger, she admitted to giving some pregnant women instructions to take quinine along with capsules containing small amounts of arsenic if they sought an abortion or if she judged they would be unfit mothers.[13]

Other doctors used eugenics as a justification to go even further. Although narratives of cultural progress liked to start by pointing out that "primitive" and "barbaric" societies deliberately withheld care from unwanted children and let them die, there was a robust movement in the medical community in the 1920s to do the same.

As early as 1910 Dr. William J. Robinson advocated euthanizing children in some circumstances, specifically with chloroform or potassium cyanide.[14] Euthanasia in this context was cast as heroic with the help of—what else?—the movies.

. . .

A gray-haired father explains to his soon-to-be-married son, Jack, "Our statute books contain many laws covering the breeding of livestock— but in the highest form of life—most precious of all living matter, almost no attention is paid to its breeding." He tells Jack about his old friend Claude, "blessed with wealth and position, but whose inheritance includes the blood taint of an indiscreet ancestor"—a reference to syphilis.

Claude marries and has a son anyway, and Dr. Dickey must operate quickly to ensure the baby's survival. Then the mother falls into a series of visions of her disabled child's future, like a twist on *It's a Wonderful Life*. When she awakens, she asks the doctor to "save him from such a fate." The child is allowed to live, but grows up beset by pain, bullying, and criminal impulses. The story has its desired effect. Jack gets tested for syphilis and gonorrhea, is pronounced fit, and the final frame holds the phrase, "Yes, we're fit to marry."

This was the 1927 film *Are You Fit to Marry?* Its director, W. H.

Stafford, had adapted it from a 1916 drama, *The Black Stork*. The newer version, which had broad distribution and was screened publicly until at least 1942, featured an actual physician, Dr. Harry Haiselden, in the role of Dr. Dickey, who counsels the young couple before their wedding.

When he took on the role, Haiselden was a known name already. In November 1915, he'd supervised a birth in Chicago and made sure the infant didn't live. Anna Bollinger was already a mother of three, married to a car repairman. Her band-new, seven-pound son, John, was born with visible deformities, was partially paralyzed, and in the days after birth he hovered between life and death.[15] The baby's most pressing need was bowel surgery. Haiselden declined to operate and John died at six days old.

"Nature has blundered at the German-American hospital, 819 Diversey Parkway," reported the *Chicago Daily Tribune*, in a bizarrely jaunty editorial. "The error is a malformed baby, which, if it lived, would grow to be a mental, and perhaps a moral defective. Death will be nature's means of righting its mistake."[16]

Haiselden had sought and received Anna's approval before withholding treatment. Once word got out, and while John still lived, reporters could and did visit the hospital to witness the "pink bit of humanity [lying] upon the white cloth . . . quite vigorously informed with life." They listened as Haiselden expounded on how he believed he was helping preserve "the race."[17]

Other doctors, social workers, members of the clergy, and ordinary people protested; many others, including the NBCL, Clarence Darrow, and Helen Keller, supported Haiselden. "No other event in recent months has been so widely discussed in the newspapers, in the pulpits, in meetings in scientific societies and in the homes of the people," claimed the *Salt Lake Telegram*.[18]

Dennett gave a revealing comment to the press, telling a *New York Tribune* reporter, "I think the physician has done a big, humanitarian thing!" arguing that John Bollinger's incurable disabilities justified

Haiselden's actions.[19] It was an unusual instance of her cheerleading drastic eugenic measures in the press. Either Sanger, who was generally more vocally keen on eugenics, avoided commenting publicly on Haiselden or her opinions have been lost to time.[20]

Once acquitted, Haiselden went public about past instances in which he had withheld treatment to hasten an infant's death, and had sometimes used narcotics toward the same end. His valorization in the press and on-screen emboldened other physicians to talk about the "mercy killings" they had brought about for eugenic reasons.[21] Haiselden chased the spotlight more than most physicians, but his notoriety came more from the fact that he was honest about his actions than from the fact that the killings themselves had happened in the first place.

. . .

Eugenics underpinned major legal decisions from the 1920s onward. The ability of the state to sterilize its citizens was affirmed by the 1927 Supreme Court decision in *Buck v. Bell*. Carrie Buck was born poor and white in Charlottesville, Virginia. She grew up with foster parents after her own mother, Emma, was committed to a state institution. As a teenager she was raped by her foster parents' nephew and became pregnant, and was thereafter committed to the state institution by her foster family.

Carrie Buck's seven-month-old daughter, Vivian, was assessed to be "not quite normal, but just what it is, I can't tell" by a social worker.[22] On that basis, plus the tarnish of her illegitimacy, Vivian was declared an imbecile in court. Her mother and grandmother, already institutionalized, had the same designation.

The word "imbecile" is derived from the Latin for "without a staff for support," as Eve Tushnet, a historian, notes, and this was the Bucks' main deficiency: they were without support.[23] In the decision, Justice Oliver Wendell Holmes justified compulsory sterilization thus: "In order to prevent our being swamped with incompetence . . . instead of waiting to execute degenerate offspring for crime, or to let them starve for their imbecility, society can prevent those who are manifestly unfit from continuing their kind. The principle that sustains compulsory vaccination is broad enough to cover cutting the Fallopian tubes. . . . Three generations of imbeciles are enough."[24] The ruling was held up by the defense at Nuremberg, and provided precedent for tens of thousands of forced sterilizations.[25]

The eugenics movement played fast and loose with physical and psychological categorizations, with brutal consequences. Many women were, like Carrie Buck and her baby, designated feebleminded without a clear definition of the term. Eugenics Record Office field-workers frequently called attention to "immorality" or "slovenliness" as evidence of disability in women; others noted "sissy" and "very feminine" men being characteristic of a "defective" family.[26]

In 1932, Mary Brewer of Forsyth County, North Carolina, was forced to undergo eugenic sterilization because neighbors testified her five children were dirty and she did not "[keep] a home like a mother should."[27] Parents sometimes arranged for their children to be sterilized, as in the infamous case of heiress Ann Cooper Hewitt, who in 1936 sued her mother and two surgeons for having sterilized her without her knowledge, telling her the surgery was to treat appendicitis. Hewitt lost, setting a precedent that a representative of paternalistic authority—parents, physicians, judges—had total control of dependents' fertility.[28]

Women who sought sterilization as a health measure, meanwhile, were often turned away. It helped if they knew or were coached into the right words to say during their initial appointment. The desire to end childbearing was not justification enough. Claiming to have severe pain or exceptionally heavy bleeding, or a diagnosis of uterine prolapse, sometimes worked.[29] Again, their fertility was not wholly their own.

Dennett's major motive for agitating against the Comstock Act was her belief in freedom of speech. But as early as the formation of the NBCL in 1915, she had agreed to include language about the so-called unfit being included in the group's founding documents. Stopes's 1921 visit had further persuaded Dennett it was only pragmatic to solicit the support of eugenicists. In early December of that year, she noted it was time for the VPL to adopt a resolution "designed to emphasize the relationship between birth control and eugenics."[30] Then, in February 1922, with the eugenics movement rising rapidly in influence, Dennett put out a press release affirming the league "supports the eugenic principles which seek the improvement of the conditions of child-breeding"—a hedging way to support eugenics, but supportive nonetheless.[31]

Sanger embraced the movement through her books, lectures, and persistent appeals to prominent eugenicists to support birth control. Her 1922 book, *The Pivot of Civilization*, advocated for birth control as an essential means toward a more "fit" future. Here, Sanger distanced herself from the pro-euthanasia physicians: "Nor do we believe," she wrote, "that the community could or should send to the lethal chamber the defective progeny resulting from irresponsible and unintelligent breeding."[32]

For readers and lecture audiences, Sanger began to envision a world in which parents would have to "apply" for babies, as immigrants apply for citizenship.[33] Eight years earlier she hadn't hesitated to compare motherhood to slavery, but now Sanger was exalting motherhood as "woman's noblest career," worthy of careful orchestration.[34]

She found that pro-eugenics rhetoric could lure a wider class of donors. One wealthy suffragist, Narcissa Cox Vanderlip, herself a mother of six, had given small amounts to the ABCL but had her secretary express her concerns to Sanger that her own class "is allowing the Anglo-Saxon race to die out while they indulge in motors, instead of babies."[35]

Most eugenicists managed to keep the birth control movement at arm's length, but Sanger was determined to overcome this hesitation. She had made her pro-eugenics sentiments clear earlier, in the *Birth*

Control Review of February 1919. She always insisted birth control
was more important. The two movements, Sanger argued, had different beliefs about women and methods of managing the population
but shared the same ultimate goal. "Eugenists imply or insist that a
woman's first duty is to the state," she wrote; "we contend that her duty
to herself is her first duty to the state."[36]

Eugenicists placed a new emphasis on inherited forms of TB.
Where previously the disease had been considered infectious and
contagious, it was now viewed as heritable as well.[37] Sanger doesn't
seem to have ever objected to the fact that having TB was enough to
classify someone as "unfit." As she had long been aware, if any eugenic authority had been called in to decide whether Anne Higgins
was fit to reproduce, or whether Margaret Sanger was, the judgment
would have been no.

In a way Sanger's memory of her mother's pain may have made
it simpler for her to take the stance that she did. Clearly, she wanted
certainty that women with TB would in the future be considered a
protected class, and that they should have access to birth control.

Eugenicists and birth controllers had one sure opponent in common: the Roman Catholic Church. The only dissenter on the bench
for *Buck v. Bell* was a Catholic justice, Pierce Butler. Catholics were
remarkably unified against compulsory sterilization.[38] Every pregnancy was part of God's plan; every child, no matter their heredity,
was part of a preordained natural order. This opposition carried real
weight in the United States. Catholics in the early twentieth century
came close to being considered an underclass, but their numbers and
political engagement were growing.

Gene Burns, a historian at Michigan State University, writes that
in the 1920s, the Catholic Church was viewed by many elite Protestants as "basically a strange, un-American, and undemocratic" religion.[39] Fearmongering rhetoric about a coming Catholic takeover of
American society helped provoke the rise of the Ku Klux Klan in the
1920s. But by then, the United States had become a significant center

of gravity for the church. A papal official wrote in 1919 that "Rome now looks to America to be the leader in all things Catholic, and to set an example to other nations."[40]

Sanger, baptized into the Catholic Church, consistently disdained its dogma. Dennett, by contrast, made a sustained effort to bridge the divide. She published pamphlets arguing that legal birth control was in line with freedom of expression that would ultimately help Catholic causes too—such as the freedom to run their own schools without government interference.[41]

In England, Stopes preached eugenics untroubled by ambivalence or any desire to make peace with Catholics. For her London clinic, she adopted the slogan "Joyful and deliberate Motherhood, A Safe Light in our Racial Darkness," accompanied by a sketch of a glowing lantern.[42] She suggested sterilizing anyone with chronic inherited disease, alcoholism, or even, as her biographer June Rose notes, "bad character."[43] (Interestingly, her aversion to bad character did not extend to dogs. Her chow, Wuffles, whom she refused to leash, was such a biter that law enforcement ordered him to be put down in 1928; for the rest of his natural life, Stopes was fined a pound a day for keeping him alive.)[44]

Perhaps the most egregious expression of Stopes's fervency for eugenics manifested in her own family. When her son, Harry, was two, realizing she was likely too old to conceive again, she began seeking to adopt another child. As Rose describes it, Stopes would consider only candidates who were male, "completely healthy, intelligent and uncircumcised."[45]

A series of boys duly came her way: Robin, whose counting and reading at age five were pronounced subpar; Dick, whom she feared wouldn't "bloom so as to be a credit to us"; John, who was dull in school; and Barry, whose toilet training accidents disqualified him.[46]

When her biological son, Harry, fell in love with a woman who wore glasses, Stopes was adamant the marriage must not go ahead. In her view it would "make a mock of our lives' work for Eugenic breeding and the Race."[47] After Harry married his Mary, she cut him out of her will, instead bequeathing much of her estate to the Royal Society of Literature and the Eugenics Society.

Undoubtedly, eugenics' popularity among middle-class white Americans gave a new sheen of decency to the language of birth control.[48] If people (and, eventually, congressmen) could discuss fertility and genetics without feeling they had touched a taboo, they might just be swayed by what Dennett and Sanger were trying to do.

Eugenics helped provide a way to discuss sex in polite company. Very quickly, however, old-guard eugenicists had to face the uncomfortable truth that young people, if the books and films are to be believed, didn't need any pretext at all.

It is hard to find a reflective woman, in these days, who is not harboring some new and startling scheme for curing the evils of monogamous marriage. . . .

Great hordes of viragoes patrol the country, instructing school-girls in the mechanics of reproduction and their mothers in obstetrics.

—H. L. Mencken, "The Sex Uproar,"
The Nation (July 1924)

EVERY INVENTION OF THE MID-1920S seemed designed to shred any last vestiges of modesty and add jingles and jitters to every formerly peaceful moment, starting with the radio. Between 1922 and 1929, radio sales rose from $60 million to $852 million.[1] The radio supplied news, entertainment, and music, which fueled a dancing craze. According to one college newspaper, dancers would "jig and hop around like a chicken on a red-hot stove, at the same time shaking the body until it quivers like a disturbed glass of jell-o."[2]

Dances like the shimmy and bunny hug gave unmarried couples an outlet to move their bodies freely and hold each other close, from cheek to ankle.[3] One thing led to another: F. Scott Fitzgerald wrote in *This Side of Paradise*, published in 1920, that "none of the Victorian mothers—and most of the mothers were Victorian—had any idea how casually their daughters were accustomed to be kissed."

Sex for pleasure, in and out of marriage, had become a pretty run-of-the-mill concept, in big cities and small towns alike. A 1925 study of fifty middle-class wives in New York City born after 1890 found thirty of them admitted to pre- or extramarital sex; out of fifty born before 1890, only seventeen claimed to have done so.[4] The people of Norphlet, Arkansas, meanwhile, decided looser morals didn't suit them and actually made extramarital sex illegal. Town leaders passed a 1925 ordinance with these provisions:

> Section 1. Hereafter it shall be unlawful for any man and woman, male or female, to be guilty of committing the act of sexual intercourse between themselves at any place within the corporate limits of said town.
> Section 3. Section One of this ordinance shall not apply to married persons as between themselves, and their husband and wife, unless of a grossly improper and lascivious nature.[5]

Now that wartime attention to STI prevention was fading, sex education was mostly left up to abstinence-focused tracts, a few daring teachers, and those birds-and-bees analogies stuttered by parents. Young people began banding together to demand the facts of life. The trend started in colleges: Barnard students agitated for a biology curriculum that included comprehensive anatomy, "the nature and power of the sex impulse," and "the pathological effects of perverse and social uses of sex and society."[6]

In 1925, Northwestern University students protested that their faculty was "old and fogeyish, and that sex hygiene is not given sufficient prominence."[7] High schoolers and middle schoolers did the same, asking their schools for "talks on menstruation—their reproductive organs and explanation of many questions that were puzzling them."[8]

The policy of ignorance was turning to dust. Young people refused to tolerate it; on screen and on the page, it was trampled and mocked again and again.

. . .

Dennett was beginning to wonder how much more resilience would
be required of her to accomplish anything of lasting value in Washington. She felt as unwelcome there as ever. "You'd think the Bill was
a 'wild, live lion,' the way the officials of Clubdom run at the mere
thought of it!" Dennett wrote in her notebook in January 1924.[9]

Dennett had once framed birth control as an issue that would
draw women voters, but now that argument fell flat. Congressmen
felt justified in their near-universal view that women didn't agree on
much and, in any case, didn't vote much, either.[10]

Since gaining the vote in 1920, women voters had not yet turned
out en masse with any unified national impact. That first year, 43 percent of eligible women voted, compared with 68 percent of male
voters.[11] A 1923 survey of all nonvoters found two-thirds of them
were women, and half of these gave their reason for failing to vote
as "inertia."[12]

Few women were lucky enough to be inert by choice, of course,
though many were homebound, which is different. One Department
of Agriculture–run survey respondent from Texas reported, "Many
farm women don't get off their own premises more than a dozen
times a year. The fathers get so accustomed to the mothers' staying at
home they seem to forget that they might enjoy a little rest and recre-
ation. . . . And the mother gets so accustomed to it she, too, seems to
forget she is human."[13]

Dennett cajoled Cummins into sponsoring the bill for one more
session. He agreed so long as he could redraft it, and in the end made
a relatively minor adjustment. He suggested leaving contraception in
the obscenity clause, simply adding the proviso that "the dissemination of information respecting the means by which conception can
be prevented, when certified by not less than five reputable graduate physicians lawfully engaged in the practice of medicine, as not
injurious to life or health, shall not be held to be forbidden by this
Section."[14]

Dennett was "aghast."[15] In Cummins's version, she thought, Comstock still held too much power. She rejected it immediately. Her rigidity on this point makes it hard not to think she brought a great deal of trouble on herself and was occasionally her own worst enemy. She had managed to persuade an unwilling Cummins, a midwesterner more than twenty years her senior, to sponsor the bill, but his efforts to make it palatable in Congress provoked only dismay and remonstrance. This moment between them is a perfect example of how Dennett's commitment to her goal was formidable, yet obstinate and unbending.

To leave contraception in the obscenity law, even if the statute was revised in such a friendly way as Cummins had suggested, would be a compromise, to be sure. And possibly Cummins's draft was wordy and inelegant—but it might achieve something. No doubt, since it came from his pen, he'd throw his best efforts behind it. Dennett saw it as an affront.

Her reaction nearly spoiled their cordial relationship. He was ready to be done at this point, and he asked her to approach senators who were physicians—there were then four—to see if they would sponsor the bill instead.

Dennett tried to make amends. She worked with Vaile to revise the bill's wording, sent it back to Cummins, and was startled when she gently nudged him on it January 31, 1924—only to be told offhand he'd introduced it the previous afternoon.

Introduced already! Dennett was "quite staggered," she admitted.[16] As senators investigated the Teapot Dome bribery scandal, Cummins had gone ahead and introduced the five-physicians version of the bill. Vaile did the same, afterward telling Dennett he'd had "a little joshing from the men in the House, but nothing bothersome."[17] (When his lumbago made him limp, colleagues like to call out, "If that's what birth control does to a fellow, better look out.")[18]

Vaile's colleagues did not, it is clear, recognize reproductive healthcare as a valid topic for political discourse. Their mockery seemed to go into gleefully misogynistic territory, as if fertility control was of no concern to men, and as if being associated with it was an absolute embarrassment.

Dennett felt the full weight of that misogyny. She hoped the bill's progress would be taken seriously, and sent out a press release on January 31: "SENATOR CUMMINS INTRODUCES BILL TO PROTECT BIRTH CONTROL KNOWLEDGE."[19] Then she got back to work.

. . .

Two congressional sessions in 1924 concluded Dennett's birth control career—in public, at least. The ordeal of that final lobbying sprint put her on a new path, back on the artist's way.

To chronicle this period in Dennett's life is to witness someone burning out by steady, excruciating degrees. Poignantly, these months brought moments of hope that made her eventual departure from Washington even more of a wrench than it otherwise might have been. Flares of support from outside groups and from within the VPL were ultimately outmatched by hostility from congressmen and partisans of Sanger's doctors-only campaign.

Despite the good news that Cummins had introduced Dennett's bill in late January 1924, by mid-February she was nervous. She'd heard Sanger was planning "some sort of a scheme for dipping into the federal work, and judging by recent straws and the past, it does not presage co-operation."[20] She knew Sanger had great means at her disposal, running a half-million-dollar organization and busy with frequent, high-profile speaking engagements, while Dennett was chronically in debt. She was justly apprehensive about what was to come.

Sanger's fame was as intimidating as her wealth. Her work to build a global birth control movement gathered steam in the mid-1920s, while her league kept active Stateside, putting on lectures and claiming radio airtime, all thanks to Slee's underwriting. Sanger's antagonism toward Dennett and the clean repeal still ran hot. In the March 1924 issue of the *Birth Control Review,* an editorial reminded readers that the ABCL "has set itself against the indiscriminate dissemination of so-called Birth Control information."[21] If Dennett had hoped for some grudging gesture of solidarity once the VPL bill was introduced as the Cummins-Vaile Bill, or, at worst, silence, she was met with this kind of sniping instead.

In the meantime, congressmen stalled, saying they were facing other bills relating to feminism and family welfare and had no time for birth control. The Equal Rights Amendment (ERA), written by Alice Paul and Crystal Eastman, was introduced in December 1923 and received substantial press attention in the months that followed. (As of 2024, the ERA has been passed by the House and Senate but missed a series of state ratification deadlines; twenty-five states have since adopted equal rights provisions into their state laws, in the spirit of the ERA.)

Midwinter cold dragged long in Washington, with snow through the end of March. Though most feminist advocacy groups considered birth control impossibly radical, Dennett reapproached two of them anyway. She began working to get endorsements for her bill from the League of Women Voters and the Federation of Women's Clubs, both of which were soon to hold conventions.[22] She needed all the ammunition she could get: her bill was about to go public.

. . .

The morning of Tuesday, April 8, Dennett's birth control bill was debated in Congress for the first time. The joint subcommittee of the Senate and House judiciary committees held a hearing focused on the VPL/Cummins-Vaile Bill, starting at ten o'clock.[23] Dennett sat ready to speak, near her colleague Sonia Bronson, her eyes sweeping the room in anticipation of a lively few hours ahead.

After the text of the legislation was read, Vaile was the first to speak. Pale and dapper, he tried to quell the misinformation he knew was running rampant among his colleagues. No one would be compelled to learn about contraception, or to practice it, he reminded them. He also pointed out that from the nation's founding until the Comstock Act of 1873, there had been no laws regarding birth control whatever on the books.

Perhaps most powerfully, though, Vaile read aloud a letter from a Catholic mother of five living children. They had a good farm, but so little cash her children wore flour-sack underclothing. "One doctor told me it was criminal to have a baby oftener than once every three years," she wrote. But when she asked how to space her pregnancies, "[He] said, 'I don't dare tell you anything.'"[24]

She described having four miscarriages, watching her oldest daughter worked to exhaustion by having to help care for the younger ones, and admitted to wondering whether life was worth living: "Can't you men see that things are too lopsided?" she wrote. "I'm not a howling suffragette. I'm only a skinny 37-year-old woman asking for a fair deal for millions who are worse off than I am, because I tell you frankly I don't need your old law now, and all the high and mighty statesmen can't compel me to have another baby."[25]

In her own testimony, Dennett battered her listeners with statistics. She pointed out the prevalence of birth control in wealthier social classes (as indicated by the average number of children in congressional families: 2.7). She gave a surprisingly sympathetic account of why the Comstock Act was passed in the first place—to combat the proliferation of pornography that was increasingly falling into the hands of young people.[26] And, ultimately, she pushed for scientific knowledge to circulate freely, in accordance with America's founding ideals.

Then eugenics came up. Mrs. Dorothy Glaser spoke on behalf of her husband, head of the biology department at Amherst College. She described government laboratories at Woods Hole, where fish eggs and sperm were manipulated and birth rates limited "so that the young fish may have a square deal. But then America wants the best possible fish," she soldiered on.[27] Another eugenicist testified in favor of the bill, but during questioning he had trouble convincing the audience birth control would boost "superior" stock while restricting "inferiors."

The humanitarian case for birth control was argued by James A. Field, a professor of political economy at the University of Chicago. Another ally read letters sent by desperate mothers to the VPL office. "I am 38 years old and am the mother of 6 living children and one dead. . . . Please do be kind and tell me just some little thing that would help. . . . I will promise not to tell no one about it. I have not been able to leave this house for 2 years now and see hardly no one if only I could talk to you in person," read one.[28] "For God's sake, can't you help me somehow. Am married three years, I have a baby two years old another five months old, and I am pregnant again. Can you imagine anything more awful. . . . I swear if I become pregnant a fourth time I will do something desperate," read another.[29]

Several reported having had stillborn babies "with instruments," meaning a doctor had quickly pulled the infant's body through the birth canal with forceps when the mother's life was thought to be in danger. One of the most striking letters was from a mother of sixteen children—with another on the way—on a hardscrabble Montana ranch.

Opposing testimony came from two Catholics, a Lutheran, and "two pathetic women, one a spiritualist . . . [the] other an elderly physician," in Dennett's memory.[30] A tremulous speaker, listed in the record as Mrs. O'Bear, argued "volunteer motherhood" could only be virtuously achieved via abstinence: "The body is a temple of God and must be kept holy, using the sex function for creation only."[31] The old argument had staying power, but on the whole Dennett felt its effect on the hearing was negligible.

The second hearing, on May 9, featured a surprise guest. Dennett had come to expect a few regular speakers for the opposition. Monsignor John A. Ryan, who directed the social action department of the National Catholic Welfare Conference, maintained an anti–birth control crusade, and relatedly a representative from the National Council of Catholic Women could be relied upon to show up.[32] Accordingly Dennett brought a list of endorsers who were clerics, including rabbis and ministers from a variety of sects, as well as physicians and educators.

This hearing also brought an actual spy. Miss Sara Laughlin of Philadelphia had been a dues-paying member of the VPL for three years. As it was revealed at the start of the hearing, Laughlin had used her VPL membership to gain access to Dennett's regular campaign reports to the league, for the purposes of surveilling and undermining the work.[33] Laughlin spoke about the moral dangers of birth control for nearly an hour, with the result that every other speaker was limited to just five minutes.

Besides that protracted moment of drama, the hearing devolved into congressmen piping up to share misgivings, impressions, and rehearsed one-liners. Representative Ira Hersey, Republican of Maine, heckled that Congress couldn't possibly pass a law authorizing "a mysterious remedy for what you [Dennett] call the evil of child birth."[34] Representative Richard Yates, Republican of Illinois, helpfully contributed that his daughter "had four babies, and she is fatter and prettier now after having the four."[35]

Then the room emptied, sending Dennett, her supporters, and everyone else shuffling through the doorway and into the spring afternoon.

. . .

After the hearing, Dennett's blitz of follow-up meetings challenged any optimism she had left. Representative Earl C. Michener, Republican of Michigan, persisted in pointing out the "danger which this bill would make for young girls."[36] (Dennett fought the urge to roll her eyes. "That girl again!" she wrote in the campaign diary. "She has nine lives!") He gestured out the window, toward a set of buildings known to house women clerks: "A lot of them are confirmed old maids . . . but I wouldn't trust what would happen to them if they all knew they could do what they pleased and no one would be the wiser."

A few days before the end of the congressional session, Dennett heard news that flustered her even further. A League of Women Voters representative, Mrs. O'Connor, told her Sanger's league was "lobbying in Washington against our [the VPL's] bill."[37] Dennett had suspected this; she'd recently seen Annie Porritt, the managing editor of the *Birth Control Review*, listed on the register at her hotel. "Within a few days," Dennett observed, "Senator Spencer announced a brand new excuse for stalling; namely, that the States should act first, before Congress could be expected to."[38]

This had long been Sanger's policy, and Dennett had suspected it came from the rival league somehow, but now she knew her suspicions were correct. Congress, she fumed "would just eat up advice from another B. C. group, which urged them to wait for the states to act first!"[39]

For now Congress adjourned, the bill swatted down yet again. Dennett took the train northward to seek refuge with her mother and her boys. Though she didn't yet know it, she would give herself—and Washington—one more brief chance.

Will you please answer my letter? I am a mother of 8 children. I am 30 years of age and my husband works by the month on a farm. My family is already larger than I can give good care like I ought to, so I am in terror of adding to it.

—Letter to Margaret Sanger (July 1927)

DENNETT SPENT THE SUMMER OF 1924 in uneasy contemplation. She was on the verge of becoming solely responsible for her mother's care. She had barely any income, and VPL committees did little to support her. They hardly realized what it was to be deeply in debt, she wrote: "The rent on our minute apartment due next Tuesday will just about land us on the sidewalk, with our grit for our sole asset. Fancy my reporting this sort of fact at a Committee meeting! No, it just isn't done."[1] She mulled over whether or not she should resign.

Carleton and Devon had jobs now, but she still worried about them. Devon hadn't been able to start college due to his mother's inability to pay tuition, and both sons were disillusioned about what they'd seen of social justice work, which seemed compromised and unsustainable. "They can't run away fast enough from everything which smacks of 'reform' or work pro bono publico," she wrote regretfully. "They feel that 'something is rotten in Denmark' when social work is dependent either upon the foundations given by the predatory rich, or on the casual donations of the moderately well to do . . . I confess I feel much the same way too."[2]

As the warmer months passed, Dennett developed a measure of sardonic distance from her work.[3] When the days grew shorter, she recognized this feeling for what it was: being broke, underappreciated, and used up. She told the VPL she was leaving, effective September 3.[4] Typically, her colleagues pulled together once Dennett was on the verge of moving on. Some money was raised, with the league's New York core trying to convince her that "one more vigorous, Congressional Campaign would probably do the trick," and Dennett represented their "best chance."[5] Despite her misgivings and responsibilities at home, she agreed to be reinstated. By October 1 she was lobbying again.

· · ·

For this final campaign the VPL rented a Washington office from Helen Hoy Greeley, an ally from Madison, Wisconsin, who was full of the newcomer's gushing enthusiasm. "You do things so ably, with such grasp and perspective and facility, so perfectly and so easily," she wrote Dennett; "yes I know you'll say, 'Illusion,' but that is the impression you produce."[6]

Dennett insisted she was "just only a plodder, feeling my way along as best I can."[7] But she was happy to have Greeley's company and adopted a scrappy tone in reports to close colleagues. She assured them she had no intention of leaving the legislative field "to the tender mercies of Margaret Sanger, and her 'doctors-only' bill and her instinct for staging a long 'fight,' full of 'militancy,' and all the excitements that careerists love."[8]

Five years into the Washington whirl, Dennett somehow found another wellspring of energy to propel her through it. Each day, she held around five lobbying appointments followed by office work, dinner, and evening correspondence. Many conversations went badly. Senator Samuel Shortridge, Republican of California, railed against "the awful jazz music at our dances, the willingness of our women to go half naked and corset less," and presenting Dennett with "a rather revolting smirk" and the line, "You know, Mrs Bennett [sic], there is a perfectly simple, easy way for people to avoid having babies. . . . As I say to my wife, if you are afraid of getting fat, why,—just don't eat,—that's all."[9]

They faced "hard sledding" in other ways, too—snowstorms, head colds, diminishing funds.[10] As a last-ditch gesture, Dennett wrote to Mrs. Coolidge, the first lady, asking for an appointment "quite as a private person, and not as Director of the Voluntary Parenthood League." No one, not even her stenographer, knew she was making this request. The Coolidges hadn't acted on her previous letters about the legislative campaign, but she wanted a chance to inform the White House of the consequences of the Comstock Act.[11] This time, Dennett's note was acknowledged—but Mrs. Coolidge's secretary firmly told her the First Lady would not discuss legislation of any kind.[12]

On January 30, the session ended and Cummins emerged with bad news. An unnamed senator had moved to indefinitely postpone the bill, and it was killed with no argument offered "except one remark that was really obscene . . . that concerned just myself," Cummins told Dennett. He came away convinced they hadn't a chance.[13]

Within the VPL, the flurry of support that had sent Dennett back to Washington a few months earlier oscillated back toward collapse. The executive committee doubted whether it was worth continuing with the legislative campaign at all, given Cummins's news. Beyond exhausted, and faced with a personal debt of several thousand dollars and the prospect of working without a strong organization behind her, Dennett again resigned.

"I shall quit without being what is called successful," she wrote to her colleagues Myra Gallert and Sonia Bronson, "but it can't be helped. My reputation will have to go as a somewhat damaged affair. But what I have done will count considerably as foundation. It may well be that the hardest part of the struggle is over."[14] She had told the committee she would stay if her salary was guaranteed, along with a paid vacation and assurance of moral support. Dennett had been through this before. Always, the money had materialized, and she had managed to propel herself and the bill through another congressional session.

But this time, the league couldn't meet her terms. Dennett recognized her lobbying hadn't produced the promised result, but she took this blow personally. The VPL executive committee, she noted with regret, "as a whole respects me . . . but they do not *like* me. (For which I do not blame them. I don't myself, but hardly for the same reasons.)"[15]

She was plunged again into the thicket of her old anxiety, rooted in that childhood moment of eavesdropping on her uncle Edwin Mead, when his offhand criticism made certain her guardians didn't find her brilliant or lovely or even tolerable for long. "It really is quite essential that the fellow who heads a campaign should be reasonably popular among his backers," Dennett continued. "I am not that."[16]

Her work ethic had been useful to the league, it had animated the entire enterprise, but she hadn't managed to make a path for herself in the hidebound institution of Congress. In addition, she was not generally known and had no money of her own. She later wrote a friend, "I think the doctors will be discovering a new disease presently, induced by the long continued keeping of 'a stiff upper lip.'"[17]

It was a hard separation. "I am sorry, deeply so, about you and your 'child,'" Greeley wrote her.[18] That was the truth: Dennett was losing something that held a permanent, dominant place in her heart.

. . .

Sanger moved with alacrity once she knew Dennett had left Washington. In March 1925, she executed the Sixth International Neo-Malthusian and Birth Control Conference at New York's Hotel McAlpin, still aggressively wooing eugenicists.

"While the United States shuts her gates to foreigners," Sanger said in her opening address, "no attempt whatever is made to discourage the rapid multiplication of undesirable aliens—and natives—within our own borders."[19]

In her league's newsletter later that year, Sanger issued a call to action: "NOW FOR THE BIG PUSH ON CONGRESS! We want to change the Federal Law."[20] Dennett and the VPL were neither invited nor mentioned.

It is hard to know exactly why Sanger was motivated to abandon her old strategy of changing state laws first. She had long objected to Dennett's lobbying in Washington and her focus on amending the Comstock Act, arguing it was pointless to tackle federal legislation before the public opinion in favor of birth control had been proven state by state.

Perhaps her earlier insistence on a states-first campaign was as an honest tactical effort: she left space for Dennett to spend five years scandalizing congressmen with the clean-repeal idea, so Sanger's doctors-only version would later be received as a safer, more conservative approach. In any case, Sanger's incursions into Washington in the spring of 1924, followed by her swiftness in picking up congressional lobbying once Dennett withdrew, suggests she had for some time been assessing that arena for herself, after all, and thought birth control now had a good chance of success.

The *Review* was still her mouthpiece, but in its pages Sanger had a very different voice from the one she used in person. While the *Review* carried headlines such as "WANTED: INTELLIGENCE TESTS FOR LEGISLATORS,"[21] a new volunteer described Sanger herself as

> small, quiet, elegant in a stone beige coat trimmed with black Persian lamb, carrying a large patent leather pocketbook . . . her Titian hair was straight and swathed around her head. Wideset in a small heart-shaped face, her incredibly deep blue eyes [actually hazel, according to reliable sources] met the gaze of acquaintances with the steadiest, most penetrating look one has ever seen. Her voice,

calm and quiet, answered questions without fuss
or unnecessary elaboration. A smile of greeting to
those who caught her eyes, then to her own office
and desk.[22]

In January 1926, Sanger and two colleagues went to Washington.
It was a "scouting expedition," Sanger wrote, "to take a survey of the
mental attitude of Congressmen" when it came to a doctors-only
birth control bill.[23] Far quicker than expected, the expedition turned
into a very different undertaking, but Dennett, at least, seemed to be
receding into the shadows.

Physicians and eugenicists, led, respectively, by Robert Latou Dickinson and Francis Sumner, now urged Dennett to support Sanger's
campaign in Washington. The best chance for legalizing birth
control, they argued, would be if there was unity in the movement.
"Mrs. Sanger is the symbol, the international figure. . . . She has a
way of delivering the goods," Dickinson wrote.[24] Sumner reiterated
to Dennett how rival bills would just confuse congressmen and give
a convenient excuse to dither, pointing out, "The time has certainly
not yet come when it is *good politics* to champion birth control."[25]

Faced with these calls to fall in line behind Sanger, Dennett withdrew further into herself. The summer of 1925 found her introspec-
tive and nearly broke. She had been turned down for a department
store job for being "too superior."[26] Every clerical agency rejected
her for being overqualified, or possibly too old—she was fifty-three—
though the phrase they used was "too intelligent."

She wrote a heartfelt letter to Stopes, saying she was "in such an
unsettled state and so depressed." She was "weary-souled indeed," she
told her friend. Sanger's "degeneration into a careerist, whose every
instinct is to develop a situation in which the agitation will last indefinitely, instead of taking those steps which will most quickly and justly
end the need for agitation" was turning out to be highly effective,
when combined with her money.

Dennett's "unfortunate lethargy" threatened to take over.[27] Though exhausted, she was keenly aware that Sanger's doctors-only bill was circulating through Congress and was likely soon to be the focus of active lobbying, while her own clean repeal was moribund.

Finally, Dennett resolved to agitate another way. She could, she thought, write a book. Sanger had written several by then, but Dennett envisioned her own very differently: not at all a memoir or a polemic. It would discuss the legal status of birth control through American history, the current struggles of the movement, and the prospects for the future.

She pinned her hopes on the book shifting public opinion, and giving the "chameleon"-like Sanger an opportunity to reconcile herself to Dennett's ideas.[28] She thought about the reviews her book might receive, and wrote her colleague Myra Gallert, "Wouldn't it be a joke if our publicity could be the means of making the Committee report in favor of a clean repeal. . . . Quite neat!"[29] It is telling about the kind of reader and thinker Dennett was that she assumed readers would be more powerfully persuaded by a book of legal reasoning than by a tale of underdog heroism or a radical manifesto, the genres Sanger was most drawn to for her own books.

Dennett called her book *Birth Control Laws: Shall We Keep Them, Change Them, or Abolish Them*. In her manuscript she referred to herself sparingly, as "the author," and emphasized the objectivity of her reporting. "It makes no pretense at literature and it is not propaganda. . . . It simply talks over the subject in an untechnical fashion, from the human standpoint, with the idea that most thinking, well-meaning people want our laws to represent common sense."[30]

But before the book could have any impact, it needed a publisher, and finding one proved difficult. Some editors, regardless of the censors, had already committed to a book on birth control; others declined to take on the topic since the book might be suppressed.[31]

Additionally, though she had been the first to take a birth control bill to Congress, Dennett didn't have name recognition like Sanger did. In fact, she'd actively resisted developing it. When Gallert and Bronson told her they had proposed putting "Founded by Mary Ware Dennett" on VPL stationery, she told them not to. "The value of the League is not who started it," she wrote, "but what it stands for and what it does."[32]

She insisted on putting ideas at the center of her narrative instead of herself. Though she knew well that a central myth, or a central martyr, could help galvanize a movement, she refused to package her own experiences for public consumption. Publishers duly made their assessments, and rejections piled up.

She no longer felt sure of her life's direction. The day after Christmas 1925, Dennett typed up a letter to loved ones. She noted the beauty of the season and confessed her own lack of energy, writing, "I tried to be oblivious of Christmas this year."[33]

Her boys were grown, and her mother increasingly frail. She quoted Christopher Morley, a *New York Post* columnist she admired: "Life is a foreign language; all men mispronounce it" and "Life is all one piece of endless pattern. No stitch in the vast fabric can be unravelled without risking the whole tapestry. It is a garment woven without seams."[34]

. . .

In early 1926, Sanger and Anne Kennedy met with sixty senators, twenty congressmen, and seventeen members of the Senate Judiciary Committee. The overall response to their doctors-only proposition was resistance.[35] Senator Henry Ashurst, Democrat of Arizona, told them he "had not been raised to discuss this matter with women."[36] Senator James E. Watson, Republican of Indiana, retorted birth control was no good because "it would permit the women to have more lap-dogs and encourage the idle to be still more idle."[37]

When they sat down with Senator Cummins, he remained doubtful any birth control bill would be taken seriously. His efforts in that direction had been "the laughing-stock of the cloakroom for several days."[38]

Unbeknownst to Sanger and Kennedy, their interviewees were being peppered with protest letters from Dennett. "I am quite certain that you will be urged by the birth control group of which Margaret Sanger is president . . . to alter your bill and to compromise of the principles on which your bill is based," she wrote Cummins. "I most earnestly hope it will be impossible to persuade you to compromise."[39]

Dennett's epistolary mischief likely made no discernible difference. Congress was hopeless, Sanger and Kennedy decided within a few weeks. The law would change only if the rest of the country went way ahead of it first. Propaganda, publicity, grassroots campaigning—all were needed to get lawmakers to come around.

Through 1925 and 1926, the ABCL ran a national charm campaign, made possible by the league's deep pockets—or rather, Noah Slee's. By 1925, nearly $50,000 of Slee's fortune was invested in the ABCL, turning him into its single greatest source of funding by far.[40]

The cause gained another masculine ally when Sanger hired a medical director for the league, Dr. James Fryer Cooper, whose job was to travel the country making birth control look manly and respectable. Cooper spoke primarily to local medical societies, but also to Lions Clubs, Kiwanis, and normal schools. He often lectured multiple times a day, delivering more than seven hundred birth control talks across the country over the course of two years.[41]

Most audiences welcomed Dr. Cooper, a tall, fair-haired, former Christian missionary. He had a tragic personal connection to the issue of maternal health: his wife had died of preeclampsia, a complication of pregnancy.[42] As he traveled, Cooper took down the names of pro–birth control doctors, and once back in New York his notes and business cards were compiled into a "Doctors File" so women writing to Sanger for help could be referred to a sympathetic local physician.[43]

Universally, doctors told Cooper they knew little about contraception—sometimes this was stated with stubborn pride, sometimes with open curiosity. Birth control was still not part of the standard medical-school curriculum. A county medical society in Portland, Maine, even told Cooper "they felt B.C. was beneath the dignity of the medical society to discuss."[44] But Cooper was undeterred, arguing with anyone who blustered about birth control being unnatural or undignified that it held exactly the same status as safety razors or vaccination.[45]

The second-most-common objection he heard was that no method of birth control was foolproof, so none should be prescribed—a point that Dennett, too, had heard in the hearings over the Cummins-Vaile Bill. Cooper remarked on the "great deal of thoughtless talk about 'no one hundred per cent method,'" writing, "Is it fair then, to ask, have we any one hundred per cent methods in medicine, or surgery, or serum, or vaccine therapy?"

Cooper urged his physician audiences to be less prescriptive and sure of themselves in *all* areas of their work. In his words, "The only ethical attitude a physician can take is to guarantee nothing. He can only promise to do his best."[46] Better-informed physicians he met said their obstacle was finding a way to order diaphragms through the mail without risking arrest.

A select few even ventured to support a change in the laws. Within the AMA, the section on obstetrics, gynecology, and abdominal surgery called in 1925 for "the alteration of existing laws so that physicians may legally give contraceptive information to their patients in the regular course of practice."[47]

Comparable policies overseas helped spur along the change. In England, in the spring of 1926, the Ministry of Health decreed that publicly funded clinics could legally distribute birth control to married women, though the new law did not compel physicians or clinics to do so. Marie Stopes's first clinic had been operating successfully for five years, and had moved from Holloway, a working-class North London neighborhood, to the more genteel Bloomsbury.

Though the American laws had not changed yet, the market was expanding, thanks to the proliferation of devices and growing social acceptance. Varieties of the "womb veil"—the Mensinga diaphragm, Mizpah pessary, and many others—had been growing in popularity since the publication of *Family Limitation* a decade earlier.

Sanger also worked to reverse or at least soften religious opposition among the largest denominations. She had recently had success in the Jewish community nearest to her. Rabbi Stephen S. Wise, a prominent antiwar, prolabor activist who had founded the Free Synagogue in Manhattan, affirmed his support of birth control in 1925, saying, "If the church and synagogue stand in the way of justice and the nobler order of human society realizable through birth control, so much the worse will it be. . . . The life of a child is a sacred thing and we ought to hold it so sacred as not to have life come into the world unless we are able to give it fair opportunity to find its highest service."[48] The Central Conference of American Rabbis would formally accept birth control in 1927, while encouraging Jewish families to have a minimum of two children.[49]

Charles Francis Potter, a Unitarian leader, spoke of the dangers of the culture of ignorance around sex and birth and praised the eugenic potential of birth control. "Knowledge does not cause vice; it is ignorance that does it," he wrote in 1925.[50] Overall, Protestant and Evangelical churches were unlikely to publicly support birth control, but neither did they systematically organize against it.[51]

Open hostility was still the domain of the Catholics. The National Catholic Welfare Conference stood firm, despite some tentative friendly overtures from Sanger. Monsignor John A. Ryan had first attacked birth control in a *Harper's Weekly* feature in 1915, and more recently he had testified at both hearings on the Cummins-Vaile bill in 1924, saying he regarded birth control as "immoral, degrading and stupid" and "quite [as] immoral as self mutilation or the practice of solitary vice."[52] He called for better wages and social supports for families instead, while blaming small families for the nation's current and future economic problems. In early 1926, the conference ramped up its countercampaign and encouraged all members to oppose any birth control legislation that made it to a hearing.

Sanger kept an open mind about whom she might convert to the cause. She took on numerous speaking engagements herself, including an infamous date with the women's auxiliary of the Ku Klux Klan in Silver Lake, New Jersey. It was, she wrote, "One of the weirdest experiences I had in lecturing" against a background of "dim figures parading with banners and illuminated crosses."[53] In the West, a few of the birth controllers who came out were intractably loyal to Dennett's clean repeal, but on the whole Sanger was satisfied the national movement was rallying around her now.[54]

. . .

In summer 1926, Dennett went through a "smash-up," as she called it to her friends. She hated admitting she suffered anything nerve related, but her mental health had collapsed.[55] The clear precipitating event was the congressional campaign and unrelenting stress of supporting her family. It's possible that some recent news from Hartley's neck of the woods contributed. In 1925 the Chases divorced, and Hartley and Margaret married the following year.[56]

More than twenty years after laying aside *guadameciles*, Dennett returned to them, finding the refuge she badly needed in handicraft. To make a living, she found part-time work writing and organizing for the American Foundation for Homeopathy.[57] She had a firm faith in homeopathy, an inclination that started during her father's cancer, when allopathic physicians had offered so little comfort.[58] Much later in her life, her polished box full of minuscule homeopathic pills became an object of fascination to her grandchildren.[59]

Helped by her art practice, her family, and manageable portions of decently paid work, she gradually revived.[60] Her book *Birth Control Laws* was on the verge of a publishing deal at last. And in May she became a grandmother when Devon and his wife, Marie, had their first child, Sally-Marie.[61] Dennett's gift to her daughter-in-law was *Radiant Motherhood* by Marie Stopes.[62]

Yet as much as she tried, it was impossible to separate her thoughts from Sanger and Washington. In June, she'd opened a letter from Myra Gallert and Vine McCasland containing a proposition. In the interest of pushing through *some* form of birth control legislation, what did Dennett think of exchanging concessions with Sanger? If Sanger would agree the Comstock Act's contraception clause should be removed, would Dennett agree the VPL could endorse an additional doctors-only amendment opening the way to birth control access? They yearned to keep working for the cause, but didn't feel they could join Sanger's group unless Dennett made an overture.

Dennett telegrammed, then sat down and wrote a letter, too.[63] Her "hair stood on end" and her "heart sank and all that," she replied. She would "far rather see the League die or go into void storage than to see it cave in as its final service to ideals."[64]

Her most loyal friends were pressing her to bend. What if *nothing* happened—what if the Comstock Act just continued to operate and be enforced? Did Dennett want to wait fifty years?[65] Her old colleagues didn't want to let the perfect be the enemy of the good.

"Taking false steps is not at all the same thing as taking a step at a time, in the right direction," Dennett insisted.[66] "Special privilege has crept in, to an appalling degree, not only in our actual legislation, but in the interpretation of laws and the enforcement of laws," she wrote. "Why deliberately add to the mess? . . . Why pile up endless work for our successors to struggle with? Why make them cuss our stupidity?"[67]

Dennett, admirably, thought the existing laws worthy of clear, concise, equitable amendment. But that same conviction meant she refused to consider any path that might have legalized birth control sooner, though in a more restricted—some would say pragmatic—

way. She also didn't hold back from letting her more pliable friends know that any compromise was not only unjust, but messy and stupid, too. Gallert and McCasland, as much as they loved her, must have grown used to her unyielding, sometimes scolding judgment.

She might have been heartened to know the rival group faced all-too-familiar difficulties in Washington. The ABCL committee retreated from federal action in May 1926. "The more I have to do with Congressmen," Sanger concluded, "the more I believe in birth control and sterilization."[68]

. . .

Sanger went to London in early 1927, and Dennett followed her. At least, her book *Birth Control Laws*, released in late 1926, did. Sanger read it quickly, furiously.

"I am heart sick over the fact that Mary Dennett's book is out & Marie Stopes is boosting it here to hurt me," she wrote Slee in late March 1927. "The book calls me all kinds of names in a cleaver [*sic*] way. Quoting from things I said in the early days & things I did not say etc. etc. . . . The poor sick woman has failed in her work & in order to explain her failure, she throws the blame on me & my work & early views. Most of them very good but *radical*."[69]

While claiming neutrality, the book was a rapier-sharp argument in favor of the clean repeal. "Would it not be best," Dennett asked in the book, "to have the laws simply provide an open field, and let the dignified authoritative scientists compete with the quacks and the spurious folk with faith that eventually the best would win, very much as the increased public knowledge of general hygiene is steadily putting quackery into the background?"[70]

Birth Control Laws actually gave Sanger a measure of credit. Sanger's arrests, Dennett wrote, "touched off the park [*sic*] that flamed into what has been called in late years, the American birth control movement."[71] It recognized Sanger's "gallant zeal" and admitted her work was crucial in crystallizing and expanding the movement.

But then, indeed, it turned. Dennett criticized the "strident tone" of the *Woman Rebel* and described the ABCL's refusal to support the VPL's efforts to change the federal law.[72] She wrote dimly of Sanger's feeling that it was "her particular function to break the laws rather than to spend effort at that time in trying to change them."[73] Sanger had hampered Dennett's prospects in Washington, inducing panic and resistance in politicians. She faulted Sanger for drawing out her entry into the federal field to inflate her own sense of self-importance. "The leaders of movements as well as play-wrights are sometimes not immune to the temptation to make a four act play out of a one act plot," she wrote.[74]

Between Dennett's book, the ABCL's frustrated efforts to change the federal law, and an upcoming world population conference, Sanger was generally chagrined. Occasionally, especially when dealing with eugenicists or Neo-Malthusians, her work was co-opted by men who behaved as though she had no business in their ranks.

That conference, held in Geneva in mid-1927, required an enormous amount of labor from Sanger. She hoped to be repaid with recognition and an academic seal of approval on birth control, but events did not play out that way. The gathering brought together daring minds like Julian Huxley, brother of the novelist Aldous, and the economist John Maynard Keynes. Yet, provokingly, birth control ended up entirely shut out of the proceedings.

Scholars expounded on population change in relation to biology, sterility rates, and nutrition—every angle except the one most important to her. "The papers of Professors East and Fairchild came perilously near mentioning the forbidden word Malthusianism, but as for birth control," Sanger wrote, "it was edged about like a bomb which might explode at any minute."[75]

Just before the conference started, its president, the English eugenicist Sir Bernard Mallet, objected to Sanger's being in the speaking program, meaning she had to put aside the talk she had written and keep to her seat.[76]

Her presence still mattered to the assembled group, though more as a symbol or token than an actual source of authority; after the farewell address the crowd sang "For She's a Jolly Good Fellow" in her honor. Still, Sanger was effectively silenced through the event she had envisioned, planned, and executed. She felt humiliated and patronized, as though her allies had "failed and compromised" her, as she wrote to Hugh de Selincourt.[77]

At this point Dennett considered herself "absolutely sworn off from causes," if they meant working with a committee or going to Washington.[78] She continued to sell *The Sex Side of Life* in sealed envelopes via first-class mail, or via express when fulfilling bulk orders. Dickinson's Committee on Maternal Health expressed interest in reissuing *The Sex Side of Life* with revisions and new illustrations by Dickinson himself, but for now Dennett was content with managing the trade herself.[79]

By July 1927, Cummins and Vaile had both died. "It puts our story really into the realm of history, doesn't it!" Dennett wrote her friends. "I wish they might both have lived to their bill [*sic*] become a law. Do you suppose *any of us* will?"[80]

As Dennett withdrew, Sanger fed as much cash as she could muster into her propaganda machine. It might have continued to churn without results had it not been for two surprising precursors to the Great Crash: the transgressive cultural turn of 1928 and an ill-conceived police raid that showed just how far attitudes to birth control had come.

Part III | *The Wandering Path to Victory*

It was harder now to cry. People were much gayer. Water
was hot in two seconds. Ivy had perished or been scraped
off houses. Vegetables were less fertile; families were much
smaller.

—Virginia Woolf, *Orlando* (1928)

THE LATE 1920S BROUGHT GLEAMING renewal and ostenta-
tion to New York. Sonia Bronson wrote Dennett, Gallert, and
McCasland in March 1927 that the city was "entirely new," with
seemingly every block under construction, while New Yorkers themselves inhabited a "mercenary atmosphere. . . . There seems to be one
mad rush to outdo the other in display of wealth, and achievement in
size. All thought for the finer and more beautiful side of things seems
to be fast becoming vestigial."[1]

Berenice Abbott, a photographer visiting from Paris, became
captivated by the glittering high-rise landscape and returned just to
capture it on film. "Old New York is fast disappearing," Abbott wrote.
"At almost any point on Manhattan Island, the sweep of one's vision
can take in the dramatic contrasts of the old and the new and the
bold foreshadowing of the future."[2] For a brief period, horse-drawn
wagons and skyscrapers overlapped.

Automobiles brought people together in close, unchaperoned
proximity. Across the United States, about 6.7 million passenger cars
were on the roads in 1919; ten years later the number was greater than
23 million, each one a potential den of iniquity.[3] Of all the women

who reported having premarital sex, 41 percent had done so in an automobile.[4]

Since the first subway had started running in 1904, more than a hundred miles of subway tunnel had been excavated, the new trains speeding up the pace of the city even further. Dennett reflected, "This is undoubtedly the most rapidly moving era which the world has ever known. . . . Life is not only speeded up, but is jazzed up as well. 'C'm on, let's go,' seems the most popular slogan. . . . Girls and women have plunged in, to an extent undreamed of heretofore. . . . Their swagger and nonchalance is appalling—equipped, as one shocked matron said, 'with nothing in their little wrist bags, but a contraceptive, a lip stick and a powder puff."[5] According to Kinsey research published much later, while a third of women born before 1900 usually kept their clothes on during sex, only 8 percent of the next cohort did.[6]

Art and music had left the age of Comstock far behind. Georgia O'Keeffe's close-ups of flowers were immediately seen by critics as erotic metaphors, to O'Keeffe's irritation, and unhesitatingly hung on gallery walls.

Gertrude "Ma" Rainey's blues recordings and Isadora Duncan's dancing drew thrilled audiences. Clara Smith, a South Carolina blues singer, sang in "Mama's Gone, Goodbye": "There's a fire in my range, bakes nice and brown. / All I need is some good Daddy turn my damper down."[7] At certain YMCAs men took refuge in the evenings, knowing they were in a rare space where it was safe to be a gay man.[8]

Women's fashion was nearly unrecognizable from that of the previous decade. Instead of ankle-length skirts over petticoats and no more makeup than a touch of powder, women now wore a single layer of clothing, showed their knees and sometimes even their shoulders, and painted their lips.

The *Journal of Commerce* recorded that over the past fifteen years, the average amount of material needed for a woman to be fully clothed shrank from 19.25 yards to 7 yards.[9] You could see more of a woman's skin and figure on a trip to the grocery store than had once been possible in a vaudeville show. Whereas in 1910 a risqué performance might feature a woman in a body stocking, by 1927, theaters in the Midwest boasted performers nude except for ribbon pasties, calling on the audience to "shake 'em up girls! Shake all you got for the boys!"[10]

A new pop culture heroine was ascendant: the good-hearted dame who didn't take the rules too seriously and knew how to look out for herself. The Ladies' Home Journal now printed occasional stories in which the protagonist had a career, did not marry, and was nonetheless portrayed positively and sympathetically.[11] The second-best-selling novel in America in 1925, Gentlemen Prefer Blondes by Anita Loos, was a caper about two such women beating the system. (Sanger's colleague Anne Kennedy got her copy as a gift from Mary Sumner Boyd—a good friend and former Twilight Sleep advocate— and praised it as a welcome break from eugenics polemics.)[12]

To critics, Loos's writing was too snappy and feminine to really be literature, but her fans included F. Scott Fitzgerald, Edith Wharton, and James Joyce, who confessed to "reclining on a sofa and reading Gentlemen Prefer Blondes for three whole days."[13] The novel mocks morality and marriage, pokes fun at propriety and inhibitions, and paints love as a form of currency most often traded in exchange for material assets.

If there was a queen avatar of the irreverent sex comedy, it was Mae West. Before she started writing her own plays, West was a darling of the revue stage. The Central Association of Obstetricians and Gynecologists even talked her up as a post-flapper-era "boon to motherhood" because she single-handedly brought "plump female figures" back in style.[14] They clearly hadn't read her work or heard her punch lines ("I used to be Snow White, but I drifted"), each word delivered as if shimmying in its own feather boa.

In 1926, West wrote a play called Sex, under the pseudonym Jane Mast. Sex was a caper of deception, blackmail, and true love with a good-hearted prostitute at its center, played by West herself. It was thought crass, vulgar, absurd, funny—and a must-see. Upward of 300,000 people filed into Daly's Sixty-Third Street Theatre on Broadway to see it, and it was trendy among the smart set to have seen it more than once.[15] The city's vice squad raided the playhouse and shut down production in February 1927.

Just before her arrest, West had drafted a new play, *The Drag*, mocking the taboos and conversion attempts foisted on gay men. But after *Sex* was shut down, *The Drag* was never permitted to open in New York.[16] Even after West reworked it as *Pleasure Man*, changing gay characters to straight, the theme of unrepentant sexuality remained—sexuality unchained to procreation.

In the 1920s women made 80 percent of consumer purchases, according to market analysis, and consumer goods and entertainment were emphatically marketed to answer the anxieties and desires of women shoppers.[17] Birth control turned into a sales hook, with the implication being that it would help secure a happy marriage.

"Young Wives Are Often Secretly Terrified," was the tagline for one product. "Can a Married Woman Ever Feel Safe?" asked another.[18] The promoter for the 1922 film *Tell Me Why* advertised it as "birth control propaganda" and sold pamphlet editions of "What Every Girl Should Know" and "What Every Mother Should Know" in theater lobbies.[19]

The pro–birth control movie *No More Children* (1929) imagined Mary and Jimmy, a couple with four children in dire financial straits. Jimmy, desperate for enough money to feed his family, is arrested for fraud, and the sympathetic judge lets him walk free but orders him and his wife to have no children for the next five years. They begin sleeping apart, and their marriage suffers. "Laws made by men—not by women—denied her the scientific knowledge which would have given her the power to decide for herself whether she would or would not become the mother of a fifth child," read a booklet released together with the film. "She knew nothing of Birth Control and Sex Hygiene."[20] Desperate, Mary finds a doctor in the phone book who is willing to surgically sterilize her. She contracts sepsis and dies after the operation. The promotional literature attached to the film praised Sanger, quoted ministers and rabbis who endorsed birth control, emphasized both the humanitarian and eugenic advantages of birth control, then put to the audience the loaded question, "What do YOU THINK?"[21]

This wasn't the first time birth control had appeared on the silver screen, however. As far back as 1916 and 1917, it briefly held the heartland's cinemas "in its grip," according to the *New York Dramatic Mirror*, which recommended four films on the topic that were showing at the same time.[22] Silent film had helped women make a case for suffrage—Dennett herself had helped make one short movie in 1912, "Votes for Women"—and the birth control movement deployed it, too.

Sanger herself had taken to the screen in 1917. She wrote a script titled *Birth Control* with the help of her colleague Frederick Blossom; the plot was likely inspired by that of the Lois Weber–directed silent feature *Where Are My Children?*, released the year before. "Although I had long since lost faith in my abilities as an actress," she wrote, "I played the part of the nurse."[23] She issued a statement that it would be her only film appearance, and all profits would go to promoting the cause. Ads for the film included a still: Sanger being handcuffed, dwarfed and surrounded by a policeman and a vice agent in a top hat.[24]

The film has been lost, but detailed descriptions and stills have survived. The first scene showed a poor mother's burdensome life juggling several small children in a ramshackle home contrasted with a middle-class mother's small family and spacious home. The narrative adapted the Sadie Sachs story, incorporating images of desperate women and disabled children. Sanger tells of her patient's suicide, her own persecution under the law; the film ends with shots of Sanger in jail, with the subtitle "No matter what happens, the work must go on."[25]

Birth Control's opening was canceled. The day before it was due to run at Columbus Circle's Park Theatre, New York License Commissioner George H. Bell issued a statement saying the film was "directly contrary to public welfare" and was banned for indecency. Sanger showed the film at her lectures, but it never had a theatrical release. The closest the public got to it was its review in *Variety*, which described Sanger as a "placid, clear eyed, rather young and certainly attractive propagandist" and concluded viewers may not be fully converted to birth control after seeing and listening to her, but that the film "will certainly make everyone think twice before denouncing the movement."[26]

By the 1920s, that movement was starting to get attention on college campuses, too. Between 1890 and 1920, the number of women moving through higher education more than doubled—the increase was three times greater for women than men—and their research now came to light.

Anthropologists who had started researching sex and women's lives in the early 1900s began publishing their findings, which were revelatory. In 1918, the sociologist Katharine Bement Davis had started a monumental survey of mainly middle-class white women. Published in 1929, the results, titled *Factors in the Sex Life of Twenty-Two Hundred Women*, indicated women were "more highly sexed" than any expert had hitherto believed.[27]

Davis's research revealed that a majority of women of marriageable age just prior to World War I practiced some form of birth control, and an even greater proportion believed contraception presented no moral issue.[28] Most admitted to masturbating, and one in five had had same-sex relationships.[29] Though Davis's sample was in no way representative of the general population, the results of her study redefined "normal" sexuality and challenged the widespread assumption that women were passionless by nature.[30]

Margaret Mead's *Coming of Age in Samoa* (1928) brought readers to the village of Tau, where, Mead wrote, sex was never exactly taboo, since groups lived in longhouses without interior walls. Casual pre- and extramarital sex was seen as natural and little emphasis was placed on female virginity. Her portrait of Samoan society was as powerful as the work of Freud or Ellis in its effect of sparking dialogue about sex and society with a quasi-academic gloss—not only among scholars of sexuality but among laypeople too, since her book became a bestseller.[31]

As Mead wrote in her autobiographical *Blackberry Winter*, "I spent most of my life studying the lives of other peoples, faraway peoples, so that Americans might better understand themselves."[32] Dennett believed this was the point of anthropology, too. Americans should read Mead's *Growing Up in New Guinea*, she thought, to "make a useful appraisal of their job as parents, and, unless I am much mistaken, the result will be illumination."[33] Mead's work let American readers view their own social structure, based on the atomized nuclear family and strictly regulated female sexuality, as a culturally relative phenomenon.

Literary publishing in 1928 was markedly more willing to accept gender fluidity, queerness, and maternal ambivalence than in years past. It was as though the social upheavals of World War I had sown the seeds for a crop of revelatory books that bloomed in this single year. *Orlando* by Virginia Woolf came out, and D. H. Lawrence's *Lady Chatterley's Lover*, two daring explorations of gender and sexuality.

In her introduction to the Oxford Classics edition of *Orlando*, Rachel Bowlby sums up this new world of cultural interrogation and transgression: "Instead of it being taken for granted, or rather for natural, that men and women were simply different, with whatever consequences followed from the specific form of the assumption . . . now the very origins of masculinity and femininity and the forms of sexual interest that might accompany them were being perceived in some quarters as being in need of explanation."[34]

A handful of the most powerful literary works of 1928 centered the experience of women propelled through life by a reproductive destiny shaped by factors beyond their control. Novels like *Quicksand* by Nella Larsen, which addresses the moral complexities of marriage and parenthood for Black women in the age of eugenics, and *The Well of Loneliness* by Radclyffe Hall, which follows a queer narrator's coming of age, brought frank portrayals of women's diverse sexual and reproductive experiences into the public eye.

Sanger dwelled on the plight of women deprived of birth control information in her book *Motherhood in Bondage*, another product of 1928. In it she quoted about four hundred letters from mothers who had written her for help over the years. Many of the letters hit the same few notes of pain and isolation, a fact Sanger embraced. "Repetition the readers will find," she wrote, "but significant repetition. It builds up the unit of this tragic communal experience. Despite all the differences, the story of motherhood in bondage is, by and large, the same story, the same pattern of pain . . . producing the same cry for deliverance."[35]

For the book's title, she wanted something provocative, something that succinctly described the physical, emotional, and financial strain of being unable to plan or space pregnancies. Her publishers thought it went too far, so she wove it into the text instead: "the inferno of maternity."[36]

An Untimely Raid

He's washing dishes and baby clothes
He's so ambitious, he even sews
But don't forget, folks
That's what you get, folks, for makin' whoopee.

—"Makin' Whoopee" by
Gus Kahn and Walter Donaldson (1928)

IN SEPTEMBER 1928, DENNETT WAS paging through *Time* when a surprising headline made her pause. Sanger was casting off old alliances again: she had resigned as president of the ABCL[1] and surrendered the editorship of the *Birth Control Review*,[2] after growing out of sync with the rest of the group. Three months later she gave a resignation speech at the Bryn Mawr Club in New York, announcing her intention to focus her work on reducing maternal mortality.[3]

The problem, Sanger had decided, was that the ABCL had "settled down." It had "the apathy which came from a fat bank balance," and had achieved the dubious honor of "being brought into the drawing room"[4] and run by "drawing room lizards."[5] She was ready to be free of it.

Turning the league into a well-run bastion of clubwomen had, of course, been a deliberate strategy on Sanger's part. The typical ABCL staff member, in the words of one volunteer, resembled "the best type of woman—those active in the Mother's Club and the League of Women Voters . . . [women] who will be extremely active and influential in the substantial conservative circles."[6]

The Colony Club, New York's most prestigious women's association, had at least nineteen members who were also in the ABCL, and the league had even relied on the Colony Club to use its enrollment lists for recruitment.[7] Now, after infusing the league with this well-heeled population and her husband's fortune, Sanger was ready to disavow what she had created.

A handful of events had made her realize the league no longer supported her unequivocally. There had, over the past year or two, been a series of pointed rebellions from Sanger's underlings at the ABCL. The league's nominal leader, Eleanor Dwight Jones, had criticized Sanger's continual emphasis on congressional lobbying as impractical.[8]

Then, while Sanger was in Europe stoking support for the World Population Conference, the ABCL had dismissed her friend Anne Kennedy, very much against Sanger's wishes.[9] Proclaiming herself "aghast"[10] at this insubordination, Sanger also suspected Jones looked down on her Irishness and bare-bones education.

When Sanger left the ABCL she managed to bring with her some of its most generous funders, including the Rockefeller-financed Bureau of Social Hygiene.[11] Now both leagues, the VPL and ABCL, seemed to have little hope of ever passing a federal law legalizing birth control. Still, Sanger made it known she had no plans to relinquish her leadership of the movement. As she wrote in her 1928 book *Motherhood in Bondage*, "My name has become a symbol of deliverance."[12]

. . .

Neither Sanger, who turned fifty in 1929, nor the debate over birth control were ingenues anymore. As Havelock Ellis wrote her, their once scandalous work had become a predictable talking point. "The BC movement was magnificent in its day and it is splendid that you should be its St. Margaret," he wrote Sanger, "but it is . . . though always important, quite dull and commonplace."[13] The venerable Charles Francis Brush, inventor of the arc light and pride of Cleveland, endowed a $500,000 fortune toward birth control research and advocacy.

By 1929, flappers were no longer outrageous. Breaking down the last generation's sexual hang-ups was no longer the winning formula for movies, plays, or the press. "Books about sex and conversation about sex," remarked Frederick Lewis Allen, "were among the commodities suffering from overproduction" in the late 1920s.[14]

Restraint was back in style. In the theater pages of the New Yorker, Robert Benchley practically yelled about needing a break from sex. "Sex, as a theatrical property, is as tiresome as the Old Mortgage," he wrote. "I don't care if all the little girls in all sections of the United States get ruined or want to get ruined or keep from getting ruined. All I ask is: don't write plays about it and ask me to sit through them."[15] The first book of prose by his colleague E. B. White, in collaboration with James Thurber, was 1929's Is Sex Necessary?, which poked fun at Freudian theorizing and the vogue for exhaustively parsing sex and relationships.

Sanger's letters to her husband suggest she was keenly aware of her status as a changemaker at the pinnacle, or, perhaps, just past the pinnacle, of her career. "A dinner was given for me tonight Upton Sinclair was at my right," she wrote Slee from Los Angeles. "Judge Lindsey brought me home."[16] Ben Lindsey was a judge whose popular 1927 book Companionate Marriage had reimagined coupledom with easy divorce, regular use of birth control, and generally less strife.

Meetings with Mary Pickford and Douglas Fairbanks were broached, but in the end Sanger was too busy, or at least that's what she reported in her letters. "I see so many people & seem to decide the fate of the cities," she mused. Fox Movietone News broadcast her to movie theaters nationally, speaking from a stage about the importance of birth control for public health and the national interest.[17]

Sanger and Slee were often apart. He still hated this, but when he protested she urged him to see their separations as his own personal sacrifice for the cause. "The movement now needs one dominating force to drive it to success," she wrote him. "Will you help me? . . . I can never believe that you have come into my life to hold me back, you who are so vigorous & glorious in your love & splendid in your ideals & generosity."[18] She enjoyed his letters far more than his proximity. It was an incompatibility that would last the rest of their life together.

Before this mismatch of expectations could erupt into conflict, however, Sanger was under attack from a very different direction.

. . .

On April 15, 1929, Sanger's downtown Clinical Research Bureau was raided by an eight-person plainclothes police squad.[19] Sanger had expanded the CRB four years earlier, moving premises to a brownstone. It had ample space that was divided into compact consultation booths and had operated with no notice from law enforcement for about six years.

As with Sanger's preceding clashes with police, the raid and ensuing trial comprised an engine of courtroom drama and newspaper publicity. But where the Brownsville raid had neatly erased the clinic from the neighborhood after less than two weeks' operation, the attempted shutdown of this clinic had a very different effect.

The raid was a tragicomedy. Detectives stalked the premises "like chickens fluttering about a raided roost," seizing sterilizers and medicine droppers at random and projecting a forbidding atmosphere.[20] They confiscated "the curio closet," a display of unusual or amateurish contraceptive devices patients had brought in for the clinic's assessment. More significantly, they took 150 medical records.[21]

Dr. Stone and the nurses stood impassively; patients sat hunched over and weeping.[22] When Sanger had the reasons for the raid investigated by a private detective, she learned many Irish, Italian, and other Catholic patients had recommended the CRB to neighbors and social workers. It had become such a standby that church leaders came to hear of it and conspired with police to shut it down.

Catholics held positions throughout the upper echelons of law enforcement. The head of the Policewomen's Bureau, Mary Agnes Sullivan, was put in charge of the raid, and an undercover detective, Anna McNamara, posed as a decoy patient, "Mrs. Tierney."

McNamara, a mother in her midthirties, walked into the clinic in late March. She struck Dr. Stone as "rather care-worn looking."[23] She said she was weaning her third baby, was found to have several conditions that would make another pregnancy hazardous, and accordingly received birth control instruction. That was enough to prompt the shutdown.[24]

Sanger now called on Morris Leopold Ernst, a forty-year-old civil rights attorney. Ernst was, as a *Life* magazine journalist would later write, "a smallish, darkish man whose birdlike eyes and manner belied his seeming physical solidity . . . [with] a general air of being about to take off."[25] Jewish, of German American parentage, he enjoyed socializing at the Algonquin Hotel and kept his Harvard rejection letter under glass in his office. (He'd gone to Williams instead.) In 1928 he had published an anticensorship book, *To the Pure*, favorably blurbed by Havelock Ellis and Aldous Huxley.

Ernst and Sanger had once shared a stage at a protest in Boston, and now, on Dickinson's recommendation, Sanger gave him a call for help. Describing himself, Ernst once said, "I'm a ham. I like publicity."[26] When he heard about Sanger's predicament, he agreed to take the case.

The day after the raid, April 16, 1929, Sanger was the honored guest at a "frolic" sponsored by the Ford Hall Forum. The Forum, a Boston educational organization, promoted the event with a poster reading "NO ONE ADMITTED UNLESS UNDESIRABLE." After Sanger had attempted to lecture in Boston in 1923, '24, and '25—being barred by the mayor each time—she got away with it this time, since the occasion was programmed as a satirical event and she never technically spoke.

Instead Sanger stood with a symbolic gag over her mouth, while the event's emcee, Arthur Schlesinger, read her speech before a crowd of about seven hundred. Her statement concluded, "As a propagandist, I see immense advantages in being gagged. It silences me, but it makes millions of others talk and think about the cause in which I live."[27]

On April 19, four days after the raid, the trial began, the proceedings witnessed by a five-hundred-person-strong crowd.[28] A surprising proportion were physicians. The raid, while futile from a criminal-prosecution viewpoint, encouraged doctors to Sanger's side in greater force than ever before. As a *New Yorker* journalist wrote, "The medical fraternity" hardly, collectively speaking, "[gave] a whoop about birth control," but they didn't like the trend of police charging in and confiscating private medical records.[29]

Physicians' interests compelled them to speak out. It was no longer so outlandish for them to be associated with birth control or an outfit like the CRB. As the *Times* asserted, Sanger was no longer a Socialist or an anarchist but the "leader in the fight for the dissemination of knowledge by physicians concerning birth control."[30]

The episode even prompted the New York Academy of Medicine to publish a friendly mention of the CRB in its journal and to officially proclaim and support the right of physicians to prescribe contraception for the cure or prevention of disease—the first open endorsement of this kind from the whole academy.[31]

Many physicians, however fervently they defended the CRB's right to operate unmolested by police, were still vague on what constituted appropriate, applicable birth control advice. In 1929 a prominent Nebraska physician on the Joint Committee on Maternal Welfare wrote, "One doctor in every eight in the country has written to the American Birth Control League for information. Over two hundred county medical societies, covering every state, have asked for talks on birth control."[32] This squared neatly with the letters piling on Sanger's desk complaining at physicians' refusal to give advice, or discovering their advice was bogus.

News coverage of the raid was almost universally incredulous. It might have been quaint if it hadn't been traumatic to patients. In the end it mainly served to boost publicity and support for Sanger's work. "Attempts to fight birth control merely advertise its possibility to the remaining members of the population who do not already know about it," remarked the *New Republic*.[33]

In *The Nation*, Dudley Nichols, then a fledgling screenwriter (he later wrote *Stagecoach* and *Bringing Up Baby*), noted, "How times had changed! This was not 1916."[34] Dr. Stone, when interviewed, thought it "fantastic"—"Only a few moments ago," she had told Sanger, "a visiting physician from the Middle West asked one of the nurses whether we ever had any police interference. 'Oh, no,' the nurse cheerfully replied. 'Those days are over.'"[35]

After two hearings, all charges were dropped and the police commissioner issued a public apology. Because birth control instruction at the CRB had been given in accordance with New York State law, which allowed contraception for the cure or prevention of disease—bolstered by Judge Crane's decision in the 1918 appeal for *People v. Sanger*—the prosecution was unsuccessful.

One courtroom spectator, the ABCL's executive secretary, Penelope Huse, wrote Ernst to congratulate him. The DA had shown "such a woeful lack of knowledge of anatomy and the sex functions," she wrote, "that one might almost have pitied him, unless one realized, as a taxpayer, that he was being paid by all of us."[36]

The fact that the trial had gone ahead at all was a glaring illustration of how determined and powerful Sanger's Catholic opposition could be. At that time, the CRB premises were owned by an Irish landlord. So, with support from Slee, the organization bought a five-story town house at 17 West Sixteenth Street in 1930. It would remain open there for forty-three years.

That spring brought a reckoning for Sanger's rival, too. Less than two weeks after Sanger left the Manhattan police court victorious, Dennett faced her own courtroom battle in Brooklyn, also defended by Morris Ernst—with very different results.

She had dared to admit that the sex union might be pleasurable; a fact universally known, but apparently unmentionable.

—Attorney Alexander Lindey in the
Birth Control Review (1930)

"I N THE YEAR OF OUR Lord 1929 a strange spectacle was to be observed in the hallowed Borough of Brooklyn of the City of New York," Ernst wrote in an essay about one of his most valuable clients.[1] That year, Mary Ware Dennett went on trial for obscenity.

For years, Dennett had been discreetly selling *The Sex Side of Life*, a slim pamphlet printed under a handsome blue cover. As journalism, scholarship, and pop-culture fanfare around sex ed ramped up through the 1920s, customers requesting *The Sex Side of Life* included physicians, clergy, educators, YMCA staff, and parents.

In his May 1926 piece "The Literature of Sex" in the *American Mercury*, H. L. Mencken praised Dennett's work as the single exception in a dispiriting genre. Most of the "disgusting treatises recommended to adolescents by Y.M.C.A. secretaries," Mencken wrote, "are written by prudes, and apparently for hogs." Dennett alone, he wrote, had "sound sense and decent thinking."[2] By 1928, *The Sex Side of Life* had gone through more than twenty small print runs, always financed by Dennett and her family. It was eventually translated into fifteen languages.

All the while, she quietly pursued legal channels to exempt *The Sex Side of Life* from suppression after it was officially banned in 1922.

First, she wrote to the lawyer Arthur Garfield Hays, a founding member of the ACLU. Hays had taken part in the Scopes trial, defending the right of a Tennessee high school teacher to teach evolution, and he would soon participate in the trials of the Italian anarchists Sacco and Vanzetti as well as that of the Scottsboro Boys. More relevant to Dennett, he had helped Mencken gain an injunction against postal authorities after the *Mercury* printed a story referring to prostitution. Hays thought Dennett's pamphlet was too risky and advised her not to pursue an injunction.

She put the idea aside for a year or two, then in mid-1928 she wrote to Ernst to see what he thought. Ernst responded enthusiastically, saying he was familiar with her work and asking whether she had "ever considered testing out the legality of the pamphlet in the court."[3] Dennett was intrigued.

Before they could plot any further, the trouble she was seeking found its way to her home address. Dennett received the envelope that held her federal indictment on January 2, 1929.[4] Though she and Ernst had started talking about provoking a test case, this came as a surprise, as the result of a good-faith sale. She had answered an inquiry from a Mrs. C. A. Miles of Grottoes, Virginia, but Mrs. Miles turned out to be a decoy.

"There is such a place as Grottoes, Virginia," Dennett later wrote of the episode, "but there is no Mrs. Miles. . . . The government even went to the length of having this little letterhead printed to serve its snooping purpose."[5] She'd been caught in a classic Comstockian trap.

Just the day before, on New Year's Day, Dennett had written her aunt Lucia to say that "nothing on the face of the earth will ever again tempt me into anything approaching a cause or an organization or a movement. I am as through with all those things as if I were dead." Instead she was absorbed in making *guadameciles*, "a new path," she wrote. "I may get lost, but I shall at least enjoy the wandering."[6] The indictment pried her out of her art studio and into the courthouse.

The first hearing was called on the frigid morning of January 7,

1929, the courthouse "jammed with the week-end collection of liquor cases," Dennett recalled.[7] Bail was set at $2,500.[8] Dennett spent the day in a holding pen alongside a woman arrested in a speakeasy raid who hadn't eaten for days.

The hours passed slowly. "The room was high but small," Dennett later wrote. "The windows were shut tight, and the air was foul. . . . The only water available was from a tank, below which was one muddy-looking glass tumbler, used by all and sundry. The adjoining toilet facilities were unspeakably horrid—no sex discrimination there."[9]

When Ernst arranged to get a chicken sandwich delivered to her, she could manage only a bite before giving it to the hungry woman beside her. Her bail was gathered from a small army of supporters, headed by the peace activist William Floyd.[10]

She returned to court January 21 and again on the 28th, wearing a blue dress and flanked by Carleton and Devon. (Ernst went in even more frequently, since his ultimately-successful defense of Radclyffe Hall's American publishers from obscenity charges was happening concurrently with the Dennett trial.) The courtroom was "crowded with an exceedingly interested audience," Dennett wrote.[11]

Judge Grover Moscowitz presided, a neutral and somewhat hesitant presence. The judge had called in a curious crew of experts. He'd invited three local faith leaders to share the bench and "aid the con-science of the court":[12] a Catholic priest, a Protestant Episcopal rector, and a Brooklyn rabbi, all of whom cast a sense of "solemnity," as Dennett recalled, over the proceedings.[13]

Ernst, donating his time on behalf of the ACLU, struck observers in the gallery as "young, vital" with "clear reasoning."[14] First he filed a motion to quash the indictment, which was denied. Ernst laid out a cogent argument against censorship, reminding the judge of Comstock's heyday, when works by Emile Zola and Walt Whitman were suppressed and Renaissance-inspired paintings covered with splotches of lamp-black. "If this pamphlet is obscene," Ernst declared, "then life itself is obscene."[15]

Assistant District Attorney James E. Wilkinson pushed to delay the trial. "This woman has had eleven [sic] years in which to find friends for the pamphlet," Wilkinson complained, "while I have had only a few weeks to find opponents."[16] A digressive debate on masturbation monopolized an hour or two. Since its first edition, the pamphlet had been revised to cast masturbation as perfectly safe. A scholar testified to the fact that the "most physically fit among Princeton freshmen" had masturbated daily since the age of thirteen.[17] The judge probed further, asking whether it did any actual harm; Wilkinson insisted it did.

Besides, Wilkinson continued, young people should have their sexual paranoia bolstered, not eased: they should "retain all their fears in order to keep themselves straight."[18] "Not one word in this about chastity!" Wilkinson scolded, the accent of his native Georgia carrying through. "Not one word about self-control! . . . Why, there's nothing a boy could see, on reading this book, except a darkened room and a woman!"[19]

The contrast in moral values between Ernst and Wilkinson neatly paralleled the split that now extended across the country between traditionalists and progressives. On Dennett's side, twenty witnesses had been called for the defense, including John Dewey, Robert Latou Dickinson, Katharine Bement Davis, and other distinguished figures from medicine, scholarship, and the clergy. There were gynecologists and psychologists alongside social workers, headmasters and superintendents alongside magazine editors.[20]

John Sumner of the New York Society for the Suppression of Vice sat slumped against the wall, beadily watching through dark-rimmed glasses.[21] Sweating, Moscowitz finally issued a decree that none of them would testify: it would draw too much publicity. Instead, he would accept a dozen letters from each side. Beset by other troubles—he was facing charges of misconduct in a separate incident—Moscowitz decided to temporarily retire from the bench and pass the *Sex Side of Life* circus on to another judge.[22]

The trial began on April 23 and lasted three days. Dennett didn't think much of the new judge, Warren Burrows of New London, Connecticut. He was appalled by *The Sex Side of Life* and didn't mind saying so. "The Judge told Ernst privately that he had never in his life before seen the term vagina in print and was inexpressibly shocked by my pamphlet," Dennett wrote.[23]

The jurors had been selected by a painstaking, depressingly unrepresentative process. All were men, and all but one were middle-aged or elderly. While the Civil Rights Act of 1957 would grant women the right to serve on federal juries, it wasn't until 1973 that every state passed concurring legislation.

Wilkinson dismissed any jurors who had read Ellis or Mencken. Ernst weeded out just one, who turned out to be a personal friend to Wilkinson. Reporters clustered, anticipating plenty to chew on.

Facing the indictment and consequent publicity left Dennett feeling alternately "benumbed or sardonically amused," she wrote Myra Gallert.[24] An editorial in the Elizabeth, New Jersey, *Times* predicted Dennett's case would "attract world-wide attention" and would "rival the 'evolution' [Scopes] trial in Tennessee, as a reflection on the intelligence of some of our judges and juries."[25] *The Nation* compared Dennett's hearing on charges of "sexological heresy" to the persecution of Galileo,[26] saying Wilkinson had given a satisfactorily fire-and-brimstone performance, his "flaming archangelic personality" in full effect.[27]

They were bruising days, but they did, on the other hand, include meaningful moments with Carleton and Devon, who lent Dennett their constant presence and loyalty. The press noted the "two tall young men who sat, quietly smouldering with anger, beside the bright-eyed, alert-minded little grandmother convicted of being a lewd and corrupt force."[28]

Dennett had little patience for the "little grandmother" description. She was also characterized as the "ever-rebellious daughter of a flintily intellectual New England house," which she allowed to pass without comment.[29] But too often, the papers fixated on the fact that she was a woman of a certain age. Though she was an energetic fifty-seven, Dudley Nichols described her in *The Nation* as "an elderly woman."[30] One headline ran, "Grandma's YWCA-endorsed sex pamphlet was found obscene."[31]

It was reminiscent of the way coverage of her divorce had reduced her to a sad suffragist and nothing more. When Dennett wrote to the *New York Times* asking the press to "let some of my accomplishments serve as an antidote to the 'silver-haired grandmother' emphasis which has been so excessively used," nothing changed.[32] As an editor at *The World* put it, Dennett's grandmotherly image "carried great weight with the newspaper reading public."[33] It made the story notable for its touch of the weird, turning her into an amiable-looking crone bent on ruining the young.

Though it wasn't much mentioned in the press, Dennett's case was a referendum on a precedent in English law often deployed in the United States called the Hicklin test. In *Regina v. Hicklin* (1868), the decision said obscenity was present if "any excerpt" of material had a tendency to "deprave and corrupt those whose minds are open to such immoral influences."[34] If a section of a book, no matter how it was taken out of context, was seen as likely to "stimulate sexual thoughts in impressionable minds," the work as a whole was classified as obscene.[35]

The imagined consciousness of the innocent reader—usually, in legal arguments, a sheltered young girl—had gone through several metamorphoses in the years since the *Hicklin* decision. Dennett hoped Judge Burrows's decision would show the world how far that standard had moved.

An avalanche of letters, both denunciation and praise, overwhelmed Burrows. Writing in support of the prosecution, several clergymen alleged that the pamphlet preached free love, birth control, and the breakdown of the family. Canon William Sheafe Chase, a Brooklyn Episcopalian minister and advocate of film censorship, blustered at

Dennett's glorification of female sexual pleasure, a rare moment of comic relief for some readers. Her elevation of the woman's physical enjoyment in *The Sex Side of Life* was "simply untrue," he wrote, "because, as my wife says, it is not to be mentioned on the same day with the joy of nursing one's own baby."[36]

Wilkinson read the entire pamphlet aloud, in a droning voice that became animated only when he considered he was reading corrupting material. Reporters noted the jury "blushed and squirmed" as anatomical terms were pronounced in court.[37] Summing things up, Wilkinson called Dennett a "polluter of the morals of young people," earning a wince from Carleton.[38]

Then came the defense and Dennett's own testimony. Ernst made a case that the pamphlet was itself practically an antique, nearly fifteen years old and not fully in tune with the significant change in the general attitude to sex that had taken place over the course of the 1920s. He showed comparable pamphlets issued by the American Social Hygiene Association and various government agencies, including the plainspoken *Sex Education* published two years earlier by the US Public Health Service.[39]

Dennett was instructed by the judge not to give any extraneous detail on the stand. The jury was solely concerned with whether she had mailed the pamphlet or not. Determined to work around this somehow, Ernst started rushing questions and Dennett piped up with responses before Burrows could sustain Wilkinson's objections. "Did you receive orders [for the pamphlet] from the Young Women's Christian Association?" Ernst said in half a breath. "Yes," she replied instantly.[40]

Ernst would not let the judge deliberately ignore the pamphlet's popularity. At the time of the indictment, more than 25,000 copies were in circulation.[41] Between April 1929 and March 1930, thanks to the publicity around the trial, another 60,000 were circulated via express delivery and booksellers, vaulting it from a labor of love and idealism to a source of meat-and-potatoes income.[42]

The ACLU's Mary Ware Dennett Defense Committee received over $3,000 in donations and held a support rally at Town Hall on May 21.[43] At that rally, a five-person committee was nominated to pursue anticensorship lobbying in Congress.[44] Sanger didn't come, but in the evening Eleanor Dwight Jones, the president of the ABCL, approached Dennett, clasped her hand, and said her league strongly supported her and also had come to support her legislative policy.[45]

More than a hundred of Dennett's supporters signed a copy of *The Sex Side of Life* and mailed it to President Hoover, in a gesture meant to make them all guilty of obscenity, too.[46] In one of the letters for the defense, Dewey argued, "Instead of being suppressed its distribution to parents and to youth should be encouraged. . . . Instead of being indecent I should have been glad to have my own children receive such information as a protection against indecency."[47]

In the end, the only written evidence submitted to the jury was the pamphlet itself. The bewildered Judge Burrows wouldn't admit any letters, or any evidence of the pamphlet's institutional uses, to be handed over.[48]

To get around this partway, in his concluding statement Wilkinson quoted the letters of protest (there had been eleven of them). One correspondent described the fate of a local young girl who had always loved babies. She'd learned about sex from a pamphlet, instructed a butcher boy in what to do, and now was pregnant out of wedlock.

In a separate incident, described in a letter heavy on hand-wringing and light on detail, an eleven-year-old girl accused a man of raping her, describing the act in detail. After a doctor examined her and questioned her further, she admitted she had made up the rape, after reading a sex education pamphlet.[49] The implication was absurdly cruel: it was better to keep children unable to name sexual acts, regardless of whether it would help them understand and resist abuse, because of the possibility that such knowledge might inspire imagined allegations. Sex education, clearly, gave young people inordinate and pernicious power.

The day of the verdict, Dennett came to court in a velvet coat and a small black hat bedecked with white flowers.[50] The jurors entered the jury room and three times voted without reaching a unanimous verdict. An attendant warned the jurors that since it was after five o'clock, they would soon pause proceedings and serve a "court supper."[51] Hastily, rogue jurors fell in line. Forty-two minutes after starting deliberations, they filed out and the foreman announced they had found Dennett guilty.

Ripples of disbelief ran through the court, turning to rage. The Rev. Dr. William Milton Hess, a pastor and Yale philosophy professor, cornered Wilkinson in the hallway and said, "In all my life I have never heard such medieval fatheadism and hot air as you spouted today."[52]

When reporters interviewed jurors, they found that many of them felt the judge had "practically directed" the conviction. When they asked Dennett what she would choose—a fine or jail term—she prepared and delivered a brief speech. "I shall not pay any fine, no matter how small, either now or later, nor shall I allow anyone to do it for me," she said. Later on, she said, "It is the government which is disgraced, not I."[53] Ernst immediately said they would appeal.

Mildred Gilman, a newspaperwoman known for covering the murders and scandals of the Roaring Twenties, got one of the most confiding quotes from Dennett: "The whole trial seemed like an Alice-in-Wonderland dream—too incredible to be true. Of course, the verdict was hard. One keeps a stiff upper lip in the face of such things, even though it is difficult."[54]

The *New York Times* reported the following day that Dennett was "quivering a trifle from the shock of the verdict . . . her two grown sons at her side," saying "she was at least glad most of the strain upon her was over." The reporter noted *The Sex Side of Life* had been circulated by the YMCA, used in the Bronxville school system, and endorsed by a wide range of health, religious, and civic agencies.

In the press, Burrows quickly emerged as the chief fool. Of the dailies, the *New York Times* and *New York Herald Tribune* covered it; the New York *World* joked the jury had been practically illiterate; the *Detroit Free Press* called Dennett's fate "A Medieval Verdict."[55] Columnist Heywood Broun of the *New York Telegram* wrote, "Quite evidently these mature men of Brooklyn [the jury] were afraid of sex. . . . The verdict seems so incomprehensible by any rule of reason that it is not fantastic to assume that it was rendered under some sort of terror."[56]

The magazines *Time, The Nation,* and *Woman's Journal,* among others, covered the case.[57] The *New Republic* connected the Dennett verdict with two other instances of censorship: the suppression of Theodore Dreiser's novel *An American Tragedy* in Boston and the NYPD's raid on Sanger's downtown clinic less than a month earlier. But compared with the other cases, "The conviction of Mrs. Dennett . . . constitutes a frightful injury not only to a principle, but to the children of the nation and to society itself."[58]

A few months later the magazine urged total tolerance of birth control, too: "Birth control is just as natural as listening in on the radio talking over the telephone, traveling in a train, riding in an automobile, flying in an airplane, writing on a typewriter, or with a fountain pen, sending a message by wire or by wireless, crossing the ocean in a steamer, or making use of any of the great inventions which have marked the progress of civilization for: ALL INVENTIONS ARE UNNATURAL [*sic*]."[59] Wilkinson never quite lived down his performance. When he resigned as assistant US district attorney two years later, a small notice in the newspapers announced, "Sex Book Foe Resigns."[60]

Sentencing was set for April 29. Dennett was fined $300, but stood in court and said clearly, "If I have corrupted the youth of America, a year in jail is not enough for me. And I will not pay the fine!"[61] The *Herald Tribune* noted the "hint of flame in her steel-blue eyes" and described her exit: "Jostled about in the corridors . . . Mrs. Dennett, hugging the bouquet of tulips and jonquils given her by the National

Suffrage Association . . . indignantly assailed the operation of the law."[62]

On June 10, in response to the Dennett trial, Representative Fiorello La Guardia of New York introduced a bill to allow sex education to circulate in "a medical or scientific publication or part thereof" or if it was "issued, approved, or circulated" by a federal, state, or local government.[63] It didn't go far, but was still a sign of solidarity.

Dennett's critics, meanwhile, did their utmost to ruin her good name. Horace J. Donnelly, solicitor of the US Post Office Department, reminisced about the 1922 incident in which the pamphlet had been originally declared unmailable, accusing Dennett of being "obviously designed to make money by appealing to mankind's lowest instincts."[64] Canon Chase took part in a public debate over the pamphlet's decency at a packed-to-overflowing Brooklyn YMCA against M. E. Kriegel, a lawyer and radio man, and was pronounced the winner.[65]

Dennett found this less objectionable than an event put on by Brooklyn's Werba's Theatre, which exploited Dennett's fame more creatively. The theater put together a stage and screen production of *The Sex Side of Life*, using Dennett's name and image, and for fifty cents, they promised "actual scenes showing everything" until one of Ernst's associates visited to protest. Despite the manager's pleas that "business [remained] very good," he agreed to drop Dennett's name and pamphlet from the show and its advertisements.[66]

Later that summer, speaking to a journalist, Constance Heck, Dennett described her hope for sex education in the future. She told Heck, "The time may come when sex physiology is taught in schools. It seems a little stupid, this present method of teaching children that humans have bones, muscles, nerves, blood circulation, digestive and respiratory organs, and omitting the fact that they have sex organs as well."[67]

She showed no remorse for offending men like Canon Chase: "I believe that the sex instruction of the future will include something regarding the technique of sex," she said. "The ill health of many wives is often due to ignorance on the part of their husbands as well as themselves concerning sex."[68] If nursing a baby was considered peak enjoyment, then indeed, sex education still had a long way to go.

. . .

Dennett's indictment and her alliance with Ernst created a surprising new dynamic: Sanger paused hostilities. The two women crossed paths in Ernst's offices one day and exchanged expressions of support and hope for federal birth control legislation in the coming years.[69] Two days after the late-May Town Hall rally for Dennett, Sanger wrote Dennett a sympathetic note saying she was "bound to win in the higher courts. I certainly hope so."[70]

The détente didn't last. In April 1929, Sanger had formed a new group, the National Committee on Federal Legislation for Birth Control. She served as national chairman, and then president.[71] By fall 1929, the committee had an office in Washington. The group's immediate priority, and Sanger's near-singular focus from 1929 through 1935, was the passage of the doctors-only bill.

Separately, Sanger's old league, the ABCL, was planning an early-winter conference at Times Square's Hotel Astor. This time, thanks to her comradely relationship with Eleanor Dwight Jones—whose own relationship with Sanger was still frosty—Dennett was invited.

The ABCL, Dennett surmised, was "pretty well disgusted with Margaret, for they have found out her unwillingness to put in hard sustained work on any program, and her insatiable desire for exclusive credit for all the work done by anyone else."[72] Standing to speak in the Astor's ballroom, Dennett could not contain a sense of unreality—especially when, during the resolutions session the following day, a motion to move the ABCL to "the Dennett policy" prompted lively debate.[73]

She began to dream of the ABCL's open defection from the

doctors-only path. She wrote Myra Gallert that it might even make sense for the VPL to disband and merge with the ABCL. In February 1930, she was convinced a public statement from the ABCL in favor of the clean repeal was imminent.[74] It never came.

The same month, Dennett wrote Sanger a letter laying her cards on the table. "You are now the *one* leader in the movement for federal birth control legislation," Dennett wrote. "I am out of campaigning for good. It is your move now, and the road is open and unimpeded."[75] She expressed hope Sanger would advance clean-repeal legislation despite her prior commitment to doctors-only. "I shall take genuine pleasure in supporting your work in every way possible, if you will now give me the chance to do so."[76]

Dennett's support had unacceptable conditions tied to it, but Sanger replied to acknowledge it was "nice to receive a cordial letter from you after all the years," and that she was "very glad to have this definite statement" that the VPL was out of Washington.[77] As she concluded the letter she wished Dennett well with her case, and sounded sincere.

Dennett was temporarily silenced, but acquaintances encouraged her to keep pushing. She'd been invited to speak to a birth control group in California by Sanger's disillusioned ex-friend Caroline Nelson—an invitation she declined only because she couldn't afford the trip.[78] The doctors-only bill, in Nelson's view, represented Sanger making "the greatest mistake of her life"; it was "one of the greatest insults offered to the American people. . . . It will turn every medical doctor into a voluntary policeman."[79] Nelson signed off saying, "Sex-education and birth control must go together, and there is certainly enough brain inside the skull of the American woman to carry it out successfully."[80]

Nelson's righteous ire buoyed Dennett, especially after word got back to her that Sanger was telling people a garbled version of their recent friendly exchange, saying Dennett now supported Sanger's leg-islative strategy and wished the doctors-only bill every success.[81] Later in the year, under the auspices of the near-dormant VPL, Dennett invited Nelson to join the legislative committee.

Nelson confessed to being done with activism—physically exhausted by it, as Dennett was—but being in cahoots stirred things up for both of them. Nelson admitted she sensed "some of the old spirit coming back," and Dennett felt the same.[82] "I do wish all manner of people and organizations had not told me 'confidentially' that they are for the clean bill and against the doctors only," Dennett wrote Nelson. "Sometimes I feel fairly bursting with the secrets."[83] One wonders what those secrets could have been.

In July 1930, between congressional sessions, Dennett wrote Sanger to urge the clean repeal yet again, saying the VPL was focused on "quiet, efficacious educational work among the leaders of opinion all over the country"—and that "interest in the clean repeal is bound to grow steadily, and that interest will inevitably be reflected in Congress."[84] Sanger withdrew from the correspondence.

Over the following months, Dennett pushed for an answer, only to be told by Sanger's secretary that she was in Europe.[85] Clearly, Sanger had returned to her earlier policy of ignoring Dennett whenever possible.

Sanger was, however, anguished enough by Nelson's endorsement of the clean repeal to write her old friend a short, poisonous retort. "It never surprises me to find you in the lead against me," she told Nelson. "So on with the dance, dear Caroline. Your opposition to a great truth does not make a ripple."[86]

Dennett's main indication of Sanger's renewed resentment was a painful incident with *The Nation*. The magazine scheduled a birth control–themed issue in 1930 and asked Dennett to contribute. But as it turned out, Sanger had donated $1,000 toward creating the issue, and when she heard of Dennett's involvement, she threatened to pull the money.[87] Quickly, the editors smoothed things over with Sanger and agreed to kill Dennett's piece. There would be no lasting truce; not yet.

. . .

Waiting for the appeal decision was excruciating, and Dennett needed to know her fate in order to finish her book, which she titled *Who's Obscene?* Stopes encouraged Dennett, telling her she was "coming into your own at last."[88]

The two friends had realized, after years of stop-and-start correspondence, that their letters sometimes went missing. It was happening too often to be happenstance: clearly, the American censors picked up on anything that bore Stopes's name. Dennett started sending her letters to "Mrs. Roe," using Stopes's husband's surname, and the disruptions ceased. "There is no doubt," Stopes concluded, "that my name on an envelope renders it liable to interference in your country."[89]

With their line of communication open again, Stopes, from her home in the English countryside, offered Dennett asylum if her appeal was not successful. A job and home would be ready for her in London.[90] Dennett loved the idea but rejected it. The only "square thing to do," she replied, was to "face the music whatever tune it may play."[91] She was too much of a stickler for rules and principles, and too engaged with her family, to leave willingly, no matter the consequences.

Between the initial verdict and appeal hearing, the Mary Ware Dennett Defense Committee grew from eight to over fifty prominent names. Still chaired by John Dewey, the group included Alice Stone Blackwell, Mary Phillips Riis, and Lillian Burton, a businesswoman. To Burton, Dennett confirmed that she had finally transcended her fear of fame. The indictment had become, in her mind, an "endurance test," worth the price of her privacy because it represented "not a matter that chiefly concerns my freedom from discomfort and unwelcome publicity, but a potential service toward freedom for everyone from government censorship and toward progress in sex education."[92]

To Ernst, Dennett's case had become "the most important in his career," according to one biographer.[93] Ernst's appeal was filed in September 1929, arguing that the "test of obscenity is a living standard. Any publication must be judged by the mores of the day."[94]

When it finally came to court on March 3, 1930, Dennett was acquitted. Judge Augustus Hand of the US Circuit Court of Appeals, cousin of the famed jurist Learned Hand, ruled that "an accurate exposition of relevant facts of the sex side of life in decent language and in manifestly serious and disinterested spirit cannot ordinarily be regarded as obscene."[95]

He disputed the Hicklin test, writing, "Any incidental tendency to arouse sex impulses which such a pamphlet may perhaps have, is apart from and subordinate to its main effect. The tendency can only exist in so far as it is inherent in any sex instruction and it would seem to be outweighed by the elimination of ignorance, curiosity, and morbid fear."[96]

As soon as Dennett heard the decision, she telegraphed Stopes. "I am just as glad as I can be," she told anyone who asked, "and not a little surprised."[97] She was too cautious to really celebrate, suspecting the government might appeal again. But although the government's attorney attempted to take the case to the Supreme Court, the solicitor general decided to let the Second Circuit's decision stand.[98]

Dennett's friends were jubilant. "I don't know when I have had such a spontaneous outburst of elation," Dewey wrote her. "I feel as if I had been let out of jail myself."[99]

The press had by now turned its focus elsewhere, as the full weight of the Depression began to lean on the country at large. Dennett, relieved and redeemed, turned to putting the finishing touches on her memoir of the trial, wondering if her ideas were finding their moment at last.

Drought, Grasshoppers, and Babies

The most frequent eternal triangle:

A HUSBAND . . . A WIFE . . . and her FEARS

Fewer marriages would flounder around in a maze of misunderstanding and unhappiness if more wives knew and practiced marriage hygiene. Without it, some minor physical irregularity plants in a woman's mind the fear of a major crisis. Let so devastating a fear recur again and again, and the most gracious wife turns into a nerve-ridden, irritable travesty of herself.

—Ad for Lysol in *McCall's* (1933)

THE GREAT DEPRESSION AND THE Dust Bowl turned babies into a national economic issue. For the average family, income shrank by about 40 percent in the four years following the crash.[1] Mass poverty and unemployment, in Sanger's words, "proved a marvelous boost for the birth control idea, although the new adherents are mainly interested in it from the economical angle."[2]

In a New Deal–era interview with the Farm Security Administration, one supervisor identified three major factors keeping American farmers poor: "drought, grasshoppers, and babies."[3] While the first two were seasonal, she warned about the "year round season of pregnancies" threatening to foil economic rehabilitation.[4] This was strong ammunition. Dennett wondered if Coolidge prosperity had worked against her.

For Dennett, who had no fortune to invest, the vagaries of the stock market mattered less than the grinding dearth of jobs in the early '30s. She remained financially unstable, as she had been for years, and, with jobs so hard to come by, her sons struggled to make a steady living, too.

Fundraising for birth control, which had always been chancy, became impossible. Donors she had once solicited every now and then, like George Eastman or Kate Crane Gartz, were either dead or too low on cash. Sanger also had far less funding for her work now, since Slee and Rublee both sustained heavy financial losses in the crash.

This scarcity had a silver lining, however. Sanger's speaking and publishing income became essential, a fact that relieved her of any obligation to be with her husband a moment longer than she wanted to.[5] Sanger intensified her lecturing and writing, and her sons both attended Cornell Medical College, the school she had once wanted to attend herself. She helped support them, especially the younger and more fragile Stuart, and also regularly sent money to Havelock Ellis.[6]

The purity movement fell on tough times, too. By the early 1930s, it had become glaringly clear that Prohibition, ratified in 1919, had done far more for bootleggers and organized crime than for public health or morals. This signal achievement of the purity crusaders had failed. Now, in lobbying meetings, birth control advocates used the terms "bootlegging" and "speakeasy" to refer to ways and means of obtaining contraceptives, arguing that banning birth control was equally unrealistic and detrimental as banning alcohol.

The reformist landscape in which Sanger and Dennett operated seemed to change almost overnight. Hunger was suddenly everywhere, a devastating spectacle, especially the hunger of children and their parents' accompanying helplessness. The humanitarian potential of family planning was now universally clear, and the moral arguments in favor of it began to carry more weight than those against it.

Dr. Hannah Stone wrote in the *Birth Control Review* in 1932, "A greater change in the temper of America toward birth control has taken place during the last two years than in the preceding decades."[7]

By 1933, American fertility rates fell below replacement level for the first time.[8]

Several factors fed into this, apart from contraception. Abortion rates rose sharply after the crash. In 1930, it is estimated that at least 800,000 American women terminated a pregnancy. (Just under 2,700 died from complications, which meant abortion accounted for one-fifth of the maternal mortality causes that year.)[9] Legally, contraceptives gained a small measure of respectability after the 1930 decision in *Youngs Rubber Corporation v. C. I. Lee and Co.*, which allowed contraceptives to be sent via interstate mail so long as they were legally prescribed.

Abortion remained illegal except in the minority of cases where it was deemed necessary by a physician and classified as a "therapeutic abortion." Among CRB patients from the Bronx, 25 percent admitted to having had an abortion, a proportion that ticked up between 1929 and 1931.[10] The Kinsey Institute would later find that among upper- and middle-class women, a similar proportion—24.3 percent—terminated pregnancies in 1930.[11] A physician-run study in 1938 found 28 percent of Black women interviewed (of a total of just 730) had had at least one abortion, slightly higher than the national average.[12]

Politically, of course, abortion was on far shakier ground than birth control. It was so unpopular that the active movement to legalize abortion was rarely even countenanced by birth control activists. A notable exception was William J. Robinson, who supported limited abortion rights in his 1933 book, *The Law against Abortion*, pointing to "the right of the woman to her own body" and advising it should be legalized through the first trimester, with exceptions for the "fourth, fifth, or sixth month."[13]

Dennett supported abortion, unambivalently but always in private. She had helped her sister, Clara, end a pregnancy and gently advised her friend Vine McCasland to do the same. In a draft of a book for young people that was never published, *Youth in the Life of Today*, she noted that an unwanted pregnancy forcibly carried to term was usually "disastrous . . . to all concerned."[14] But Dennett never spoke about it publicly with any hint of the tolerance she so clearly felt at heart, and she never sought to remove "abortion" from the Comstock Act along with contraception.

Sanger toed the same line. In her clinical work, she put her personal beliefs into exceedingly quiet practice. In 1932 she was called up to consult with a CRB patient, a young woman: due to marry in March, she had had sex with her fiancé in January. She then missed her period and went to a physician for a urine test—still a rare procedure—which came back positive for pregnancy. Her fiancé refused to marry her or visit the clinic with her, so she had come to the CRB.

Sanger was glad to refer her for a termination, but urged the CRB nurse handling the case, Marjorie Prevost, to be discreet. "I have been exceedingly careful," Prevost wrote Sanger, "did not even write Dr. Siegel's address for her but had her do so herself on a piece of blank paper."[15]

In time Sanger became firmer on her policy of never referring patients for abortions, conscious of the risk to the rest of the clinic's operations. When a staff member was discovered to be helping patients in this way in 1942, Sanger wrote to the clinic supervisor, saying, "Don't be too hard on her humanitarian spirit. It was not graft or for gain. . . . I'd be the last to throw a stone. Discipline must be kept—So in the supply room she goes."[16]

As poverty exerted its destructive pressure on ordinary Americans, faith leaders began to bend. The Depression pushed American Protestants toward accepting birth control.[17] The New York East Conference of the Methodist Episcopal Church and the American Unitarian Association had both endorsed it, and in March 1931, the Committee on Marriage and the Home of the Federal Council of the Churches of Christ in America, a Protestant coalition group, formally approved of it, too.[18] Their report stated that "the careful and restrained use of contraceptives by married people is valid and moral" and that "sex between husbands and wives as an expression of mutual affection, without relation to procreation, is right."[19] The previous year, authorities of the Church of England decided not to condemn birth control and pointed out it was too widespread to suppress.[20]

Catholics remained unmovable in their position, affirmed by their highest earthly authority. Pope Pius XI issued the encyclical *Casti Conubii* on December 31, 1930, asserting the righteousness and naturalness of patriarchy. "The man is the rule of the family, and the head of the woman," read the text, and an essential part of family life was "the ready subjection of the wife and her willing obedience."[21]

Birth control represented a "criminal abuse" and was "intrinsically against nature."[22] People had no right to use contraceptives, have abortions, be sterilized, or obtain a divorce; sexual intercourse belonged within marriage, and both required a total giving of the self, including an embrace of the risk of conception.[23]

States, likewise, had no right to sterilize citizens or deny marriage to them. The encyclical was so influential to lawmakers in the Republic of Ireland that contraception was made illegal in 1935, a ban that was overturned only in 1980.

In Massachusetts, historically a bastion of Irish Catholicism, birth control opponents rebranded the movement "anti-procreation."[24] Besides Monsignor John A. Ryan, one of the most prominent voices of the Catholic protest against birth control was Father Charles E. Coughlin of Detroit. From early 1934, Coughlin's radio lectures fixated on birth control as a symbol of moral decay and a means of turning marriage into "a legalized bed of prostitution."[25] In later broadcasts, he emphasized his fears that "Celtic" Americans would soon be outnumbered by Jewish, Black, and foreign people.[26] Within a century, "Washington will be Washingtonski" if birth control were legal, he warned.[27]

Where Ryan had paired his anti–birth control arguments with demands for a guaranteed living wage, Coughlin was more interested in a total social transformation, preferably with a fascist-style leader at the helm. The two priests hated each other, and their combative editorials occupied many column inches in the Catholic press in the mid-1930s, but they saw eye to eye on birth control.

Sanger knew there was no hope of persuading the likes of Ryan and Coughlin. She responded to *Casti Conubii* in an article in *The Nation*. There she noted the rise of the birth control movement in the United States, where Catholic women, at least those she had encountered at the CRB, "were showing a gradual but persistent spirit of independence."[28] Answering the charge that birth control frustrated the will of nature, she wrote, "The Pope frustrates nature by getting shaved and having his hair cut."[29]

. . .

Into these choppy waters sailed *The Rhythm*. If the pope had hoped to settle the matter with *Casti Conubii*, this book, by Dr. Leo J. Latz of Loyola University, Chicago, brought a blockbuster-bestselling complication.

Fully titled *The Rhythm of Sterility and Fertility in Women*, it was first published in 1932. Latz drew on studies from Japan and Austria that separately concluded ovulation preceded menstruation by twelve to sixteen days for the majority of women.[30]

Although it held some questionable science—for example, stating "extraordinary ovulation" could happen "under extraordinary circumstances . . . as for instance, in the case of adultery," and saying the rhythm method would not work "when used illicitly"—the rhythm method was specifically designed for Catholics, and it clarified how sex could be timed to avoid or encourage conception.[31] Thus family planning without actual contraceptives was to some extent possible, since Latz's fertility-awareness method proved more effective than any calendar-based systems that had come before.

The church first issued guidance based on cycles of fertility in 1853, after the theory that female ovaries release eggs according to a cycle (and not in response to sexual intercourse) first came into wide acceptance in the 1840s. Couples were permitted to abstain during the fertile period, according to that ruling.[32] Conversely, they were not required to abstain after menopause.

But with *The Rhythm*, Catholics were drawn into an even more nuanced debate. In Latz's view, "the procreation of children is not essential to marriage," and "there is nothing reprehensible in enjoying the pleasures of sex without having to bear the burdens ordinarily resulting therefrom, provided no violence is done to nature, no law of God is violated."[33] The flyleaf held the line "Published with ecclesiastical approbation," though it was repudiated by some Catholics, and it was the only birth control–related volume permitted by the postmaster general to circulate through the mail.[34]

By 1942, the book had sold 200,000 copies; companies began producing ten-cent calendars, wheels, and graphic slide rules to help track fertility. Despite all this, the Vatican would not accept the rhythm method until 1951.

Congressmen looked to *The Rhythm* with hope and relief. Wasn't this sufficient—was the sordid matter of birth control not settled? Why did they have to consider the availability of things like pessaries and douches in the first place? Sanger pushed back, saying women felt more desire during the fertile period and were generally more liable to "repulse the idea of relationship" during the "safe period."[35]

The book's appearance and influence helped people get used to the idea that it wasn't necessarily immoral to separate intercourse from procreation, though the church was still set against barrier or chemical contraceptives. As H. L. Mencken commented, "It is now quite lawful for a Catholic woman to avoid pregnancy by a resort to mathematics, though she is still forbidden to resort to physics or chemistry."[36]

More recently there have been glimmers that Catholic dogma is beginning to shift. In 1968, Pope Paul VI reaffirmed the church's stance against all forms of "artificial" birth control as "intrinsically wrong,"[37] but in 2022, the Vatican's publishing house released the book *Theological Ethics of Life*, which proposed that it was time for renewed dialogue about complex bioethical issues, including contraception.

A majority of American Catholics use birth control regardless. Recent studies, such as the National Survey of Family Growth of 2015–17, showed that among Catholic respondents, 92 percent of men had used condoms and 68 percent of women had tried the pill.[38]

The Rhythm was useful to Sanger, in that she set to work trying to provoke a test case to see whether the book was obscene in the eyes of the law. Throughout the mid-1930s, as her bill was repeatedly raised and killed in Congress, Sanger and Ernst were constantly either mailing or importing books and pamphlets to determine what exactly was deemed admissible under the Tariff Act, which in 1930 had adopted a section essentially quoting the Comstock Act in prohibiting the importation of contraceptives and contraceptive information.

Ernst was certain the test-case strategy would whittle the Comstock Act into oblivion far more efficiently than a legislative campaign.[39] In 1933 he and Sanger began planning to deliberately mail *The Rhythm* in the same package as a pamphlet or two by Dr. Stone. Sanger, Stone, and Ernst even started drafting a "dummy" pamphlet about birth control solely for the purpose of bringing it outside the United States and sending it back in, hoping to provoke the authorities.[40]

In the fall of 1934, a small, high-tempered woman, just landed in New York after a steamer trip from England, had her suitcase searched by customs officials. Her name was Hazel Moore, and she worked for Sanger. Her luggage held *The Rhythm* along with samples of new contraceptive products and books by Dr. Stone and Sanger: exactly the kind of provocative collection Sanger had planned.[41]

Latz's book was confiscated after a bumbling interview. The customs agent found several tubes with unfamiliar medical labels in Moore's bag, and took these too, saying, "We'll take these on the assumption that if you brought them in they must be contraceptives." She came close to laughing: "I also brought in tubes of toothpaste and cold cream," she told them. "Sure you don't want those? You can't tell what I might use them for."[42]

Nothing landed Sanger with precisely the kind of court case she was hoping for, however. Assistant Collector H. C. Stuart became a frequent correspondent, often sending a note to inform Sanger of yet further confiscations.[43] The authorities were, for now, satisfied with removing and destroying anything they didn't like. But they couldn't avoid a courtroom reunion with Sanger forever.

. . .

The Rhythm, intentionally or not, was part of a wave of books set to pry open the grip of censorship that had long kept books about sex and fertility out of the marketplace. In a way, with its careful description of the cycle of fertility, it had some substance in common with *Married Love* by Marie Stopes. That book, too, was now circulating freely.

After her acquittal and before parting from Ernst, Dennett had asked him to help lift the ban on *Married Love* in America,[44] and in 1931, he successfully represented the book's publisher, G. P. Putnam's Sons, in doing so.

In his ruling, Judge John Munro Woolsey stated that Stopes's book "may fairly be said to do for adults what Mrs. Dennett's book does for adolescents."[45] "I do not find anything exceptionable anywhere in the book, and I cannot imagine a normal mind to which this book would seem to be obscene," he wrote.[46]

Stopes was elated. While *Married Love* had sold more than 750,000 copies in Britain, she had been deprived of American royalties; only pirated copies had circulated there since the ban.[47] The same year, Stopes's book *Contraception* came before the court, again defended by Ernst, and was also pronounced decent, again by Judge Woolsey.[48] Dennett was "simply staggered" by that ruling.[49]

Two years later, Ernst was defending James Joyce's *Ulysses*. Once more, Woolsey ruled it wasn't pornographic. At the appeal hearing

Augustus and Learned Hand were both on the bench, and, drawing on the Dennett ruling as precedent, ruled: "It is settled, at least as far as this court is concerned, that works of physiology, medicine, science, and sex instruction are not within the [Comstock] statute, though to some extent and among some persons they may tend to promote lustful thoughts. We think the same immunity should apply to literature as to science, where the presentation, when viewed objectively, is sincere, and the erotic matter is not introduced to promote lust and does not furnish the dominant note of the publication."[50]

Analyzing the *Ulysses* verdict in 1938, the *Harvard Law Review* called the decision, which stemmed directly from Dennett's ordeal, "a new deal for literature."[51] It helped define our modern conception of literature as an art primarily concerned with creative innovation, emotional power, and social relevance, rather than reinforcing an existing moral code.

Sociologists, meanwhile, now took for granted the transformative potential of family planning and the fact that most people practiced it already. And the more privileged they were, the more options they had.

In 1929 the first volume of *Middletown*, a sociological study of life in a small American city between 1890 and 1925 by the husband-and-wife team of Robert and Helen Merrell Lynd, finally proved this beyond a doubt. *Middletown* was one of the greatest publishing triumphs of its year, reviewed on the front page of the *New York Times* and never out of print since. Its scope included chapters on earning a living, making a home, training the young, leisure, religious practice, and community activities.

The Lynds chose the title *Middletown* to suggest they had studied a profoundly average community. The real subject of their study was Muncie, Indiana, which in one particular way, at least, diverged from the average—its population was 5 percent Black, well above the national average. Yet the Lynds ignored the nonwhite population.

Their reason for studying only the "homogeneous, native-born population" was to investigate how class differences operated and how people pursued status. An overall effect of this decision was to make their portrayal more of a mythical evocation of "real America," with plentiful data masking the fundamental erasure that had happened.[52]

Their work did shed light on how family life was changing within their limited survey pool. The Lynds wrote about how men and women saw each other as two elements in a dichotomy, specifically how husbands spoke of women "as creatures purer and morally better than men but as relatively impractical, emotional, unstable, given to prejudice, easily hurt, and largely incapable of facing facts or doing hard thinking."[53]

They found most teenagers had access to a car, went to the movies weekly, and listened to the radio constantly. Religious observance was on the decline. People married earlier, became parents later, and were more likely to divorce than their parents had been. Among married couples, wives increasingly worked outside the home, but assumed full homemaking duties as well.

Muncie families had gotten smaller, from 4.6 per household in 1890 to 3.8 in 1920. The Lynds ascribed this to "the diffusion of knowledge of means of contraception."[54] Family planning access didn't apply equally across classes, however: it had a pyramid shape. "At the top, among most of the business group, the use of relatively efficacious contraceptive methods appears practically universal," they wrote, "while sloping down from this peak is a mixed array of knowledge and ignorance, until the base of ignorance is reached."[55]

After the Dennett appeal verdict, movie directors were ready to exploit the new public consensus that sex ed was part of good modern parenting. *Guilty Parents* (1934) joined the genre of the teen-exploitation film, prefaced by an intertitle that could have been drawn from the racier journalism around the Dennett trial. Movies had started talking, but moviemakers liked putting some noble text at the opening of an otherwise run-of-the-mill melodrama. "Foreword: sex ignorance, the black plague of adolescence, continues to augment the mass of ignorant youth in the abyss of despair. . . . Youth, caught in the current of flaunted worldly independence, demands not restriction, but instruction!"[56]

Guilty Parents opens in a courtroom, where a young woman is on trial. Because her mother deprived her of timely, sensible sex ed, she was seduced, fled Ohio for a big city, had an abortion, wound up in an unsuitable marriage, and was drawn into a blackmail plot. After one of her friends dies following a botched abortion, she kills a man.[57] It's a classic good-girl-gone-wrong story, with a sex ed pamphlet held up as a beacon of hope and protection.

The Hays Code went into effect later in 1934, suppressing any on-screen reference to sex hygiene, childbirth, or "sex perversions."[58] Afterward, radio was often less vulnerable to censorship than film. In November 1929, RCA's National Broadcasting Company (NBC) declined to cover the ABCL's conference.[59] The CEO of RCA, Owen D. Young, said birth control "was not yet ripe for introduction through the radio to the homes of America, available for any member of the family, of any age or condition, to turn on."[60]

But in 1934, the Federal Radio Commission was replaced with the Federal Communications Commission (FCC), which was more supportive of what it viewed as educational programming. In February 1935, Congressman Walter N. Pierce delivered a broadcast on NBC about birth control legislation; the next day a Newark, New Jersey, radio host conducted a radio poll on birth control, finding that about 95 percent of listeners supported it.[61]

Dennett wrote her way through the Depression. A year after publishing her memoir of the indictment and trial, *Who's Obscene?*, in 1930, she produced a sequel to *The Sex Side of Life*, titled *The Sex Education of Children: A Book for Parents*. She warned readers of conflating a high-status background with a healthy one, suggesting her willingness to ally herself with eugenics had soured. "It is among the folks of Anglo-Saxon background," she wrote, "that prudes and 'nice Nellies' of both sexes most abound."[62]

She loved to write. "There is no comfort on earth, I'm thinking, like some form of creative effort," she wrote an English friend, the journalist George Bedborough. "It is likewise a kind of misery,— lovely misery,—because one can never, never do one's very best. . . . Still, it is exhilarating to try."[63] Mulling over her ever-present money issues, she concluded poignantly, "I think most of my work will have posthumous value, if any."

When the government opted not to appeal her case to the Supreme Court, the ACLU's Mary Ware Dennett Defense Committee was reorganized as the National Committee on Freedom from Censorship, a cause Dennett would remain attached to for the rest of her life. A few days after Judge Hand's ruling, the ACLU sent a bulletin to members announcing rallies at local broadcasting stations, to capitalize on the momentum of Dennett's case and lift the ban on mentioning birth control on the airwaves.[64] The Detroit Free Press printed that Dennett's vindication had "torn the veil of Victorian cant from sex relationship and opened the way for the discussion of it on a scientific basis."[65]

Sanger was writing a new book, too. Hers embraced the form of a character-driven story, centered on herself, which always aroused in Dennett suspicion, distaste, and a powerful desire to rewrite it in her own words.[66] Sanger's My Fight for Birth Control was published in 1931. It received lavish publicity and critical praise but was, like her other autobiographical works, selective with the facts. It barely mentioned Dennett, only retelling the episode in which Dennett, speaking for the NBCL, had declined to support Sanger in her Woman Rebel trial.[67]

This book, contrasted with Dennett's Birth Control Laws, reflects the unbridgeable gap between the authors' points of view. Dennett's book emphasized the importance of principles over her own individual perspective, "with the idea that most thinking, well-meaning people want our laws to represent . . . justice and practicability; and that they want them to harmonize with our heritage of American ideals of freedom and self-government."[68] Sanger instead provided a David-and-Goliath narrative with herself as the embattled heroine.

William J. Robinson, always touchy about his own importance to the movement, reviewed Sanger's book viciously, calling it "false and lopsided," quibbling with the fact that she mentioned his own name only twice when "I started my B.C. work at least ten years before she did," calling her a "not very cultured nurse," and indicting her desire "to be the whole pooh-bah."[69] In conclusion, "the crown of martyrdom sits badly on Margaret's head. She *never* fought alone, and *she* never bore the expenses of the fight."[70]

A few weeks earlier, Robinson had bought a ticket for a dinner hosted by Sanger in honor of H. G. Wells, which he seems to have endured solely for the purpose of making poisonous comments about it later. "The thing was a flop," he huffed in an article. "Mrs. Sanger made some platitudinous, egoistic remarks that she has made a hundred times before, and Wells was so hoarse that his words could be heard only with the greatest difficulty." The meal itself, he reported with deliciously petty detail, was cheap and unsatisfying ("*pea soup* [not even a fruit cocktail or melon], *lamb, salad, ice cream* and *demitasse*"). He observed, however, that "the Birth Control cause has certainly become respectable, for at the speakers' table we had a princess, a grand duchess, the wife of a cabinet minister, besides some professors and reverends."[71]

Despite the public panic over the Depression, Sanger was a highly public persona in 1931, aided by her new book's publication and allies in the press. The *New York World-Telegram* ran a story by Ruth Millard praising Sanger's "wit and eloquence," her "inspired shrewdness," the way "[her] mild blue [*sic*] eyes blazed with the light of martyrdom," and how "[with] a fiery belligerence that transformed her frail, modest prettiness, she struck out at her persecutors."[72]

She had become practically an establishment figure in the eyes of the press and public. "Opinions about Margaret Sanger are much gentler than they used to be," noted another journalist, Mildred Adams.[73]

She stringently maintained her presence as "small and slender and shy she is, looking not at all like one's preconceived idea of a great woman leader. She is too slim and too essentially feminine."[74]

"One does not look for dynamite in baby blue frocks," commented another reporter in 1933.[75] Yet Sanger had enough firepower left to use the crisis of the Depression as best she could—in Washington.

The few bits of public service which I have made a stab
at have always seemed to me like errands that needed
doing by somebody or other. . . . Ambition for achievement
seems more and more to be satisfying to one's soul, when it
is a part of the general concept of being alive as a human
being, a part of an alive universe, in which one tries to be
an active element, however small.

> —Mary Ware Dennett to Missouri civil rights
> activist Fannie Frank Cook (1938)

AFTER HER ACQUITTAL IN 1930, journalists besieged Dennett,
trying to turn her time in the spotlight into an extended drama.[1]
Her desk became a clearinghouse for the general public, too: people
needing sex advice, abortions, or a chance to vent marital and familial woes, and those seeking feedback on their manuscripts.[2]

An old friend asked her to resell a "thingamajig"—in this case, an
intrauterine device with two prongs—that "worked O. K. But it hurt
me so like the dickens having it yanked in and out (not to speak of the
bother and expense) that I've decided to fall back on the old and well
known preventives."[3] A pharmacist asked her for instructions for the
contraceptive devices sold in his own store.[4] She was offered contracts
for product endorsements, lecture tours, and even vaudeville.[5]

When Dennett looked at her days, she was flooded with what she
described as the "joyful misery of seeing ahead endless worthwhile
things to do, and going to bed each night with the list even longer."[6]
She spent considerable time referring people to one of Sanger's clinics
or suggesting they read Dr. Antoinette Konikow's books. Money was

still tight, but she secured a $5,000 loan from her friend Evelyn Marshall Field, then married to the heir of a department-store fortune.[7] When she could, she turned to her *guadameciles*.

Stopes kept prodding her friend to return to lobbying, but Dennett stayed firm. Solitude and privacy were more precious to her than they were to Stopes or Sanger; one of her pet remarks to friends was, "If they have committees in heaven, I won't stay there."[8]

Vonie now needed daily care, and she lived with Dennett in Astoria. But Dennett and her sister, Clara, had a secret. After years without contact, their brother, Willie, whose health had been frail since childhood and who had vanished into the Midwest decades earlier, had resurfaced in 1928. He was in Ohio, in such fragile mental and physical health he was confined to a hospital, as Dennett saw when she made a quick visit by train.[9] They thought it would be too troubling for Vonie to know, so for now, they kept quiet about Willie.

As usual in the summer, much of New York seemed to melt away. For Dennett, this was the season when Vonie went to stay with Clara outside Boston. In other words, it was the closest thing Dennett had to a holiday. Carleton and his wife, Catherine, had a baby daughter now, Nancy, Dennett's third grandchild. Catherine, she wrote, "had the baby beautifully. . . . No stress, no complications, nothing but the maximum of happiness and the very minimum of pain."[10] But the Depression soon took Carleton's job, and when Hartley offered the young family rent-free use of part of his New Hampshire property, they went.[11]

In solitary hot-weather moments such as these, Dennett sometimes shopped around her fiction. Her short story "A Middle Class Mother's Day" had been kicking around her desk for a decade. Instead of putting her own name on it, she wrote in the initials I. C., which she used for several of her unsigned pieces.

The story is a "slice of life" of a privileged but servantless mother going about her day: cooking, tidying, tending to her sons and dog, paying bills, corresponding with a charitable program committee, and drafting a suffrage talk. At the end she falls asleep in the dark, "a little nap, before I start in doing these things all over again." Everything is done in short bursts, with no chance to focus deeply on anything. She wonders, half-conscious, "if this kind of thing will long be considered the normal thing for mothers." She doesn't mind her life, but she suspects "fifteen or twenty years of it would successfully prevent me being either a good mother or an intelligent woman."

She knows she has it easy—"Thousands, if not millions of American women are doing just this kind of thing, many of them under far less tolerable conditions than mine." But she is stumped as to who will push for systemic change when most mothers were "too busy by day, and too sleepy by night, to get their heads together and plan a way out? I wonder."[12] Dennett had submitted the story to Collier's, Harper's, and the Woman's Home Companion, but it was universally rejected.

Such projects helped ward off an insistent sadness—"The blue devils get me," she once confessed to Vine McCasland.[13] Writing, art, music on the radio, the sense of her mother resting peacefully in the next room, her window-box flowers—these brought some comfort and true purpose. But, as McCasland wrote her, "being a work-horse is an insidious thing. One forgets how to play, or is very clumsy at it. I think the two of us need to get into a fine rage at life, Mary, and break up the furniture, instead of plugging along straining at the yoke."[14]

· · ·

When Sanger returned from Europe, she decided that she would give Washington another try. She'd heard and absorbed Ernst's doubts. Sanger had a new strategy, however. Whereas the birth control movement had been shoehorned in with the campaign to eradicate syphilis and gonorrhea twenty years before, now Sanger attached the cause to the government's panic over "relief babies."

Despite the continuing national trend toward smaller families, high fertility among the poor and the resulting public expense was a matter of browbeating in the papers and in politics. Politicians and psychologists alike disdained "the modern woman . . . who has short hair and short skirts, painted cheeks, lips and eyebrows, who understands how to steer a motor car, but not how to guide her children."[15]

President Hoover himself blamed "ignorant parents" and "ill-constructed children" for declining national morals. In a radio address, he mused, "If we could have but one generation of properly born, trained, educated and happy children, a thousand other problems of government would vanish."[16] The judgment was implicit—no generation he'd seen yet had been "properly born."

Lawmakers felt increasing pressure to do something about all these "ill-constructed" babies. Just as they had done during the anti-immigration panic a decade earlier, eugenicists stepped up to say it was time for the government to have a firmer hand in planning the population. Large broods of "unfit," "unproductive" children haunted the rhetoric of fiscally conservative politicians and pro–birth control reformers alike.[17]

As she had in the past, Sanger tried to take advantage of eugenicists' political clout to further her goals for birth control. In a 1934 hearing she presented striking numbers: birth rates for families on relief were nearly 50 percent higher than for families with an employed breadwinner.[18] Was birth control not the logical answer? This angle was received with more friendliness in Congress than any humanitarian argument, and Sanger held out grand hopes for what it could achieve.

But now another means of fertility control was in favor: sterilization. The widespread popularity of compulsory sterilization programs among white, able-bodied voters created a political tailwind for the eugenics movement. At a local Woman's Civic League meeting in Pasadena in 1930, the eugenicist Paul Popenoe gave a talk titled "Outstanding Results in Sterilization for Human Betterment"—and the crowd liked it. Sanger was in attendance; reporters took note and were disappointed not to hear her speak as well.[19]

Popenoe himself never warmed to Sanger. He called her league "a lot of sob sisters, grandstand players and anarchists" and urged the American Eugenics Society to avoid getting involved with any kind of "lunatic fringe," clearly of the opinion that birth control was more an "ornament" to eugenics than a comparable movement.[20]

Instead he threw his support behind sterilization, which he deemed more conducive to preserving white supremacy. "If charity begins at home, Birth Control should begin abroad," he wrote. "Continued limitation of offspring in the white race simply invites the black, brown, and yellow races to finish the work already begun by Birth Control."[21] Popenoe's version of the birth control movement called less for individual rights than for government mandates aimed at creating a whiter population.

When he praised the German sterilization program, which was implemented in July 1933 and permitted the forced sterilization of Germans with disabilities, Popenoe was joining a chorus of authoritative American voices. In a favorable review of another eugenic text, the *New York Times* outlined a worldview many white readers saw as reality, their "eventual submersion beneath vast waves of yellow men, brown men, black men and red men, whom the Nordics have hitherto dominated . . . with Bolshevism menacing us on the one hand and race extinction through warfare on the other."[22]

In early 1932, Sanger lectured on "My Way to Peace," sponsored by New York's New History Society, a speech that exposed her thinking on eugenics at that moment. She spoke of keeping immigration closed to the "feeble-minded, idiots, morons, insane, syphiletic [*sic*], epileptic, criminal, professional prostitutes." She idealized a "stern and rigid policy of sterilization," and the segregation of already-tainted bodies, as well as those of "illiterates, paupers, unemployables . . . [and] dope-fiends" to "farm lands and homesteads where these segregated persons would be taught to work under competent instructors for the period of their entire lives."[23] In Sanger's pitch to this audience, women's health was now a minor part of her plan, at least the version she brandished in public, which instead prioritized protecting Americans from "hereditary taints."[24]

These were widely accepted ideas among white American voters, considered practical, sanitary solutions, not yet tarnished by their association with Nazism. One 1935 ad in the Boston *Transcript*, sponsored by the Birth Control League of Massachusetts, read: "TAXPAYERS! Nearly a quarter of a million children were born last year to families entirely supported by you through public relief. Our organization exists to help those parents have only those many children as they can support. Will You Help Us Do This Preventive Work?"[25]

In Pennsylvania a more chilling version read, "Nobody Wanted Jimmy . . . But He Was Born Anyhow . . . And Died Three Weeks Later." It went on to tabulate the costs to taxpayers of supporting Jimmy's brief presence on earth, which, after prenatal appointments, a hospital birth, and the funeral, was about $300.[26]

Like the "welfare queen" of the 1980s, the "relief baby" of the 1930s was a myth bent on doing damage, a pretext for an insecure, ill-gotten authority to seize more power.

. . .

Bureaucracy, hostility, and moments of desperate hope characterized Sanger's 1931 congressional lobbying campaign, just as they had Dennett's—though Sanger was better staffed and better funded, and commanded greater press attention.

At just past fifty, Sanger was described by a *New Yorker* journalist as "one of those harmless, meek-appearing little women whom wise men are wary of arousing. With her soft, dark eyes and the absence of dash in her attire she seems about as dangerous as a little brown wren. Perhaps you have noticed, however, that her full, firm lips press shut in an upward curve . . . the expression of one who bites off nails with all the amiability in the world."[27]

When Sanger was given a chance to describe herself, she muted the militant aspects of her character. "I am merely the mother of three children with a message to mothers," she said after a lecture in Detroit.[28]

She easily admitted to reporters that she could be prickly. "They'll tell you I'm hard to work with, and I'm afraid they're right," she told journalist Mildred Adams, adding that she never joined clubs or went to teas.[29] "Margaret was rather like a lion tamer," her longtime friend and colleague Dorothy Brush once told an interviewer. "She kept us each on our boxes until she needed us—then we jumped and jumped fast. Weeks might go by without a word from her. Then perhaps a telephone call and I had to be down at 17 West 16th Street in an hour."[30]

In Congress, just over a decade after Dennett's first lobbying season, Sanger found more nervous hesitation than open scoffing—which was progress, at least. She faced skirmishes elsewhere, however. In May 1931, she took the train to Atlanta to take part in a debate, "Should the Federal Laws Be Changed?"

Her opponent, Richard B. Russell, chief justice of Georgia's supreme court, was a fiery, white-bearded father of eighteen who seemed determined to work a kind of exorcism on Sanger. She was impressed by the way he "flam[ed] with rage," but also noted specimens like him were growing harder to find. "I always welcomed a debate," she wrote, but over time "it had been almost impossible" to find someone willing to share the stage with her and argue against birth control.[31]

She wrote that senators and representatives were by contrast "full of fears—fear of prejudices, fear of cloakroom joshings, mainly fear of Catholic opposition."[32] Determined to keep Catholic constituents happy, they dismissed news that the Methodist Episcopal Church had joined the ranks of the Unitarians, Universalists, and Jewish communities in approving birth control as a part of marriage, followed by the Presbyterian General Assembly in the spring of 1931.[33]

Still, Sanger cleared the first hurdle beautifully: Senator Frederick H. Gillett of Massachusetts agreed to sponsor the doctors-only bill. Kicking off her first legislative season that year, Sanger printed "The Mothers Bill of Rights": "Parenthood when it is responsible can be a noble trust, a proud commission—an honored assignment," she told her readers, "and this can be accomplished only by taking it out of the sphere of accident and placed into the sphere of conscious responsibility."[34] Though the bill died in committee, the hearings were lively, packed with senators' wives and journalists, with supportive testimony from clergymen, eugenicists, and the Junior League of New York.[35]

Dennett learned of the Gillett bill three days before the hearing, and decided to speak out against it.[36] She sent an open letter arguing for a clean repeal to Sanger, Gillett, and the Senate Judiciary Committee, and she forwarded it to influential contacts, including the editors of the *New York Times*, *The New Yorker*, *The Nation*, and several others.[37]

Ten days later, Sanger wrote to her in anger, sending a terse note she redrafted several times. Dennett's arguments were "unbelievable . . . incredible," she began. "Most people who received your confusing, unsportsmanlike letter agree that if you are out of the running, why not stay out and give others a chance to win out. You had your day, you had an open field, and we are still cleaning up the messy confusion in Washington as a result of the 'Open Bill.'"[38]

She leaned on a formidable group for support. The board of directors of Sanger's National Committee included Slee; Rublee; Henry Pratt Fairchild, a sociologist and eugenicist; Rabbi Sidney Goldstein; and one particularly valuable asset: Katharine Houghton Hepburn, the namesake—and mother—of the famous actor.

Hepburn came to the campaign from Connecticut, which had some of the nation's most stringent "little Comstock" laws. Coincidentally, she had relatives in Sanger's hometown of Corning, New York, but there, the similarity between her background and Sanger's ended. Hepburn was related to the head of Corning Glass Works.[39] Sanger's sister Mary had cleaned house for a time for Hepburn's aunt and uncle.[40]

Hepburn had gone to Bryn Mawr, married a doctor, moved to Connecticut, and had six children: a predictable path for a woman of her social class. When her sister, Edith Houghton Hooker, joined the Society for Sanitary and Moral Prophylaxis with the aim of helping society transcend what she called "the dark ages of sex," Hepburn was pulled in.[41]

She and her husband sympathized with the focus of the social hygiene movement on outdoorsy physical health. She didn't ally herself with Sanger right away—it is unclear when and where they first met—but over the years, they developed a close and enduring friendship.

Sanger had an aunt-like bond with Hepburn's daughter Kate, the budding film actor.[42] In 1933, Kate Hepburn starred in *Christopher Strong*, the story of an aviatrix who becomes pregnant by her married lover. Released months before the Hays Code descended on the film industry, *Christopher Strong* was directed by Dorothy Arzner, one of the only women who succeeded both in Hollywood's silent era and in the talkies.

Kate Hepburn enjoyed telling the press of her own support for the birth control movement and her mother's work for the cause. "My mother is important," she liked to say; "I am not."[43] When Sanger wrote Katharine Houghton Hepburn a thank-you note for her daughter's courageous stance, the reply read, "I'd have spanked her if she hadn't."[44]

Dennett had won over her own powerful supporters, including Ernst,[45] William J. Robinson, and much of the ABCL.[46] But while the public was more likely to recognize her name now, more people knew her for her anticensorship battle than for her birth control work. That was firmly Sanger's domain. *Time* magazine covered the Gillett bill's hearing and misstated that Sanger had been behind the Cummins-Vaile bill, too. The editor later told Dennett the error had actually been deliberate, because "in the eyes of the American public Mrs. Sanger *was* the movement, and naturally everything that happened was credited to her."[47]

A few individuals came out in support of Dennett merely as a means of tearing down Sanger. In response to Dennett's open letter,

Robinson sent her a note of encouragement, which mainly consisted of bitter words about her rival: "I feel," he wrote, "that the time has come to stop pussy footing (you won't like that word, and perhaps it is not exactly right) to M.S." He decried "her inconsistencies, her back treading, her determination to keep clinics etc in her own hands" and praised Dennett's "amazing way of never actually hitting her and yet making the blows fly rather close."[48]

Puzzlingly, Dennett could not internalize just how far she had alienated Sanger at that point. According to her confidences to Stopes, she thought her coercive messages to Sanger were "quite sensible" in "forcing her to the realization that the clean repeal was the thing she better learn to want."[49] She wrote to Sanger yet again, at length, reiterating all the hazards of keeping contraception in the Comstock Act, and justifying her continued activism by saying, "I shall never be out of the running as a responsible individual citizen, who is keen to have laws which are decent, unhypocritical and enforceable."[50] She'd transferred her obsessive energy from lobbying Congress to lobbying Sanger.

In the most artful letter of that early-1931 campaign, she conjured a vision of the Sanger she wanted to see, the Sanger of her earliest acquaintance: "I vividly recall the day back in 1915 when you lunched with me at my apartment, and the shine in your eyes when you talked of your determination not to rest till people had the knowledge and help they needed and birth control was rescued from indecency. I do earnestly want to see you swing back to that fine fervor."[51]

Her final plea blended sincerity with something less positive: "Forget, please, that you have not liked me any too well. Forget about everything except your big opportunity as a leader. You and I are in totally different positions. I have never had any ambition or bent toward being a public character. You are that by force of personality and the course of events. I shall be only too glad to help you if you will rise to your present chance to be both big and true, and my help will be quiet in proportion as your stand is forthright and steadfast."[52]

Immediately after reading this, Sanger drafted a reply, which may never have been sent. The version in Sanger's archive is typed, with a scrawl over it, dated just a day after learning the Gillett bill had been killed in committee: "I cannot bother now to reply."[53] Sanger was determined to remain civil. Regarding Dennett's line "you have not liked me any too well," she wrote, "I disagree with that emphatically. . . . Repeatedly I have said 'If M W D & I had been friends & co workers we would have won hands down on bc long ago,' I still believe that to be true."[54]

She glossed over her deep-set dislike of Dennett, which she had made clear to Rublee and Selincourt (and Stopes), among others. Presumably the only feasible grounds for them to work together would have been if Dennett had had a drastic change of heart and come over to Sanger's league to promote Sanger's bill, fully accepting Sanger's authority.

Sanger too remembered their first meeting, but wondered that "with all the fire of an idealist *you* did not back me up. . . . You called me 'Radical' 'Red' 'Bomb thrower,' 'free lover.' . . . I was as you have repeatedly told to strangers not so clever as you, & with not the same background." On the other hand, she wrote, Dennett lacked practicality and instead clung to a "political quality of mind." It was not a compliment, and, as Sanger concluded, placing herself and Dennett in opposition, "Politics & Science do not see eye to eye just yet."[55]

. . .

In 1932, a change in politics brought new hope to Sanger and to the movement. "So we are on our way!" Sanger wrote Havelock Ellis after Franklin D. Roosevelt won the presidency that November.[56]

She had never agitated for a presidential candidate before—her son Grant quipped that she didn't give "a damn who was President of the United States," and she voted for Norman Thomas, a Socialist, until he stopped running—but had to admit the new Roosevelt administration was promising.[57] Eleanor Roosevelt had even served on the ABCL board before her husband became New York's governor in 1928.[58]

Though Eleanor Roosevelt's initial public support proved controversial in the press and her policy was now to stay silent on birth control, Sanger pushed for an alliance.[59] In September 1933, she spoke at a dinner honoring Eleanor Roosevelt at the Exposition of Women's Arts and Industries, calling for a "new deal" for women through legalizing birth control.[60]

The paradox between birth control's position in society and its legal status drew journalists to try to explain it. In the February 1932 *New Republic*, James Rorty wrote, "Public opinion today accepts birth control and in the middle and upper classes it is very generally practiced."[61] Lawmakers would not accept birth control, he theorized, until it was a *"fait accompli . . .* If it is done, we shall be entitled to consider ourselves almost as civilized as, say, Holland, about fifty years ago. Would it be worth while?"[62]

He pointed out birth control's gradual incursion into medical-school curricula. Out of sixty-seven reputable medical schools surveyed by Dr. S. Adolphus Knopf in 1930, fourteen now had courses on fertility control, twenty-eight gave "incidental instruction which was considered inadequate," twenty did not touch on it at all, and four covered sterilization but not contraception.[63] Rorty laid most of the blame for birth control's failure in Congress at the feet of physicians as well as social workers, calling out "the tragic inertia" of both professions.[64]

Sanger's committee asked the first woman senator elected to a full term, Hattie Caraway of Arkansas, to sponsor her bill in the next legislative session. Caraway had replaced her husband, the irascible Thaddeus Caraway, whose argument with Dennett a decade previously had included his challenge, "If you want to make everybody prostitutes, then go ahead." Hattie Caraway was interested in birth control, she confessed to Sanger, but "her secretary would not let her touch it" for fear of losing credibility with voters.[65]

As she worked the halls of Congress, Sanger solicited messages of support from a wide array of experts: not just doctors and clubs but also military surgeons, anatomists, ophthalmologists, even zoologists. It didn't seem to matter much. In many of their meetings in Washington, Sanger's lobbyists found congressmen on both sides of the aisle settled into mulish opposition.

Representative Charles A. Eaton, Republican of New Jersey, said he was "in favor of killing half the population and keeping the other nine-tenths from being born."[66] Representative John C. Lehr, Democrat of Michigan, had sat "back in his chair with thumbs hitched in his suspenders" and proclaimed, "As a member of this Committee I want to go on record there have never been any contraceptives used in my home. I have six children too."[67]

In late May 1932, the bill had another hearing. Hepburn gave opening remarks, Sanger gave the main address, and her statement was followed by supporting testimony from two public-health experts, a rabbi, and Charlotte Perkins Gilman. The discussion got mired in the question of whether the purpose of douching was primarily contraceptive. Writing to a social worker friend afterward, Sanger noted, "Oh Mary you would love to see the look on the mens faces (17 in the Ways & Means Com in the House who sat & listened for 2 1/2 days) when I replied to pertinent questions & talked about 'douches.' . . . Poor darlings they wanted to escape but they had to sit & listen to what women endure."[68] Sanger tried to stick to eugenics-based arguments, and was rewarded a few months later when, in 1933, the American Eugenics Society finally endorsed birth control.[69]

Dennett, now sixty, maintained her behind-the-scenes campaign going strong. Aside from keeping close tabs on news regarding the Lindbergh baby kidnapping—an event that had mesmerized her, perhaps because she, too, had lost a beloved baby boy—she wrote again to influential voices in Congress, philanthropy, and the press, still objecting to the bill, liberally mailing out copies of her book *Birth Control Laws*.

She asked Bruce Bliven, the editor of the *New Republic*, to write an editorial supporting clean repeal. He declined, saying he agreed with her in theory but "things have now gone so far that unanimous support of a half-way measure is better than a quarrel in the ranks which will only lend comfort to the enemy."[70]

This view was echoed in other responses, notably by Dewey—a defection that sorely disappointed her—and Michael Davis, the medical director of the Julius Rosenwald Fund. Davis, an important funding channel for the birth control movement, found Dennett's behavior nonsensical and stated, "In a word, even though I have the appetite for a whole loaf of bread, I am willing to buy half a loaf provided, as I believe is the case in this instance, the half is sound quality."[71] Dennett again wrote to Sanger, urging her to move over to a clean repeal and assuring her she would "gladly *give you all the credit*."[72] Sanger never responded.

Undeterred nearly to the point of mania, Dennett intensified her protest.[73] In the fall session she wrote to the president to plead for clean repeal, and in February 1933 she issued letters to magazine editors about it again.[74] She sent warm notes to activists who had worked with Sanger asking them to wire her and ask her to switch over to the clean repeal.[75] When occasionally someone replied, as Bliven did, to suggest Dennett ought to be pragmatic and throw her support behind whichever bill had a chance, she sent lengthy letters of self-justification.

In time Sanger blamed the government's "impenetrable wall of inertia and subterfuge" for the way her bill had failed to progress.[76] Her committee had persistently negotiated meeting after meeting only to be brushed off by senators claiming to be "old fashioned."[77]

More frequently now, anticipated unrest in Europe was cited as another reason to defer. In Germany, Adolf Hitler had just come to power. "When war is in the air," Representative Effie Wingo, Democrat of Arkansas, told Sanger's colleague Hazel Moore, "we cannot consider something that cannot come about for years."[78]

Sanger returned home to Fishkill in frail health after the bill died in committee yet again. Maybe after all, as Ernst kept telling her, it was time to change course and pursue her goal through the courts.[79] But first, she had some business to tie up in Harlem.

The white world is feverishly anxious to know of our thoughts, our hopes, our dreams. Organization is our strongest weapon.

—Jessie Redmon Fauset (1921)

ON WHAT WAS OTHERWISE AN unremarkable Saturday in February 1930, a clinic opened its doors on Seventh Avenue near 138th Street, within sight of Harlem's Abyssinian Baptist Church. Inside, visitors could find stacks of free pamphlets about family planning. A few curious souls came to read them, or quietly packed them into their purses.[1]

If they asked for an appointment, patients were examined by Nurse Antoinette Field and her assistant Mrs. Margaret Ensign, who were both white, even though the neighborhood was predominantly Black.[2] After examination, women were given a diaphragm and spermicidal jelly and shown how to use them.

Later that same year, as women began trickling into the Harlem CRB, a Black newspaper, the *Pittsburgh Courier*, ran a serialization of the novel *Bad Girl* by Viña Delmar. The protagonist, Dot, becomes pregnant and seeks an abortion.

"The hospitals are wide open to the woman who wants to have a baby," Dot is told, "but to the woman who doesn't want one—that's a different thing. High price, fresh doctors. It's a man's world, Dot. The woman who wants to keep her body from pain and her mind from worry is an object of contempt."[3]

Though set in Harlem, *Bad Girl* was about a working-class white couple. The book had been a surprise bestseller two years earlier, another startling literary specimen of 1928. Its publishers marketed it simultaneously as pulp and as something more serious. First it was banned in Boston—at that point practically a literary badge of honor—then the Literary Guild made it its monthly selection in April 1928. Delmar was the youngest author to achieve that honor.

She was twenty-three, white, with the bobbed hair and waspish wit of a practiced vaudeville performer, which she was.[4] Her career trajectory overlapped with Anita Loos's. Both wrote novels and screenplays packed with social commentary deftly stitched onto a plot that could just about be packaged as frothy melodrama. They told women's stories, with slightly edgy implications about the power dynamics between the sexes.

Why was the Black press boosting *Bad Girl* in 1930? It was entertaining, and sure to draw readers with its treatment of risqué topics like maternal ambivalence and abortion, but the novel's rerelease coincided with another development. Where Harlemites had previously had to travel a full eight miles to go over contraceptive options and techniques at the downtown CRB, now Sanger had come to them.

This new branch of the CRB had been eight years in the making and, in the early '30s, after the birth control movement had ascended into familiar and long-established territory, its significance for people of color became the focus of fraught debate.

Black authors had long been the authoritative voices on Black motherhood in society, the stakes of which Dennett and Sanger could hardly understand. In the "New Emancipation"–themed October 1919 issue of the *Birth Control Review*, the story "The Closing Door" by Angelina Weld Grimké depicts a young Black woman, married and yearning to be a mother, overjoyed to discover she is pregnant.

Then she hears the news that her brother has just been lynched.[5] She begins to be suspicious of her own joy, and winds up overwhelmed by the conviction she is simply "an instrument of reproduction!— another of the many!—a colored woman—doomed!—cursed!—put here!—willing or unwilling!—For what?—to bring children here—for the sport—the lust—of possible orderly mobs."[6] After giving birth, she smothers her baby with a pillow. Grimké's story was powerfully, tragically timely; its publication came just after the "Red Summer" of 1919, when white supremacist violence erupted in more than thirty cities, from Georgia to Arizona.

Grimké, a Black great-niece of the white reformers Sarah Grimké and Angelina Grimké Weld, had woven the same theme into her 1916 play *Rachel* (originally titled "Blessed Are the Barren"). "The white women of this country are about the worst enemies with which the colored race has to contend," Grimké's script reads. "[But] if anything can make all women sisters underneath their skins, it is motherhood."[7] In the spring of 1916, in Washington, DC, *Rachel* became the first American play written by a Black person and performed by an all-Black cast for an integrated theater audience.

In the first act of *Rachel*, a young Black woman sits with her family and listens as her mother confesses that on that day, ten years earlier, her first husband and one of their sons had been lynched. Suddenly, Rachel's aspirations toward a family of her own start to seem naive. "Everywhere, throughout the South, there are hundreds of dark mothers who live in fear, terrible, suffocating fear," she thinks, "whose rest by night is broken, and whose joy by day in their babies on their hearts is three parts pain."[8] Critics praised the beauty and power of *Rachel*, but noted its pessimism.[9]

That pessimism was amply justified. Black people lived much closer to death than their white neighbors. In June 1932, the *Birth Control Review* bore the title "A Negro Number." In his article "Quantity or Quality," George S. Schuyler noted, "The Negro death rate is twice as high as that of the white people; the death rate from tuberculosis is three times as high. There are 100 per cent more stillbirths among Negroes than among Caucasians. . . . The Negro expectancy of life is only 45 years as compared with the Caucasian expectancy of 55 years. In other words, Negro health is just about where white health was 40 years ago."[10] In Mississippi, maternal mortality among Black women was actually increasing; it stood at 10.9 per 1,000 Black mothers compared with 6.6 for whites.[11]

While the bodies of Black women were depicted in eugenics polemics and much of the white-run media as if they were dangerous and disposable, people of color debated fertility control in a very different light. They had no guarantee of the freedom to give birth with the same degree of safety and comfort as white people did, to feed their children and secure them opportunities for the future, and to get healthcare that didn't try to suppress their fertility.

That guarantee of equal access to healthcare is still far from becoming a reality. According to the Centers for Disease Control, Black women in 2023 were two to three times more likely than white women to die from pregnancy-related complications, and they were also more likely to experience life-threatening postpartum conditions like preeclampsia and hemorrhage.[12] After Mississippi passed a 1928 sterilization law aimed at "persons who are afflicted with hereditary forms of insanity that are recurrent, idiocy, imbecility, feeble-mindedness or epilepsy," and yet another sterilization law in 1964, thousands of Black women were sterilized without their consent well into the twenty-first century.[13] Fannie Lou Hamer, an activist and herself a survivor, called the procedure a "Mississippi appendectomy."[14] Unlike an appendectomy, however, these surgeries were done without any health-related justification and without the patient's consent.

In 1922 members of the Harlem Community Forum first approached Sanger about opening a branch of the CRB in their neighborhood. It took nearly eight years, with a failed attempt in 1924 at opening a clinic in a mostly Black neighborhood near Midtown,[15] but eventually a new clinic grew out of her meetings with that influential advocacy group.[16] Besides the Harlem Community Forum's invitation, Sanger was also solicited in 1929 by leaders at the Hope Day Nursery for Colored Children, run by a group of Black women who wrote her that they'd heard a rumor a clinic was coming and wanted her to know they thought it would be "of untold value" to the people of Harlem.[17]

The same year, Sanger met with members of the New York Urban League and Harlem Social Workers Club to discuss opening a new branch of the CRB.[18] Planning moved forward efficiently, helped by influential community voices and funding from Caroline Bamberger Fuld, of Bamberger's department stores, and Julius Rosenwald.[19]

In tracking this series of meetings and collaborations, the issue of Sanger's alliance with the eugenics movement comes to mind. Could she have been personally motivated to control the Black population? Eugenics, after all, was an inherently racist ideology, and she was at that point a long-standing ally of the eugenics movement.

Sanger certainly never declined a donation from anyone who supported population control for racist reasons, and she willingly accepted a speaking engagement with the KKK's women's auxiliary. Her ease and enthusiasm when it came to promoting eugenics, especially antidisability eugenics, indicate she personally believed what she was saying.

In Sanger's own speeches and writing, her emphasis when it came to birth control for eugenic reasons dwelled consistently on "defectives": on disabilities, not race. Such ableist and morally compromised words glare at us today, unsurprising yet disturbing, impossible to excuse or brush aside. Planned Parenthood, the organization directly descended from Sanger's clinics, took her name off of a Manhattan clinic in 2020, citing her troubling embrace of eugenics. More recently, politicians calling for abortion bans point to Sanger's racism in their arguments: "The abortion industry has nefarious roots in hatred and racism. Margaret Sanger, the founder of Planned Parenthood, was a eugenicist who systematically targeted 'inferior races' for decades," claimed Ohio state senator Michele Reynolds in the fall of 2023.[20]

Yet it is also true that Sanger designed studies and services that supported women of color. While she was still involved with the Harlem branch, Sanger wrote to Norman Himes, a sociologist, to refute what the majority of white physicians claimed—that people of color had no interest in or aptitude for using contraception correctly. Instead, Sanger wrote, "negro women learn the technique of procedure with greater ease and facility than does the average white woman," according to Harlem clinicians.[21]

She was convinced the reason had more to do with social factors than race, especially the "intensity of the desire to apply contraceptive knowledge effectively."[22] Her readiness to publicize a study that was contrary to "common knowledge"—and to try to make a white male professor reflect on the bias that permeates that category—indicates she had the energy and intent to try to change at least one of the racist narratives around her.

Then there was the actual clinical work, the slowly accumulating stacks of case files and steady distribution of diaphragms. Sanger's endeavors in Harlem, and later in the South, brought direct and tangible benefits to the community and little profit to Sanger herself. Seen through this lens, it makes sense that the Harlem Community Forum a century earlier did not hesitate to invite her into the neighborhood.

Sanger initially knew little of Harlem. The neighborhood had the largest concentration of Black people in the United States, and their numbers were growing: between 1900 and 1940, Manhattan's Black population grew from about 60,000 to more than 400,000.[23] More women than men participated in the Great Migration, and consequently women made up an outsize share of new Harlem residents.

In 1900, in New York City, there were 124 Black women to every 100 men.[24] Many were domestic workers, hard-pressed to afford large families even if they wanted them. In 1920, 80 percent of Black women in America cooked, cleaned, or did laundry for a living.[25] Prior to the new clinic's opening, a few women traveled from Harlem to the Greenwich Village CRB, but the vast majority could not take the time off work or away from their households.

When Black servicemen returned from Europe after the First

World War, many of them came to Harlem. Harlem was, of course, a cultural mecca as well, and it was flooded with thousands of white clubgoers from all parts of the city every night of the week. The lively neighborhood, with new high-rise buildings packed with families and newcomers and cultural heavyweights, swelled.

Jazz and civil rights, poetry and the blues, painting, sculpture, and journalism: in the Harlem Renaissance, the lived experience of Black people was central to both art and activism. But political—and medical—institutions lagged behind the cultural flourishing of Black New York, and thus several local groups had decided to court Sanger.

At first, despite the fact that the new clinic was open seven days a week, it was sleepier than expected. In areas like Harlem, drugstores were plentiful and anonymity relatively easy to come by. Women were accustomed to handling things themselves. They could buy Vaseline and quinine to be placed over the cervix, and Puf, a powder-and-applicator product, was promoted as "marriage hygiene" with the tagline "End Calendar Worries Now!"[26]

It was the same in other cities: the *Pittsburgh Courier* ran ads for solutions, jellies, powders, and suppositories that promised to destroy "foreign germs."[27] The Baltimore *Afro-American* listed pencils, nails, and hatpins as common tools, while the *Birth Control Review* noted the widespread rural practice of drinking turpentine.[28] City dwellers were also more likely to seek out a doctor-administered abortion, though this was so expensive it was common practice to instead end a pregnancy at home, using household implements.

Between February and November, the clinic saw 742 patients, only about half of whom were Black.[29] As members of the advisory council pointed out, the Black community was suspicious—with good reason—of a white-run birth control organization attempting to target Black patients specifically. The word "research" in the CRB's name evoked doubts about what kind of research or experimentation was being done on patients.[30]

Black women's sexuality and maternity were flattened in white culture, which perpetuated the Jezebel and Mammy stereotypes and contributed to a pervasive theory in the white medical establishment that Black women were not responsible stewards of their own fertility.[31]

"Reproductive liberty must encompass more than the protection of an individual woman's choice," wrote the sociologist Dorothy Roberts in 1997, in her landmark book *Killing the Black Body*. "It must encompass the full range of procreative activities, including the ability to bear a child, and it must acknowledge that we make reproductive decisions within a social context, including inequalities of wealth and power."[32] As soon as the birth control movement sought an alliance with eugenics, Roberts points out, race became an integral part of the birth control discourse.[33]

Most Black Americans didn't have positive or long-lasting experiences with the medical establishment to begin with. One of the immediate impacts of the Flexner Report back in 1910 had been to shut down several of the medical colleges that admitted people of color. In the late 1930s the proportion of physicians who were Black hovered between 2 and 3 percent of the total.[34]

People of color anticipated that white clinicians and activists would doubt or minimize their experiences. Sanger's colleague Hazel Moore described how one woman had come to a 1937 rural outreach event "carrying in her arms and tugging at her skirts her five children who had walked 'a good piece' to get to the birth control advice."[35] When someone asked why she hadn't left them with the neighbors, she answered she'd brought them as "my evidence" so that she could "get [that] control."[36] She'd been so accustomed to having her concerns dismissed that she came armed with flesh-and-blood proof, hiking miles with five children, to back up her case.

Much of the pro–birth control propaganda in the Black press came from men, who assigned to Black parents a "duty to help uplift the race."[37] Specifically, this meant raising and educating children who could attain the trappings of middle-class American life. Smaller families were thought to have a better chance of getting ahead. In 1932, the Black New York newspaper *New Amsterdam News* printed an editorial answering concerns about Sanger's racism: "This branch was not opened in Harlem as a segregation measure, but rather to suit the convenience of Harlem wives. . . . When we have healthier and fewer babies," the editor wrote, "our mortality rate is going to decrease and we, as a race, will be offered better rates in the various insurance companies."[38] This may read like a strangely bloodless argument to us today, but at a time when insurance companies charged Harlemites high fees based on the neighborhood's dismal health data, it mattered.

The Reverend Adam Clayton Powell Jr. of the Abyssinian Baptist Church welcomed Sanger, brushing aside the cult of "false modesty" around any topic linked to sex.[39] For the Mother's Day service in 1933, Sanger stood in the church to deliver a "sermon" titled "Is Motherhood Sacred?" The clinic also revised its pamphlets to include a section explaining the difference between contraception and sterilization, emphasizing that birth control is "merely a temporary means of preventing undesired pregnancies. It never affects the ability of the mother to have children when she so desires."[40]

W. E. B. Du Bois had long been enthusiastic about the birth control movement. As early as 1922, he wrote in *The Crisis*, published by the NAACP, that while "marriage and birth control are still slightly improper subjects" among middle-class Black readers, "few women can bear more than two or three children and retain strength for the other interests of life. And there are other interests for women as for men and only reactionary barbarians deny this." Du Bois then argued for controlled intervals between pregnancies, to "allow for the physical, economic and spiritual recovery of the parents."[41]

He saw early on what eugenic sterilization policies would mean for Black Americans. State-sanctioned, compulsory sterilization programs would "fall upon colored people and it behooves us to watch the law and the courts and stop the spread of the habit," Du Bois wrote in 1936.[42]

A vocal countermovement, headed by Black Nationalist leader Marcus Garvey, distrusted the birth controllers and urged Black people to reject their gospel. Birth control interfered with the course of nature and the will of God, Garvey argued.[43] It was inherently complicit in a larger campaign by white people to monopolize power, including the power in high population numbers. Black motherhood was a profoundly meaningful calling, elevated and blessed, in a world that kept trying to destroy Black bodies. In Garvey's vision—which had greater popularity with men than women—birth control was akin to genocide.[44]

By 1933, the uptown CRB had moved a couple of blocks away to a New York Urban League property, integrated its staff, and started gaining trust in the neighborhood. On Dr. Stone's recommendation, the suggested fee was decreased from $5 to $1. The clinic's books showed that more than 90 percent of patients there did not pay the full fee, and more than half of Black patients were not required to pay at all.[45]

A survey that year compiled visitors' assessments of how birth control had affected their lives. "Our home relationships improved"; "I'm not so nervous"; "I used to become pregnant once every year before using it, no more fear of this"; "First year in 13 of marriage I've not had baby or miscarriage"; "We both enjoy relations now"; "I now feel free"; and "My salvation" were some of the answers.[46]

After operating the uptown CRB for four years, Sanger had a better handle on whom the Harlem clinic really served, and in what numbers. The clinic saw around one thousand women annually, equally divided between Black and white.[47] The average first-time visitor had been married for seven years, nearly all were mothers already, and most reported having sex around twice a week. As with the downtown clinic, the prevailing reason for a visitor's failure to follow up was lack of time, childcare, or carfare.[48]

There were clear differences between Black and white patients' circumstances. Among the Black clients, each family had an average of four children, as opposed to three for the whites. The age of first pregnancy was more likely to be in the early or mid-teens.[49] Preferences for birth control differed. In white families, men were more likely to use withdrawal or condoms. Black women were more likely to take charge of it themselves, relying often on postcoital douche.[50] And, as in other surveys, this one showed that the likelihood of maternal or infant mortality among Black families was twice as high as among whites.

One of the most illuminating articles in the *Birth Control Review*'s "Negro Number" came from a Black social worker, Constance Fisher. She reported family case workers were fielding requests for birth control information more and more often, as women who had once felt guilty or ashamed no longer did. Couples were hard-pressed to make ends meet, pregnancy scares fueled resentment, and relationships dissolved due to the stresses of "constant pregnancy," Fisher noted.[51] Social workers in Harlem found themselves referring clients to Sanger's clinic with increasing frequency.

In mid-1935, with the clinic's finances in trouble, the ABCL took over management. After a brief closure, it stayed open for another rocky decade.[52] A Black nurse, Mabel Staupers, who eventually became the head of the National Association of Colored Graduate Nurses, wrote Sanger a frank letter protesting negative interactions she'd had with ABCL representatives. She hoped both Sanger and birth control reformers generally would "discontinue the practice of looking on us as children to be cared for," pointing out, "I feel that we should be treated with the proper courtesy that is due us and not with the usual childish procedure that is maintained with any work that is being done for Negroes."[53]

Staupers's words should have been broadcast to public-health authorities well beyond Harlem. Far away in Tuskegee, Alabama, three years earlier, the US Public Health Service had launched its study of syphilis in Black men. None of the six hundred people being studied knew the true purpose of the experiment: to track the progression of untreated syphilis. Over the course of forty years, even after straight-forward treatment for syphilis with penicillin became protocol in the 1940s, none of the men were treated, regardless of worsening symp-toms, spread of disease, deaths, and children born with congenital disease. The Tuskegee syphilis study has today become a historical monument to the brutal consequences of racism in medical research.

Sanger replied to Staupers to say she was "utterly shocked" to hear that dynamic was present at the Harlem clinic, but by then it was out of her hands and she abandoned the issue.[54] She had gone back to Washington one last time.

Margaret, don't try to get a law changed. You'll never get a
law changed. You've gotta get it reinterpreted.

—Morris Ernst to Margaret Sanger (1935)

I N FEBRUARY 1935, MARGARET SANGER put on a satiny evening dress and threw a party in a grand dining room in Washington: the Birth Control Comes of Age Dinner. Katharine Houghton
Hepburn, flanking her for much of the night, was more sober in a
shirtwaist and tie. Charlotte Perkins Gilman sent a poem; the novelist
Pearl Buck stood to speak.

With high color in her cheeks and flowers pinned to her dress,
Buck told a crowd of seven hundred that a "final triumph" was "coming and coming quickly"[1] for the birth control movement. "And in
that future to come," she told the assembled listeners, "people will
be astonished, as we are now astonished, that the things for which
Margaret Sanger fights should ever have been opposed or wondered
at or taken for anything else than a matter of inevitable human
right and reason. The time will come in our country, as it has already in countries older and wiser than ours, when birth control
and the dissemination of scientific birth control knowledge will be
a commonplace."[2]

Their bill had died in congressional committee again a week
earlier. Its failure seemed freshly nonsensical at a moment when a
panel of American scholars had just named *Married Love* one of the
most important books of the past fifty years, along with Freud's *The
Interpretation of Dreams* and Marx's *Capital*.

Women were traversing gulfs and boundaries, both literally and in the ranks of public power. Nineteen-year-old Gertrude Ederle of Manhattan, slathered in grease and snacking on chicken legs, had set a new record for swimming the English Channel in the summer of 1926—not just as the first and fastest woman, but the fastest all-round. A Black woman, Mary McLeod Bethune, was a leader in Roosevelt's unofficial "kitchen cabinet" and advised both the president and Eleanor Roosevelt, at the same time that a white woman, Frances Perkins, was appointed to the cabinet, in 1929. In 1932, Amelia Earhart flew solo across the Atlantic.

"Feminism," in 1933, made its debut in the *Oxford English Dictionary*, as "the opinions and principles of the advocates of the extended recognition of the achievements and claims of women; advocacy of women's rights."[3] The following year, a group of seventeen women organized by the Austrian feminist Anna H. Askanasy drafted the "International Manifesto of Women: A New Proclamation of Rights, by Women." This ten-page typescript was foundational to the Women's Organization for World Order, formed in Geneva in 1935. The "masculine civilization in which we live is on the point of breaking down," the manifesto announced. Women were on the cusp of seizing control of their collective destiny, playing a greater role in public life and working toward a more equitable, peaceful world.[4]

In Washington, Sanger did her utmost to link birth control to other social policy talking points at every turn. By now, membership of her National Committee was substantial and growing. Over the course of the Depression, the committee grew from one thousand in 1931 to about fifty thousand in 1935.[5] At the American Conference on Birth Control and National Recovery, a well-attended Washington event in January 1934, some sessions attracted nearly a thousand listeners.[6] Earhart was one of the featured speakers.[7]

Compulsory sterilization had been a pressing issue at that conference. The governments of the United Kingdom, Sweden, and Poland were considering passing laws requiring individuals with specific conditions thought to be inherited, including the broad designation of mental incompetence, to be sterilized, and Sanger boosted the idea of the United States doing the same.[8] Several states had already done so, and in time more than thirty created their own sterilization laws.

Under Nazi Germany's eugenic sterilization law, which first passed in July 1933, qualifying conditions included intellectual disability, schizophrenia, blindness, deafness, syphilis, epilepsy, alcoholism, and "asocial elements," which included homosexuality. People who were Roma and Afro-German were targeted, too.

By some estimates, about four hundred thousand people were sterilized under the Nazis, dwarfing the scale of other nations' campaigns several times over. American eugenicists, at least for the first decade or so, looked on agog. One state hospital superintendent summed up the early prevailing feeling after the law went into effect, telling a reporter, "The Germans are beating us at our own game."[9] Sanger was troubled by reports of sterilization on grounds of faith or ethnicity, but she still felt winning over eugenicists was essential to getting her bill passed.

The morning after the January conference ended, Sanger and Hepburn marched, surrounded by supporters, into a hearing for their bill. The room quickly filled past capacity, so the meeting moved to the House caucus room, which soon filled up, too. Father Coughlin, the Detroit "radio priest," showed up to protest; Hepburn, genteel and poised with her hat set at an angle, fought back.[10] Still, it didn't pass.

The National Committee yet again brought its bill to a Senate Judiciary Committee hearing in March 1934. Sanger took this as an opportunity to frame contraception as a branch of medicine, not a new medium for free speech, as Dennett had. "It is just the same as the 10-cent pair of glasses in a 10-cent store. That is no way for people who need to have them to have glasses fitted," she told assembled congressmen. "We want this subject [contraception] removed from the 10-cent store and the gasoline stations and placed in the hands of those who are qualified in every way to explain the relations of parenthood properly."[11]

Despite her bill being repeatedly "smothered" and shuffling sponsors, Sanger came breathtakingly close.[12] In April 1934 her bill actually passed, before being recalled fifteen minutes later by Senator Pat McCarran, Democrat of Nevada and an observant Catholic. Sanger, needing a change of scene, booked steamer tickets abroad.

She toured Russia and northern Europe that summer. Besides her dissatisfaction with Washington and ambitions for the global birth control movement, there was a third reason Sanger was tempted to leave America on at least a semipermanent basis: her husband. In mid-1935, she and Slee saw the need to create a new contract, their gritted teeth evident in every line.

"To my beloved wife," Slee wrote, "I acknowledge my weakness & from this date, I shall never again critizise [sic] any of your actions, (even if in my mind I disagree) I shall never *find fault with you in any way.*" She wrote, "*We* hereby agree from June 1st 1935 to avoid: getting on each others nerves by saying anything that comes into our minds." Penalties for contract-breaking were steep: "When ever the above are violated the person who starts any of the above shall pay the other $1,000 for each offense, providing the other person does not reply in like manner."[13]

Cohabitation held few pleasures for the couple in the late 1930s. In her diary Sanger referred to him as "the Sadist" and vented her contempt for his rigid routines and querulous attitude to her work.[14] In 1936, after a bout of bad health and a brief affair with a Scottish doctor in Penang, Sanger told Slee not to expect a physical relationship with her ever again.[15]

. . .

Sanger's outlook for a breakthrough in the public realm, meanwhile, kept getting better. Under the New Deal, enacted between 1933 and 1939, family planning centers drawing from a mix of public funds and private sources opened across the country. By this time, nearly every state had adopted the standard that physicians could prescribe contraception for the prevention or cure of disease; only Massachusetts and Connecticut maintained total bans.

New clinics turned to Sanger for advice on everything from instructional literature to pessary brands.[16] In 1929 only thirty clinics offering contraception had existed in the United States; five years later, there were around two hundred.[17] Most were in cities, though, and large swaths of the population had little hope of access to them.

Although publicly run programs offering birth control were piloted in Lynchburg, Virginia, and Greene County, Missouri, with Works Progress Administration (WPA) workers on staff, the WPA was not supposed to directly fund contraception. Due in large part to Catholic lobbying, the 1935 Social Security Act had reinstated maternal and child-wellness programs while deliberately excluding birth control.[18]

As has always been the case, women did whatever they could to end unwanted pregnancies. Since the WPA itself fired workers who were found to be pregnant, many went to extreme lengths to keep their fieldwork jobs. "Rather than lose their jobs, they are lacing themselves with corsets and bandages and are having their abortions in the WPA toilets," Lydia DeVilbiss wrote Sanger in 1936.[19]

By the late 1930s, however, birth control was enough of an industry that it was covered in *Fortune*. A humorous preface to the article mentioned how difficult it was still to mention the topic in polite society: "Though it is a matter bearing upon the most basic act of life, the discussion of it is not supposed to be in good taste. It is fenced around by verbal taboos of the most primitive sort . . . this strange, half-lighted world is not one that a lay magazine enters casually."[20] Then the editors got down to business: "In the midst of this Walpurgisnacht of fears and witches' potions there exists an industry—a peculiar industry, half legitimate, half bootleg, prosperous, and growing."[21]

Among the chemical contraceptives, Ortho-Gynol vied with

Hex Solution, O&C Eugenic Creme, and Marvel Whirling Spray.[22] The Lanteen diaphragm was sold as a "universal" cap that could be bought "without the necessity of performing a fitting."[23] Condom vending machines had been installed in gas stations and men's rooms in many cities. The condom even made its first appearance in poetry: in George Orwell's "St. Andrew's Day, 1935," the speaker curses the forces of economics and fear that place "the sleek, estranging shield / Between the lover and his bride."[24]

In the decade that followed, birth control became a $250-million-a-year industry, not quite on par with the jewelry business but larger than the barbershop trade,[25] with the lion's share of spending going to "feminine hygiene"–branded contraceptive products sold in drugstores.[26] "O tempora! O mores! . . . With jazz and knowledge of matters sexual taught the young, especially the female, with condom-filled compacts, the age has indeed become fast," remarked Louis Frank, MD, in a medical journal in the early 1930s.[27]

Birth control got its first history book, a milestone for any movement. *A Medical History of Contraception* by Norman Himes, a sociologist, was published in 1936. While spurious in many of its assertions—Himes claimed girls were infertile for three to four years after first menstruation, for instance—it lent further respectability to the cause.

In the section titled "Inevitability of Birth Control," Himes drew from the fact that contraception had existed in some form throughout the entire history of human society and that suppressing it was not just useless, but immoral. "We are gradually emerging from the night of blind prejudice and of brutal force. . . . Violence yields to benevolence, compulsion to kindness, the letter of the law to the spirit of justice," he concluded.[28]

Congress seemed reluctant to join this age of benevolence. After Sanger's bill was killed yet again in 1935—introduced, this time, by Senator Royal S. Copeland, who years earlier had evaded Dennett before deciding he was pro–birth control—it didn't reach a hearing again. But by the time of its demise, the prevailing rationale for opposing birth control had noticeably changed.

As Senator Ellison D. Smith, Democrat of South Carolina, "snapped" at Sanger, "We should let it alone. It jars me. It is revolting to interfere in people's personal affairs."[29] There is a hint here that, though sex and contraception were still seen as private matters, mentioning them was gauche rather than obscene, crass but no longer morally heinous.

Tired of seeing her bill repeatedly killed, but far from demoralized, Sanger now intended to try the line of attack Ernst had recommended: the courts. An opportunity had lately presented itself. She had been impressed by the design of a new Japanese pessary, the conical "Koyama Suction" brand, at the 1930 birth control conference in Zurich. The physician who invented them, Dr. Sakae Koyama, wrote, "I had twelve children, so there was much trouble and care to raise and educate them."[30]

Sanger was intrigued. She ordered a box of about 120 of them from Tokyo.[31] On June 14, 1932, they were confiscated and destroyed by US customs, so Sanger, thinking strategically, wrote her Japanese contact that he "might try sending some direct to our Medical Director, Hannah Stone, 17 West 16th Street."[32]

As a licensed physician in New York, Dr. Stone had the right to import contraceptives for the prevention or cure of disease. When customs again refused to transmit her shipment, Sanger recalled what Ernst said to her at a lunch earlier in 1935: "Margaret, don't try to get a law changed. You'll never get a law changed. You've gotta get it reinterpreted."[33] Given how congressmen were stonewalling her, she was game, though she first had to ask a wealthy friend for a $500 loan to cover the coming legal fees. When the government seized those pessaries, she was ready.

The morning of Tuesday, December 10, 1935, at ten thirty, in the federal court at the Old Post Office building in Manhattan, Ernst stood before Assistant District Attorney John F. Davidson and Judge

Grover Moscowitz, who had been the first judge on Dennett's obscenity trial six years earlier. Sanger, who was in India, asked her colleague Florence Rose to attend in her stead.

United States v. One Package of Japanese Pessaries was a fairly straightforward case, though a wondrous twist presented itself in the form of the government's only witness. He was a surgeon, Frederic Wolcott Bancroft, and he seemed unaware he was supposed to testify *against* Sanger and Ernst. Bancroft told the judge he himself distributed diaphragms to help remedy various conditions, and that he believed in the health benefits of spacing pregnancies. Rose noted he was "so helpful to our side that one wondered whose witness he really was!!"[34]

To the general amusement of the court, the pessaries themselves vanished in the course of the hearing, with many murmuring that Bancroft had been keen to get hold of them. Moscowitz, ruling that federal restrictions didn't apply to contraceptives being distributed for legitimate medical purposes, dismissed the case.

The decision initially brought relief, then the beginnings of a great reversal of fortunes for Sanger. Rose telegrammed her immediately, glad to share such news at the beginning of a new year: "JAPANESE CASE VICTORY CONGRATULATIONS."[35]

The government appealed the decision. In the circuit court of appeals decision in November 1937, Judges Augustus Hand, Learned Hand, and Thomas Swan upheld the Moscowitz decision, based on the opinion that "conscientious and competent physicians"[36] had the right to bring contraceptives into the country and send them through the mails "for the purpose of saving life or promoting the well being of their patients."[37]

The opinion mirrored the wording of the doctors-only bill, and had much the same effect. Now doctors were at liberty to decide for themselves the circumstances that justified prescribing contraception.

Ernst was triumphant, but Sanger felt differently; she wasn't so sure she had won yet. She retreated with a group of colleagues, and for two days they discussed how to interpret the decision. Betraying a deep-buried alignment with Dennett in a letter to colleagues, she posited, "We will never be free from worry until Sec. 211 [the part of the Comstock Act referring to contraception] is redrafted and classified."[38] The chairman of the House Judiciary Committee, hearing she was considering returning with a bill, told the committee, "If I were you people, I would just go right ahead and act as if it were all settled."[39]

Finally, once she was confident the government wouldn't appeal the case to the Supreme Court, Sanger decided she agreed with Ernst. To the public, she described the moment as "an emancipation proclamation to the motherhood of America."[40]

This achievement had been "for twenty years," Sanger reflected, "the object of my earnest endeavor." She saw "little point" in continuing to lobby for federal legislation. Later that spring, the National Committee disbanded.[41]

After her years of defying the law, and more recently the National Committee's herculean efforts—nearly two thousand lectures sponsored across the country, more than 68,000 letters mailed out, radio broadcasts, the chasing down of evasive senators—they had broken through.[42] "The birth control movement is *free*," she proclaimed in disbelief.[43]

. . .

Dennett, meanwhile, was submerged in a many-layered grief. The youngest child of her sister, Clara, had died around Christmas 1935 after a brief illness, aged twenty-three. Hartley and Margaret died in early in 1936, succumbing to the same flu-pneumonia within a week of each other.[44] Devon built his father's coffin, and Carleton played the organ at their funeral near their home in New Hampshire.

Vonie died in April 1936, just before her ninety-third birthday, after a difficult few days in a partial coma. Devon hosted the memorial, to which Dennett brought homemade pomegranate wine. As consuming as it had been for her to care for her mother, Vonie had also been a ballast to Dennett, a source of love, comfort, and common sense. As Clara once wrote to Dennett, "Do be good to your self. . . . You won't have mother now to tell you when to go and lie down and you must be *over* careful rather than the other thing."[45]

Dennett and Clara had informed Vonie of Willie's reappearance during her final illness. The sisters communicated with Willie's nursing home and sent him care packages for the rest of his life, but Dennett was mystified at how their family had come so unraveled.[46]

Lucia Ames Mead died in November. "Well, as soon as I can get my legs under me, and overcome my wobbly head, I'll be beginning life over again," Dennett wrote her friends. "It is turning a sharp corner for me."[47] Her aunt had left her an annuity of just over $500. With sales of *The Sex Side of Life* still steady and recent endorsements from Dale Carnegie and *Better Homes and Gardens*, Dennett was relieved, at least for now, of worrying about how to make rent.[48]

In the midst of these losses, she disagreed with Sanger's decision to take the *One Package* ruling as a victory. She had little faith that one legal precedent would reliably protect every American. A year earlier she had written an ABCL representative who sought her advice on strategy: "Whittling away the meaning of the present laws by a succession of loop-hole decisions is an immensely clever use of legal talent," Dennett wrote. "Yet, while these decisions do instant good . . . they do not take the place of definite law revision, and they are actually detrimental on two counts."[49]

She argued "anti-social interests" would be able to deploy activist judges toward their own ends, and secondly that relying so heavily on one or two legal decisions where a new law, passed by Congress, was called for made "a monkey of the law."[50] It was again an argument based as much on principles and aesthetic standards as on the way the law worked. Her words must have seemed impractical, but in 2022, when *Roe v. Wade* was overturned, they proved prescient.

She was frustrated to see the *One Package* decision celebrated as the end of the campaign. It made for a convenient narrative, to be sure, but a false one. "The oft quoted statement from Margaret Sanger and others that B.C. has now become legal in the U.S. is quite misleading," Dennett wrote Myra Gallert in late 1937. "There has been no real change in the laws."[51]

The *One Package* decision, however, could help make "the road nicely open" for federal legislation to pass at last. In her letters, Dennett allowed herself to keep dreaming about this. "Wouldn't it be delightful if victory should come soon!"[52]

She kept trying to build a coalition to carry out this plan. In December 1935, she'd exchanged letters with Katherine Houghton Hepburn, whom she'd met in her suffrage days. A frank and fun lunch with the ABCL leadership at the Colony Club followed. "Their experiences" with Sanger and with lobbying, Dennett noted, "are not at all unlike mine."[53] By mid-1937 Dennett was hoping Hepburn, the ABCL, and the Women's Joint Congressional Committee, a group of eighteen national women's organizations, could build momentum around birth control legislation using the *One Package* decision as a starting point.

Physicians seemed to agree with Dennett—at least, at first. In April 1937, the AMA *Journal* stated the *One Package* decision "has no reference to the right of physicians to advise the practice of contraception . . . or to prescribe or supply articles for the prevention of conception. . . . This propaganda [by Sanger's committee] is essentially misleading."[54]

Weeks later, however, reading the newspapers on a June morning at Willowlake, Sanger saw an arresting announcement. The AMA's Committee on Contraception had informed a convention of doctors they had the legal right to prescribe birth control, and it recommended that current contraceptive methods and techniques should be taught in medical schools.

The AMA formally supported research into developing contraceptives, with the line "The intelligent voluntary spacing of pregnancies may be desirable for the health and general well being of mothers and children."[55] Birth control was part of a responsible marriage and family life, and prescribing it did not need to be justified by threat of disease or death. These were strong words.

When it came to birth control clinics, the AMA's statement of support had stricter conditions. "All [contraceptive-providing] dispensaries, clinics, and similar establishments," read recommendation no. 4, should not only "be under legal licensure and supervision" but should be "under medical control."[56] Still, in essence, the AMA was claiming birth control as part of standard medical education and practice.

The *New York Times* announced the endorsement as a "landmark in the annals of American medicine" in a front-page story.[57] "In my excitement," Sanger wrote, "I actually fell downstairs." It was, wonderfully and truly, "a dream come true."[58] Sanger went on the radio to proclaim that the AMA's announcement "marks the end of a long and arduous fight against fear and taboo, inertia, and bigotry."[59]

Winning over the doctors was, she decided, "really a greater victory" than the *One Package* decision.[60] With this formal approval from the medical establishment, the government would be freer to allocate funds and programs to birth control. Clinics could more easily find supplies and staff, and the police would leave them alone. More doctors would learn about birth control options during their education, and, one way or another, more patients would find the help they sought.

In Sanger's final bulletin to the National Committee, she set out a new, expanded scope for the movement—a surprising one, given all the focus and energy she had dedicated to the doctors-only bill. She called for "an army of equipped, sympathetic nurses" to convey birth control to "mountain women, farm women, mothers on distant homesteads." Nurses, social workers, public-health officials who went and cared for people in the far-flung places where they lived: all of them should, Sanger affirmed, have the same right as physicians to dispense contraception.[61]

She had first pushed for this vision two decades earlier, petitioning Judge Crane after his decision in *People v. Sanger*. It had remained her ultimate goal, despite her frequent public insistence on the doctors-only provision and her cautionary arguments against the free circulation of contraception.

Sanger's latest proposal reflected how she saw the evolution of birth control in the realm of politics and the law. First she surmounted the hurdle of legalization, and later she would address the problem of gatekeeping. Means of access would multiply, she hoped. Dennett, meanwhile, had envisioned instead a single-stroke change in the law, one that would have achieved everything in one important deletion from the Comstock Act. She refused to accept that paternalistic gatekeeping, while incompatible with quintessentially American freedoms, was central to how many lawmakers at that time defined their purpose.

And yet it's tempting to imagine Dennett could have come to support Sanger's latest proposal. It didn't privilege physicians above other health workers, and it prioritized the needs of poor and rural women. But Sanger, who for years held tight to the doctors-only provision because it had a greater chance of passing, had no interest in collaborating with someone who, in her eyes, was a proven—and relatively powerless—adversary.

Sanger quickly relinquished that expanded vision again, at least in public. By the time she published her autobiography a year later, she was once again reiterating her argument that birth control was a matter for doctors, that specialized gynecological training was necessary. Clinics, she wrote, "ought not to be placed in the hands of unskilled midwives, social workers, or even nurses."[62]

It's likely that in conversations and correspondence she was clearer about her intentions for the future of the movement than she was in her memoir. In any case, for a brief moment after a heady success, she envisioned what it might look like to create a network of birth control access that actually met people where they lived.

In March 1938, the *Ladies' Home Journal* made birth control the topic of its regular "What Do the Women of America Think?" survey column. "The women of America believe in birth control," the magazine reported; 79 percent of respondents were in favor. The editors claimed their surveys ran nationwide, among married and unmarried women, widowed and divorced, from all races, creeds, and income levels.[63]

The results also confirmed that motherhood was still a status to which most women aspired: "They believe, just as firmly, in having children," the *Journal* reassured readers. Most women wanted four. About 2 percent admitted they regretted having children in the first place—a subversive answer for the magazine's readership at that time.[64]

Congress still didn't like dealing with anything to do with fertility, but its members were by now used to hearing about it. What was once taboo, or silently mandated by dogma or nature, could now be debated in legislative committees, boosted from the pulpit, discussed in the classroom, dispensed by a vending machine, and obtained at the doctor's office. So long, that is, as you were married and had a physician who kept up with the news.

Through the hands of Dennett, who never let go of her dream of changing the law, and Sanger, who still had a long career ahead of her, contraception attained its modern status. It went from radical fringe to the pages of the *Ladies' Home Journal* and *Fortune*, from esoteric to mainstream, from the sawdust-floor bars of Greenwich Village to the tea tables of Connecticut and beyond. Birth control became not just decent, but emblematic of safety, responsibility, and common sense.

Epilogue

We strongly sensed that with the pill, life would never be the same again. We'd be so free in our bodies it was frightening. Free as a man.

—Annie Ernaux, *The Years* (2008)

I N THE FALL OF 1937, just a few months after the AMA's endorsement, fifty-eight-year-old Margaret Sanger moved to Tucson, Arizona, where she and Slee built a house near her son Stuart and his family. Growing closer with them, she wrote, "made me envy mothers who had leisure to grow along with their children or, at least, to watch them develop." But, she went on philosophically, "it is possible we are all the better friends in adult life; at least we adhere to the rights of individuality for ourselves and for each other."[1]

She had less congenial musings about her husband, and he expressed equivalent exasperation. "God help me for having married a cause!!" Slee wrote his wife on May 4, 1939, threatening to leave her and spend his remaining years in South Africa, where he had been born. "I am more than weary trying to please you & from now on I am not even going to try!!"[2]

She seemed tickled by the idea. Just try it, her response suggested, and be "a pawn for every goldigger & baby face thats in the game to catch such fish [sic]."[3] They remained married until Slee's death in 1943.

Work consumed her through the 1950s. Once the CRB and ABCL combined into the Birth Control Council of America in May 1937, there was finally a single umbrella organization for the birth control movement. Two years later, the group became the Birth Control Federation of America (BCFA), and in 1942 it was renamed again as the Planned Parenthood Federation of America (PPFA), a name Sanger heartily disliked. She resented its exclusion of the term she'd long claimed to have coined herself—birth control.

As she wrote Kenneth Rose, who took on leadership of Planned Parenthood in the 1940s, the original movement for birth control had been "a fighting, forward, no fooling movement, battling for the freedom of the poorest parents and for women's biological freedom. . . . The P.P.F. has left all this behind and has no interest in any fight."[4]

After the *One Package* decision, Sanger moved her focus to developing new contraceptive methods and reaching more people. She regretted how the larger institutionalization of the movement required her to relinquish a measure of direct control over its priorities, but she compensated by investing in brand-new hormonal birth control technologies, which eventually led to the pill.

As early as 1930, Sanger helped fund a study into hormonal anovulants at the University of Edinburgh. When the project's leaders announced their findings at a conference the same year, they pointed out both the significance and the probable uselessness of their results: "It is doubtful," they said, "whether we shall ever wish to obtain a point where these dangerous weapons will be at the disposal of man."[5]

Sanger recognized that the doctors-only victory privileged people with access to physicians, who were majority urban and white. She took action to rectify the imbalance to the extent she now could. The BCFA set up the Negro Project, envisioned to bring birth control clinics to rural Black communities in the South, in 1939. Its advisory council included Du Bois, Mary McLeod Bethune, and the Reverend Adam Clayton Powell. Sanger secured philanthropic interest, starting with a $20,000 grant from the businessman Albert Lasker.

While planning this endeavor, Sanger wrote the sentence that has been held against her more than any other. "We do not want word to go out that we want to exterminate the Negro population and the minister is the man who can straighten out that idea if it ever occurs to any of their more rebellious members," she wrote Clarence Gamble in December 1939.[6] The editors of the Sanger Papers accurately say that this line "has condemned Sanger to a perpetual waltz with Hitler and the KKK."[7] They also point to how it has been taken out of context.

She had, in this particular case, been arguing for the need for a true coalition with Black clergy, writing also, "I do not believe that this project should be directed or run by white medical men. The Federation should direct it with the guidance and assistance of the colored group—; perhaps, particularly and specifically formed for the purpose."[8]

Sanger knew what justifiable suspicions Black communities had toward white reformers trying to interfere in their family planning. She believed at least a year of research and trust-building was necessary before launching a program. But once she had connected the BCFA with money, they disregarded her. The project was handled mainly by white clinicians, with some of its more notable successes coming in communities where Black nurses were hired on to participate.

The man to whom that infamous letter was addressed, Dr. Clarence Gamble, was emblematic of the new generation of birth controllers. He came from money—his forebears founded Ivory Soap—and wanted WASPs to have larger families. He was instrumental in running birth control programs, mostly self-funded, in several states and in Puerto Rico. Gamble advocated for the FDA to test condoms, piloted the door-to-door delivery of spermicidal jelly in West Virginia, distributed condoms in North Carolina, and funded the distribution of foam powder and sponge kits in Florida.[9]

Sometimes Gamble's programs addressed a desperate situation. In North Carolina in 1939, maternal mortality was twice as likely as in Connecticut, and infant mortality was well above average.[10] A director of the State Board of Health told a reporter from The Atlantic that he frequently saw young wives who had married in their teens and had

six children by their midtwenties, birthing them at home, sometimes
with no reliable water supply or barrier from insects and livestock.

He told of a couple who had had twenty children in seventeen
years, losing twelve of them in infancy. The mother told a reporter:
"I'm for any way that will keep me from having another child. Any way
so long as I keep from losing that man I got."[11] By 1939, thanks in part
to Gamble, North Carolina had more birth control clinics than any
state but New York. Nationally, by the end of the 1930s, more than
300,000 American women had visited a birth control clinic.[12]

In Puerto Rico, the Emergency Relief Administration funded a
pilot program distributing contraceptive information and supplies
starting in 1935, and the territorial legislature legalized birth control
in 1937, aiming to stem the fertility rate of Puerto Ricans.[13] Because of
this push, the territory became a kind of laboratory for new population-
control policies.[14] Fertility did decline, but plans for a network of birth
control clinics ran out of money, and pilot programs in Puerto Rico
were notorious for sterilizing women without informed consent. In
the late 1960s the territory held the highest percentage in the world
of women of childbearing age who had been sterilized.[15]

American birth controllers' work abroad, meanwhile, was done
with the assumption of superior Western expertise and colonialist
beneficence. Birth control programs overseas were less likely to be
covered by the media at home, allowing directors to experiment with
uncertain methods or funnel in defective or shoddily made products.
Gamble, for instance, trained missionaries bound for India in demonstrating the use of a basic barrier method of a rag soaked in brine.[16]

Sanger, too, spent time in India, having first gone there in the fall
of 1935, hauling trunks full of life-size, three-dimensional models of
the female reproductive tract.[17] She and Gandhi spent days in conversation at his ashram in December 1935, debating the virtues of birth
control (Sanger) as opposed to sexual self-restraint (Gandhi). The
same year, Nehru's Indian National Congress adopted a resolution in
favor of state-sponsored birth control distribution.[18]

Sanger's involvement with Planned Parenthood waxed and waned. She didn't consistently click with its leadership. Helping develop the pill from a preliminary experimental stage to a commercial product fascinated her more than the machinations of any league or federation. "I've got herbs from Fiji which are said to be used to prevent Conception," she wrote Gamble in 1939. "Im hoping this may prove to be the 'magic pill' I've been hoping for since 1912 when women used to say 'Do tell me the secret' 'cant I get some of the medicine too? [sic]'"[19]

In the early 1950s, she matched two scientists, Gregory Pincus and subsequently John Rock, with funding for hormonal contraceptive research. In 1956, two studies on the first pill, Enovid, were run in Puerto Rico and California. It was approved by the FDA on June 10, 1957.

Sanger's final decade was difficult, with a series of heart attacks and pains contributing to anxiety and a dependence on painkillers. She witnessed the breakthrough of 1965's *Griswold v. Connecticut*, which gave married people the right to contraception, as she battled through a haze of illness. She died September 6, 1966, aged eighty-six, and is buried next to Slee and her sister Nan in Fishkill Rural Cemetery.

In the final paragraph of her autobiography, Sanger quoted Nietzsche: "Build thou beyond thyself."[20] She did exactly that, with a Nietzschean regard for her own power-hunger. Part of her spirit, at least, entered the pantheon of pop culture in the unlikely guise of a comic book heroine: in 1941, Wonder Woman made her debut, the creation of the psychologist William Moulton Marston. Readers had little inkling she was partly inspired by Sanger, whose niece Olive Byrne lived with Marston and his wife. Wonder Woman's creator echoed Sanger closely in his belief that "the only hope for civilization is the greater freedom, development and equality of women."[21]

. . .

"Life is prodigiously interesting, although difficult, in these tense days of transition toward something which we can hope will be based upon better principles than those which have produced the world depression," Dennett wrote in early 1934. She herself, now sixty-one, had been "very nearly demolished" by the hard times, "but I am still here."[22]

Dennett's postindictment fame and her stand for free speech turned her into a minor living legend. Sherwood Anderson invited her to join the Writers Delegation to the President of the National Committee for the Defense of Political Prisoners.[23] Into the early 1940s, she was listed in various editions of *Who's Who*. Colleagues from the past wrote letters of admiration, with sentiments like "Whether you do remember me or not—yours was always such a busy and wonderful life—I will never forget you, and the glimpse into and beyond the great horizon that meeting people of your type gives a youngster."[24]

She continued to make *guadameciles*. For all her humility about her art, it was a serious pursuit. After a small show on the West Coast, Marlene Dietrich bought a pair of Dennett-made leather bookends.[25]

From the late 1930s, Dennett lived with Devon and his family in Woodside, Queens, maintaining her memberships in Heterodoxy (until it disbanded in 1940), the Pen and Brush Club, the Civic Club, the Society of Arts and Crafts, and several other groups.[26] To her grandchildren, she was "scary and nice," to quote her granddaughter Nancy, a scratchy but engaging figure who would take her knitting out to concerts and click the needles in time with the music.[27]

Her room was filled with dried flowers and a stationary bicycle she would hike her skirts up to ride, and she was always making clothes for herself and her family.[28] She continued to follow Sanger's doings, without engaging with them. "It is wonderful how time makes the burial of hatchets a simple and painless process!" she wrote a VPL colleague in 1938.[29]

A series of strokes precipitated her move from Devon's to a nursing home in Valatie, New York, where she died July 25, 1947, aged sixty-five.

Her *New York Times* obituary called her a "suffrage leader," retold the saga of *United States v. Dennett,* and summarized the various leagues Dennett had helped lead. It neglected to mention the VPL at all.[30]

Committed as she was to helping the next generation understand sex and have children only when they wanted to, Dennett would doubtless still find much to revolt against today. Abstinence-only sex ed programs, which receive $110 million in federal funds every year, would be contrary to the spirit of her commonsense, science-based approach. (No federal funds at all are currently dedicated to developing and expanding access to comprehensive sex ed, meanwhile, which is based in medical research, covers relationship health and communication, is LGBTQ-inclusive, and frames sexuality as a normal part of life.)[31]

Contemporary debates over banned books, school boards censoring teachers, and classical art blocked from high school courses for depicting the human body echo Comstock's "blunder" loud and clear. Given Dennett's impatience with any framework that places one gender at a power advantage over the other in the eyes of the law, one also wonders what she would have made of the trans rights movement, whether she could have mapped her simple yet controversial "Women Are People" stance onto the rallying cry of all genders to be recognized as worthy of rights, respect, and compassionate medical care.

Unlike Sanger, she did not live long enough to see her ideas come into near-universal respectability. Her comparatively early death, combined with her commitment to promoting the cause while *not* promoting herself, helps account for her relative obscurity. Her most palpable presence, these days, lies in her stuff. Dennett left steamer trunks full of correspondence, diaries, scrapbooks, sketchbooks, her much-mended "duds," jewelry, and *guadameciles.*

Almost as if she anticipated biographers, she organized and labeled her things for those who came after her. She never wrote out her life story for the wider public, but left notebooks for her sons. Compared with Sanger, she was hardly photographed at all, and unlike her rival she never appeared on television. Still, if her carefully kept archive is any evidence, she seems to have expected future generations would hail her singular importance in American history. In the end, this was a certainty she shared with Sanger, a sign she had a healthy ego after all.

As she had made clear when she was a teenager, Dennett's preference was to be cremated. Carleton kept her ashes in his Alstead house until one night, when he took them out to Hartley's grave and scattered them, reuniting his parents once more.[32]

He kept a copy of *The Sex Side of Life* on the back of the toilet, where his children could read it whenever they liked.[33] Free speech and tolerance were the family's watchwords. "Purists," Dennett once said, "can live according to their light, although to the rest of us it may seem but a tallow dip,—but they should not claim that no other light exists."[34]

In an article Dennett wrote about how birth control would transform family life, she predicted, "The results, in much shorter a time than four or five generations, will be happier homes; greater mutual respect between husband and wife; honeymoons lasting two to three years before children arrive. . . . That is what makes the difference between feeding and dining, being covered against the elements and being charmingly dressed, living in a cave and having a hospitable home."[35] In other words, we live with the miracles of human ingenuity every day. In Dennett's imagining, they promise not only survival, but joy.

. . .

When Dennett's granddaughter Nancy went to be fitted for a diaphragm, she did as her peers did: borrowed money from her mother and a wedding ring from a friend.[36] In this way contraception's cultural role was redefined in the 1940s and '50s. It was an important recourse for practical wives, or people playing that role.

Physicians gradually absorbed contraception into mainstream healthcare, as med-school curricula embraced it after the *One Package* decision and the AMA's endorsement. Since legalization and the medical monopoly were affirmed around the same time, doctors were effectively made the gatekeepers for methods like the diaphragm, the IUD, and, eventually, the pill.

In the three decades between 1936's *One Package* decision, which legalized birth control by individual prescription only, and 1965's *Griswold v. Connecticut,* which finally legalized birth control for married people, the initial impetus for the birth control movement— that it was a humanitarian necessity, born of a larger feminist movement—was consistently minimized.

Of the *Griswold* decision, one scholar, Jessica L. Furgerson, writes, "The word 'wife' appears five times . . . the word 'woman' is never utilized, and the word 'women' is used only once as a collective noun in a sentence wholly unrelated to the rights of women." *Griswold* was "about facilitating responsible reproduction among married couples," not making a statement about gender equality or bodily autonomy.[37] It took another seven years for unmarried people to gain the right to birth control too, via 1972's *Eisenstadt v. Baird.*

Today, birth control is a pillar of global health. The World Health Organization recommends birth spacing of two to three years, citing evidence there is higher risk of complications for both mother and baby for shorter-interval pregnancies.[38] In the United States, public expenditure on family planning exceeds $2 billion annually,[39] and federal law requires insurers to offer a wide array of FDA-approved contraceptive options. Birth control has been woven into policy: Title X, established in 1970, became the only federal program in the United States dedicated to family planning services as part of the Public Health Service Act.

In one very basic sense, Dennett's vision was realized in 1971: "contraception" was struck from the Comstock Act. Yet in 2022, in the ruling *Dobbs v. Jackson Women's Health Organization*, which overruled *Roe v. Wade*, Justice Clarence Thomas expressed doubt about the legal right to birth control, pointing out the rationale behind the *Dobbs* decision would likely overrule *Griswold*, too.[40] Like *Roe*, after all, the *Griswold* decision centered on the right to privacy.

Nationally, there is broad bipartisan consensus in favor of contraception, but it has still been stymied on the level of federal legislation, even after robust post-*Dobbs* efforts. The legal right to contraception has been codified in only thirteen states as of this writing.[41] In Congress, meanwhile, the Right to Contraception Act was introduced in 2023, in the aftermath of *Dobbs*, but failed to pass the Senate; opponents called it "completely unnecessary" and "a Trojan horse for more abortions." Birth control was, in this context, still both too unimportant and somehow too drastic.

If there doesn't seem to be a clear threat to the right to birth control at this very moment, that may come soon. The *Dobbs* decision brought us an urgent awareness that no aspect of reproductive healthcare can be taken for granted, regardless of precedent. Federal legislation affirming the right to birth control has joined an array of causes with broad popular support—commonsense gun control, abortion rights, the right to IVF, protection from discrimination for LGBTQ+ Americans—similarly languishing in Congress.

Design and technological innovations have shaped the contraception landscape far beyond the battle for the diaphragm. The pill, the patch, the vaginal ring, a variety of IUDs, all promise highly effective long-term contraception. The Today sponge, the most popular over-the-counter method in the 1980s, ran up against regulatory issues in the mid-1990s and was discontinued; morning-after contraception and fertility awareness method (FAM) apps have won FDA approval.

One consequence of Sanger's doctors-only path has been the

problem that, long after many countries made the pill available over the counter in pharmacies, Americans could get it only with a prescription. Finally, in 2023 the brand Opill was approved for over-the-counter sale. This represents not only a carefully considered FDA decision but also the AMA's admirable crusade against the "scope creep," the unnecessary expansions to physicians' scope of work that compromise patients' well-being while maintaining a measure of paternalism in healthcare.[42]

Though the prohibition on contraception has been repealed, the Comstock Act remains largely unchanged, and it is easy to imagine Comstock deciding that the internet, as well as the mail, presents *"the most powerful agent, to assist this nefarious business, because it goes everywhere and is secret."*[43] Project 2025, an 887-page blueprint produced by the right-leaning Heritage Foundation and designed to set priorities for a future presidential administration, explicitly states the Comstock Act should be revived and enforced.[44]

Relying on the Comstock Act to halt the distribution of FDA-approved drugs suggests an immediate threat to birth control methods often misrepresented in political discourse as abortifacients, such as IUDs, Plan B, and even hormonal birth control. This despite the fact that these methods prevent fertilization and implantation and should not, according to the American College of Obstetricians and Gynecologists and the FDA, be viewed as abortion methods.[45]

Confusion over how chemical methods work persists, and the conflation between contraception and abortion continues to happen in a political climate in which evidence-based recommendations are routinely dismissed. In 2022, Colorado representative Lauren Boebert repeatedly introduced amendments that would prevent "abortifacient contraceptive drugs" from being included in the appropriations process, while Montana representative Matt Rosendale attempted a bill with a similar goal.[46] The problem is multigenerational: in 2017, Kristan Hawkins, the president of Students for Life, told an MSNBC reporter that the pill and IUDs should be illegal, and the group's social media posts have indicated that hormonal birth control is another form of abortion.[47]

"Man is not an economic, but a social being," wrote Karl Polanyi, a Hungarian economic historian, in 1947. *We live in a society, not an economy* is a position that has infused arguments among policy-makers (and whose brevity has made it a favorite on social media) ever since. And yet arguments for fertility control as a social good, as a means of improving people's quality of life, have not fared well in the political arena unless attached to an economic justification or population-shaping measure.

Tracing the two rationales for birth control over the last century—one humanitarian, the other essentially concerned with money and eugenics together—illustrates their strikingly different chances for success. The latter has always had more traction politically. Because of the way our political institutions work, even when humanitarian messaging might have hit home—at the worst of the Depression, for instance—it was concern about the economy that hastened birth control clinics into being.

Similarly, looking at Dennett's and Sanger's parallel efforts to legal-ize birth control grants an illuminating perspective on how activism makes headway. A *Harvard Business Review* article by Greg Satell, "What Successful Movements Have in Common" (2016), notes the importance of five elements: a clear purpose, values prioritized above slogans, the participation of small groups and not just one large crowd, steadily overcoming thresholds of resistance, and relying on engage-ment rather than rhetoric.[48]

Both Dennett and Sanger shared a clear purpose. Dennett, however, was arguably more values-driven and less easily lured by compromise. Sanger led the crowd, undoubtedly, and was a clear-eyed and motivated pragmatist, but she underestimated Dennett's deeply American vision and what it added to the movement.

Even after it became clear neither wished for renewed collabora-tion, it would have strengthened the movement had they at least been able to coordinate, or to agree on complementary agendas. All too quickly, the two leaders became suspicious and prejudiced against each other to the extent that their communication broke down, and every letter was read as a loaded, insinuating jab.

The blame for this breakdown is unevenly shared. While Dennett was uncompromising to a fault, Sanger dismissed the boldness and usefulness of Dennett's efforts in Washington and, at certain points, seemed actively determined to sink Dennett if she could. Sanger had the greater share of power and renown; the fact that she did not find a way to turn Dennett's efforts to her advantage suggests that, in addition to sheer competitiveness, there had been a personal insult between them that she couldn't forgive.

That grudge came at a cost. The bitterness between them became a distraction and a source of delay as both sought the approval of the medical establishment and elected leaders.

The lack of real communication between them shortchanged the movement more than their actual differences of opinion. Heavyweight activism benefits from a combination of incremental legal change and an ability to capture the public imagination (Sanger's style) as well as the dogged pursuit of fundamental, big-picture change (Dennett's). If these strands are isolated and alienated from each other, if leaders insist on personal loyalty above loyalty to the larger cause, no one profits except those who would rather see the movement fail.

Dennett and Sanger shared at least one shortcoming that cast a long shadow on the current reproductive rights movement. Today's activists are aware of the concept of intersectionality: of the importance of creating movements by and for people who claim a range of identities, across race, class, and gender. The birth control movement of a century ago had no such framework to base itself on, and it was consequently blind to many of its own limitations.

The legacy of eugenics is very much with us. It is, to repeat a metaphor often attached to it, the foundation we must somehow redesign while continuing to live in the floors above. Activists in the birth

control movement at worst accelerated, and at best failed to counteract, some of the most bigoted policies our country has ever put into
play. The campaign for reproductive rights has long ignored priorities
proposed by Black and brown people, including improving prenatal
and birth care and ending forced sterilization.[49] Further betraying its
ancestral ties to the eugenics movement, it has tried to separate itself
from the disability rights movement, which includes the right to have
children.

State-sanctioned sterilizations continued long beyond Sanger's or
Dennett's lifetime. It is estimated that sixty thousand people were
forcibly sterilized in the United States between 1907 and 1964.[50] In
the 1970s, a campaign of forced sterilization targeting Native Americans resulted in between 20 percent and 30 percent of women of
childbearing age losing their fertility.[51]

This was not a southern problem, or a rural problem; the *Boston
Globe* revealed Boston City Hospital regularly performed medically
unnecessary hysterectomies on Black patients as late as 1972, justifying that medical residents needed the practice.[52] In California state
prisons, the sterilization program wasn't officially ended until 2010.
As of February 2022, thirty-one states still have laws on the books
regarding state-approved sterilization, including minors with disabilities and people under guardianship.[53] It is also legal for judges
to mandate defendants to use long-term contraceptives, offering a
reduced prison term so long as the defendant accepts a birth control
implant, for instance.[54]

Dorothy Roberts, a sociologist and the author of *Killing the Black
Body* (1997), notes of the original feminist vision for the birth control
movement, "It was superseded by the concern for the nation's fiscal
security and ethnic makeup" and co-opted by population-control
enthusiasts.[55] This helps account for the Black maternal health crisis
that is a mark of shame on the United States today.

It still isn't accurate to say, as Justice Thomas wrote in a 2019
dissent, that "from the beginning, birth control and abortion were

promoted as a means of effectuating eugenics."[56] For Dennett and Sanger, fertility control represented a basic human right first and foremost. But they clearly accepted the tenets of the "fit versus unfit" school of thought, and if eugenics happened to be the train that carried birth control through Congress, they were ready to claim a car and ride it all the way through.

Today, as fertility in many high-income nations falls below replacement level, governments have tried to encourage reproduction with short-term benefits, like tax breaks, housing assistance, or "baby bonuses" (offered in Canada, Australia, France, and South Korea, among other nations). The trend persists despite evidence that shows policies supporting universal work-family balance have the best long-term results.[57]

Despite the title of this book, it is too neat to say Dennett was driven purely by ideals and Sanger by ambition. For someone who rejected lawbreaking as a strategy, Dennett didn't apply the same rules to herself when she mailed out *The Sex Side of Life*. Defensive as she was of her preeminence in the birth control movement, Sanger could not have worked so tirelessly and ingeniously without a sense of calling. Sanger's readiness to grant physicians a gatekeeping role, and Dennett's rejection of any substantial compromise, both turned out to be wildly flawed positions.

Had Dennett been less rigid in her ideals and intentions, and had Sanger been firmer with her intent to expand prescribing privileges to nurses and social workers, families might have met a kinder world. However, both their visions were warped by the hostile systems they had to work through to get something done: fearful and uninformed physicians, politicians who found the topic generally icky.

New technologies and values battered by World War I, the Roaring Twenties, and the Great Depression meant old frameworks no longer worked. Dennett's and Sanger's work was in this sense bigger than birth control. They were instrumental in forcing lawmakers to recognize the kind of world Americans actually lived in, one where fertility control was nearly universally practiced, instead of one constrained by hypocrisy, silence, and loyalty to an oppressive past.

Reproduction inspires countless metaphors and resists all of them. In the language of legal and political debate, the fetus shows up either a cluster of cells or a fully formed person, a trespasser or a soul. Whichever analogy dominates has the knock-on effect of imposing a new status on the person carrying the fetus, determining what rights they have or must relinquish. Closely related is the question of whether motherhood is the most essential function for those capable of it; or, as historians have noted, whether the childbearers of the world are "a means to an end rather than as ends in themselves."[58]

A consistent challenge threading its way through writing about this historical episode has been the difficulty of handling reproduction's multiplicity of images and the slippery legal status attached to pregnancy. On one hand, childbearing is part of private family life. On the other, it shapes the collective, swelling or shrinking the population. It is deeply personal and just as fully social. How counterintuitive it is, then, that something so weighty, both for the individual and society, has relatively little dedicated legislation.

Dennett's story might be a source of ballast at a time when it is especially hard to view the American experiment as a steady march toward justice. Her life in activism is ripe for reappraisal as we continue to reckon with the need to affirm free speech and reproductive rights.

She did the unexpected, as a middle-aged, middle-class, educated, straight white woman with scant interest in revolution or free love. Yet Dennett believed—vociferously, at great cost to her own well-being—that full citizenship shouldn't be restricted by gender, and that individuals should know and control their own bodies, and she wanted that reflected in the Constitution.

She made one mistake after another in trying to make this a reality, but her activism was monumental in effort and visionary in nature.

"There is another thing to remember," Dennett wrote in an unpublished manuscript. "We never come to the end of learning. We should not let our prejudices stand in the way of more knowledge. We should keep on learning, and correcting things that we thought we knew if we come to understand them better." Especially when it came to sex, she urged her readers "to keep on asking questions, and to improve our understanding as long as we live."[60]

Author's Note

My understanding of this moment in history and the early-twentieth-century movement for women's rights rests on the work of the scholars who have done the foundational work, including Nicola Beisel, Janet Farrell Brodie, Beth Widmaier Capo, Nancy Cott, Carl Degler, John D'Emilio and Estelle Freedman, Linda Gordon, Cathy Moran Hajo, Helen Lefkowitz Horowitz, Rose Holz, Esther Katz, Wendy Kline, Judith Walzer Leavitt, Carole McCann, James Reed, Robyn Rosen, Andrea Tone, and Laura Weinrib. I also could not have pieced together the story as clearly without the expertise of Constance Chen, Ellen Chesler, Peter C. Engelman, Jessica Furgerson, Anya Jabour, Margaret Grace Myers, Lauren MacIvor Thompson, and Sharon Spaulding. I wish every biographer had such riches, delivered with such style, to learn from.

The Icon and the Idealist is far from being the first book about the birth control movement. Sanger is the subject of several comprehensive biographies. Likewise, Dennett's achievements and shortfalls have been explored and put into context by generations of historians, though she is frequently relegated to a sidebar.

The historical record is rife with unrecorded stories. For the majority of Americans in 1910 through 1930, sex and pregnancy were intensely private topics, better suited for whispers and insinuations than detailed confessions on the page. Daniel Scott Smith, a quantitative historian, has described this general trend: "Women in the family do not generate written documents describing their ordinary life experiences. It is easier, for example, to describe historical attitudes toward women's proper role than to determine what the roles actually were at any given time."[1] Sometimes couples wrote to each other about their sexual selves, but they nearly always used metaphors, euphemisms, or abbreviations—endeavoring to assign the topic to a private, semisecret language.

Collecting the life stories of women and low-income individuals has not been a priority for much of history, abetting the self-censorship that silenced people from recording what they deemed unimportant, unserious, or undignified. Sheer embarrassment had a singular power to discourage people from telling the whole truth about their lives— even when they had cause to seek urgent help.

When the birth control campaign got underway in earnest in the 1910s, society and medical expertise decreed gender was synonymous with sex assigned at birth. A birthing person was always a woman and a mother. Donna Drucker, a historian, has written of the need to balance "women" and "men" as categories without erasing the historical presence of transgender and nonbinary people whose ability to bear children, or to impregnate others, has little bearing on their gender identity.[2] In this book, therefore, my guiding rule has been to assume cisgendered terms where the characters and context would have demanded it.

The enduring legacy of white supremacy plays a role in shaping the archives of maternity and medicine in America. The first published surveys of sexual and contraceptive habits in America came in the 1890s, and their target demographic was white, married, and middle class. Where archives turn up diaries and letters that mention sex and birth, their creation nearly always rested on the fact that the authors had the time and education—and often, the household help—to sit down and write.

One historian, Jessie Rodrique, quotes a Florida librarian who replied, when asked about the records of a local hospital that primarily served Black people, "These are black records, honey, what did you expect?"[3] Retracing the story of the birth control movement means recognizing the tidal volume of experiences that died with the teller's voice or were seen as unworthy of preservation. This book is shaped as much by those silences as by what has survived.

Acknowledgments

The opportunity to discover and draw a detailed portrait of Mary Ware Dennett was as daunting as it was irresistible. I was inspired to continue by Sharon Spaulding, a feminist historian and the curator of the Sharon Spaulding / Dennett Family Archives, whose contributions were central to this project. In early 2021, I began corresponding with Sharon and made a series of visits to Alstead, New Hampshire, and Sandy, Utah, rifling through steamer trunks full of papers and ephemera, admiring *guadameciles*, and even looking over Mary's jewelry.

Sharon has been a well of engaging ideas and necessary guidance all along. She and her husband, Carl, opened up their homes to me, made it possible for me to interview Dennett's remarkable granddaughter, and sent me home with a sampling of Dennett's sex-book collection. I am deeply indebted to them and to Nancy Dennett.

Many institutional archives were essential to this project, and I'm especially grateful to Teddy Schneider at the Schlesinger Library; the British Library; Edith A. Sandler at the Library of Congress's Manuscript Division; Stephanie Krauss at the Countway Library of Medicine; the Sophia Smith Collection of Women's History at Smith College; the Harry Ransom Center at the University of Texas at Austin; Scout Noffke at Dartmouth's Rauner Special Collections; and Ruthann Tomassini at the Framingham History Center, as well as Gwendolyn Holbrow, who now lives in the Framingham home once shared by Mary and Hartley Dennett, and Alexander Sanger. I relied greatly on the Margaret Sanger Papers Project at New York University, led by Esther Katz, Cathy Moran Hajo, and Peter C. Engelman.

Lanham Bundy of the Providence Public Library made this book possible. Despite pandemic-related obstructions, Lanham summoned hundreds of books, articles, and reels of microfilm to Empire Street. My unwieldy, aspirational research spreadsheet was magicked into reality. Lanham, thank you.

Nicholas Aaron Friesner: it was a stroke of luck you opened that beseeching email, and thank you for opening up several more sources for me.

I am grateful to the Logan Nonfiction Program at the Carey Institute for Global Good: the spring 2021 virtual session allowed me to participate even with a baby around. I was also fortunate the Massachusetts Historical Society offered me an Alyson R. Miller Fellowship for 2022–23: the MHS is a blissful place to work.

Molly Atlas: meeting you twenty years ago was ridiculously lucky. Thanks for midwifing this book into being and for your acuity and kindness. Thanks to editor Sara Birmingham for having faith in the project and for the energy and precision that went into the edit. Dan Crissman gave the book its structure and is as far-sighted and generous a reader as I could imagine. Srdjan Smajic contributed invaluable queries and revisions (AWK forever).

At Ecco, Helen Atsma and Miriam Parker have assembled the best team possible. I'm especially grateful to Rachel Sargent, Frieda Duggan, Doug Johnson, Pam Rehm, Janet Renard, Vivian Rowe, Patrick Barry, Nina Leopold, Daniela Salazar, and Meghan Deans.

I'm indebted to the individuals and groups who kept me company and spurred me to keep going as I wrote this book, especially through the pandemic. Thanks to the Ronald McDonald House of Providence Running Club, brainchild of Bob and Anne Rothenberg. Thanks to my fellow activists here in RI: working with you is the way work should be, and taking part in the real stuff of activism alongside you for years now has helped me feel especially close to this project. Thanks to the Biographers International Organization, the NBCC, and LitArtsRI.

For solid-gold friendship and writerly commiseration, thanks to

Ginny McReynolds, Kristina Gaddy, Memsy Price, Neda Toloui-Semnani, Rachel Dickinson, and the Goucher Nonfiction community. For the chance to work alongside brilliance and shun distraction for a while: Kristen McNeill and the Forest app. For long friendship and lending me a car when I needed it: Laura Richardson and Rone Tempest. For your creativity, conversation, and friendship through big transitions: Ellen Reeves, Lindsey Beal, Lisa Gendron, and Melissa Lê-Hoa Võ. For all the necessary eating, reading, and swimming, and for being the smartest and funniest: Jacqueline, Maija, Mara, Pauline, and Suzanne. For making the Mom Chat a thing of beauty: Angie, Bonnie, Bonnie, Laura, Melanie, Nicole, Stephanie, and Tiffany.

My family changed shape in the course of writing this book. Our second child was born in August 2020, and my dad, Theodore Johnston "Ted" Gorton, died in October 2022. His memory is a blessing, though his company was far better. My mother, Andrée Feghali Gorton, has always been my greatest teacher. Thank you also, Mom, for ordering the packages of books that showed up at my door during the lockdown days of 2020–21 and enabled me to keep working: what a gift. Much love to my siblings, Haig, Maya, and Alex Gorton, and my in-laws, Ginny and Paul T. Murphy, who have shown up for us again and again.

Paul: to misquote Hartley, how lucky I am that "your North Star and mine are in the same quarter of the sky." Love always to you, Josephine, Miriam, and Quahog.

Notes

INTRODUCTION

1. Constance Chen, *"The Sex Side of Life": Mary Ware Dennett's Pioneering Battle for Birth Control and Sex Education* (New York: The New Press, 1996), 293.
2. Laura Weinrib, "The Sex Side of Civil Liberties: United States v. Dennett and the Changing Face of Free Speech," *Law and History Review* 30, no. 2 (May 2012): 329.
3. Janet Farrell Brodie, *Contraception and Abortion in Nineteenth-Century America* (Ithaca, NY: Cornell University Press, 1994), 51.
4. Kara Platoni, "The Sex Scholar," *Stanford Magazine*, March/April 2010, https://stanfordmag.org/contents/the-sex-scholar.
5. Margaret Talbot, "The Pill's Difficult Birth," *The New Yorker*, November 11, 2014, https://www.newyorker.com/culture/cultural-comment/pills-difficult-birth.
6. Angela Davis, *Blues Legacies and Black Feminism: Gertrude "Ma" Rainey, Bessie Smith, and Billie Holiday* (New York: Pantheon Books, 1998), 5.
7. Untitled typescript by Dennett, Sharon Spaulding / Dennett Family Archives, Alstead, NH & Sandy, UT.
8. "Contraceptive Deserts," Power to Decide, https://powertodecide.org/what-we-do/contraceptive-deserts.
9. "State Family Planning Funding Restrictions," Guttmacher Institute Public Policy Office, September 1, 2023, https://www.guttmacher.org/state-policy/explore/state-family-planning-funding-restrictions.
10. Peter C. Engelman, "The Rivalry between Margaret Sanger and Mary Ware Dennett," ProQuest, accessed April 21, 2022, https://pq-static-content.proquest.com/collateral/media2/documents/casestudy-histvault-engelman.pdf.

CHAPTER 1: MAMIE WARE

1. Mary Ware Dennett, "Curriculum Vitae," n.d., Mary Ware Dennett papers, Schlesinger Library, Radcliffe Institute for Advanced Study at Harvard University (MWD papers).
2. *New York Times*, April 4, 1872, https://timesmachine.nytimes.com/timesmachine/1872/04/04/issue.html.
3. Mary Ware Dennett, *The Sex Education of Children: A Book for Parents* (New York: The Vanguard Press, 1931), 47–48.
4. Dennett, 66.
5. Dennett, "Curriculum Vitae."
6. Dennett, "Curriculum Vitae."
7. Mary Ware Dennett to Lucia Ames Mead, September 28, 1933, MWD Papers.
8. Lynn Lederer, "'The Dynamic Side of Life'—The Emergence of Mary Coffin Ware Dennett as a Radical Sex Educator" (PhD diss., Rutgers University, 2011), 53–54.
9. Lederer, 73, and Susan E. Hollister, "Rare Species Identified: A Discussion of the Life and Work of Hartley Dennett" (master's thesis, 1985), 4, Sharon Spaulding / Dennett Family Archives, Alstead, NH & Sandy, UT.

10. Mary Ware Dennett, "For My Sons after My Death," Sharon Spaulding / Dennett Family Archives, Alstead, NH & Sandy, UT, 8–9.

11. Dennett, 9–10.

12. Dennett, 187.

13. Abigail Adams to John Adams, March 31–April 5, 1776, in *Adams Family Papers: An Electronic Archive*, Massachusetts Historical Society, accessed June 16, 2023, https://www.masshist.org/digitaladams/archive/doc?id=L17760331aa.

14. Mary Beth Norton, "The Constitutional Status of Women in 1787," *Minnesota Journal of Law & Inequality* 6, no. 1 (June 1988): 7, https://scholarship.law.umn .edu/cgi/viewcontent.cgi?article=1558&context=lawineq (accessed April 21, 2022).

15. Abigail Adams to John Adams, March 31–April 5, 1776, in *Adams Family Papers: An Electronic Archive*, Massachusetts Historical Society, accessed June 16, 2023.

16. History.com editors, "Abigail Adams Urges Husband to 'Remember the Ladies,'" History.com, October 22, 2009, https://www.history.com/this-day-in-history/abigail -adams-urges-husband-to-remember-the-ladies.

17. Barbara Ehrenreich and Deirdre English, *Witches, Midwives & Nurses*, 2nd ed. (New York: Feminist Press, 2010), 76.

18. Maya Salam, "*Vagina Obscura* Demystifies Female Anatomy," *New York Times* March 29, 2022, https://www.nytimes.com/2022/03/29/books/vagina-obscura-rachel -gross.html.

19. Kimberly A. Hamlin, *From Eve to Evolution: Darwin, Science, and Women's Rights in Gilded Age America* (Chicago: University of Chicago Press, 2014), 105.

20. Ann Douglas Wood, "'The Fashionable Diseases': Women's Complaints and Their Treatment in Nineteenth-Century America" in *Clio's Consciousness Raised: New Perspectives on the History of Women*, ed. Mary S. Hartman and Lois Banner (New York: Octagon Books, 1976), 3.

21. John Wiltbank, quoted in Carroll Smith-Rosenberg, *Disorderly Conduct: Visions of Gender in Victorian America* (New York: Knopf, 1985), 183–84.

22. Fernando Tadeu Andrade-Rocha, "On the Origins of the Semen Analysis: A Close Relationship with the History of the Reproductive Medicine," *Journal of Human Reproductive Sciences* 10, no. 4 (October–December 2017): 242–55, https://doi .org/10.4103/jhrs.JHRS_97_17.

23. Judith Walzer Leavitt, *Brought to Bed: Childbearing in America, 1750 to 1950*, 30th anniversary ed. (New York: Oxford University Press, 2016), 65–66.

24. Dorothy M. Brown, *Setting a Course: American Women in the 1920s* (Boston: Twayne Publishers, 1987), 35.

25. Mary Ware Dennett, "Crematoria," MWD School Papers, MWD Papers.

26. Drexel hire letter, December 12, 1894, MWD Papers.

27. Author interview with Sharon Spaulding, Sandy, UT, May 12, 2022.

28. Chen, "*The Sex Side of Life*," 24.

29. Chen, 33.

30. Lederer, "'The Dynamic Side of Life,'" 95.

31. Mary Ware Dennett, handwritten notebook, "For my dear boys Carleton and Devon," Sharon Spaulding / Dennett Family Archives, Alstead, NH & Sandy, UT, 11–12.

32. Dennett, 12.

33. Dennett, 14.

34. Chen, "*The Sex Side of Life*," 30.

35. "William Morris and His Legacy," National Portrait Gallery, London, for the exhibition *Anarchy & Beauty: William Morris and His Legacy, 1860–1960*, 2014–2015,

https://www.npg.org.uk/whatson/anarchy-beauty-william-morris-and-his-legacy-1860-1960/new.
36. Chen, *"The Sex Side of Life,"* 45.
37. Chen, 35.
38. Chen, 35.
39. Author interview with Sharon Spaulding, Sandy, UT, May 14, 2022.
40. Dennett, "Curriculum Vitae."
41. Chen, *"The Sex Side of Life,"* 41.
42. Hollister, "Rare Species Identified," 7.
43. Mary Ware Dennett to Annie O. Dennett, June 10, 1900, Sharon Spaulding / Dennett Family Archives, Alstead, NH & Sandy, UT.
44. Mary Ware Dennett to Annie O. Dennett, August 16, 1900, Sharon Spaulding / Dennett Family Archives, Alstead, NH & Sandy, UT.
45. Mary Ware Dennett, "The Sex Side of Life: An Explanation for Young People," 6th printing (New York: privately printed by the author, 1919), https://www.gutenberg.org/files/31732/31732-h/31732-h.htm.
46. Dennett.
47. Hartley Dennett to Annie O. Dennett, December 23, 1900, Sunday night, Sharon Spaulding / Dennett Family Archives, Alstead, NH & Sandy, UT.
48. Mary Ware Dennett to Marie Stopes, marked private, October 31, 1921, Sharon Spaulding / Dennett Family Archives, Alstead, NH & Sandy, UT.
49. Chen, *"The Sex Side of Life,"* 50.
50. Chen, 55.
51. Dennett to Marie Stopes, October 31, 1921.
52. Dennett to Stopes, October 31, 1921.
53. Dennett to Stopes, October 31, 1921.
54. Dennett to W. F. Robie, January 25, 1920, Sharon Spaulding / Dennett Family Archives, Alstead, NH & Sandy, UT.

CHAPTER 2: MAGGIE HIGGINS

1. H. G. Wells, quoted in Gloria Steinem, "Margaret Sanger," *Time,* international ed., 151, no. 14 (April 13, 1998), https://content.time.com/time/subscriber/article/0,33009,988152,00.html (accessed April 20, 2024).
2. Jill Lepore, *The Secret History of Wonder Woman* (New York: Vintage, 2015).
3. *The Selected Papers of Margaret Sanger,* ed. Esther Katz, asst. ed. Cathy Moran Hajo and Peter C. Engelman, vol. 1, *The Woman Rebel, 1900–1928* (Urbana: University of Illinois Press, 2003), xxi.
4. Ellen Chesler, *Woman of Valor:* Margaret Sanger and the Birth Control Movement in America (New York: Simon & Schuster, 1992), 41.
5. Margaret Sanger, *Margaret Sanger: An Autobiography* (New York: W. W. Norton, 1938), chap. 9, chap. 1, https://www.gutenberg.org/files/56610/56610-h/56610-h.htm (accessed April 22, 2022).
6. Sanger, *Autobiography,* ch. 1; Jean Baker, *Margaret Sanger: A Life of Passion* (New York: Hill and Wang, 2011), 9.
7. *Selected Papers,* 1:xxiv.
8. Sanger, *Autobiography,* chap. 1.
9. Quoted in Sanger, epigraph to chap. 2.
10. Schlesinger-Rockefeller Oral History Project interview with Grant Sanger, MD, by Ellen Chesler, August 1976.

11. Sanger, *Autobiography*, chap. 3.

12. Sanger, chap. 4.

13. *The Selected Papers of Margaret Sanger*, ed. Esther Katz, asst. ed. Cathy Moran Hajo and Peter C. Engelman, vol. 2, *Birth Control Comes of Age, 1928–1939* (Urbana: University of Illinois Press, 2007), 261n8.

14. James F. McKenzie, Robert R. Pinger, and Jerome E. Kotecki, *An Introduction to Community Health*, 6th ed. (Sudbury, MA: Jones and Bartlett, 2007), 121–22.

15. Judith Walzer Leavitt, *Brought to Bed: Childbearing in America, 1750 to 1950*, 30th anniversary ed. (New York: Oxford University Press, 2016), 20.

16. Andrea Tone, *Devices and Desires: A History of Contraceptives in America* (New York: Hill and Wang, 2001), 137.

17. Elizabeth Hlavinka, "Racial Bias in Flexner Report Permeates Medical Education Today," *Medpage Today*, June 18, 2020, https://www.medpagetoday.com /publichealthpolicy/medicaleducation/87171.

18. Tone, *Devices and Desires*, 128.

19. Carl N. Degler, *At Odds: Women and the Family in America from the Revolution to the Present* (New York: Oxford University Press, 1980), 238.

20. Jennifer Schuessler, "The Fight Over Abortion History," *New York Times*, May 4, 2022, https://www.nytimes.com/2022/05/04/arts/roe-v-wade-abortion-history .html.

21. S. Josephine Baker, *Fighting for Life* (New York: The Macmillan Company, 1939), 115–16; Barbara Ehrenreich and Deirdre English, *Witches, Midwives & Nurses*, 2nd ed. (New York: Feminist Press, 2010), 86.

22. Leavitt, *Brought to Bed*, 121.

23. Leavitt, 121.

24. Vivienne Souter et al., "Comparison of Midwifery and Obstetric Care in Low-Risk Hospital Births," *Obstetrics & Gynecology* 134, no. 5 (November 2019): 1056–65, https://doi.org/10.1097/aog.0000000000003521.

25. Chesler, *Woman of Valor*, 52.

26. Chesler, *Woman of Valor*, 54.

27. Sanger, *Autobiography*, chap. 5.

28. Sanger, chap. 5.

29. Chesler, *Woman of Valor*, 207.

30. Sanger, *Autobiography*, chap. 5.

31. Sanger, chap. 5.

32. Sanger, chap. 5.

33. Sanger, chap. 5.

34. Peter C. Engelman, *A History of the Birth Control Movement in America* (Santa Barbara, CA: Praeger, 2011), 28.

35. Margaret Sanger, quoted in Carole R. McCann, *Birth Control Politics in the United States, 1916–1945* (Ithaca, NY: Cornell University Press, 1994), 12.

36. Baker, *Margaret Sanger*, 49.

37. Sanger, *Autobiography*, chap. 7.

38. Constance Chen, *"The Sex Side of Life": Mary Ware Dennett's Pioneering Battle for Birth Control and Sex Education* (New York: The New Press, 1996), 165.

39. Sanger, *Autobiography*, chap. 7.

40. Sanger, chap. 7.

41. Sanger, chap. 7.

42. Quoted in Baker, *Margaret Sanger*, 50.

CHAPTER 3: THIS NEFARIOUS BUSINESS

1. Advertisement quoted in Amy C. Sarch, "Dirty Discourse: Birth Control Advertising in the 1920s and 1930s" (PhD diss., University of Pennsylvania, 1994), 43.
2. Anthony Comstock, *Traps for the Young* (New York: Funk & Wagnalls, 1883), 7.
3. Comstock, 240.
4. Janet Farrell Brodie, *Contraception and Abortion in Nineteenth-Century America* (Ithaca, NY: Cornell University Press, 1994), 5.
5. Brodie, 191.
6. Wayne E. Fuller, *Morality and the Mail in Nineteenth-Century America* (Urbana: University of Illinois Press, 2003), 180–81.
7. Fuller, 180–81.
8. Brodie, *Contraception and Abortion*, 192.
9. Helen Lefkowitz Horowitz, "Victoria Woodhull, Anthony Comstock, and Conflict over Sex in the United States in the 1870s," *Journal of American History* 87, no. 2 (September 2000): 433.
10. Amy Sohn, *The Man Who Hated Women: Sex, Censorship, and Civil Liberties in the Gilded Age* (New York: Farrar, Straus & Giroux, 2021), 62.
11. Sohn, 26.
12. Sohn, 25.
13. Constance Chen, *"The Sex Side of Life": Mary Ware Dennett's Pioneering Battle for Birth Control and Sex Education* (New York: The New Press, 1996), xiv.
14. Edward De Grazia, *Girls Lean Back Everywhere: The Law of Obscenity and the Assault on Genius* (New York: Random House, 1992), 6.
15. Molly McGarry, "Spectral Sexualities: Nineteenth-Century Spiritualism, Moral Panics, and the Making of U.S. Obscenity Law," *Journal of Women's History* 12, no. 2 (Summer 2000): 17.
16. Nicola Kay Beisel, *Imperiled Innocents: Anthony Comstock and Family Reproduction in Victorian America* (Princeton, NJ: Princeton University Press, 1997), 170.
17. Comstock, quoted in Beisel, 72.
18. "An Act for the Suppression of Trade in, and Circulation of, obscene Literature and Articles of immoral Use," https://wams.nyhistory.org/industry-and-empire/fighting-for-equality/comstock-act/, accessed June 20, 2023.
19. McGarry, "Spectral Sexualities," 1.
20. Brodie, *Contraception and Abortion*, 264.
21. "Letter against the Comstock Act," March 18, 1879, History, Art & Archives of the US House of Representatives, https://history.house.gov/Records-and-Research/Listing/c_019/, accessed June 20, 2023.
22. Sohn, *Man Who Hated Women*, 130.
23. Brodie, *Contraception and Abortion*, 266.
24. Sohn, *Man Who Hated Women*, 33.
25. Sohn, 83–84.
26. Chen, *"The Sex Side of Life,"* xx.
27. "History of Birth Control," online exhibit, Case Western Reserve College of Arts and Sciences, Dittrick Medical History Center, https://artsci.case.edu/dittrick/online-exhibits/history-of-birth-control/, accessed June 20, 2023.
28. Peter C. Engelman, *A History of the Birth Control Movement in America* (Santa Barbara, CA: Praeger, 2011), 10–11.
29. Andrea Tone, "Black Market Birth Control: Contraceptive Entrepreneurship and

Criminality in the Gilded Age," *Journal of American History* 87, no. 2 (September 2000): 435–59, https://doi.org/10.2307/2568759.

30. Beisel, *Imperiled Innocents*, 88.
31. Heywood, quoted in Beisel, 65.
32. Tone, "Black Market Birth Control," 443.
33. Tone, 452.
34. Sohn, *Man Who Hated Women*, chap. 8.
35. Tone, "Black Market Birth Control," 455.
36. Donna J. Drucker, *Contraception: A Concise History* (Cambridge, MA: MIT Press, 2020), chap. 2.
37. Trent MacNamara, *Birth Control and American Modernity: A History of Popular Ideas* (New York: Cambridge University Press, 2018), 12.
38. Daniel Scott Smith, "Family Limitation, Sexual Control, and Domestic Feminism in Victorian America," in *Clio's Consciousness Raised: New Perspectives on the History of Women*, ed. Mary S. Hartman and Lois Banner (New York: Octagon Books, 1976), 129.
39. MacNamara, *Birth Control and American Modernity*, 12.
40. Angela Y. Davis, *Women, Race & Class* (New York: Random House, 1981), 206.
41. "History of Birth Control," online exhibit.
42. Etienne Van De Walle and Virginie de Luca, "Birth Prevention in the American and French Fertility Transitions: Contrasts in Knowledge and Practice," *Population & Development Review* 32, no. 3 (September 2006): 539.
43. MacNamara, *Birth Control and American Modernity*, 10.
44. Jefferson, quoted in Dorothy Roberts, *Killing the Black Body: Race, Reproduction, and the Meaning of Liberty* (New York: Pantheon Books, 1997), 25.
45. Davis, *Women, Race & Class*, 204–5.
46. Brodie, *Contraception and Abortion*, 53.
47. Treva B. Lindsey, "What Did the Suffragists Really Think about Abortion?," *Smithsonian*, May 26, 2022, https://www.smithsonianmag.com/history/what-did-the-suffragists-really-think-about-abortion-180980124/.
48. Sarch, "Dirty Discourse," 58.
49. Grimké, quoted in Davis, *Women, Race & Class*, 207.
50. Kristin Luker, "Sex, Social Hygiene, and the State: The Double-Edged Sword of Social Reform," *Theory and Society* 27, no. 5 (October 1998): 608.
51. Carl N. Degler, *At Odds: Women and the Family in America from the Revolution to the Present* (New York: Oxford University Press, 1980), 201.
52. Briana Bierschbach, "This Woman Fought to End Minnesota's 'Marital Rape' Exception, and Won," NPR, May 4, 2019, https://www.npr.org/2019/05/04/719635969/this-woman-fought-to-end-minnesotas-marital-rape-exception-and-won.
53. Brodie, *Contraception and Abortion*, 78.
54. Brodie, 216–17.
55. Brodie, 221.
56. Quoted from copy in *Medical Adviser and Marriage Guide*, editions from 1854 to 1870, featured in Brodie, *Contraception and Abortion*, 219.
57. Brodie, 221.
58. Engelman, *History of the Birth Control Movement*, 11.
59. Cari Romm, "Before There Were Home Pregnancy Tests," *The Atlantic*, June 17, 2015, theatlantic.com/health/archive/2015/06/history-home-pregnancy-test/396077/.
60. Jessica L. Furgerson, *The Battle for Birth Control: Exploring the Lasting*

Consequences of the Movement's Early Rhetoric (Lanham, MD: Lexington Books, 2022), 87.

61. John M. Riddle, *Eve's Herbs: A History of Contraception and Abortion in the West* (Cambridge, MA: Harvard University Press, 1997), 219.
62. Cary Aspinwal, "'They Railroad Them': The States Using 'Fetal Personhood' Laws to Criminalize Mothers," *The Guardian*, July 25, 2023, https://www.theguardian.com/world/2023/jul/25/states-using-fetal-personhood-laws-to-criminalize-mothers.
63. "ACOG Statement on 'Personhood' Measures," American College of Obstetricians and Gynecologists, November 9, 2022, https://www.acog.org/clinical-information/policy-and-position-statements/position-statements/2022/acog-statement-on-personhood-measures.
64. Gerard Letterie and Dov Fox, "The Irony of Pro-life Efforts to Grant Embryos Legal Personhood," *Bill of Health* (blog), May 15, 2023, https://blog.petrieflom.law.harvard.edu/2023/05/15/the-irony-of-pro-life-efforts-to-grant-embryos-legal-personhood/.
65. Letterie and Fox.
66. Linda Gordon, *The Moral Property of Women: A History of Birth Control Politics in America* (Urbana: University of Illinois Press, 2007, paperback edition; substantially revised and updated from *Woman's Body, Woman's Right*, 1974), 30.
67. Sohn, *Man Who Hated Women*, 115.
68. Chesler, *Woman of Valor*, 64–65.
69. Andrea Tone, *Devices and Desires: A History of Contraceptives in America* (New York: Hill and Wang, 2001), 42.
70. MacNamara, *Birth Control and American Modernity*, 1.
71. Brodie, *Contraception and Abortion*, 2.
72. James Reed, *The Birth Control Movement and American Society: From Private Vice to Public Virtue* (Princeton, NJ: Princeton University Press, 1978), 17.
73. Judith Walzer Leavitt, *Brought to Bed: Childbearing in America, 1750 to 1950*, 30th anniversary ed. (New York: Oxford University Press, 2016), 19–20.
74. Beth Widmaier Capo, *Textual Contraception: Birth Control and Modern American Fiction* (Columbus: Ohio State University Press, 2021), 15–16.
75. Jessie M. Rodrique, "The Afro-American Community and the Birth Control Movement, 1918–1942" (PhD diss., University of Massachusetts Amherst, 1991), 6.
76. Engelman, *History of the Birth Control Movement*, 5.
77. Owen, quoted in Van De Walle and Luca, "Birth Prevention in the American and French Fertility Transitions," 535.
78. Katha Pollitt, "Abortion in American History," *The Atlantic*, May 1997, https://www.theatlantic.com/magazine/archive/1997/05/abortion-in-american-history/376851.
79. Brodie, *Contraception and Abortion*, 99.
80. Brodie, 112.
81. Helen Lefkowitz Horowitz, *Rereading Sex: Battles over Sexual Knowledge and Suppression in Nineteenth-Century America* (New York: Vintage, 2003), 91.
82. Horowitz, *Rereading Sex*, 113.
83. Brodie, *Contraception and Abortion*, 113.
84. Carl N. Degler, "What Ought to Be and What Was," *American Historical Review* 79, no. 5 (December 1974): 1468.
85. Horowitz, *Rereading Sex*, 276.
86. Brodie, *Contraception and Abortion*, 64–65.
87. Brodie, 206.
88. M. E. Melody and Linda M. Peterson, *Teaching America about Sex: Marriage*

Guides and Sex Manuals from the Late Victorians to Dr. Ruth (New York: New York University Press, 1999), 31.

89. Chesler, *Woman of Valor*, 197.

90. Safar Saydschoev, "History of Medicine Book of the Week: *Tokology* (1883)," Indiana University School of Medicine, June 5, 2020, https://medicine.iu.edu/blogs /medical-library/history-of-medicine-book-of-the-week–tokology.

91. Norman E. Himes, *The Medical History of Contraception* (New York: Schocken Books, 1936 [1970 ed.]), 276.

92. Marsha Silberman, "The Perfect Storm: Late Nineteenth-Century Chicago Sex Radicals: Moses Harman, Ida Craddock, Alice Stockham and the Comstock Obscenity Laws," *Journal of the Illinois State Historical Society* 102, no. 3/4 (Fall-Winter 2009): 324–67, https://www.jstor.org/stable/25701240.

93. Kara Platoni, "The Sex Scholar," *Stanford Magazine*, March/April 2010, https:// stanfordmag.org/contents/the-sex-scholar.

94. John D'Emilio and Estelle B. Freedman, *Intimate Matters: A History of Sexuality in America* (New York: Harper & Row, 1988), 180.

95. Brodie, *Contraception and Abortion*, 202.

96. Degler, *At Odds*, 214.

97. Tone, *Devices and Desires*, 78.

98. Brodie, *Contraception and Abortion*, 58.

99. Reed, *Birth Control Movement*, 32.

100. Platoni, "The Sex Scholar."

101. Robert Latou Dickinson, "Marital Maladjustment—The Business of Preventive Gynecology," *Long Island Medical Journal* 2 (1908): 1–5, quoted in David M. Kennedy, *Birth Control in America: The Career of Margaret Sanger* (New Haven, CT: Yale University Press, 1970), 54.

102. Lillian Faderman, *Woman: The American History of an Idea* (New Haven, CT: Yale University Press, 2022), ebook loc. 4,381.

103. Chesler, *Woman of Valor*, 71.

104. Platoni, "The Sex Scholar."

CHAPTER 4: A BUTTERFLY ON THE WHEEL

1. "Mr. and Mrs. Hartley Dennett Succumb to Pneumonia," unknown magazine, 1936, Sharon Spaulding / Dennett Family Archives, Alstead, NH & Sandy, UT.

2. Mary Ware Dennett, "For My Sons after My Death," Spaulding typescript, Sharon Spaulding / Dennett Family Archives, Alstead, NH & Sandy, UT, 105.

3. Constance Chen, *"The Sex Side of Life": Mary Ware Dennett's Pioneering Battle for Birth Control and Sex Education* (New York: The New Press, 1996), 61–62.

4. Mary Ware Dennett to Marie Stopes, October 31, 1921, Stopes papers, British Library.

5. Dennett, "For My Sons after My Death," 105.

6. Mary Ware Dennett, handwritten notebook, "For my dear boys Carleton and Devon," Sharon Spaulding / Dennett Family Archives, Alstead, NH & Sandy, UT, 4.

7. Chen, *"The Sex Side of Life,"* 57.

8. "Divorce History: How the Divorce Process Changed for the Better," Law Office of Polly A. Tatum: Mediation Advantage, accessed April 22, 2022, https://www .lawofficeofpollytatum.com/blog/divorce-history-how-the-divorce-process-changed -for-the-better/.

9. William L. O'Neill, *Divorce in the Progressive Era* (New Haven, CT: Yale University Press, 1967), 70–71.

10. William L. O'Neill, "Divorce in the Progressive Era," *American Quarterly* 17, no. 2 (Summer 1965): 203–17, https://doi.org/10.2307/2711354.
11. David M. Kennedy, *Birth Control in America: The Career of Margaret Sanger* (New Haven, CT: Yale University Press, 1970), 42.
12. Dorothy M. Brown, *Setting a Course: American Women in the 1920s* (Boston: Twayne, 1987), 122.
13. Jill Lepore, "Fixed," *The New Yorker*, March 22, 2010, https://www.newyorker.com /magazine/2010/03/29/fixed.
14. Lepore.
15. Kevin Brownlow, *Behind the Mask of Innocence: Sex, Violence, Prejudice, Crime: Films of Social Conscience in the Silent Era* (New York: Knopf, 1990), 41.
16. Kate Chopin, *The Awakening* (Chicago: Herbert S. Stone, 1899), 300.
17. Claire Vaye Watkins, "The Classic Novel That Saw Pleasure as a Path to Freedom," *New York Times*, February 5, 2020, https://www.nytimes.com/2020/02/05/books /review/kate-chopin-the-awakening.html.
18. Mary Ware Dennett, divorce folder, MWD Papers.
19. Dennett, divorce folder.
20. Hartley Dennett notebook, n.d., Sharon Spaulding / Dennett Family Archives, Alstead, NH & Sandy, UT.
21. Chen, *"The Sex Side of Life,"* 89.
22. Chen, 79–80.
23. Chen, 78.
24. Chen, 77.
25. Dennett, divorce folder, MWD Papers.
26. Dennett, "For my dear boys Carleton and Devon," 1.
27. Dennett, 2.
28. Transcript of custody hearing, February 15, 1913, before Judge F. W. Dallinger, MWD Papers.
29. Lynn Lederer, "'The Dynamic Side of Life'—The Emergence of Mary Coffin Ware Dennett as a Radical Sex Educator" (PhD diss., Rutgers University, 2011), 142–43.
30. Chen, *"The Sex Side of Life,"* 92.
31. Hartley Dennett to Mary Ware Dennett, December 4, 1909, MWD Papers.
32. Transcript of custody hearing, February 15, 1913.
33. Divorce folder, MWD Papers.
34. Divorce folder.
35. Mary Ware Dennett, petition before Judge Chamberlain, September 22, 1909, MWD Papers.
36. Dennett, petition.
37. Divorce folder, MWD Papers.
38. Divorce folder.
39. Divorce folder.
40. *Report of Referee, Mary Ware Dennett, Libellant, vs. Hartley Dennett, Libellee*, Commonwealth of MA Superior Court, n.d., Sharon Spaulding / Dennett Family Archives, Alstead, NH & Sandy, UT.
41. *Report of Referee.*
42. Chen, *"The Sex Side of Life,"* 104–5.
43. Chen, 101.
44. Hartley Dennett to Mary Ware Dennett, January 20, 1911, from Alstead, Sharon Spaulding / Dennett Family Archives, Alstead, NH & Sandy, UT.
45. Chen, *"The Sex Side of Life,"* 105.

46. Mary Ware Dennett to Carleton Dennett, April 28, 1913, MWD Papers.
47. Mary Ware Dennett to Carleton Dennett, June 12, 1918, Sharon Spaulding
    / Dennett Family Archives, Alstead, NH & Sandy, UT.
48. "Play Paralleled in Divorce Court," *Boston Journal*, February 12, 1913, MWD
    Papers.
49. "Mrs. Dennett Will Not Join 'Golden Rule Triangle,'" *The World*, February 1, 1913,
    divorce folder, MWD Papers.
50. Chen, *"The Sex Side of Life,"* 178.

CHAPTER 5: THE ROAD TO 81 SINGER STREET

1. Mary Ware Dennett, "For My Sons after My Death," Spaulding typescript, Sharon
   Spaulding / Dennett Family Archives, Alstead, NH & Sandy, UT, 133.
2. Dennett, 176.
3. Constance Chen, *"The Sex Side of Life": Mary Ware Dennett's Pioneering Battle for
   Birth Control and Sex Education* (New York: The New Press, 1996), 106.
4. Carleton Dennett to Hartley Dennett, January 10, 1915, Sharon Spaulding
   / Dennett Family Archives, Alstead, NH & Sandy, UT.
5. Dennett, "For My Sons after My Death," 181.
6. Chen, *"The Sex Side of Life,"* 112.
7. Author interview with Sharon Spaulding, Sandy, UT, May 13, 2022.
8. 1911 New Year's card, MWD Papers.
9. "Suffrage Parade in New York City, ca. 1912," Records of the Office of War
   Information, accessed April 22, 2022, https://www.docsteach.org/documents/
   document/suffragette-parade-nyc.
10. "Suffrage Will Own 'The Town' To-Night," *The Sun* (New York), November 9, 1912, p. 9.
11. "Suffrage Parade in New York City, ca. 1912"; "The Two 1912 New York
    Suffrage Parades," Suffragette City 100, accessed December 18, 2023, https://
    suffragettecity100.com/57.
12. Ad for the Suffragist Special of *The Sun* (New York), May 2, 1914, p. 8.
13. Lynn Lederer, "'The Dynamic Side of Life'—The Emergence of Mary Coffin Ware
    Dennett as a Radical Sex Educator" (PhD diss., Rutgers University, 2011), 145.
14. Dennett, quoted in Lederer, 146.
15. Dennett, quoted in Lederer, 146.
16. Barbara Leaming, *Katharine Hepburn* (New York: Crown, 1995), 153.
17. Lederer, "'The Dynamic Side of Life,'" 153–54.
18. Joan Johnson, *Funding Feminism: Monied Women, Philanthropy, and the Women's
    Movement, 1870–1967* (Chapel Hill: University of North Carolina Press, 2017), 71.
19. "Memorandum Concerning the Prosecution of Mrs. Margaret H. Sanger of New
    York, U.S.A., for Her Advocacy of Birth Control and Her Issue of a Pamphlet
    entitled 'Family Limitation' Describing Various Methods of Restricting Families,"
    International Neo-Malthusian Bureau of Correspondence and Defence (Founded
    at the Third International Neo-Malthusian Conference at the Age, July 1910),
    MWD Papers.
20. Emmeline Pethick-Lawrence and Charlotte Perkins Gilman, pamphlet, [1911],
    MWD Papers, 12–13.
21. Gilman, quoted in Kimberly A. Hamlin, *From Eve to Evolution: Darwin, Science,
    and Women's Rights in Gilded Age America* (Chicago: University of Chicago Press,
    2014), 147–48.

22. Mary Ware Dennett, "Letter to the Freewoman," April 17, 1912, quoted in Lederer, "The Dynamic Side of Life," 205.
23. Dennett, quoted in Chen, *"The Sex Side of Life,"* 191.
24. Chen, 157.
25. Judith Schwarz, *Radical Feminists of Heterodoxy: Greenwich Village, 1912–1940* (Norwich, VT: New Victoria Publishers, 1986), 29. See also Joanna Scutts, *Hotbed: Bohemian Greenwich Village and the Secret Club that Sparked Modern Feminism* (New York: Seal Press, 2022).
26. Christine Stansell, *American Moderns: Bohemian New York and the Creation of a New Century* (New York: Metropolitan Books, 2000), 259.
27. Scutts, *Hotbed*, 200.
28. Schwarz, *Radical Feminists of Heterodoxy*, 25.
29. Chen, *"The Sex Side of Life,"* 158.
30. Schwarz, *Radical Feminists of Heterodoxy*, 1.
31. Mabel Dodge Luhan, *Movers and Shakers* (Albuquerque: University of New Mexico Press, 1936), 143.
32. Schwarz, *Radical Feminists of Heterodoxy*, 37.
33. "Nurseries in Flats Is Feminist Plea," *The Sun* (New York), May 26, 1914, p. 11.
34. Schwarz, *Radical Feminists of Heterodoxy*, 16.
35. *Variety*, September 1912, p. 18, https://archive.org/details/variety28-1912-09/page /n61/mode/2up (accessed July 2, 2023).
36. W. E. B. Du Bois, "The Damnation of Women," in *Darkwater: Voices from within the Veil* (New York: Harcourt & Brace, 1920).
37. Typescript by Mary Ware Dennett, n.d., Sharon Spaulding / Dennett Family Archives, Alstead, NH & Sandy, UT.
38. Kathleen Rooney, "Alice Duer Miller's Evergreen Question in 'Are Women People?,'" *Los Angeles Review of Books*, August 17, 2020, https://lareviewofbooks .org/article/alice-duer-millers-evergreen-question-in-are-women-people/.
39. Chen, *"The Sex Side of Life,"* 160.
40. Ellen Chesler, *Woman of Valor: Margaret Sanger and the Birth Control Movement in America* (New York: Simon & Schuster, 1992), 16.
41. Sanger, quoted in Lederer, "The Dynamic Side of Life," 205.
42. Lederer, 205.
43. Margaret Sanger, *Margaret Sanger: An Autobiography* (New York: W. W. Norton, 1938), chap. 9, https://www.gutenberg.org/files/56610/56610-h/56610-h.htm (accessed April 22, 2022).
44. Sanger, chap. 9.
45. Sanger, chap. 9.
46. Sanger, chap. 9.
47. Mabel Dodge Luhan, *Movers and Shakers* (Albuquerque: University of New Mexico Press, 1936), 69–70.

CHAPTER 6: REBEL WOMEN

1. Margaret Sanger, *Margaret Sanger: An Autobiography* (New York: W. W. Norton, 1938), chap. 6, https://www.gutenberg.org/files/56610/56610-h/56610-h.htm (accessed April 22, 2022).
2. Sanger, chap. 6.
3. Gene Burns, *The Moral Veto: Framing Contraception, Abortion, and Cultural Pluralism*

in the United States (Cambridge, UK: Cambridge University Press, 2005), 51.

4. "Outcome for the Socialist Party," part of the online exhibition *1912: Competing Visions for America*, Ohio State University, n.d., https://ehistory.osu.edu/exhibitions/1912/content/debs_outcome (accessed April 22, 2022).

5. Ellen Chesler, *Woman of Valor: Margaret Sanger and the Birth Control Movement in America* (New York: Simon & Schuster, 1992), 57.

6. Chesler, 75.

7. Christopher Klein, "The Strike That Shook America," History.com, November 26, 2019, https://www.history.com/news/the-strike-that-shook-america.

8. Klein, "Strike That Shook America."

9. James Reed, *The Birth Control Movement and American Society: From Private Vice to Public Virtue* (Princeton, NJ: Princeton University Press, 1978), 74–75.

10. Constance Chen, *"The Sex Side of Life": Mary Ware Dennett's Pioneering Battle for Birth Control and Sex Education* (New York: The New Press, 1996), 161.

11. Goldman, quoted in Chen, 161.

12. Linda Gordon, *The Moral Property of Women: A History of Birth Control Politics in America* (Urbana: University of Illinois Press, 2007, paperback edition; substantially revised and updated from *Woman's Body, Woman's Right*, 1974), 148.

13. "The New York Foundling Hospital," National Orphan Train Complex, accessed April 10, 2024, https://orphantraindepot.org/history/the-new-york-foundling-hospital/.

14. Amy Sohn, *The Man Who Hated Women: Sex, Censorship, and Civil Liberties in the Gilded Age* (New York: Farrar, Straus & Giroux, 2021), 253.

15. Candace Falk, *Love, Anarchy, & Emma Goldman: A Biography* (New York: Holt, Rinehart and Winston, 1984), 222.

16. Jean Baker, *Margaret Sanger: A Life of Passion* (New York: Hill and Wang, 2011), 47.

17. Sanger, quoted in Baker, 70.

18. Quoted in Baker, 70.

19. Peter C. Engelman, *A History of the Birth Control Movement in America* (Santa Barbara, CA: Praeger, 2011), 32.

20. *The Selected Papers of Margaret Sanger*, ed. Esther Katz, asst. ed. Cathy Moran Hajo and Peter C. Engelman, vol. 1, *The Woman Rebel, 1900–1928* (Urbana: University of Illinois Press, 2003), 43.

21. Sanger, *Autobiography*, chap. 8.

22. Chesler, *Woman of Valor*, 81.

23. Schwarz, quoted in Baker, *Margaret Sanger*, 63.

24. Hapgood, quoted in Chesler, *Woman of Valor*, 92.

25. Sanger, *Autobiography*, chap. 8.

26. Sanger, chap. 8.

27. Sanger, chap. 8.

28. Etienne Van De Walle and Virginie de Luca, "Birth Prevention in the American and French Fertility Transitions: Contrasts in Knowledge and Practice," *Population & Development Review* 32, no. 3 (September 2006): 529.

29. Bibia Pavard, "The Right to Know? The Politics of Information about Contraception in France (1950s–80s)," *Medical History* 63, no. 2 (April 2019), https://doi.org/10.1017%2Fmdh.2019.4.

30. Sanger, *Autobiography*, chap. 8.

31. Sanger, chap. 8.

32. Sanger, chap. 8.
33. Chesler, *Woman of Valor*, 95.
34. Chesler, *Woman of Valor*, 94.
35. Sanger, *Autobiography*, chap. 11.
36. Chesler, *Woman of Valor*, 91.
37. Chesler, 95.
38. *Selected Papers*, 1:69.
39. Baker, *Margaret Sanger*, 76–77.
40. Sanger, quoted in Beth Widmaier Capo, *Textual Contraception: Birth Control and Modern American Fiction* (Columbus: Ohio State University Press, 2021), 27.
41. *Selected Papers*, 1:72.
42. Sanger, *Autobiography*, chap. 9.
43. Margaret Sanger, *My Fight for Birth Control* (New York: Farrar & Rinehart, 1931), 81.
44. *Selected Papers*, 1:71.
45. *Selected Papers*, 1:75n4.
46. *Selected Papers*, 1:81.
47. *Selected Papers*, 1:84.
48. Baker, *Margaret Sanger*, 83.
49. Sanger, *Autobiography*, chap. 9.
50. Chesler, *Woman of Valor*, 102.
51. Margaret Sanger, *Family Limitation*, 6th ed. (privately published, 1917), MWD Papers.
52. Sanger, *Family Limitation*.
53. Sanger, quoted in Chesler, *Woman of Valor*, 103.
54. Sanger, *Autobiography*, chap. 9.
55. Sanger, quoted in Engelman, *History of the Birth Control Movement*, 44–45.
56. Engelman, 44.
57. Caroline Nelson to Mary Ware Dennett, April 1, 1930, MWD Papers.
58. Nelson to Dennett, April 1, 1930.
59. Sanger, quoted in Carole R. McCann, *Birth Control Politics in the United States, 1916–1945* (Ithaca, NY: Cornell University Press, 1994), 11.
60. Engelman, *History of the Birth Control Movement*, xviii.

CHAPTER 7: TWILIGHT SLEEP

1. G. A. Skowronski, "Pain Relief in Childbirth: Changing Historical and Feminist Perspectives," *Anaesthesia and Intensive Care*, July 2015, https://journals.sagepub.com/doi/pdf/10.1177/0310057X150430S106.
2. Ann Finkbiner, "Labor Dispute," review of *What a Blessing She Had Chloroform: The Medical and Social Response to the Pain of Childbirth from 1800 to the Present*, by Donald Caton, *New York Times*, October 31, 1999, Sunday Book Review, p. 20, https://www.nytimes.com/1999/10/31/books/labor-dispute.html.
3. Mary Boyd and Marguerite Tracy, *Painless Childbirth: A General Survey of All Painless Methods with Special Stress on "Twilight Sleep" and Its Extension to America* (New York: Frederick A. Stokes, 1915), 27.
4. Boyd and Tracy, 29.
5. Ellen Barry, "Chloroform in Childbirth? Yes, Please, the Queen Said," *New York Times* May 6, 2019, https://www.nytimes.com/2019/05/06/world/europe/uk-royal-births-labor.html.

6. Grimké, quoted in Angela Y. Davis, *Women, Race & Class* (New York: Random House, 1981), 207.

7. Kat Eschner, "It Didn't Take Very Long for Anesthesia to Change Childbirth," *Smithsonian*, December 27, 2017, https://www.smithsonianmag.com/smart-news /it-didnt-take-very-long-anesthesia-change-childbirth-180967636/.

8. Lawrence G. Miller, "Pain, Parturition, and the Profession: Twilight Sleep in America," in *Health Care in America: Essays in Social History*, ed. Susan Reverby and David Rosner (Philadelphia: Temple University Press, 1979), 22.

9. "Mrs. Dennett Will Not Join 'Golden Rule Triangle,'" *The World*, February 1, 1913.

10. Miller, "Pain, Parturition, and the Profession," 22.

11. Sarah Laskow, "In 1914, Feminists Fought for the Right to Forget Childbirth," *Atlas Obscura*, February 23, 2017, https://www.atlasobscura.com/articles/twilight-sleep -childbirth-1910s-feminists.

12. *Washington Herald*, January 22, 1915, p. 6, https://chroniclingamerica.loc.gov/lccn /sn83045433/1915-01-22/ed-1/seq-6/.

13. *Washington Herald*, January 22, 1915, p. 6.

14. "Society Women Spread Twilight Sleep Gospel to Prevent Future Suffering by the Mothers of the United States," *Washington Post*, January 3, 1915.

15. Report of the Executive Secretary [Marie Virginia Smith] of the Twilight Sleep Association, January 20–November 1, 1915, MWD Papers.

16. Judith Walzer Leavitt, "Birthing and Anesthesia: The Debate Over Twilight Sleep," *Signs* 6, no. 1 (Autumn 1980): 148; Finkbiner, "Labor Dispute."

17. Miller, "Pain, Parturition, and the Profession," 21.

18. Miller, 23.

19. Judith Walzer Leavitt, *Brought to Bed: Childbearing in America, 1750 to 1950*, 30th anniversary ed. (New York: Oxford University Press, 2016), 63.

20. Report of the Executive Secretary [Marie Virginia Smith] of the Twilight Sleep Association.

21. Leavitt, "Birthing and Anesthesia," 158.

22. Leavitt, 138.

23. Tamar Lindenbaum, "Patient's Orders: Twilight Sleep and the Female Medical Consumer in the Turn-of-the-Century United States, 1880–1920" (senior thesis, Barnard College , 2018), 62, https://history.barnard.edu/sites/default/files/inline -files/TamarLindenbaum_Patient%27s%20Orders_2018.pdf.

24. Jacqueline H. Wolf, *Deliver Me from Pain: Anesthesia and Birth in America*, reprint ed. (Baltimore: Johns Hopkins University Press, 2012), 60.

25. "American Experiments with Twilight Sleep," *St. Louis Post*, November 15, 1914.

26. Boyd and Tracy, *Painless Childbirth*, 145.

27. Report of the Executive Secretary [Marie Virginia Smith] of the Twilight Sleep Association.

28. Mary Ware Dennett, "Statement of the Executive Committee of the Twilight Sleep Association Concerning the report of the Temporary Finance Committee," August 11, 1916, MWD Papers.

29. Undated letters from MV Smith to MWD, MWD Papers.

30. Mary Ware Dennett, "For My Sons after My Death," Spaulding typescript, Sharon Spaulding / Dennett Family Archives, Alstead, NH & Sandy, UT, 184.

31. Laskow, "In 1914, Feminists Fought for the Right to Forget Childbirth."

32. "Doctors Disagree on Twilight Sleep," *New York Times*, August 24, 1915, p. 7, https://timesmachine.nytimes.com/timesmachine/1915/08/24/100174786. html?pageNumber=7.

33. Theodore Roosevelt, "Remarks Before the Mothers' Congress, March 13, 1905,"
    American Presidency Project, University of California, Santa Barbara, https://www
    .presidency.ucsb.edu/documents/remarks-before-the-mothers-congress (accessed
    June 23, 2023).
34. Leavitt, "Birthing and Anesthesia," 159.
35. Boyd and Tracy, *Painless Childbirth*, 196.
36. Sylvia Plath, *The Bell Jar* (New York: Harper Perennial, 2005), 50.
37. J. H. Salidsbury, "The Twilight Sleep in Obstetrics," letter to the editor, *Journal
    of the American Medical Association*, October 17, 1914, https://doi.org/10.1001
    /jama.1914.02570160076033.
38. Neel Shah, "I'm an OB/GYN Who Attended Thousands of Deliveries Before
    Wondering Why Americans Give Birth in Bed," *The Conversation*, January 8, 2020,
    https://theconversation.com/im-an-ob-gyn-who-attended-thousands-of-deliveries
    -before-wondering-why-americans-give-birth-in-bed-127894.

CHAPTER 8: NAUGHTY PAMPHLETS

1. Margaret Sanger, *Margaret Sanger: An Autobiography* (New York: W. W. Norton, 1938),
   chap. 10, https://www.gutenberg.org/files/56610/56610-h/56610-h.htm (accessed April
   22, 2022).
2. Sanger, chap. 11.
3. Ellen Chesler, *Woman of Valor: Margaret Sanger and the Birth Control Movement
   in America* (New York: Simon & Schuster, 1992), 118.
4. Sanger, *Autobiography*, chap. 10.
5. Chesler, *Woman of Valor*, 104.
6. Chesler, 107.
7. "Disorder in Court as Sanger Is Fined," *New York Times*, September 11, 1915,
   https://www.nytimes.com/1915/09/11/archives/disorder-in-court-as-sanger-is-fined
   -justices-order-room-cleared.html.
8. Chesler, *Woman of Valor*, 109.
9. Sanger, *Autobiography*, chap. 13.
10. Margaret Sanger to Anna E. Higgins, from Barcelona, March 25 or 26, 1915, in *The
    Selected Papers of Margaret Sanger*, ed. Esther Katz, asst. ed. Cathy Moran Hajo
    and Peter C. Engelman, vol. 1, *The Woman Rebel, 1900–1928* (Urbana: University
    of Illinois Press, 2003), 130.
11. Linda Gordon, *The Moral Property of Women: A History of Birth Control Politics in
    America* (Urbana: University of Illinois Press, 2007, paperback edition; substantially
    revised and updated from *Woman's Body, Woman's Right*, 1974), 178.
12. Sanger, *Autobiography*, chap. 12.
13. Sanger, quoted in Joan M. Jensen, "The Evolution of Margaret Sanger's 'Family
    Limitation' Pamphlet, 1914–1921, *Signs* 6, no. 3 (1981): 550.
14. June Rose, *Marie Stopes and the Sexual Revolution* (London: Faber & Faber, 1992), 90.
15. Sanger, *Autobiography*, chap. 14.
16. Stopes papers, British Library.
17. Rose, *Marie Stopes and the Sexual Revolution*, 90.
18. Rose, 78.
19. Sanger, *Autobiography*, chap. 14.
20. Marie Carmichael Stopes, *Married Love or Love in Marriage* (New York: The Critic
    and Guide Company, 1918), chap. 11, http://digital.library.upenn.edu/women
    /stopes/married/1918.html (accessed June 23, 2023).

21. Stopes, chap. 3.
22. Rose, *Marie Stopes and the Sexual Revolution*, 95.
23. Rose, 117.
24. Rose, 140.
25. Rose, 186.
26. Rose, 130.
27. Stopes, *Married Love*, Ch. 9.
28. Virginia Woolf to Molly McCarthy, 1923, in Virginia Woolf, *Letters*, 3:6, quoted in Layne Parish Craig, *When Sex Changed: Birth Control Politics and Literature between the World Wars* (New Brunswick, NJ: Rutgers University Press, 2013), epigraph to introduction.
29. Margaret Sanger to Marie Stopes, September 15, 1915, in *Selected Papers*, 1:161.
30. Stopes to President Wilson, September 1915, Stopes papers, British Library.
31. Edwin Black, *War against the Weak: Eugenics and America's Campaign to Create a Master Race* (New York: Four Walls Eight Windows, 2003), 16.
32. Black, 88.
33. Black, 94.
34. Daniel Okrent, *The Guarded Gate: Bigotry, Eugenics, and the Law That Kept Two Generations of Jews, Italians, and Other European Immigrants Out of America* (New York: Scribner, 2019), 353.
35. Jessica L. Furgerson, *The Battle for Birth Control: Exploring the Lasting Consequences of the Movement's Early Rhetoric* (Lanham, MD: Lexington Books, 2022), 197.
36. Victor Robinson, *Pioneers of Birth Control in England and America* (New York: Voluntary Parenthood League, 1919), 78.
37. Daylanne K. English, *Unnatural Selections: Eugenics in American Modernism and the Harlem Renaissance* (Chapel Hill: University of North Carolina Press, 2004), 13.
38. English, 14, 39.
39. "Disorder in Court as Sanger Is Fined," *New York Times*.
40. Chesler, *Woman of Valor*, 126.
41. "Disorder in Court as Sanger Is Fined," *New York Times*.
42. Bill Sanger, quoted in Furgerson, *Battle for Birth Control*, 5.
43. "Disorder in Court as Sanger Is Fined," *New York Times*.
44. Chesler, *Woman of Valor*, 126.
45. "Disorder in Court as Sanger Is Fined," *New York Times*.
46. Jean Baker, *Margaret Sanger: A Life of Passion* (New York: Hill and Wang, 2011), 100.
47. Chesler, *Woman of Valor*, 72.
48. Peter C. Engelman, *A History of the Birth Control Movement in America* (Santa Barbara, CA: Praeger, 2011), 56–57.

CHAPTER 9: FORBIDDEN KNOWLEDGE

1. Mary Ware Dennett to Carleton Dennett, January 10, 1915, MWD Papers.
2. Mary Ware Dennett, "For My Sons after My Death," Spaulding typescript, Sharon Spaulding / Dennett Family Archives, Alstead, NH & Sandy, UT, 178.
3. Dennett to Carleton Dennett, January 10, 1915, MWD Papers.
4. Jeffrey P. Moran, *Teaching Sex: The Shaping of Adolescence in the 20th Century* (Cambridge, MA: Harvard University Press, 2000), 52–53.
5. Moran, 52–53.

6. Moran, 63.
7. Moran, 111.
8. Moran, 23.
9. Moran, 28.
10. John D'Emilio and Estelle B. Freedman, *Intimate Matters: A History of Sexuality in America* (New York: Harper & Row, 1988), 204.
11. Prince Morrow, quoted in Bryan Strong, "Ideas of the Early Sex Education Movement in America, 1890–1920," *History of Education Quarterly* 12, no. 2 (Summer 1972): 136.
12. Madeline Hodgman, "On the Island of Dr. Morrow," College of Physicians of Philadelphia, December 5, 2016, http://histmed.collegeofphysicians.org/on-the -island-of-dr-morrow/.
13. Guidelines at Annual Meeting of ASHA, 1914, quoted in Strong, "Ideas of the Early Sex Education Movement in America," 139.
14. Eliot, quoted in D. M. Ferd. Krogh, "Physiology and Hygiene," *Mind and Body* 20 (March 1913–February 1914): 248.
15. Mary Ware Dennett to sons, October 31, 1915, MWD Papers.
16. Constance Chen, *"The Sex Side of Life": Mary Ware Dennett's Pioneering Battle for Birth Control and Sex Education* (New York: The New Press, 1996), 171.
17. Mary Ware Dennett, *The Sex Side of Life: An Explanation for Young People*, 6th printing (privately printed, 1919), p. 2, https://www.gutenberg.org/ files/31732/31732-h/31732-h.htm (accessed June 16, 2023).
18. Strong, "Ideas of the Early Sex Education Movement in America," 151.
19. Strong, 152.
20. Dennett, *Sex Side of Life*, 5.
21. Dennett, 5.
22. Dennett, 9–10.
23. Dennett, *Who's Obscene?* (New York: The Vanguard Press, 1930), https://archive .org/stream/b29814601/b29814601_djvu.txt (accessed December 9, 2019).
24. "A friend" to Dennett, February 11, 1916, MWD Papers.
25. Havelock Ellis to Dennett, May 11, 1916, MWD Papers.
26. Ellen Chesler, *Woman of Valor: Margaret Sanger and the Birth Control Movement in America* (New York: Simon & Schuster, 1992), 129.
27. *Harper's Weekly*, April 24, 1915, quoted in Peter C. Engelman, *A History of the Birth Control Movement in America* (Santa Barbara, CA: Praeger, 2011), 49.
28. *Harper's Weekly*, April 24, 1915, quoted in Dolores Flamiano, "The Birth of a Notion: Media Coverage of Contraception, 1915–1917," *Journalism & Mass Communication Quarterly* 75, no. 3 (September 1998): 565.
29. Chesler, *Woman of Valor*, 130.
30. Linda Gordon, *The Moral Property of Women: A History of Birth Control Politics in America* (Urbana: University of Illinois Press, 2007, paperback edition; substantially revised and updated from *Woman's Body, Woman's Right*, 1974), 395n113.
31. Jessie Ashley to Mary Ware Dennett, n.d., from White Mountains, MWD Papers.
32. Ashley to Dennett, n.d.
33. Chen, *"The Sex Side of Life,"* 180.
34. "Typescript of Speech at the Meeting Which Organized the National Birth Control League—March 1915 at Clara Stillman's House," MWD Papers.
35. Chen, *"The Sex Side of Life,"* 184.
36. Chen, 183–84.
37. Anthony Comstock to Clara Gruening Stillman, April 28, 1915, MWD Papers.

38. Mary Alden Hopkins, "Birth Control and Public Morals: An Interview with Anthony Comstock," *Harper's Weekly*, May 22, 1915, p. 490.

39. Unsigned, undated mailing from NBCL, MWD Papers.

CHAPTER 10: MATTERS OF THE HEART

1. Mary Ware Dennett, "For My Sons after My Death," Spaulding typescript, Sharon Spaulding / Dennett Family Archives, Alstead, NH & Sandy, UT, 62.

2. Dennett, 18–19.

3. Dennett, 20.

4. Dennett, 20.

5. Dennett, 24.

6. Dennett, 24.

7. Dennett, 32.

8. Dennett, 33.

9. Constance Chen, *"The Sex Side of Life": Mary Ware Dennett's Pioneering Battle for Birth Control and Sex Education* (New York: The New Press, 1996), 90.

10. Mary Ware Dennett to Hartley Dennett, January 20, 1915, Sharon Spaulding / Dennett Family Archives, Alstead, NH & Sandy, UT.

11. Dennett, "For My Sons after My Death," 43.

12. Annie O. Dennett to Hartley Dennett, March 1 and 2, 1915, quoted in Chen, *"The Sex Side of Life,"* 355n557.

13. "'Eternal Triangle' Proves Satisfactory to These 3 People," *Tacoma Times*, February 13, 1915, p. 1.

14. Dennett, "For My Sons after My Death," 44.

15. Dennett, 56.

16. Dennett, 56.

17. Dennett, 61–62.

18. Dennett, 62.

19. Dennett, 68.

20. Dennett, 68.

21. Dennett, 79.

22. Dennett, 85.

23. Dennett, 94.

24. Dennett, 69–70.

25. Lynn Lederer, "'The Dynamic Side of Life'—The Emergence of Mary Coffin Ware Dennett as a Radical Sex Educator" (PhD diss., Rutgers University, 2011), 144.

26. Dennett, quoted in Lederer, 144.

27. Dennett, "For My Sons after My Death," 99.

28. Dennett, 136.

29. Dennett, 139.

30. Dennett, 144.

31. Dennett, 149.

32. Dennett, 206.

33. Dennett, 39.

34. I. C., "The Winner," *The Century*, February 1917, p. 475, MWD Papers.

35. I. C., "The Winner."

36. Mary Ware Dennett to Hartley Dennett, July 21 [? 1 could be /], 1916, from East Fifty-Fifth Street, Sharon Spaulding / Dennett Family Archives, Alstead, NH & Sandy, UT.

37. Hartley Dennett to Mary Ware Dennett, August 5, 1916, Sharon Spaulding / Dennett Family Archives, Alstead, NH & Sandy, UT.
38. Hartley Dennett to Mary Ware Dennett, from Alstead, March 3, 1915, Sharon Spaulding / Dennett Family Archives, Alstead, NH & Sandy, UT.
39. Nancy Dennett interview with author, March 7, 2021, Zoom.
40. Dennett, "For My Sons after My Death," 208.
41. Mary Ware Dennett to Carleton Dennett, June 12, 1918, Sharon Spaulding / Dennett Family Archives, Alstead, NH & Sandy, UT.
42. Dennett, "For My Sons after My Death," 208.
43. Dennett, 159.

CHAPTER 11: FACING THE INEXORABLE

1. Margaret Sanger, *Margaret Sanger: An Autobiography* (New York: W. W. Norton, 1938), chap. 15, https://www.gutenberg.org/files/56610/56610-h/56610-h.htm (accessed April 22, 2022).
2. Sanger, chap. 15.
3. Sanger, chap. 15.
4. Sanger, chap. 15.
5. Sanger, chap. 15.
6. Robin Pokorski, "'The Joy in the Fullness of Life': Peggy Sanger," Margaret Sanger Papers Project Research Annex, November 6, 2013, https://sangerpapers.wordpress.com/2013/11/06/the-joy-in-the-fullness-of-life-peggy-sanger/.
7. Editorial note, *The Selected Papers of Margaret Sanger*, ed. Esther Katz, asst. ed. Cathy Moran Hajo and Peter C. Engelman, vol. 1, *The Woman Rebel, 1900–1928* (Urbana: University of Illinois Press, 2003), 376.
8. Quoted in David M. Kennedy, *Birth Control in America: The Career of Margaret Sanger* (New Haven, CT: Yale University Press, 1970), 14.
9. Emma Goldman to Margaret Sanger, December 7, 1915, quoted in Candace Falk, *Love, Anarchy, & Emma Goldman: A Biography* (New York: Holt, Rinehart and Winston, 1984), 242.
10. Sanger, *Autobiography*, chap. 6.
11. Peter C. Engelman, *A History of the Birth Control Movement in America* (Santa Barbara, CA: Praeger, 2011), 30.
12. Sanger, *Autobiography*, chap. 16.
13. Falk, *Love, Anarchy, & Emma Goldman,* 243–44.
14. Falk, 244.
15. Sanger to T. J. Mead, September 27, 1929, in *The Selected Papers of Margaret Sanger*, ed. Esther Katz, asst. ed. Cathy Moran Hajo and Peter C. Engelman, vol. 2, *Birth Control Comes of Age, 1928–1939* (Urbana: University of Illinois Press, 2007), 39.
16. Sanger, *Autobiography*, chap. 16.
17. Emma Goldman, *Living My Life* (New York: Dover, 1970), 2:591.
18. Quoted in Ellen Chesler, *Woman of Valor: Margaret Sanger and the Birth Control Movement in America* (New York: Simon & Schuster, 1992), 87.
19. Sanger, *Autobiography*, chap. 15.
20. *Selected Papers*, 1:177.
21. Pokorski, "'Joy in the Fullness of Life.'"

CHAPTER 12: THE LAWBREAKER

1. Margaret Sanger, *Margaret Sanger: An Autobiography* (New York: W. W. Norton, 1938), chap. 17, https://www.gutenberg.org/files/56610/56610-h/56610-h.htm (accessed April 22, 2022).
2. Sanger, *Autobiography*, chap. 17.
3. Editorial note, *The Selected Papers of Margaret Sanger*, ed. Esther Katz, asst. ed. Cathy Moran Hajo and Peter C. Engelman, vol. 1, *The Woman Rebel, 1900–1928* (Urbana: University of Illinois Press, 2003), 199.
4. Ellen Chesler, *Woman of Valor: Margaret Sanger and the Birth Control Movement in America* (New York: Simon & Schuster, 1992), 150.
5. Sanger, *Autobiography*, chap. 17.
6. Victor Robinson, *Pioneers of Birth Control in England and America* (New York: Voluntary Parenthood League, 1919), 100.
7. Robinson, 100.
8. Chesler, *Woman of Valor*, 150.
9. Peter C. Engelman, *A History of the Birth Control Movement in America* (Santa Barbara, CA: Praeger, 2011), 83.
10. Cathy Moran Hajo, *Birth Control on Main Street: Organizing Clinics in the United States, 1916–1939* (Urbana: University of Illinois Press, 2010), 127.
11. Engelman, *History of the Birth Control Movement*, 86–87.
12. Sanger, *Autobiography*, chap. 18.
13. Sanger, chap. 18.
14. Sanger, chap. 18.
15. Hajo, *Birth Control on Main Street*, 137.
16. Chesler, *Woman of Valor*, 153.
17. Sanger, *Autobiography*, chap. 18.
18. Chesler, *Woman of Valor*, 153.
19. Chesler, 154.
20. Dolores Flamiano, "The Birth of a Notion: Media Coverage of Contraception, 1915–1917," *Journalism & Mass Communication Quarterly* 75, no. 3 (September 1998): 563.
21. Flamiano, 563.
22. Chesler, *Woman of Valor*, 154.
23. Chesler, 154.
24. Chen, *"The Sex Side of Life,"* 184.
25. "Sanger on Trial: The Brownsville Clinic Testimony," newsletter no. 25, Fall 2000, Margaret Sanger Papers Project, New York University, https://sanger.hosting.nyu.edu/articles/sanger_on_trial/ (accessed January 8, 2024).
26. Sanger, *Autobiography*, chap. 18.
27. Jill Lepore, "Birthright," *The New Yorker*, November 6, 2011, https://www.newyorker.com/magazine/2011/11/14/birthright-jill-lepore.
28. Sanger, *Autobiography*, chap. 18.
29. Sanger, 18.
30. Editorial note, *Selected Papers*, 1:195.
31. Sanger, *Autobiography*, chap. 16.
32. Warner Fite, "Birth-Control and Biological Ethics," published in New York [originally in October 1916 *Ethics*], MWD Papers.
33. Fite, "Birth-Control and Biological Ethics."
34. Chesler, *Woman of Valor*, 147.

35. Chesler, 148.
36. William J. Robinson, *Practical Prevenception, or The Technique of Birth Control* (Hoboken, NJ: American Biological Society, 1929), 1.
37. William J. Robinson, quoted in Robinson, *Pioneers of Birth Control in England and America*, 71.
38. Robinson, *Practical Prevenception*, 10–18.
39. Chesler, *Woman of Valor*, 148.
40. Antoinette Konikow, *Voluntary Motherhood: A Study of the Physiology and Hygiene of Prevention of Conception* (1st edition, 1923, no copyright information printed in book), 4, https://archive.org/details/23KonikowVoluntarymotherhood/page/n3/mode/1up (accessed June 23, 2023).
41. Konikow, *Voluntary Motherhood*, 5.
42. Konikow, 21.
43. Sanger, *Autobiography*, chap. 17.
44. Robinson, *Practical Prevenception*, 23.
45. Sanger, *Autobiography*, chap. 19.
46. Margaret Sanger, "Shall We Break This Law?," *Birth Control Review* 1, no. 1 (February 1917): 4, https://babel.hathitrust.org/cgi/pt?id=hvd.hnp3k3&view=1up&seq=10.
47. Sanger, *Autobiography*, chap. 20.
48. Beth Widmaier Capo, *Textual Contraception: Birth Control and Modern American Fiction* (Columbus: Ohio State University Press, 2021), 22n3.
49. Aimee Armande Wilson, *Conceived in Modernism: The Aesthetics and Politics of Birth Control* (New York: Bloomsbury Academic, 2016), 36.
50. Brett Gary, *Dirty Works: Obscenity on Trial in America's First Sexual Revolution* (Stanford, CA: Stanford University Press, 2021), 13–14.
51. Invite card to Testimonial Dinner to Margaret Sanger and Ethel Byrne, MWD Papers.
52. Executive Committee of NBCL to Members, January 11, 1917, MWD Papers.
53. Sanger, *Autobiography*, chap. 20.
54. Sanger, chap. 20.
55. Sanger to Rublee, undated, Juliet Barrett Rublee papers, Rauner Special Collections, Dartmouth.
56. Booklet titled *The Birth Control Movement*, stamped by the National Birth Control League, 21 West Forty-Sixth Street, New York City, MWD Papers.
57. Melissa Doak and Kristy Horaz, *Why Did Congressional Lobbying Efforts Fail to Eliminate Contraception from Obscenity Laws, 1916–1937?* (Binghamton, NY: State University of New York at Binghamton, 1999); introduction to "Letters collected by the Committee of 100, 1917, Papers of Mary Ware Dennett and the Voluntary Parenthood League."
58. Letters collected by the Committee of 100, 1917.
59. Letters collected by the Committee of 100, 1917.
60. Jessica L. Furgerson, *The Battle for Birth Control: Exploring the Lasting Consequences of the Movement's Early Rhetoric* (Lanham, MD: Lexington Books, 2022), 164.

CHAPTER 13: WHAT ARE PEOPLE FOR?

1. "Head of American Red Cross Tells the Women to Keep Cool," *New Britain Daily Herald*, April 22, 1914, 4, https://chroniclingamerica.loc.gov/lccn/sn82014519/1914-04-22/ed-1/seq-4/.

2. Mary Ware Dennett to Devon Dennett, September 30, 1917, MWD Papers.
3. Author interview with Sharon Spaulding, Sandy, UT, May 12, 2022.
4. "Mrs. Dennett, 75, Suffrage Leader," *New York Times*, July 26, 1947.
5. Mary Ware Dennett to Devon Dennett, September 30, 1917.
6. Mary Ware Dennett to Gertrude Minturn Pinchot, December 20, 1917, MWD Papers.
7. Sanger, *Autobiography*, chap. 20.
8. Matthew Connelly, *Fatal Misconception: The Struggle to Control World Population* (Cambridge, MA: The Belknap Press of Harvard University Press, 2008), xi.
9. *Medical Review of Reviews* 25, no. 3 (March 1919): 142.
10. Virginia Woolf, *Mrs. Dalloway* (New York: Harcourt, Brace & World, 1925), 135.
11. Michelle Millar Fisher and Amber Winick, eds., *Designing Motherhood: Things That Make and Break Our Births* (Cambridge, MA: MIT Press, 2021), 131.
12. Bertolt Brecht, "The Ballade of Paragraph 218," Museum of Contraception and Abortion, https://muvs.org/en/topics/literary-quotes/bertolt-brecht-the-ballade-of-paragraph-218-1929-en/ (accessed June 23, 2023).
13. Frederick Lewis Allen, *Only Yesterday: An Informal History of the 1920s* (New York: John Wiley & Sons, 1997 reprint of 1931 Harper & Row edition), chap. 5, https://xroads.virginia.edu/~Hyper/Allen/provenance.html (accessed June 23, 2023).
14. Undated NBCL press release, MWD Papers.
15. Frederick Holmes, "Medicine in the First World War: Venereal Disease," University of Kansas School of Medicine, https://www.kumc.edu/school-of-medicine/academics/departments/history-and-philosophy-of-medicine/archives/wwi/essays/medicine/venereal-disease.html (accessed June 23, 2023).
16. Gertrude M. Williams, "Race Conservation in War Time Makes Birth Control a Necessity," undated printed pamphlet, MWD Papers.
17. Jeffrey P. Moran, *Teaching Sex: The Shaping of Adolescence in the 20th Century* (Cambridge, MA: Harvard University Press, 2000), 73.
18. Andrea Tone, *Devices and Desires: A History of Contraceptives in America* (New York: Hill and Wang, 2001), 99.
19. Alexandra M. Lord, *Condom Nation: The U.S. Government's Sex Education Campaign from World War I to the Internet* (Baltimore: Johns Hopkins University Press, 2010), 31.
20. Lord, "Models of Masculinity: Sex Education, the United States Public Health Service, and the YMCA, 1919–1924," *Journal of the History of Medicine and Allied Sciences* 58, no. 2 (April 2003): 123.
21. Lord, *Condom Nation*, 27–8.
22. Lord, "Models of Masculinity," 132.
23. Lord, "Models of Masculinity," 150.
24. Scott W. Stern, *The Trials of Nina McCall: Sex, Surveillance, and the Decades-Long Government Plan to Imprison "Promiscuous" Women* (New York: Beacon Press, 2018), 126.
25. Wendy Kline, *Building a Better Race: Gender, Sexuality, and Eugenics from the Turn of the Century to the Baby Boom* (Berkeley: University of California Press, 2005), ebook loc. 669.
26. Stern, *Trials of Nina McCall*, 98.
27. Andrea Tone, "Making Room for Rubbers: Gender, Technology, and Birth Control Before the Pill," *History and Technology* 18, no. 1 (2002): 65, https://doi.org/10.1080/07341510290028756.
28. "History of Birth Control," online exhibit, Case Western Reserve College of Arts and Sciences, Dittrick Medical History Center, https://artsci.case.edu/dittrick/online-exhibits/history-of-birth-control/ (accessed June 20, 2023).

29. James W. Reed, "The Birth Control Movement Before *Roe v. Wade*" in *The Politics of Abortion and Birth Control in Historical Perspective,* ed. Donald T. Critchlow (University Park: Pennsylvania State University Press, 1996), 35.
30. Victor Robinson, "A Rational Sex Primer," *Medical Review of Reviews* 24 (1918): 67.
31. Robinson, 68.
32. Mary Ware Dennett, *The Sex Side of Life: An Explanation for Young People,* 6th printing (privately printed, 1919), p. 14, https://www.gutenberg.org/files/31732/31732-h/31732-h.htm (accessed June 16, 2023).
33. M. E. Melody and Linda M. Peterson, *Teaching America about Sex: Marriage Guides and Sex Manuals from the Late Victorians to Dr. Ruth* (New York: New York University Press, 1999), 36–37.
34. [Redacted] to Mary Ware Dennett, January 15, 1928[?], MWD Papers.
35. K. French to Dennett, June 14, 1918, MWD Papers.
36. Mary Ware Dennett to Carleton Dennett, March 12, 1918, MWD Papers.
37. Jessica L. Furgerson, *The Battle for Birth Control: Exploring the Lasting Consequences of the Movement's Early Rhetoric* (Lanham, MD: Lexington Books, 2022), 15.
38. Mary Ware Dennett to sons, undated [1918], MWD Papers.
39. Allen, *Only Yesterday,* chap. 2.

CHAPTER 14: A WASHINGTON DEBUT

1. Mary Ware Dennett to her sons, January 30, 1919, MWD Papers.
2. Dennett to her sons, January 30, 1919.
3. Mary Ware Dennett to league members, March 5, 1919, MWD Papers.
4. Mary Ware Dennett, July 22, 1919, confidential, Report to the National Council, MWD Papers.
5. Constance Chen, *"The Sex Side of Life": Mary Ware Dennett's Pioneering Battle for Birth Control and Sex Education* (New York: The New Press, 1996), 213.
6. S. Josephine Baker, *Fighting for Life* (New York: The Macmillan Company, 1939), 144.
7. Baker, 145.
8. Chen, *"The Sex Side of Life,"* 159–60.
9. Joan Johnson, *Funding Feminism: Monied Women, Philanthropy, and the Women's Movement, 1870–1967* (Chapel Hill: University of North Carolina Press, 2017), 190.
10. Johnson, 182.
11. Mary Ware Dennett to Agnes Engelhard, December 29, 1929, MWD Papers.
12. Johnson, *Funding Feminism,* 192.
13. Chen, *"The Sex Side of Life,"* 206.
14. Ellen Chesler, *Woman of Valor: Margaret Sanger and the Birth Control Movement in America* (New York: Simon & Schuster, 1992), 167.
15. Chen, *"The Sex Side of Life,"* 212.
16. Mary Ware Dennett, July 22, 1919, Report to the National Council.
17. Loomis Institute to Mary Ware Dennett, March 10, 1919, Sharon Spaulding / Dennett Family Archives, Alstead, NH & Sandy, UT.
18. Mary Ware Dennett to Carleton Dennett, November 19, 1917, MWD Papers.
19. Mary Ware Dennett, Confidential Report No. 4, August 2, 1919, MWD Papers.
20. Dennett, July 22, 1919, Report to the National Council.
21. Dennett, report, August 2, 1919, MWD Papers.
22. Dennett, Report No. 8, undated, MWD Papers.

23. Eleanor Kinsella McDonnell, "Keeping the Stork in his Place," *Pictorial Review*, 1919–1920, https://prod-cdn.atria.nl/wp-content/uploads/2018/09/14103242/keeping-the-stork-in-his-place-eleanor-kinsella-mcdonnell.pdf (accessed June 23, 2023).

24. Dennett, Report No. 8.

25. Dennett, "Yes, But—," 1919, MWD Papers.

26. Dennett, Campaign Diary, September 12, 1919, MWD Papers.

27. Dennett, notes of May 7, 1924, MWD Papers.

28. Dennett, Sen. Nelson meeting notes, 1919 Congressional Diary, MWD Papers.

29. Dennett, Confidential Report No. 4.

30. Dennett, Confidential Report No. 4.

31. *Medical Review of Reviews* 25, no. 3 (March 1919): 131.

32. *Medical Review of Reviews* 25, no. 3: 141.

33. *Medical Review of Reviews* 25, no. 3: 135.

34. Quoted in Peter C. Engelman, *A History of the Birth Control Movement in America* (Santa Barbara, CA: Praeger, 2011), 53.

35. *Medical Review of Reviews* 25, no. 3 (March 1919): 135.

36. Margaret Sanger, "How Shall We Change the Law," *Birth Control Review* 3, no. 7 (July 1919): 8–9.

37. Sanger, "How Shall We Change the Law."

38. Mary Ware Dennett, Congressional Report, December 30, 1920, MWD Papers.

39. Dennett, Congressional Diary, September 4, 1919, MWD Papers.

CHAPTER 15: TRAITOROUS DAYS

1. New Year card, 1920, MWD Papers.

2. Loomis Institute to Mary Ware Dennett, March 10, 1919, Sharon Spaulding / Dennett Family Archives, Alstead, NH & Sandy, UT.

3. Dennett, Report No. 12, September 17, 1920, MWD Papers.

4. Carleton Dennett to Hartley Dennett, December 22, 1919, Sharon Spaulding / Dennett Family Archives, Alstead, NH & Sandy, UT.

5. Frederick Lewis Allen, *Only Yesterday: An Informal History of the 1920s* (New York: John Wiley & Sons, 1997 reprint of 1931 Harper & Row edition), chap. 5, https://xroads.virginia.edu/~Hyper/Allen/provenance.html (accessed June 23, 2023).

6. Allen, chap. 5.

7. Allen, chap. 5.

8. Dennett, Report No. 12, September 17, 1920.

9. Margaret Sanger, "A Birth Strike to Avert World Famine," *Birth Control Review* 4, no. 1 (January 1920): 1.

10. Sanger, 1.

11. Mary Ware Dennett to Board of NY Woman's Publishing Co., January 20, 1920, MWD Papers.

12. Dennett to Board of NY Woman's Publishing Co.

13. Dennett, Report No. 9, March 20, 1920, MWD Papers.

14. "THE PRESENT SITUATION—AS TO THE BILL," n.d., MWD Papers.

15. Mary Ware Dennett, Report No. 11, June 16, 1920, MWD Papers.

16. Freda Kirchwey, "Alice Paul Pulls the Strings," *The Nation*, March 2, 1921.

17. Dorothy M. Brown, *Setting a Course: American Women in the 1920s* (Boston: Twayne, 1987), 60.

18. Mary Ware Dennett, Campaign Diary, February 15, 1921.

19. Dennett, Campaign Diary, February 15, 1921.
20. Dennett to Mrs. Lane, Stone, and Tompkins, Washington Report, February 21, 1921, MWD Papers.
21. Dennett, Report No. 13, November 1, 1920, MWD Papers.
22. Dennett, memo, "CONFIDENTIAL MESSAGE TO COUNCIL/VOLUNTARY PARENTHOOD LEAGUE, 51 East 59th Street/Jan. 3, 1921," MWD Papers.
23. Dennett, Campaign Diary, December 16, 1920, MWD Papers.
24. Dennett, Congressional Report, December 7, 1920, MWD Papers.
25. Carole R. McCann, *Birth Control Politics in the United States, 1916–1945* (Ithaca, NY: Cornell University Press, 1994), 90.
26. Dennett, Campaign Diary, December 16, 1920.
27. S. Josephine Baker, *Fighting for Life* (New York: The Macmillan Company, 1939), 138.
28. Baker, 138.
29. Dennett, Campaign Diary, December 16, 1920.
30. Author interview with Sharon Spaulding, Sandy, UT, May 12, 2022.
31. Constance Chen, *"The Sex Side of Life": Mary Ware Dennett's Pioneering Battle for Birth Control and Sex Education* (New York: The New Press, 1996), 217.
32. Chen, 218.
33. Chen, 218.
34. Vine McCasland to Mary Ware Dennett, n.d. [probably late June 1920], Sharon Spaulding / Dennett Family Archives, Alstead, NH & Sandy, UT.
35. Dennett to McCasland, July 2, 1920, Sharon Spaulding / Dennett Family Archives, Alstead, NH & Sandy, UT.
36. Dennett to W. F. Robie, August 18, 1921, MWD papers.
37. Dennett to Lucia Ames Mead, letter fragment from 1920, MWD Papers.
38. Dennett to Lucia Ames Mead, letter fragment from 1920.

CHAPTER 16: DIGGING TRENCHES, SHARPENING KNIVES

1. Ellen Chesler, *Woman of Valor: Margaret Sanger and the Birth Control Movement in America* (New York: Simon & Schuster, 1992), 190.
2. "The Passionate Friends: H. G. Wells and Margaret Sanger," newsletter no. 12, Spring 1996, Margaret Sanger Papers Project, New York University, https://sanger.hosting.nyu.edu/articles/passionate_friends/.
3. Margaret Sanger, *Margaret Sanger: An Autobiography* (New York: W. W. Norton, 1938), 268, https://www.gutenberg.org/files/56610/56610-h/56610-h.htm (accessed April 22, 2022).
4. Chesler, *Woman of Valor*, 184.
5. *The Selected Papers of Margaret Sanger*, ed. Esther Katz, asst. ed. Cathy Moran Hajo and Peter C. Engelman, vol. 1, *The Woman Rebel, 1900–1928* (Urbana: University of Illinois Press, 2003), 185n6.
6. Marie Stopes to Margaret Sanger, July 8, 1920, Stopes papers, British Library.
7. Sanger to Stopes, April 11, 1921, Stopes papers, British Library.
8. Sanger, *Autobiography*, chap. 22.
9. Editorial note, *Selected Papers*, 1:287.
10. Margaret Sanger, *Woman and the New Race* (New York: Brentano's, 1920): 1.
11. Sanger, 2.
12. Sanger, 15, 29.
13. Sanger, 40, 42.

14. *Selected Papers*, 1:311–13.
15. Mary Ware Dennett to Carleton Dennett, November 4, 1921, MWD Papers.
16. Author interview with Sharon Spaulding, Sandy, UT, May 13, 2022.
17. Mary Ware Dennett to sons, April 9, 1921, MWD Papers.
18. Dennett to sons, June 19, 1921, Sharon Spaulding / Dennett Family Archives, Alstead, NH & Sandy, UT.
19. *Birth Control Review* 5, no. 3 (March 1921): 4.
20. *Birth Control Review* 5, no. 3, quoted in an editorial note, *Selected Papers*, 1:294.
21. Mary Ware Dennett to Sanger, March 12, 1921, MWD Papers.
22. Dennett to Sanger, March 12, 1921.
23. Dennett to Sanger, March 31, 1921, MWD Papers.
24. June Rose, *Marie Stopes and the Sexual Revolution* (London: Faber & Faber, 1992), 153.
25. Dennett, Report No. 18, June 23, 1921, MWD Papers.
26. Carrie Chapman Catt to Margaret Sanger, November 24, 1920, in *Selected Papers*, 1:290.
27. Sanger, quoted in David M. Kennedy, *Birth Control in America: The Career of Margaret Sanger* (New Haven, CT: Yale University Press, 1970), 94.
28. Mary Ware Dennett to Sanger, July 29, 1921, MWD Papers.
29. Dennett to Sanger, July 29, 1921.
30. Dennett, Report No. 20, August 10, 1921, MWD Papers.
31. Dennett, Report No. 21, August 31, 1921, MWD Papers.
32. Dennett, Campaign Diary, August 11, 1921, MWD Papers.
33. Dennett to Marie Stopes, June 14, 1921, Stopes papers, British Library.
34. NY Women's Publishing Co. to Marie Stopes, draft invitation dated July 19, 1921, Sharon Spaulding / Dennett Family Archives, Alstead, NH & Sandy, UT.
35. Margaret Sanger to Juliet Barrett Rublee, July 20, [1921], in *Selected Papers*, 1:301.
36. Sanger to Rublee, July 30, 1921, in *Selected Papers*, 1:306–7.
37. Sanger to Rublee, July 30, 1921.
38. Sanger to Marie Stopes, July 29, 1921, Stopes papers, British Library.
39. Sanger to Mary Ware Dennett, September 23, 1921, MWD Papers.
40. Dennett to Sanger, September 26, 1921, MWD Papers.
41. Mary Ware Dennett to Carleton Dennett, November 4, 1921, MWD Papers.
42. "Verbatim Report of the Town Hall Meeting under the Auspices of the VOLUNTARY PARENTHOOD LEAGUE at Which the Chief Speaker Was Dr. Marie C. Stopes, of London, President of the Society of Constructive Birth Control and Racial Progress," October 27, 1921, MWD Papers.
43. Verbatim Report, October 27, 1921.
44. Matthew Connelly, *Fatal Misconception: The Struggle to Control World Population* (Cambridge, MA: The Belknap Press of Harvard University Press, 2008), 54.
45. Connelly, 54.
46. Warren G. Harding, quoted in Ian Frazier, "When W. E. B. Du Bois Made a Laughingstock of a White Supremacist," *The New Yorker*, August 19, 2019, https://www.newyorker.com/magazine/2019/08/26/when-w-e-b-du-bois-made-a-laughingstock-of-a-white-supremacist.
47. Mary Ware Dennett to Carleton Dennett, November 4, 1921, MWD Papers.
48. Mary Ware Dennett, Report No. 22, November 30, 1921, MWD Papers.
49. Marie Stopes to Margaret Sanger, October 28, 1921, Stopes Papers, British Libraray

50. Stopes to Juliet Barrett Rublee, October 28, 1921, Stopes Papers, British Library.
51. Mary Ware Dennett to Margaret Sanger, October 31, 1921, MWD Papers.

CHAPTER 17: THE LIMITS OF SOLIDARITY

1. *Birth Control—What It Is, How It Works, What It Will Do*, Proceedings of the First American Birth Control Conference (November 1921), p. 17, https://babel.hathitrust .org/cgi/pt?id=hvd.hwikw8&view=1up&seq=5.
2. "The Voluntary Parenthood League, by Mary Ware Dennett—Director/Prepared for Mrs. Sanger's Conference—November 11, 13, '21," MWD Papers.
3. "Voluntary Parenthood League, by Mary Ware Dennett."
4. Peter C. Engelman, *A History of the Birth Control Movement in America* (Santa Barbara, CA: Praeger, 2011), 123.
5. *Birth Control—What It Is, How It Works.*
6. *Birth Control—What It Is, How It Works.*
7. Anna Julia Cooper, quoted in Lillian Faderman, *Woman: The American History of an Idea* (New Haven, CT: Yale University Press, 2022), ebook loc. 4,036.
8. Memo, "Note Passed to Mrs. Sanger during 1st Session of Her Conference, November 1921," MWD Papers.
9. Mary Ware Dennett, *Birth Control Laws: Shall We Keep Them, Change Them, or Abolish Them* (New York: Frederick H. Hitchcock, 1926), 288.
10. Dennett to Marie Stopes, [November 25, 1921], Stopes papers, British Library.
11. *Birth Control—What It Is, How It Works.*
12. *Birth Control—What It Is, How It Works.*
13. Engelman, *History of the Birth Control Movement*, 124–25.
14. Margaret Sanger, *Margaret Sanger: An Autobiography* (New York: W. W. Norton, 1938), chap. 23, https://www.gutenberg.org/files/56610/56610-h/56610-h.htm (accessed April 22, 2022).
15. Sanger, chap. 23.
16. Ellen Chesler, *Woman of Valor: Margaret Sanger and the Birth Control Movement in America* (New York: Simon & Schuster, 1992), 203.
17. Chesler, 203.
18. Engelman, *History of the Birth Control Movement*, 126.
19. Sanger, *Autobiography*, chap. 24.
20. Kathleen A. Tobin, *The American Religious Debate over Birth Control, 1907–1937* (Jefferson, NC: McFarland, 2001), 80.
21. Tobin, 85.
22. Mary Ware Dennett to Marie Stopes, [November 25, 1921], Stopes papers, British Library.
23. Dennett to Margaret Sanger, November 15, 1921, MWD Papers.
24. Memo, "Re: Mrs. Sanger's Arrest at the Town Hall Meeting, Nov 13, 1921," MWD Papers.
25. Sanger, *Autobiography*, chap. 23.
26. Joan Johnson, *Funding Feminism: Monied Women, Philanthropy, and the Women's Movement, 1870–1967* (Chapel Hill: University of North Carolina Press, 2017), 183.
27. Mary Ware Dennett to Juliet Barrett Rublee, November 13, 1921, MWD Papers.
28. Dennett, "A Special Message to the Council, Contributors and Friends of the Voluntary Parenthood League—Nov. 18, 1921," memo, MWD Papers.
29. Dennett, "Special Message to the Council."
30. Dennett, "Special Message to the Council."

31. Margaret Sanger to Henry John Gibbons, December 7, 1921, MWD Papers.
32. Margaret Sanger, "Unity!" *Birth Control Review* 5, no. 11 (November 1921), 3–4.
33. Sanger, 3–4.
34. Sanger, 3–4.
35. "Minutes of meeting called by Mrs. Leslie J. Tompkins [Jean Burnet Tompkins] at her home at 8 o'clock January 3rd, 1922, to consider what steps should be taken in reference to Mrs. Sanger's attacks on Mrs. Dennett and the V.P.L. and to consider questions of reorganization," MWD Papers.
36. Constance Chen, *"The Sex Side of Life": Mary Ware Dennett's Pioneering Battle for Birth Control and Sex Education* (New York: The New Press, 1996), 230–31.
37. Chesler, *Woman of Valor*, 224.
38. Jean Burnet Tompkins, Attorney and Counselor at Law, 55 Central Park West, NYC, to Dennett, February 4, 1922, MWD Papers.
39. Tompkins to Dennett, February 4, 1922.
40. Dennett to Vera Lane, September 23, 1922, MWD Papers.
41. Dennett, "Birth Control's Hunt for Sponsor," *New York Times*, February 26, 1922, pp. 86, 93, https://timesmachine.nytimes.com/timesmachine/1922/02/26/issue.html.
42. Dennett, "Birth Control's Hunt for Sponsor."
43. Dennett, "Birth Control's Hunt for Sponsor."
44. Dennett, "Birth Control's Hunt for Sponsor."
45. Dennett to sons, September 15, 1922, MWD Papers.
46. Arthur Miller, "Before Air-Conditioning," *The New Yorker*, June 14, 1998, https://www.newyorker.com/magazine/1998/06/22/before-air-conditioning.
47. Mary Ware Dennett, "An Open Letter to President Harding on Respect for the Law Which Forbids Birth Control Knowledge," March 31, 1922, MWD Papers.
48. Dennett, Report No. 23, March 31, 1922, MWD Papers.
49. Mary Ware Dennett to Carleton Dennett, August 1, 1922, MWD Papers.
50. Mary Ware Dennett, "To the Members of the V.P.L.," September 29, 1922, MWD Papers.
51. Dennett, "To the Members of the V.P.L."
52. Dennett, "To the Members of the V.P.L."
53. Dennett to Marie Stopes, October 4, 1922, MWD Papers.

CHAPTER 18: NEW BEGINNINGS

1. Margaret Sanger to Juliet Barrett Rublee, June 22, 1921, from the British Museum, in *The Selected Papers of Margaret Sanger*, ed. Esther Katz, asst. ed. Cathy Moran Hajo and Peter C. Engelman, vol. 1, *The Woman Rebel, 1900–1928* (Urbana: University of Illinois Press, 2003), 300.
2. Sanger, quoted in David M. Kennedy, *Birth Control in America: The Career of Margaret Sanger* (New Haven, CT: Yale University Press, 1970), 98.
3. Ellen Chesler, *Woman of Valor: Margaret Sanger and the Birth Control Movement in America* (New York: Simon & Schuster, 1992), 244.
4. Editorial note, *Selected Papers*, 1:350.
5. Margaret Sanger to Hugh de Selincourt, November 5, 1922, in *Selected Papers*, 1:354.
6. Chesler, *Woman of Valor*, 248.
7. Chesler, 186.
8. Andrea Tone, *Devices and Desires: A History of Contraceptives in America* (New York: Hill and Wang, 2001), 124, 126.

9. Margaret Sanger, *Margaret Sanger: An Autobiography* (New York: W. W. Norton, 1938), chap. 28, https://www.gutenberg.org/files/56610/56610-h/56610-h.htm (accessed April 22, 2022).

10. *Selected Papers*, 1:367n8.

11. Mary Ware Dennett to Heterodoxy, March 28, 1934, MWD Papers.

12. Dennett to Fannie Cook, September 23, 1938, MWD Papers.

13. Constance Chen, *"The Sex Side of Life": Mary Ware Dennett's Pioneering Battle for Birth Control and Sex Education* (New York: The New Press, 1996), 230.

14. Mary Ware Dennett to Marie Stopes, October 4, 1922, MWD Papers.

15. Dennett to Stopes, October 4, 1922.

16. Minutes, November 3, 1922, MWD Papers.

17. Mary Ware Dennett to Carleton Dennett, November 17, 1922, MWD Papers.

18. Asst. Sec. of VPL to Stopes, December 15, 1922, MWD Papers.

19. Dennett, Campaign Diary, December 11, 1922, MWD Papers.

20. Robyn L. Rosen, *Reproductive Health, Reproductive Rights: Reformers and the Politics of Maternal Welfare, 1917–1940* (Columbus: Ohio State University Press, 2003), 85–86.

21. Mary Ware Dennett to Dr. McGraw, June 4, 1932, MWD Papers.

22. "SENATOR NELSON M.W.D. and E.S.P.," February 3, 1923, MWD Papers.

23. Jessica L. Furgerson, *The Battle for Birth Control: Exploring the Lasting Consequences of the Movement's Early Rhetoric* (Lanham, MD: Lexington Books, 2022), 74.

24. Anthony M. Ludovici, *The Night-Hoers, or The Case against Birth-Control and an Alternative* (London: Herbert Jenkins, 1928), 131–33.

25. "Medicine: Birth Control Hearing," *Time*, February 23, 1931, https://content.time.com /time/subscriber/article/0,33009,930381-1,00.html.

26. "Annual Report of Voluntary Parenthood League," May 1, 1922–March 4, 1923, MWD Papers.

27. February 26 notes, MWD Papers.

28. Mary Ware Dennett, Campaign Diary, February 19, 1923, MWD Papers.

29. Fundraising circular from VPL, April 1923, MWD Papers.

30. VPL to ABCL, May 3, 1923, MWD Papers.

31. Anne Kennedy to Mary Ware Dennett, June 6, 1923, MWD Papers.

32. Kennedy to Dennett, June 6, 1923.

33. Kennedy to Members of the Voluntary Parenthood League, n.d., MWD Papers.

34. Kennedy to Members of the Voluntary Parenthood League, n.d.

35. Kennedy to Members of the Voluntary Parenthood League, n.d.

36. Mary Ware Dennett, December 21, 1923, MWD Papers.

37. Sanger, *Autobiography*, chap. 23.

38. Sanger, chap. 29.

39. "Medical Indications For Contraceptive Advice," [signed by Sanger and Hannah Stone], Margaret Sanger Papers, Library of Congress (MS LOC).

40. Chesler, *Woman of Valor*, 275.

41. Cathy Moran Hajo, *Birth Control on Main Street: Organizing Clinics in the United States, 1916–1939* (Urbana: University of Illinois Press, 2010), 64.

42. Wangui Muigai, "Looking Uptown: Margaret Sanger and the Harlem Branch Birth Control Clinic," newsletter no. 54, Spring 2010, Margaret Sanger Papers Project, New York University, https://sanger.hosting.nyu.edu/articles/harlem.

43. Peter C. Engelman, *A History of the Birth Control Movement in America* (Santa Barbara, CA: Praeger, 2011), 153.

44. Mary McCarthy, *The Group* (New York: Signet: 1963), 72.
45. Sylvia Plath, *The Bell Jar* (New York: Harper Perennial, 2005), 171.
46. Client to Margaret Sanger, May 31, 1921, in *Selected Papers*, 1:296–97.
47. Client to Sanger, Fayetteville, WV, November 21, 1923, in *Selected Papers*, 1:378.
48. Hajo, *Birth Control on Main Street*, 140–41.
49. Kennedy, *Birth Control in America*, 187–88.
50. Martha Gruening to Mary Ware Dennett, August 31, 1923, MWD Papers.
51. Dennett, letters with Louis Kaufman, MWD Papers.
52. Dennett, Campaign Diary, November 13, 1923, MWD Papers.
53. Dennett, Campaign Diary, November 13, 1923.
54. Dennett, Campaign Diary, November 13, 1923.

CHAPTER 19: PROTOPLASM

1. Daniel Okrent, *The Guarded Gate: Bigotry, Eugenics, and the Law That Kept Two Generations of Jews, Italians, and Other European Immigrants Out of America* (New York: Scribner, 2019), 352–53.
2. Okrent, 352–53.
3. Laura L. Lovett, *Conceiving the Future: Pronatalism, Reproduction, and the Family in the United States, 1890–1938* (Chapel Hill: University of North Carolina Press, 2007), 143.
4. Margaret Sanger, *Margaret Sanger: An Autobiography* (New York: W. W. Norton, 1938), chap. 30, https://www.gutenberg.org/files/56610/56610-h/56610-h.htm (accessed April 22, 2022).
5. Madison Grant, quoted in Ian Frazier, "When W. E. B. Du Bois Made a Laughingstock of a White Supremacist," *The New Yorker*, August 19, 2019, https:// www.newyorker.com/magazine/2019/08/26/when-w-e-b-du-bois-made-a-laughingstock -of-a-white-supremacist.
6. Frazier, "When W. E. B. Du Bois."
7. Edwin Black, *War against the Weak: Eugenics and America's Campaign to Create a Master Race* (New York: Four Walls Eight Windows, 2003), 140.
8. Ruth Clifford Engs, "Eugenics, Immigration Restriction and the Birth Control Movements," in Katherine A. S. Sibley, ed., *A Companion to Warren G. Harding, Calvin Coolidge, and Herbert Hoover* (Hoboken, NJ: John Wiley & Sons, 2014), 6.
9. Kathleen A. Tobin, *The American Religious Debate over Birth Control, 1907–1937* (Jefferson, NC: McFarland, 2001), 93.
10. "The Immigration Act of 1924 (The Johnson-Reed Act)," Office of the Historian, US State Department, https://history.state.gov/milestones/1921-1936/immigration-act (accessed June 26, 2023).
11. Okrent, *Guarded Gate*, epigraph.
12. Margaret Sanger to Lydia Allen DeVilbiss, June 16, 1933, in *The Selected Papers of Margaret Sanger*, ed. Esther Katz, asst. ed. Cathy Moran Hajo and Peter C. Engelman, vol. 2, *Birth Control Comes of Age, 1928–1939* (Urbana: University of Illinois Press, 2007), 230.
13. Ellen Chesler, *Woman of Valor: Margaret Sanger and the Birth Control Movement in America* (New York: Simon & Schuster, 1992), 379.
14. Black, *War against the Weak*, 252.
15. Peter C. Engelman, *A History of the Birth Control Movement in America* (Santa Barbara, CA: Praeger, 2011), 59.
16. "Doctor to Let Patient's Baby Defective Die," *Chicago Daily Tribune*,

November 17, 1915, https://www.disabilitymuseum.org/dhm/lib/detail
.html?id=1231&&print=1&page=1 (accessed June 26, 2023).

17. "Doctor to Let Patient's Baby Defective Die."

18. Engelman, *History of the Birth Control Movement*, 59.

19. "Defective Baby Divides Doctors," *New York Tribune*, November 18, 1915, quoted
in Jessica L. Furgerson, *The Battle for Birth Control: Exploring the Lasting
Consequences of the Movement's Early Rhetoric* (Lanham, MD: Lexington Books,
2022), 67.

20. Engelman, *History of the Birth Control Movement*, 61.

21. Engelman, 61.

22. Black, *War against the Weak*, 115.

23. Eve Tushnet, "'An Image of God': The Catholic Struggle against Eugenics and Its
Lessons for Today," *Patheos*, November 30, 2019, https://www.patheos.com/blogs
/evetushnet/2019/11/an-image-of-god-the-catholic-struggle-against-eugenics-and
-its-lessons-for-today.html.

24. Oliver Wendell Holmes, quoted in Beth Widmaier Capo, *Textual Contraception:
Birth Control and Modern American Fiction* (Columbus: Ohio State University
Press, 2021), 122.

25. Andrea DenHoed, "The Forgotten Lessons of the American Eugenics Movement,"
review of *Imbeciles: The Supreme Court, American Eugenics, and the Sterilization
of Carrie Buck*, by Adam Cohen, *The New Yorker*, April 27, 2018, https://www
.newyorker.com/books/page-turner/the-forgotten-lessons-of-the-american-eugenics
-movement.

26. Daylanne K. English, *Unnatural Selections: Eugenics in American Modernism and
the Harlem Renaissance* (Chapel Hill: University of North Carolina Press, 2004),
161, 169.

27. John D'Emilio and Estelle B. Freedman, *Intimate Matters: A History of Sexuality in
America* (New York: Harper & Row, 1988), 81.

28. Audrey Clare Farley, "Eugenics, Racism, and the Foreced Sterilization of Heiress
Ann Cooper Hewitt," *Salon*, April 20, 2021, https://www.salon.com/2021/04/20
/eugenics-racism-and-the-forced-sterilization-of-heiress-ann-cooper-hewitt/.

29. Martha C. Ward, *Poor Women, Powerful Men: America's Great Experiment in Family
Planning* (Boulder, CO: Westview Press, 1986), 15–16.

30. "Minutes of Conference of Council and Near-by Contributors, Thursday,
December 8, 1921 at 4:30 P.M. in the V.P.L. Office," MWD Papers.

31. Mary Ware Dennett, press release, February 2, 1922, MWD Papers.

32. Black, *War against the Weak*, 252.

33. Sanger, quoted in David M. Kennedy, *Birth Control in America: The Career of
Margaret Sanger* (New Haven, CT: Yale University Press, 1970), 117.

34. Furgerson, *Battle for Birth Control*, 40.

35. Secretary of Narcissa Cox Vanderlip to Sanger, Scarborough-on-Hudson, NY,
November 5, 1919, in Sanger, *The Selected Papers of Margaret Sanger*, ed. Esther
Katz, asst. ed. Cathy Moran Hajo and Peter C. Engelman, vol. 1, *The Woman Rebel,
1900–1928* (Urbana: University of Illinois Press, 2003), 261.

36. "Birth Control and Racial Betterment," February 1919, in *Selected Papers of
Margaret Sanger*, 1:252–54.

37. Philip K. Wilson, "Confronting 'Hereditary' Disease: Eugenic Attempts to
Eliminate Tuberculosis in Progressive Era America," *Journal of Medical Humanities*
27 (April 2006): https://doi.org/10.1007/s10912-005-9001-6.

38. Eve Tushnet, "An Image of God," https://www.patheos.com/blogs

/evetushnet/2019/11/an-image-of-god-the-catholic-struggle-against-eugenics-and-its
-lessons-for-today.html.

39. Gene Burns, *The Moral Veto: Framing Contraception, Abortion, and Cultural Pluralism in the United States* (Cambridge: Cambridge University Press, 2005), 286.

40. Tobin, *American Religious Debate over Birth Control*, 26–27.

41. Burns, *Moral Veto*, 119.

42. June Rose, *Marie Stopes and the Sexual Revolution* (London: Faber & Faber, 1992), 144.

43. Rose, 134.

44. Rose, 188.

45. Rose, 191.

46. Rose, 192.

47. Rose, 244.

48. Carole R. McCann, *Birth Control Politics in the United States, 1916–1945* (Ithaca, NY: Cornell University Press, 1994), 125–26.

CHAPTER 20: FLAMING YOUTH

1. Dorothy M. Brown, *Setting a Course: American Women in the 1920s* (Boston: Twayne, 1987), 8.

2. Jeffrey P. Moran, *Teaching Sex: The Shaping of Adolescence in the 20th Century* (Cambridge, MA: Harvard University Press, 2000), 79.

3. Lillian Faderman, *Woman: The American History of an Idea* (New Haven, CT: Yale University Press, 2022), ebook loc. 4435.

4. Linda Gordon, *The Moral Property of Women: A History of Birth Control Politics in America* (Urbana: University of Illinois Press, 2007, paperback edition; substantially revised and updated from *Woman's Body, Woman's Right*, 1974), 130.

5. Frederick Lewis Allen, *Only Yesterday: An Informal History of the 1920s* (New York: John Wiley & Sons, 1997 reprint of 1931 Harper & Row edition), chap. 5, https://xroads.virginia.edu/~Hyper/Allen/provenance.html (accessed June 23, 2023).

6. Moran, *Teaching Sex*, 101.

7. Moran, 101.

8. Moran, 101.

9. Mary Ware Dennett, notes of Monday, January 14, 1924, MWD Papers.

10. Nancy Cott, *The Grounding of Modern Feminism* (New Haven: Yale University Press, 1987), 102.

11. Faderman, *Woman*, ebook loc. 4988.

12. Cott, *The Grounding of Modern Feminism*, 102.

13. Carl N. Degler, *At Odds: Women and the Family in America from the Revolution to the Present* (New York: Oxford University Press, 1980), 406–7.

14. Mary Ware Dennett, notes of January 26, 1924, MWD Papers.

15. Dennett, notes of January 26, 1924.

16. Dennett, Campaign Diary, January 31, 1924, MWD Papers.

17. Dennett, Campaign Diary, February 1, 1924, MWD Papers.

18. Dennett, Campaign Diary, May 23, 1924, MWD Papers.

19. For immediate release, January 31, 1924, MWD Papers.

20. Dennett, Campaign Diary, February 13, 1924, MWD Papers.

21. "Birth Control and Federal Legislation," *Birth Control Review*, 8 (March 1924): 69–70.

22. Mary Ware Dennett, notes of March 15, 1924, MWD Papers.

23. *Cummins-Vaile Bill*, April 8 and May 9, 1924 (Washington, DC: Government Printing Office, 1924), https://babel.hathitrust.org/cgi/pt?id=umn.31951d02092034 u&view=1up&seq=1 (accessed June 27, 2023).

24. *Cummins-Vaile Bill*.

25. *Cummins-Vaile Bill*.

26. Dennett, "Testimony in Favor of the Cummins-Vaile Bill," April 8, 1924, reproduced by Speaking While Female, https://speakingwhilefemale.co/ reproductive-dennett/ (accessed June 27, 2023).

27. "Cummins-Vaile Bill Joint Hearings, April 8 and May 9, 1924," https://books.google .com/books?id=ksyxLfngQdAC&printsec=frontcover&source=gbs_ge_summary_r &cad=0#v=onepage&q&f=false (accessed July 26, 2023).

28. From collection of letters from mothers to VPL, MWD Papers.

29. From collection of letters from mothers to VPL.

30. Dennett, Campaign Diary, April 9, 1924, MWD Papers.

31. *Cummins-Vaile Bill*.

32. Kathleen A. Tobin, *The American Religious Debate over Birth Control, 1907–1937* (Jefferson, NC: McFarland, 2001), 117.

33. *Cummins-Vaile Bill*.

34. Mary Ware Dennett, notes of May 9, 1924, MWD Papers.

35. *Cummins-Vaile Bill*.

36. Mary Ware Dennett, notes of May 24, 1924, MWD Papers.

37. Dennett, notes of May 31, 1924, MWD Papers.

38. Constance Chen, *"The Sex Side of Life": Mary Ware Dennett's Pioneering Battle for Birth Control and Sex Education* (New York: The New Press, 1996), 235.

39. Dennett, notes of May 31, 1924.

CHAPTER 21: THE AGONY OF DEFEAT

1. "Mary D" to Myra Gallert and Vine McCasland, June 27, 1924, MWD Papers.

2. "Mary D" to Gallert and McCasland, June 27, 1924.

3. Summer 1924 correspondence between Mary Ware Dennett and Myra Gallert, MWD Papers.

4. Dennett to VPL Executive Committee, September 3, 1924, MWD Papers.

5. "Secretary" [Sonia Bronson] to Members of VPL National Council, September 19, 1924, MWD Papers.

6. Helen Hoy Greeley to Mary Ware Dennett, December 11, 1924, MWD Papers.

7. Dennett to Greeley, December 13, 1924, MWD Papers.

8. Supplement to Diary of December 20th (for Executive Committee only), MWD Papers.

9. Mary Ware Dennett, notes of January 27, 1925, MWD Papers.

10. Dennett, notes of January 12, 1925, MWD, MWD Papers.

11. Dennett to Mrs. Coolidge, January 3, 1925, MWD Papers.

12. Laura Harlan, secretary to Mrs. Coolidge, to Dennett at Grace Dodge Hotel, Washington, DC, January 6, 1925, MWD Papers.

13. Helen Hoy Greeley, notes of January 30, 1925, MWD Papers.

14. Mary Ware Dennett to Myra Gallert and Sonia Bronson, January 25, 1925, MWD Papers.

15. Dennett to Gallert, May 29, 1925, MWD Papers.

16. Dennett to Gallert, May 29, 1925.

17. Dennett to George Bedborough, June 11, 1932, MWD Papers.
18. Helen Hoy Greeley to Dennett, April 15, 1925, MWD Papers.
19. *Cummins-Vaile Bill*, April 8 and May 9, 1924 (Washington, DC: Government Printing Office, 1924), p. 23, https://babel.hathitrust.org/cgi/pt?id=umn.31951d020 92034u&view=1up&seq=1 (accessed June 27, 2023).
20. Sanger newsletter, quoted in Myra Gallert letter to VPL Members, December 2, 1925, MWD Papers.
21. Robyn L. Rosen, *Reproductive Health, Reproductive Rights: Reformers and the Politics of Maternal Welfare, 1917–1940* (Columbus: Ohio State University Press, 2003), 84.
22. Ellen Chesler, *Woman of Valor: Margaret Sanger and the Birth Control Movement in America* (New York: Simon & Schuster, 1992), 220.
23. Margaret Sanger, *Margaret Sanger: An Autobiography* (New York: W. W. Norton, 1938), chap. 34, https://www.gutenberg.org/files/56610/56610-h/56610-h.htm (accessed April 22, 2022).
24. Chesler, *Woman of Valor*, 285.
25. F. B. Sumner to Myra Gallert, December 6, 1925, MWD Papers.
26. Mary Ware Dennett to Gallert, August 29, 1925, MWD Papers.
27. Dennett to Marie Stopes, August 15, 1925, MWD Papers.
28. Dennett to Myra Gallert, November 4, 1925, MWD Papers.
29. Dennett to Gallert, November 4, 1925, MWD Papers.
30. Mary Ware Dennett, *Birth Control Laws: Shall We Keep Them, Change Them, or Abolish Them?* (New York: Frederick H. Hitchcock, 1926), iv.
31. Dennett to Myra Gallert, July 24, 1925, MWD Papers.
32. Dennett to Gallert and Sonia Bronson, September 19, 1925, MWD Papers.
33. Dennett, memo dated "the day after Christmas" [1925], MWD Papers.
34. Dennett, memo dated "the day after Christmas" [1925].
35. Jill Lepore, "Birthright," *The New Yorker*, November 6, 2011, https://www .newyorker.com/magazine/2011/11/14/birthright-jill-lepore.
36. Lepore, "Birthright."
37. James Reed, *The Birth Control Movement and American Society: From Private Vice to Public Virtue* (Princeton, NJ: Princeton University Press, 1978), 104.
38. Sanger, *The Selected Papers of Margaret Sanger*, ed. Esther Katz, asst. ed. Cathy Moran Hajo and Peter C. Engelman, vol. 1, *The Woman Rebel, 1900–1928* (Urbana: University of Illinois Press, 2003), 438–9n1.
39. Rosen, *Reproductive Health, Reproductive Rights*, 88.
40. Chesler, *Woman of Valor*, 254.
41. Andrea Tone, *Devices and Desires: A History of Contraceptives in America* (New York: Hill and Wang, 2001), 129.
42. Trent MacNamara, *Birth Control and American Modernity: A History of Popular Ideas* (New York: Cambridge University Press, 2018), 123.
43. MacNamara, 113.
44. J. F. Cooper, Report on Portland, Maine, February 26, 1926, ABCL Papers, Harvard Houghton Library.
45. MacNamara, *Birth Control and American Modernity*, 138.
46. Cooper, *Technique of Contraception*, quoted in Reed, *Birth Control Movement*, 145–46.
47. James Rorty, "What's Stopping Birth Control?," *The New Republic*, February 3, 1932, pp. 313–14.
48. Kathleen A. Tobin, *The American Religious Debate over Birth Control, 1907–1937* (Jefferson, NC: McFarland, 2001), 97.

49. Tobin, 143.
50. Tobin, 97.
51. Joyce Berkman, "The Question of Margaret Sanger," *History Compass* 9, no. 6 (June 2011): 480.
52. Tobin, *American Religious Debate over Birth Control*, 68.
53. Sanger, *Autobiography*, chap. 29.
54. Sanger, chap. 34.
55. Mary Ware Dennett to Warner Fite, January 28, 1927, MWD Papers.
56. Constance Chen, *"The Sex Side of Life": Mary Ware Dennett's Pioneering Battle for Birth Control and Sex Education* (New York: The New Press, 1996), 240.
57. Mary Ware Dennett to Myra Gallert, April 23, 1926, and "Curriculum Vitae," MWD Papers.
58. Author interview with Sharon Spaulding, Zoom, March 7, 2022.
59. Author interview with Nancy Dennett, Zoom, March 7, 2022.
60. Mary Ware Dennett to Marie Stopes, November 27, 1926, MWD Papers.
61. Myra Gallert to Dennett, May 30, 1926, MWD Papers.
62. Dennett to Stopes, November 27, 1926.
63. Dennett to Myra Gallert, telegram and letter, June 22, 1926, MWD Papers.
64. Dennett to Gallert, June 22, 1926.
65. Dennett to Gallert and Vine Colby McCasland, July 6, 1926, MWD Papers.
66. Dennett to Gallert and McCasland, July 6, 1926.
67. Dennett to Gallert and McCasland, July 6, 1926.
68. Introduction, *The Selected Papers of Margaret Sanger*, ed. Esther Katz, asst. ed. Cathy Moran Hajo and Peter C. Engelman, vol. 2, *Birth Control Comes of Age, 1928–1939* (Urbana: University of Illinois Press, 2007), xxvi.
69. Sanger to Noah Slee, March 30, 1927, in *Selected Papers*, 1:454.
70. Dennett, *Birth Control Laws*, 255.
71. Dennett, 66.
72. Dennett, 170, 95.
73. Dennett, 67.
74. Dennett, 172.
75. Sanger, *Autobiography*, 387.
76. Matthew Connelly, *Fatal Misconception: The Struggle to Control World Population* (Cambridge, MA: The Belknap Press of Harvard University Press, 2008), 69–70.
77. "From Geneva to Cairo: Margaret Sanger and the First World Population Conference," newsletter no. 8, Spring 1994, Margaret Sanger Papers Project, New York University, https://www.sanger.hosting.nyu.edu/articles/from_geneva _to_cairo/.
78. Dennett to Fite, January 28, 1927, MWD Papers.
79. Dr. Louise Bryant, Committee on Maternal Health, letter to Dennett on behalf of Dr. Dickinson on September 9, 1927, and Dennett's next-day reply to Dr. Bryant, September 10, 1927, MWD Papers.
80. Dennett to Myra Gallert and Vine Colby McCasland, July 4, 1927, MWD Papers.

CHAPTER 22: THE INFERNO

1. Sonia Bronson to Mary Ware Dennett, Myra Gallert, and Vine Colby McCasland, March 2, 1927, MWD Papers.
2. "Berenice Abbott," MoMa profile, https://www.moma.org/artists/41 (accessed June 28, 2023).

3. Dorothy M. Brown, *Setting a Course: American Women in the 1920s* (Boston: Twayne, 1987), 7.

4. Amy C. Sarch, "Dirty Discourse: Birth Control Advertising in the 1920s and 1930s" (PhD diss., University of Pennsylvania, 1994), 89.

5. Mary Ware Dennett, *The Sex Education of Children: A Book for Parents* (New York: The Vanguard Press, 1931), 81–82.

6. John D'Emilio and Estelle B. Freedman, *Intimate Matters: A History of Sexuality in America* (New York: Harper & Row, 1988), 268.

7. Lillian Faderman, *Woman: The American History of an Idea* (New Haven, CT: Yale University Press, 2022), ebook loc. 4732.

8. D'Emilio and Freedman, *Intimate Matters*, 227.

9. Frederick Lewis Allen, *Only Yesterday: An Informal History of the 1920s* (New York: John Wiley & Sons, 1997 reprint of 1931 Harper & Row edition), chap. 5, https://xroads.virginia.edu/~Hyper/Allen/provenance.html (accessed June 23, 2023).

10. Leigh Ann Wheeler, *Against Obscenity: Reform and the Politics of Womanhood in America, 1873–1935* (Baltimore: Johns Hopkins University Press, 2004), 99.

11. Beth Widmaier Capo, *Textual Contraception: Birth Control and Modern American Fiction* (Columbus: Ohio State University Press, 2021), 62.

12. Anne Kennedy to Mary Sumner Boyd, April 13, 1926, ABCL Papers.

13. James Joyce to Harriet Shaw Weaver, November 8, 1926, reproduced by the James Joyce Digital Archive, https://jjda.ie/main/JJDA/f/FF/fbiog/fwlett.htm (accessed July 14, 2023).

14. Wheeler, *Against Obscenity*, 156.

15. Allison McNearney, "How Mae West's Play 'Sex' Scandalized Broadway—and Landed Her in Jail," *Daily Beast*, October 15, 2021, https://www.thedailybeast.com/how-mae-wests-play-sex-scandalized-broadwayand-landed-her-in-jail; see also "The 'Sex' Scandal that Made Mae West," *Decoder Ring* (Slate), August 16, 2022, https://slate.com/podcasts/decoder-ring/2022/08/the-sex-scandals-of-mae-west.

16. Polly Stenham, "Brutal! Vulgar! Dirty! Mae West and the Gay Comedy that Shocked 1920s America," *The Guardian*, July 5, 2017, https://www.theguardian.com/stage/2017/jul/05/polly-stenham-mae-west-gay-pride-the-drag-national-theatre.

17. Nancy Cott, *The Grounding of Modern Feminism* (New Haven: Yale University Press, 1987), 172.

18. Andrea Tone, *Devices and Desires: A History of Contraceptives in America* (New York: Hill and Wang, 2001), 494.

19. Anne Kennedy to Annie Porritt, April 15, 1926, ABCL Papers.

20. *No More Children* (Cliff Broughton Productions, 1929), 28, https://archive.org/details/NoMoreChildren1929FilmBooklet/page/n31/mode/2up (accessed July 5, 2023).

21. *No More Children*, 34.

22. Manon Parry, *Broadcasting Birth Control: Mass Media and Family Planning* (New Brunswick, NJ: Rutgers University Press, 2013), 16.

23. Brownlow, *Behind the Mask of Innocence*, 48.

24. Parry, *Broadcasting Birth Control*, 20.

25. Brownlow, *Behind the Mask of Innocence*, 48.

26. Brownlow, 48.

27. Brown, *Setting a Course*, 35–36.

28. Capo, *Textual Contraception*, 15.

29. Estelle B. Freedman, "Sexuality in Nineteenth-Century America: Behavior, Ideology, and Politics," *Reviews in American History* 10, no. 4 (December 1982): 200.

30. Anya Jabour, "Abortion Opponents Are Gunning for Contraception, Too," *Washington Post*, March 25, 2022, https://www.washingtonpost.com/outlook /2022/03/25/abortion-opponents-are-gunning-contraception-too/.

31. Brown, *Setting a Course*, 45.

32. Margaret Mead, quoted in Brown, 47.

33. Dennett, *Sex Education of Children*, 141.

34. Rachel Bowlby, introduction to *Orlando: A Biography*, by Virginia Woolf (New York: Mariner Books, 1973), xliv.

35. Margaret Sanger, quoted in Jessica L. Furgerson, *The Battle for Birth Control: Exploring the Lasting Consequences of the Movement's Early Rhetoric* (Lanham, MD: Lexington Books, 2022), 30.

36. Helena Huntington Smith, "They Were Eleven," *The New Yorker*, June 28, 1930, https://www.newyorker.com/magazine/1930/07/05/they-were-eleven.

CHAPTER 23: AN UNTIMELY RAID

1. Mary Ware Dennett to Myra Gallert, October 6, 1928, MWD Papers.

2. Margaret Sanger, *Margaret Sanger: An Autobiography* (New York: W. W. Norton, 1938), chap. 32, https://www.gutenberg.org/files/56610/56610-h/56610-h.htm (accessed April 22, 2022).

3. Clipping from *Herald* of September 15, 1928, Joseph Lee papers, carton 19, Massachusetts Historical Society.

4. Sanger, *Autobiography*, chap. 32.

5. Sanger, quoted in Jean Baker, *Margaret Sanger: A Life of Passion* (New York: Hill and Wang, 2011), 158.

6. ABCL volunteer, quoted in Nancy Cott, *The Grounding of Modern Feminism* (New Haven: Yale University Press, 1987), 91.

7. Joan Johnson, *Funding Feminism: Monied Women, Philanthropy, and the Women's Movement, 1870–1967* (Chapel Hill: University of North Carolina Press, 2017), 188–89.

8. Ellen Chesler, *Woman of Valor: Margaret Sanger and the Birth Control Movement in America* (New York: Simon & Schuster, 1992), 240.

9. Editorial note, *The Selected Papers of Margaret Sanger*, ed. Esther Katz, asst. ed. Cathy Moran Hajo and Peter C. Engelman, vol. 1, *The Woman Rebel, 1900–1928* (Urbana: University of Illinois Press, 2003), 422.

10. Sanger to Rublee, November 4 [1928?], Rublee papers, Dartmouth.

11. Chesler, *Woman of Valor*, ebook loc. 4264.

12. Editorial note, in *The Selected Papers of Margaret Sanger*, ed. Esther Katz, asst. ed. Cathy Moran Hajo and Peter C. Engelman, vol. 2, *Birth Control Comes of Age, 1928–1939* (Urbana: University of Illinois Press, 2007), 2.

13. Chesler, *Woman of Valor*, 241.

14. Frederick Lewis Allen, *Only Yesterday: An Informal History of the 1920s* (New York: John Wiley & Sons, 1997 reprint of 1931 Harper & Row edition), chap. 14, https:// xroads.virginia.edu/~Hyper/Allen/provenance.html (accessed June 23, 2023).

15. Allen, chap. 14.

16. Margaret Sanger to Noah Slee, December 5, 1928, in *Selected Papers*, 2:13.

17. Editorial note, *Selected Papers*, 2:19.

18. Chesler, *Woman of Valor*, 256.

19. Sanger, *Autobiography*, chap. 33.

20. Sanger, chap. 33.

21. Brett Gary, *Dirty Works: Obscenity on Trial in America's First Sexual Revolution* (Stanford, CA: Stanford University Press, 2021), 217.
22. Sanger, *Autobiography*, chap. 33.
23. Hannah Stone, "The BC Raid," *Eugenics*, August 1929, p. 24.
24. Sanger, *Autobiography*, chap. 33.
25. Fred Rodell, quoted in Gary, *Dirty Works*, 19.
26. Morris Leopold Ernst, quoted in Gary, 19–20.
27. Chesler, *Woman of Valor*, 219.
28. Gary, *Dirty Works*, 231.
29. Helena Huntington Smith, "They Were Eleven," *The New Yorker*, June 28, 1930, https://www.newyorker.com/magazine/1930/07/05/they-were-eleven.
30. Gary, *Dirty Works*, 231–32.
31. Chesler, *Woman of Valor*, 285.
32. Jessica L. Furgerson, *The Battle for Birth Control: Exploring the Lasting Consequences of the Movement's Early Rhetoric* (Lanham, MD: Lexington Books, 2022), 170.
33. *The New Republic*, May 8, 1929, clipping in Sharon Spaulding / Dennett Family Archives, Alstead, NH & Sandy, UT.
34. Dudley Nichols, "Sex and the Law," *The Nation* 128, no. 3331 (May 8, 1929): 552.
35. Sanger, *Autobiography*, chap. 33.
36. Gary, *Dirty Works*, 237.

CHAPTER 24: A STRANGE SPECTACLE

1. Morris Leopold Ernst, foreword to *Who's Obscene?*, by Mary Ware Dennett (New York: The Vanguard Press, 1930), https://archive.org/stream/b29814601/b29814601_djvu.txt (accessed 12/9/19).
2. H. L. Mencken, "The Literature of Sex," *The American Mercury*, May 1926, 127.
3. Morris Leopold Ernst, quoted in Laura Weinrib, "The Sex Side of Civil Liberties: United States v. Dennett and the Changing Face of Free Speech," *Law and History Review* 30, no. 2 (May 2012): 352.
4. Constance Chen, *"The Sex Side of Life": Mary Ware Dennett's Pioneering Battle for Birth Control and Sex Education* (New York: The New Press, 1996), 269.
5. Dennett, *Who's Obscene?*
6. Dennett calls Mead "Ah Loo" in occasional letters, including one sent New Year's Day 1929.
7. Dennett, *Who's Obscene?*
8. Dennett.
9. Chen, *"The Sex Side of Life,"* 271.
10. Chen, 270–71.
11. Dennett, *Who's Obscene?*
12. Chen, *"The Sex Side of Life,"* 276.
13. Dennett, *Who's Obscene?*
14. Weinrib, "Sex Side of Civil Liberties," 352.
15. Ernst, foreword to *Who's Obscene?*
16. Dennett, *Who's Obscene?*
17. Dennett.
18. Dennett.
19. Dudley Nichols, "Sex and Our Children," *The Nation* 128, no. 3318 (February 1929): 154–55.

20. Dennett, *Who's Obscene?*
21. Nichols, "Sex and Our Children," 154–55.
22. Layne Parish Craig, *When Sex Changed: Birth Control Politics and Literature between the World Wars* (New Brunswick, NJ: Rutgers University Press, 2013), 152.
23. Mary Ware Dennett to Myra Gallert, May 15, 1929, MWD Papers.
24. Dennett to Gallert, May 15, 1929.
25. Quoted in Craig, *When Sex Changed*, 153.
26. Nichols, "Sex and Our Children," 154–55.
27. Nichols, 552.
28. "What Constitutes Obscenity? Jury at New York Says Dennett Book," *Greencastle Herald*, May 7, 1929, p. 4.
29. "What Constitutes Obscenity?," 4.
30. Dolores Flamiano, "'The Sex Side of Life' in the News: Mary Ware Dennett's Obscenity Case, 1929–1930," *Journalism History* 25, no. 2 (Summer 1999): 71.
31. Chen, *"The Sex Side of Life,"* 293.
32. "Mary Ware Dennett Excepts" (letter to the editor), *New York Times*, May 3, 1929, Sharon Spaulding / Dennett Family Archives, Alstead, NH & Sandy, UT.
33. W. P. Beazell to Dennett, May 1, 1929, MWD Papers.
34. Edward De Grazia, *Girls Lean Back Everywhere: The Law of Obscenity and the Assault on Genius* (New York: Random House, 1992), xi–xii.
35. Chen, *"The Sex Side of Life,"* xvii.
36. Leigh Ann Wheeler, *Against Obscenity: Reform and the Politics of Womanhood in America, 1873–1935* (Baltimore: Johns Hopkins University Press, 2004), 180.
37. Untitled clipping, Sharon Spaulding / Dennett Family Archives, Alstead, NH & Sandy, UT.
38. Mildred Gilman, "Sons Stand by Author Fighting Sex Verdict," undated clipping, Sharon Spaulding / Dennett Family Archives, Alstead, NH & Sandy, UT.
39. Ernst, foreword to *Who's Obscene?*
40. Brett Gary, *Dirty Works: Obscenity on Trial in America's First Sexual Revolution* (Stanford, CA: Stanford University Press, 2021), 49.
41. Nichols, "Sex and Our Children," 154–55.
42. Flamiano, "'The Sex Side of Life' in the News," 64.
43. Gary, *Dirty Works*, 53.
44. "Mrs. Dennett, 75, Suffrage Leader," *New York Times*, July 26, 1947, Sharon Spaulding / Dennett Family Archives, Alstead, NH & Sandy, UT.
45. Mary Ware Dennett to Marie Stopes, June 2, 1929, MWD Papers.
46. Clipping, "Sex Pamphlet Mother Hears Sentence Today," Sharon Spaulding / Dennett Family Archives, Alstead, NH & Sandy, UT.
47. Dennett, *Who's Obscene?*
48. Weinrib, "Sex Side of Civil Liberties," 355.
49. Chen, *"The Sex Side of Life,"* 292.
50. Flamiano, "'The Sex Side of Life' in the News," 72.
51. Nichols, "Sex and Our Children," 553.
52. Chen, *"The Sex Side of Life,"* 293.
53. Dennett, *Who's Obscene?*
54. Gilman, "Sons Stand by Author."
55. Dennett, *Who's Obscene?*
56. Heywood Broun, "It Seems to Me," *New York Telegram*, 1929, Sharon Spaulding / Dennett Family Archives, Alstead, NH & Sandy, UT.

57. Flamiano, "'The Sex Side of Life' in the News," 65.
58. *The New Republic*, May 8, 1929, clipping in Sharon Spaulding / Dennett Family Archives, Alstead, NH & Sandy, UT.
59. *New Republic* of October 16, 1929, quoted in course book for "The Family," Walpole High School, 1934–35, Frank Irving Howe Jr. family papers carton 3, Massachusetts Historical Society.
60. "Sex Book Foe Resigns," *New York World-Telegram*, April 16, 1931.
61. Chen, *"The Sex Side of Life,"* 294.
62. Flamiano, "'The Sex Side of Life' in the News," 72.
63. "Dennett Conviction Resolution Subject," *Herald* (New Britain, CT), June 12, 1929, p. 15.
64. Clipping, Sharon Spaulding / Dennett Family Archives, Alstead, NH & Sandy, UT.
65. "Canon [William Sheafe] Chase Wins Debate on Sex Book," *New York Telegram*, May 24, 1929, Sharon Spaulding / Dennett Family Archives, Alstead, NH & Sandy, UT.
66. Craig, *When Sex Changed*, 156.
67. "Pioneers against Prudery: Mary Ware Dennett and Margaret Sanger are interviewed by Constance Heck," *Food & Health Review* 1, no. 2 (July–August 1929): 20–24.
68. "Pioneers against Prudery," 20–24.
69. Dennett to Stopes, June 2, 1929.
70. Margaret Sanger to Dennett, May 24, 1929, MWD Papers.
71. "Birth Control Organizations—National Committee on Federal Legislation on Birth Control," Margaret Sanger Papers Project, New York University, https://sanger .hosting.nyu.edu/aboutms/organization_ncflbc/ (accessed June 28, 2023).
72. Mary Ware Dennett to Marie Stopes, October 24, 1929, MWD Papers.
73. Dennett to Winifred Duncan, December 4, 1929, MWD Papers.
74. Robyn L. Rosen, *Reproductive Health, Reproductive Rights: Reformers and the Politics of Maternal Welfare, 1917–1940* (Columbus: Ohio State University Press, 2003), 101.
75. Mary Ware Dennett to Margaret Sanger, February 15, 1930, MWD Papers.
76. Dennett to Sanger, February 15, 1930.
77. Sanger to Dennett, March 4, 1930, MWD Papers.
78. Dennett to Caroline Nelson, March 23, 1930, MWD Papers.
79. Nelson to Dennett, April 1, 1930, MWD Papers.
80. Nelson to Dennett, April 1, 1930.
81. Dennett to Agnes Engelhard, March 1, 1930, MWD Papers.
82. Dennett to Caroline Nelson, September 7, 1930, MWD Papers.
83. Dennett to Nelson, July 20, 1930, MWD Papers.
84. Dennett to Margaret Sanger, July 16, 1930, MWD Papers.
85. Anna Lifshiz, Sanger office to Dennett, July 23, 1930, MWD Papers.
86. Caroline Nelson to Dennett, July 18, 1930, MWD papers.
87. Chen, *"The Sex Side of Life,"* 301.
88. Marie Stopes to Mary Ware Dennett, November 5, 1929, MWD Papers.
89. Stopes to Dennett, July 4, 1929, MWD Papers.
90. Stopes to Dennett, August 23, 1929, MWD Papers.
91. Dennett to Stopes, September 5, 1929, MWD Papers.
92. Quoted in Craig, *When Sex Changed*, 155.
93. Chen, *"The Sex Side of Life,"* 280.
94. Gary, *Dirty Works*, 57.
95. Quoted in *The Selected Papers of Margaret Sanger*, ed. Esther Katz, asst. ed. Cathy Moran Hajo and Peter C. Engelman, vol. 2, *Birth Control Comes of Age, 1928–1939* (Urbana: University of Illinois Press, 2007), 158n6.

96. Quoted in Craig, *When Sex Changed*, 157–58.
97. Craig, 158.
98. Weinrib, "Sex Side of Civil Liberties," 359.
99. John Dewey to Mary Ware Dennett, March 3, 1930, MWD Papers.

CHAPTER 25: DROUGHT, GRASSHOPPERS, AND BABIES

1. Wendy Kline, *Building a Better Race: Gender, Sexuality, and Eugenics from the Turn of the Century to the Baby Boom* (Berkeley: University of California Press, 2005), ebook loc. 1322.

2. Introduction to chap. 4, *The Selected Papers of Margaret Sanger*, ed. Esther Katz, asst. ed. Cathy Moran Hajo and Peter C. Engelman, vol. 2, *Birth Control Comes of Age, 1928–1939* (Urbana: University of Illinois Press, 2007), 204.

3. Johanna Schoen, *Choice and Coercion: Birth Control, Sterilization, and Abortion in Public Health and Welfare* (Chapel Hill: University of North Carolina Press, 2005), 39.

4. Schoen, 39.

5. Ellen Chesler, *Woman of Valor: Margaret Sanger and the Birth Control Movement in America* (New York: Simon & Schuster, 1992), 338.

6. Chesler, 253.

7. Hannah M. Stone, "Birth Control in America," in "A Negro Number," special issue, *Birth Control Review* 16, no. 6 (June 1932): 188.

8. Matthew Connelly, *Fatal Misconception: The Struggle to Control World Population* (Cambridge, MA: The Belknap Press of Harvard University Press, 2008), 83.

9. Rachel Benson Gold, "Lessons from Before Roe: Will the Past Be Prologue?," *Guttmacher Policy Review* 6, no. 1 (March 2003): https://www.guttmacher.org/gpr/2003/03/lessons-roe-will-past-be-prologue.

10. Chesler, *Woman of Valor*, 300.

11. Donald T. Critchlow, *Intended Consequences: Birth Control, Abortion, and the Federal Government in Modern America* (New York: Oxford University Press, 2001), 133.

12. Jessie M. Rodrique, "The Black Community and the Birth Control Movement," in *Passion and Power: Sexuality in History*, ed. Kathy Peiss and Christina Simmons with Robert A. Padgug (Philadelphia: Temple University Press, 1989), 141.

13. Robinson, quoted in David J. Garrow, *Liberty & Sexuality: The Right to Privacy and the Making of Roe v. Wade* (New York: Macmillan, 1994), 273.

14. Mary Ware Dennett, "Youth in the Life of Today," undated draft, p. 83, MWD Papers.

15. Marjorie Prevost to Margaret Sanger, February 15, 1932, in *Selected Papers*, 2:159–60.

16. Sanger quoted in Cathy Moran Hajo, *Birth Control on Main Street: Organizing Clinics in the United States, 1916–1939* (Urbana: University of Illinois Press, 2010), 57.

17. Connelly, *Fatal Misconception*, 83.

18. Margaret Sanger, *Margaret Sanger: An Autobiography* (New York: W. W. Norton, 1938), chap. 33, https://www.gutenberg.org/files/56610/56610-h/56610-h.htm (accessed April 22, 2022).

19. Laura Weinrib, "The Sex Side of Civil Liberties: United States v. Dennett and the Changing Face of Free Speech," *Law and History Review* 30, no. 2 (May 2012): 377–78.

20. The Very Reverend W. R. Inge, "Birth Control and the Moral Law," reprinted from the *Atlantic Monthly* [1930] for the CFLBC, MS LOC.

21. Quoted in Connelly, *Fatal Misconception*, 85.

22. James P. McCartin, "Sex Is Holy and Mysterious: The Vision of Early Twentieth-Century Catholic Sex Education Reformers," in *Devotions and Desires: Histories of Sexuality and Religion in the Twentieth-Century United States*, ed. Gillian Frank, Bethany Moreton, and Heather R. White (Chapel Hill: University of North Carolina Press, 2018), 83.

23. Elizabeth Bruenig, "Sex Is Serious," *Boston Review*, January 12, 2015, https://www.bostonreview.net/articles/feminists-christians-sex-ethics-affirmative-consent-elizabeth-stoker-bruenig/.

24. Clipping from *Post* of January 26, 1930, Joseph Lee papers carton 19, Massachusetts Historical Society.

25. Chesler, *Woman of Valor*, 345.

26. Chesler, 345.

27. David M. Kennedy, *Birth Control in America: The Career of Margaret Sanger* (New Haven, CT: Yale University Press, 1970), 149.

28. Margaret Sanger, "The Pope's Position on Birth Control," January 27, 1932, in *Selected Papers*, 2:151.

29. Sanger, "My Answer to the Pope on Birth Control," *The Nation*, January 27, 1932, pp. 102–4, quoted in Kennedy, *Birth Control in America*, 153.

30. Leo J. Latz, *The Rhythm of Sterility and Fertility in Women* (Chicago: Latz Foundation, 1950), https://collection.maas.museum/object/345735 (accessed June 29, 2023).

31. Marie Stopes to Mary Ware Dennett, July 1, 1935, quoting *Birth Control News* of July 1935, review of "The Rhythm," MWD Papers.

32. Kathleen A. Tobin, *The American Religious Debate Over Birth Control, 1907–1937* (Jefferson, NC: McFarland, 2001), 42.

33. Quoted in *Selected Papers*, 2:210n5.

34. "Even Natural Birth Control Can't Get By N.Y. Customs," *Birth Control News*, January 1935, p. 98.

35. Editorial note, *Selected Papers*, 2:256.

36. H. L. Mencken, quoted in Alan Levinovitz, *Natural: How Faith in Nature's Goodness Leads to Harmful Fads, Unjust Laws, and Flawed Science* (New York: Beacon Press, 2020), 171.

37. Tom Gjelten, "50 Years Ago, the Pope Called Birth Control 'Intrinsically Wrong,'" *Morning Edition*, NPR, July 3, 2018, https://www.npr.org/2018/07/03/620105604/50-years-ago-the-pope-called-birth-control-intrinsically-wrong.

38. Ryan Burge, "Is Catholic Teaching on Birth Control Driving People from the Pews?," *National Catholic Reporter*, January 13, 2023, https://www.ncronline.org/opinion/catholic-teaching-birth-control-driving-people-pews.

39. "Tracing *One Package*—The Case that Legalized Birth Control," newsletter no. 59, Winter 2011, Margaret Sanger Papers Project, New York University, https://sanger.hosting.nyu.edu/articles/tracing_one_package/ (access June 29, 2023).

40. "Tracing *One Package*."

41. "Even Natural Birth Control Can't Get By N.Y. Customs," 98.

42. John O'Donnell and Doris Fleeson, "Birth Control Clash Puzzle to Advocates," Capital Stuff, *New York News*, October 3, 1934, MS LOC.

43. O'Donnell and Fleeson, "Birth Control Clash."

44. Marie Stopes to Mary Ware Dennett, April 4, 1930, MWD Papers.

45. EXTRACT FROM THE JUDGMENT United States DISTRICT COURT SOUTHERN DISTRICT OF New York APRIL 6th 1931 John Woolsey, U.S.

District Judge United States OF AMERICA, Libelant, Versus ONE Obscene Book Entitled "MARRIED LOVE," https://law.justia.com/cases/federal/district-courts/F2/48/821/1569043/ (accessed June 29, 2023).

46. EXTRACT FROM THE JUDGMENT.
47. Brett Gary, *Dirty Works: Obscenity on Trial in America's First Sexual Revolution* (Stanford, CA: Stanford University Press, 2021), 66.
48. Weinrib, "Sex Side of Civil Liberties," 373.
49. Marie Stopes to Mary Ware Dennett, July 31, 1931, MWD Papers.
50. Layne Parish Craig, *When Sex Changed: Birth Control Politics and Literature between the World Wars* (New Brunswick, NJ: Rutgers University Press, 2013), 159.
51. Weinrib, "Sex Side of Civil Liberties," 377.
52. Gary Younge, "The View from Middletown: A Typical US City that Never Did Exist," *The Guardian*, October 11, 2016, https://www.theguardian.com/membership/2016/oct/18/view-from-middletown-us-muncie-america.
53. Robert Lynd and Helen Merrell Lynd, quoted in Kennedy, *Birth Control in America*, 138.
54. Robert Lynd and Helen Merrell Lynd, quoted in Beth Widmaier Capo, *Textual Contraception: Birth Control and Modern American Fiction* (Columbus: Ohio State University Press, 2021), 15–16.
55. Robert Lynd and Helen Merrell Lynd, quoted in Capo, 15–16.
56. Megan Lynn Minarich, "Hollywood's Reproduction Code: Regulating Contraception and Abortion in American Cinema, 1915–1952" (PhD diss., Vanderbilt University, 2014), 170.
57. Minarich, 177.
58. Manon Parry, *Broadcasting Birth Control: Mass Media and Family Planning* (New Brunswick, NJ: Rutgers University Press, 2013), 28–29.
59. Parry, 33.
60. Parry, 33.
61. Parry, 36.
62. Mary Ware Dennett, *The Sex Education of Children: A Book for Parents* (New York: The Vanguard Press, 1931), 31.
63. Dennett to George and Louie Bedborough, February 25, 1934, MWD Papers.
64. Weinrib, "Sex Side of Civil Liberties," 368.
65. *Public Opinion*, n.d., Sharon Spaulding / Dennett Family Archives, Alstead, NH & Sandy, UT.
66. Editorial note, *Selected Papers*, 2:70–71.
67. *Selected Papers*, 2:113n6.
68. Mary Ware Dennett, *Birth Control Laws: Shall We Keep Them, Change Them, or Abolish Them?* (New York: Frederick H. Hitchcock, 1926), iv.
69. Review of *My Fight for Birth Control*, signed Dr. WJR, December 1931, MWD Papers.
70. Review of *My Fight for Birth Control*.
71. William J. Robinson, "Ten Dollars for a 75 Cent Dinner," MWD Papers.
72. Ruth Millard, "Birth Control Fight Opened by Margaret Sanger in 1914," *New York World-Telegram*, March 28, 1931.
73. Mildred Adams, "Crusader," *Delineator* 123, no. 3 (September 1933): 49.
74. Introduction to chap. 4, *Selected Papers*, 2:205.
75. Introduction to chap. 4, *Selected Papers*, 2:205.

CHAPTER 26: WAR IN THE AIR

1. Mary Ware Dennett to Myra Gallert and Vine Colby McCasland, July 13, 1930, MWD Papers.
2. Dennett to Gallert and McCasland, July 13, 1930, MWD Papers.
3. Winifred Duncan to Mary Ware Dennett, most undated, 1922–29, MWD Papers.
4. Constance Chen, *"The Sex Side of Life": Mary Ware Dennett's Pioneering Battle for Birth Control and Sex Education* (New York: The New Press, 1996), 245.
5. Mary Ware Dennett to Mrs. Marshall Field, July 31, 1930, MWD Papers.
6. Dennett to Vonie [Livonia Ware], July 24, 1932, Sharon Spaulding / Dennett Family Archives, Alstead, NH & Sandy, UT.
7. Dennett to Field, July 31, 1930.
8. Dennett to Edward Krehbiel, March 11, 1919, MWD Papers.
9. Dennett to Kenneth Parmenter, September 7, 1928, MWD Papers.
10. Dennett to Gallert and McCasland, July 13, 1930.
11. Nancy Dennett interview, March 7, 2022.
12. "A Middle Class Mother's Day," initialed I. C., MWD Papers.
13. Mary Ware Dennett to Vine Colby McCasland, September 29, 1934, Sharon Spaulding / Dennett Family Archives, Alstead, NH & Sandy, UT.
14. McCasland to Dennett, July 29, [?], Sharon Spaulding / Dennett Family Archives, Alstead, NH & Sandy, UT.
15. Van de Velde, quoted in M. E. Melody and Linda M. Peterson, *Teaching America about Sex: Marriage Guides and Sex Manuals from the Late Victorians to Dr. Ruth* (New York: New York University Press, 1999), 109.
16. Wendy Kline, *Building a Better Race: Gender, Sexuality, and Eugenics from the Turn of the Century to the Baby Boom* (Berkeley: University of California Press, 2005), ebook loc. 1404, 1400.
17. Robyn L. Rosen, "Federal Expansion, Fertility Control, and Physicians in the United States: The Politics of Maternal Welfare in the Interwar Years," *Journal of Women's History* 10, no. 3 (Autumn 1998): 65.
18. Ellen Chesler, *Woman of Valor: Margaret Sanger and the Birth Control Movement in America* (New York: Simon & Schuster, 1992), 342.
19. Vine Colby McCasland to Mary Ware Dennett, Myra Gallert, and Sonia Bronson, [?] 1930, from Pasadena, MWD Papers.
20. Paul Popenoe to Madison Grant, April 13, 1928, quoted in Edwin Black, *War against the Weak: Eugenics and America's Campaign to Create a Master Race* (New York: Four Walls Eight Windows, 2003), 139.
21. Popenoe, quoted in Jill Lepore, "Fixed," *The New Yorker*, March 22, 2010, https://www.newyorker.com/magazine/2010/03/29/fixed.
22. Ian Frazier, "When W. E. B. Du Bois Made a Laughingstock of a White Supremacist," *The New Yorker*, August 19, 2019, https://www.newyorker.com/magazine/2019/08/26/when-w-e-b-du-bois-made-a-laughingstock-of-a-white-supremacist.
23. Margaret Sanger, quoted in Alexander Sanger, "Eugenics, Race, and Margaret Sanger Revisited: Reproductive Freedom for All?," *Hypatia* 22, no. 2 (2007): 216.
24. *The Selected Papers of Margaret Sanger*, ed. Esther Katz, asst. ed. Cathy Moran Hajo and Peter C. Engelman, vol. 2, *Birth Control Comes of Age, 1928–1939* (Urbana: University of Illinois Press, 2007), 134–35.
25. Robyn L. Rosen, *Reproductive Health, Reproductive Rights: Reformers and the Politics of Maternal Welfare, 1917–1940* (Columbus: Ohio State University Press, 2003), 135–36.

26. Rosen, 137.
27. Helena Huntington Smith, "They Were Eleven," *The New Yorker*, June 28, 1930, https://www.newyorker.com/magazine/1930/07/05/they-were-eleven.
28. Peter C. Engelman, *A History of the Birth Control Movement in America* (Santa Barbara, CA: Praeger, 2011), 64–65.
29. Mildred Adams, "Crusader," *Delineator* 123, no. 3 (September 1933): 49.
30. Brush, quoted in James Reed, *The Birth Control Movement and American Society: From Private Vice to Public Virtue* (Princeton, NJ: Princeton University Press, 1978), 109.
31. Margaret Sanger, *Margaret Sanger: An Autobiography*: (New York: W. W. Norton, 1938), chap. 34, https://www.gutenberg.org/files/56610/56610-h/56610-h.htm (accessed April 22, 2022)
32. Sanger, chap. 34.
33. Transcript of April 27, 1931, Joseph Lee Papers, carton 19, Massachusetts Historical Society.
34. The Mothers Bill of Rights, Sanger Papers, Libary of Congress.
35. "Medicine: Birth Control Hearing," *Time*, February 23, 1931, https://content.time.com/time/subscriber/article/0,33009,930381-1,00.html.
36. Mary Ware Dennett to Marie Stopes, February 15, 1931, MWD Papers.
37. Dennett, "An Open Letter to Margaret Sanger, Hon. Frederick H. Gillette, and the Judiciary Committee of the Senate," February 11, 1931, MWD Papers.
38. Sanger to Dennett, February 21, 1931 [several drafts in file], MWD Papers.
39. Barbara Leaming, *Katharine Hepburn* (New York: Crown, 1995), 5.
40. "Backstage with Sanger and Hepburn," newsletter no. 34, Fall 2003, Margaret Sanger Papers Project, New York University, https://sanger.hosting.nyu.edu/articles/hepburn/.
41. Leaming, *Katharine Hepburn*, 264.
42. "Backstage with Sanger and Hepburn."
43. Leaming, *Katharine Hepburn*, unpaginated insert caption.
44. Chesler, *Woman of Valor*, 326.
45. Morris Leopold Ernst to Mary Ware Dennett, February 14, 1931, MWD Papers.
46. Dennett to Marie Stopes, February 4, 1931, MWD Papers.
47. Dennett to Stopes, July 17, 1931, MWD Papers.
48. WJR [William J. Robinson] to Dennett, April 13, 1931, MWD Papers.
49. Dennett to Stopes, February 4, 1931.
50. Dennett to Margaret Sanger, February 28, 1931, MWD Papers.
51. Dennett to Sanger, February 28, 1931.
52. Dennett to Sanger, February 28, 1931.
53. Sanger to Dennett, March 3, 1931, in *Selected Papers*, 2:95.
54. Sanger to Dennett, March 3, 1931.
55. Sanger to Dennett, March 3, 1931.
56. Introduction to chap. 4, *Selected Papers*, 2:203.
57. Schlesinger-Rockefeller Oral History Project Interview with Grant Sanger, MD, by Ellen Chesler, August 1976, p. 21.
58. Chesler, *Woman of Valor*, 339.
59. Chesler, 339.
60. *Selected Papers*, 2:240.
61. James Rorty, "What's Stopping Birth Control?," *The New Republic*, February 3, 1932, p. 313.
62. Rorty, 314.
63. Rorty, 313.
64. Rorty, 314.

65. Sanger, *Autobiography*, chap. 34.
66. Alice Palache report, January 8, 1932, MS LOC.
67. Sanger, *Autobiography*, chap. 34.
68. Sanger to Mary Hope Macaulay, May 21, 1932, in *Selected Papers*, 2:190.
69. Chesler, *Woman of Valor*, 343.
70. Bruce Bliven, editor of *The New Republic*, to Mary Ware Dennett, May 13, 1932, MWD Papers.
71. Michael Davis (Julius Rosenwald Fund) to Dennett, May 26, 1932, MWD Papers.
72. Dennett to Margaret Sanger, May 18, 1932, MWD Papers.
73. Dennett to Mrs. Otis, May 17, 1932, MWD Papers.
74. Dennett to *Herald Tribune*, February 1, 1933, MWD Papers.
75. Dennett to Mrs. Porter, May 23, 1932, MWD Papers.
76. Cathy Moran Hajo, *Birth Control on Main Street: Organizing Clinics in the United States, 1916–1939* (Urbana: University of Illinois Press, 2010), 153.
77. "Birth Control and the Good Old Boys in Congress," newsletter no. 26, Winter 2000/2001, Margaret Sanger Papers Project, New York University, https://sanger.hosting.nyu.edu/articles/good_old_boys/.
78. "Birth Control and the Good Old Boys in Congress."
79. *Selected Papers*, 2:116.

CHAPTER 27: EIGHT MILES NORTH

1. Jessie M. Rodrique, "The Afro-American Community and the Birth Control Movement, 1918–1942" (PhD diss., University of Massachusetts Amherst, 1991), 124.
2. "Research Bureau Has 'Open House': Margaret Sanger, Director, Reveals Startling Facts about Many Families," *New York Amsterdam News*, November 26, 1930, p. 11.
3. Quoted in Rodrique, "Afro-American Community," 98.
4. Cliff Alperti, "Viña Delmar and Uptown New York (1932)—World Wide's Bad Girl," *Immortal Ephemera*, January 4, 2016, https://immortalephemera.com/64040/uptown-new-york-1932-vina-delmar/.
5. Beth Widmaier Capo, *Textual Contraception: Birth Control and Modern American Fiction* (Columbus: Ohio State University Press, 2021), 94.
6. Grimké, quoted in Capo, 94.
7. Grimké, quoted in Allison Berg, *Mothering the Race: Women's Narratives of Reproduction, 1890–1930* (Urbana: University of Illinois Press, 2001), 15.
8. Blake Wilson, "Art as Protest: Angelina Weld Grimke's *Rachel*," *Boundary Stones*, WETA, April 2, 2019, https://boundarystones.weta.org/2019/04/02/art-protest-angelina-weld-grimk%C3%A9s-rachel.
9. Wilson, "Art as Protest."
10. George Schuyler, "Quantity or Quality," in "A Negro Number," special issue, *Birth Control Review* 16, no. 6 (June 1932): 165.
11. Charles S. Johnson, "A Question of Negro Health," in "A Negro Number," special issue, *Birth Control Review* 16, no. 6 (June 1932): 168.
12. Annalies Winny and Rachel Bervell, "How Can We Solve the Black Maternal Health Crisis?," Public Health On Call, Bloomberg School of Public Health, Johns Hopkins University, May 12, 2023, https://publichealth.jhu.edu/2023/solving-the-black-maternal-health-crisis.
13. Andrea DenHoed, "The Forgotten Lessons of the American Eugenics Movement," review of *Imbeciles: The Supreme Court, American Eugenics, and the Sterilization of Carrie Buck*, by Adam Cohen, *The New Yorker*, April 27, 2018, https://www

.newyorker.com/books/page-turner/the-forgotten-lessons-of-the-american-eugenics
-movement.

14. Lutz Kaelber, "Mississippi," segment of presentation about eugenic sterilizations in comparative perspective at the 2012 Social Science History Association, https://www .uvm.edu/~lkaelber/eugenics/MS/MS.html#:~:text=Mississippi%20was%20the%20 twenty%2Dsixth%20state%20to%20pass%20a%20sterilization%20law.&text=In%20 the%20sterilization%20law%20that,91).

15. "Looking Uptown: Margaret Sanger and the Harlem Branch Birth Control Clinic," newsletter no. 54, Spring 2010, Margaret Sanger Papers Project, New York University, https://sanger.hosting.nyu.edu/articles/harlem/.

16. Rodrique, "Afro-American Community," 81.

17. Rodrique, 137.

18. Carole McCann, introduction to the document selection *What Perspectives Did African American Advocates Bring to the Birth Control Movement and How Did Those Perspectives Shape the History of the Harlem Branch Birth Control Clinic?* (Binghamton: State University of New York at Binghamton, 2006), https:// documents.alexanderstreet.com/d/1000671764.

19. McCann, introduction.

20. Michele Reynolds, "Abortion Is Killing the Black Community," On the Record, Ohio Senate, 135th General Assembly, October 18 2023, https://ohiosenate.gov/news/on-the -record/abortion-is-killing-the-black-community.

21. Margaret Sanger to Norman Himes, January 10, 1933, in *The Selected Papers of Margaret Sanger*, ed. Esther Katz, asst. ed. Cathy Moran Hajo and Peter C. Engelman, vol. 2, *Birth Control Comes of Age, 1928–1939* (Urbana: University of Illinois Press, 2007), 211–12.

22. Sanger to Himes, January 10, 1933.

23. "New York City: The Harlem Renaissance and Beyond," Smithsonian American Art Museum, https://americanexperience.si.edu/wp-content/uploads/2014/07/ New-York-City_The-Harlem-Renaissance-and-Beyond.pdf (accessed June 30, 2023).

24. Rodrique, "Afro-American Community," 65.

25. Rodrique, 65.

26. Rodrique, "The Black Community and the Birth Control Movement," in *Passion and Power: Sexuality in History*, ed. Kathy Peiss and Christina Simmons with Robert A. Padgug (Philadelphia: Temple University Press, 1989), 140.

27. Rodrique, "Afro-American Community," 79.

28. Rodrique, "Black Community," 141.

29. "Research Bureau Has 'Open House,'" 11.

30. "Looking Uptown," Margaret Sanger Papers Project.

31. Dorothy Roberts, *Killing the Black Body: Race, Reproduction, and the Meaning of Liberty* (New York: Pantheon Books, 1997), 12–13.

32. Roberts, 6.

33. Roberts, 80.

34. Enrique Rivero, "Proportion of Black Physicians in U.S. Has Changed Little in 120 Years, UCLA Research Finds," *UCLA Newsroom*, April 19, 2021, https://newsroom .ucla.edu/releases/proportion-black-physicians-little-change.

35. Hazel Moore, "Report," 1937, Rose Papers, quoted in Rodrique, "Afro-American Community," 128.

36. Moore, 128.

37. McCann, introduction.

38. T. E. B. [Thelma Edna Berlack], "Harlem Not Interested," The Feminist Viewpoint, *New York Amsterdam News*, September 5, 1932, p. 1.
39. Rodrique, "Afro-American Community," 99.
40. "Looking Uptown," Margaret Sanger Papers Project.
41. W. E. B. Du Bois, "Opinion," *The Crisis* 24, no. 6 (October 1922): 247.
42. Rodrique, "Afro-American Community," 108.
43. Rodrique, "Black Community," 142.
44. Roberts, *Killing the Black Body*, 99.
45. Carole McCann, Introduction to Document 27: Advisory Council Meeting Minutes, 25 January 1933, collected in *What Perspectives Did African American Advocates Bring to the Birth Control Movement and How Did Those Perspectives Shape the History of the Harlem Branch Birth Control Clinic?*, documents selected and interpreted by Carole McCann, University of Maryland, June 2006.
46. Rodrique, "Afro-American Community," 155.
47. McCann, introduction.
48. Rodrique, "Afro-American Community," 153.
49. Rodrique, 141.
50. Marie Levinson Warner, "Birth Control and the Negro" (1934), in McCann, ed., *What Perspectives Did African American Advocates Bring to the Birth Control Movement and How Did Those Perspectives Shape the History of the Harlem Branch Birth Control Clinic?*
51. Constance Fisher, "The Negro Social Worker Evaluates Birth Control," in "A Negro Number," special issue, *Birth Control Review* 16, no. 6 (June 1932): 174.
52. McCann, introduction.
53. Mabel Staupers to Margaret Sanger, August 2, 1935, MS LOC.
54. Sanger to Staupers, August 7, 1935, MS LOC.

CHAPTER 28: BREAKTHROUGH

1. Editorial note, *The Selected Papers of Margaret Sanger*, ed. Esther Katz, asst. ed. Cathy Moran Hajo and Peter C. Engelman, vol. 2, *Birth Control Comes of Age, 1928–1939* (Urbana: University of Illinois Press, 2007), 308.
2. "New Drive Mapped for Birth Control," *New York Times*, February 13, 1935, p. 8.
3. Nancy Cott, *The Grounding of Modern Feminism* (New Haven: Yale University Press, 1987), 4.
4. Editorial note, *Selected Papers*, 2:318.
5. Vanessa Murphree and Karla K. Gower, "Mission Accomplished: Margaret Sanger and the National Committee on Federal Legislation for Birth Control, 1929–1937," *American Journalism* 25, no. 2 (2008): 13–14.
6. Editorial note, *Selected Papers*, 2:263.
7. Ellen Chesler, *Woman of Valor: Margaret Sanger and the Birth Control Movement in America* (New York: Simon & Schuster, 1992), 345.
8. Editorial note, *Selected Papers*, 2:272–73.
9. Edwin Black, "Hitler's Debt to America," *The Guardian*, February 5, 2004, https://www.theguardian.com/uk/2004/feb/06/race.usa.
10. Barbara Leaming, *Katharine Hepburn* (New York: Crown, 1995), 290–91.
11. Extract from testimony on Sanger 1842, in *Selected Papers*, 2:282.
12. "Birth Control Bill Approval Is Voted," *New York Times*, April 24, 1934, https://timesmachine.nytimes.com/timesmachine/1934/04/24/94515171html?pageNumber=4.
13. Sanger and Slee, Contract, May 12, 1935, in *Selected Papers*, 2:339.

14. Sanger, "Journal entry," January 1, 1938, in *Selected Papers*, 2:425.

15. Editorial note, *Selected Papers*, 2:356.

16. Editorial note, *Selected Papers*, 2:295.

17. Editorial note, 2:295.

18. Cathy Moran Hajo, *Birth Control on Main Street: Organizing Clinics in the United States, 1916–1939* (Urbana: University of Illinois Press, 2010), 167.

19. Chesler, *Woman of Valor*, 354.

20. "The Accident of Birth," *Fortune*, February 1938, p. 83.

21. "Accident of Birth," 83.

22. Cataloged in Amy C. Sarch, "Dirty Discourse: Birth Control Advertising in the 1920s and 1930s" (PhD diss., University of Pennsylvania, 1994).

23. "Accident of Birth," 112.

24. George Orwell, "St. Andrew's Day, 1935," reproduced by the Orwell Foundation, https://www.orwellfoundation.com/the-orwell-foundation/orwell/poetry/st-andrews-day-1935/ (accessed June 30, 2023).

25. "Accident of Birth," 84.

26. Donald T. Critchlow, *Intended Consequences: Birth Control, Abortion, and the Federal Government in Modern America* (New York: Oxford University Press, 2001), 35.

27. *International Journal of Medicine and Surgery*, June 1932, MS LOC.

28. Norman E. Himes, *The Medical History of Contraception* (New York: Schocken Books, 1936 [1970 ed.)]), 226.

29. Introduction to chap. 4, *Selected Papers*, 2:203.

30. "Tracing *One Package*—The Case that Legalized Birth Control," newsletter no. 59, Winter 2011, Margaret Sanger Papers Project, New York University, https://sanger.hosting.nyu.edu/articles/tracing_one_package/.

31. Margaret Sanger, *Margaret Sanger: An Autobiography* (New York: W. W. Norton, 1938), chap. 34, https://www.gutenberg.org/files/56610/56610-h/56610-h.htm (accessed April 22, 2022).

32. Murphree and Gower, "Mission Accomplished," 23–24.

33. Schlesinger-Rockefeller Oral History Project Interview with Grant Sanger, MD, by Ellen Chesler, August 1976, p. 23.

34. "Tracing *One Package*."

35. "Tracing *One Package*."

36. "Tracing *One Package*."

37. Sanger, *Autobiography*, chap. 34.

38. Sarch, "Dirty Discourse," 233.

39. Sarch, 233.

40. Sanger, quoted in David J. Garrow, *Liberty & Sexuality: The Right to Privacy and the Making of* Roe v. Wade (New York: Macmillan, 1994), 42.

41. Editorial note, *Selected Papers*, 2:357.

42. Manon Parry, *Broadcasting Birth Control: Mass Media and Family Planning* (New Brunswick, NJ: Rutgers University Press, 2013), 30.

43. "Tracing *One Package*."

44. "Mr. and Mrs. Hartley Dennett Succumb to Pneumonia," unknown magazine, 1936, Sharon Spaulding / Dennett Family Archives, Alstead, NH & Sandy, UT.

45. Clara Ware Hill to Mary Ware Dennett, n.d., MWD Papers.

46. Mary Ware Dennett to Carleton Dennett, December 19, 1939, Sharon Spaulding / Dennett Family Archives, Alstead, NH & Sandy, UT.

47. Mary Ware Dennett to Vine Colby McCasland and Myra Gallert, April 20, 1936, Sharon Spaulding / Dennett Family Archives, Alstead, NH & Sandy, UT.

48. "Memorandum for Carl and Devon Dennett re: Resources of M.W.D.," July 17, 1938, Sharon Spaulding / Dennett Family Archives, Alstead, NH & Sandy, UT.
49. Mary Ware Dennett to Marguerite Benson, March 18, 1936, MWD Papers.
50. Dennett to Benson, March 18, 1936.
51. Mary Ware Dennett to Myra Gallert, October 25, 1937, Sharon Spaulding / Dennett Family Archives, Alstead, NH & Sandy, UT.
52. Dennett to Gallert, October 25, 1937.
53. Dennett to Gallert, June 7, 1937, Sharon Spaulding / Dennett Family Archives, Alstead, NH & Sandy, UT.
54. Garrow, *Liberty & Sexuality*, 43.
55. Peter C. Engelman, *A History of the Birth Control Movement in America* (Santa Barbara, CA: Praeger, 2011), 169.
56. Rose Holz, "Nurse Gordon on Trial: Those Early Days of the Birth Control Clinic Movement," *Journal of Social History* 39, no. 1 (Autumn 2005): 129.
57. Garrow, *Liberty & Sexuality*, 43–44.
58. Sanger, *Autobiography*, chap. 34.
59. Engelman, *History of the Birth Control Movement*, 170.
60. Garrow, *Liberty & Sexuality*, 44.
61. Chesler, *Woman of Valor*, 376.
62. Sanger, *Autobiography*, chap. 12.
63. Henry Pringle, "What Do the Women of America Think? (Birth Control)," *Ladies' Home Journal*, March 1938, p. 114.
64. Pringle, 114.

EPILOGUE

1. Margaret Sanger, *Margaret Sanger: An Autobiography* (New York: W. W. Norton, 1938), chap. 35, https://www.gutenberg.org/files/56610/56610-h/56610-h.htm (accessed April 22, 2022).
2. Noah Slee to Sanger, May 4, 1939, in *The Selected Papers of Margaret Sanger*, ed. Esther Katz, asst. ed. Cathy Moran Hajo and Peter C. Engelman, vol. 2, *Birth Control Comes of Age, 1928–1939* (Urbana: University of Illinois Press, 2007), 486.
3. Sanger to Slee, May 7, 1939, in *Selected Papers*, 2:487.
4. Joan Johnson, *Funding Feminism: Monied Women, Philanthropy, and the Women's Movement, 1870–1967* (Chapel Hill: University of North Carolina Press, 2017), 197.
5. David M. Kennedy, *Birth Control in America: The Career of Margaret Sanger* (New Haven, CT: Yale University Press, 1970), 209.
6. "Birth Control or Race Control? Sanger and the Negro Project," newsletter no. 28, Fall 2001, Margaret Sanger Papers Project, New York University, https://sanger.hosting.nyu.edu/articles/bc_or_race_control/.
7. "Birth Control or Race Control?"
8. "Birth Control or Race Control?"
9. James W. Reed, "The Birth Control Movement Before *Roe v. Wade*," in *The Politics of Abortion and Birth Control in Historical Perspective*, ed. Donald T. Critchlow (University Park: Pennsylvania State University Press, 1996), 36.
10. Don Wharton, "Birth Control: The Case for the State," *The Atlantic*, October 1939, https://www.theatlantic.com/magazine/archive/1939/10/birth-control-the-case-for-the-state/308924/.
11. Wharton, "Birth Control."

12. Cathy Moran Hajo, *Birth Control on Main Street: Organizing Clinics in the United States, 1916–1939* (Urbana: University of Illinois Press, 2010), 126.

13. Andrea Tone, *Devices and Desires: A History of Contraceptives in America* (New York: Hill and Wang, 2001), 221.

14. Donald T. Critchlow, *Intended Consequences: Birth Control, Abortion, and the Federal Government in Modern America* (New York: Oxford University Press, 2001), 36.

15. Dorothy Roberts, *Killing the Black Body: Race, Reproduction, and the Meaning of Liberty* (New York: Pantheon Books, 1997), 95.

16. Reed, "Birth Control Movement Before *Roe v. Wade*," 36.

17. Ellen Chesler, *Woman of Valor: Margaret Sanger and the Birth Control Movement in America* (New York: Simon & Schuster, 1992), 361.

18. John Sharpless, "World Population Growth, Family Planning, and American Foreign Policy," in Critchlow, ed., *Politics of Abortion and Birth Control*, 75–76.

19. Margaret Sanger to Clarence Gamble, August 15, 1939, in *Selected Papers*, 2:495.

20. Sanger, *Autobiography*, chap. 39.

21. Nurith Aizenman, "Remember That Time When Wonder Woman Was a U.N. Ambassador?," *Goats and Soda* (newsletter), NPR, June 1, 2017, https://www.npr.org/sections/goatsandsoda/2017/06/01/531106299/remember-that-time-when-wonder-woman-was-a-u-n-ambassador.

22. Mary Ware Dennett to Marie Stopes, February 23, 1934, MWD Papers.

23. Sherwood Anderson to Dennett, August 18, 1932, MWD Papers.

24. Edith Flaster to Dennett, February 13, 1942, MWD Papers.

25. Constance Chen, *"The Sex Side of Life": Mary Ware Dennett's Pioneering Battle for Birth Control and Sex Education* (New York: The New Press, 1996), 302.

26. Chen, 302.

27. Nancy Dennett interview, March 7, 2022.

28. Dennett interview.

29. Mary Ware Dennett to Agnes Engelhard, March 11, 1938, MWD Papers.

30. "Mrs. Dennett, 75, Suffrage Leader," *New York Times*, July 26, 1947, Sharon Spaulding / Dennett Family Archives, Alstead, NH & Sandy, UT.

31. "Federally Funded Sex Education: Strengthening and Expanding Evidence-Based Programs," Guttmacher Institute Fact Sheet, June 2021, https://www.guttmacher.org/fact-sheet/sex-education.

32. Dennett interview, March 7, 2022.

33. Dennett interview.

34. Mary Ware Dennett, untitled, undated, addresses a piece by "Miss Irwin" and envisions the world in one hundred years, Sharon Spaulding / Dennett Family Archives, Alstead, NH & Sandy, UT.

35. Dennett, untitled, undated, "Miss Irwin" world in one hundred years.

36. Nancy Dennett interview, March 7, 2022.

37. Jessica L. Furgerson, *The Battle for Birth Control: Exploring the Lasting Consequences of the Movement's Early Rhetoric* (Lanham, MD: Lexington Books, 2022), 235.

38. "Birth Spacing—Report from a WHO Technical Consultation," World Health Organization Policy Brief, 2006, https://apps.who.int/iris/bitstream/handle/10665/73710/RHR_policybrief_birthspacing_eng.pdf.

39. "Publicly Supported Family Planning Services in the United States," Guttmacher Institute Fact Sheet, October 2019, https://www.guttmacher.org/fact-sheet/publicly-supported-FP-services-US.

40. Sheryl Gay Stolberg, "A Year after Dobbs, Advocates Push in the States for a Right

to Birth Control," *New York Times*, June 17, 2023, https://www.nytimes.com/2023
/06/17/us/politics/birth-control-dobbs-clarence-thomas.html.

41. Mabel Felix, Laurie Sobel, and Alina Salganicoff, "The Right to Contraception,"
    KFF, October 26, 2023, https://www.kff.org/womens-health-policy/issue-brief/the
    -right-to-contraception-state-and-federal-actions-misinformation-and-the-courts/.

42. Andis Robeznieks, "Why Stopping Scope Creep Is about Protecting Patients,"
    American Medical Association, September 7, 2022, https://www.ama-assn.org/print
    /pdf/node/91596.

43. Amy Sohn, *The Man Who Hated Women: Sex, Censorship, and Civil Liberties in the
    Gilded Age* (New York: Farrar, Straus & Giroux, 2021), 33.

44. Tessa Stuart, "Inside the MAGA Plan to Attack Birth Control, Surveil Women and
    Ban the Abortion Pill," *Rolling Stone*, December 22, 2023, https://www.rollingstone
    .com/politics/politics-features/maga-plan-attack-birth-control-surveil-women-ban
    -abortion-pill-1234934807/.

45. Stolberg, "Year after Dobbs."

46. "Don't Be Fooled: Birth Control Is Already at Risk," National Women's Law Center,
    June 17, 2022, https://nwlc.org/resource/dont-be-fooled-birth-control-is-already-at-risk/.

47. Itay Hod, "Anti-Abortion Activist Tells Shocked Joy Reid Birth Control Should Be
    Illegal (Video)," *The Wrap*, January 28, 2017, https://www.thewrap.com/anti
    -abortion-activist-tells-joy-reid-birth-control-should-be-illegal-video/.

48. Greg Satell, "What Successful Movements Have in Common," *Harvard Business
    Review*, November 30, 2016, https://hbr.org/2016/11/what-successful-movements
    -have-in-common.

49. Manon Parry, *Broadcasting Birth Control: Mass Media and Family Planning* (New
    Brunswick, NJ: Rutgers University Press, 2013), 7.

50. Daylanne K. English, *Unnatural Selections: Eugenics in American Modernism and
    the Harlem Renaissance* (Chapel Hill: University of North Carolina Press, 2004), 39.

51. Brianna Theobald, "A 1970 Law Led to the Mass Sterilization of Native American
    Women. That History Still Matters," *Time*, November 27, 2019, https://time
    .com/5737080/native-american-sterilization-history/.

52. Roberts, *Killing the Black Body*, 91.

53. Sara Luterman, "31 States Have Laws that Allow Forced Sterilization, New Report
    Shows," *The 19th*, February 4, 2022, https://19thnews.org/2022/02/forced-sterilization
    -guardianship-reproductive-justice/.

54. Roberts, *Killing the Black Body*, 151–52.

55. Roberts, 58.

56. Susan Rinkunas, "Republican Men Are Openly Questioning Our Right to Use
    Birth Control," *Jezebel*, February 23, 2022, https://jezebel.com/republicans
    -question-birth-control-supreme-court-case-1848577898.

57. Olivier Thévenon and Anne H. Gauthier, "Family Policies in Developed Countries:
    A 'Fertility Booster' with Side-Effects," *Community, Work & Family* 14, no. 2 (2011):
    https://doi.org/10.1080/13668803.2011.571400.

58. Nancy Lurkins, " 'You Are the Race, You Are the Seeded Earth': Intellectual
    Rhetoric, American Fiction, and Birth Control in the Black Community," *Historia*
    (2008): 56.

59. Jill Lepore, "The United States' Unamendable Constitution," *The New Yorker*,
    October 26, 2022, https://www.newyorker.com/culture/annals-of-inquiry/the-united
    -states-unamendable-constitution.

60. Mary Ware Dennett, "Youth in the Life of Today," undated draft, 3–4, MWD Papers.

AUTHOR'S NOTE

1. Daniel Scott Smith, "Family Limitation, Sexual Control, and Domestic Feminist in Victorian America" in *Clio's Consciousness Raised: New Perspectives on the History of Women*, ed. Mary S. Hartman and Lois Banner (New York: Octagon Books, 1976), 119.
2. Donna Drucker, *Contraception* (Cambridge, MA: MIT Press, 2020), preface.
3. Jessie M. Rodrique, "The Afro-American Community and the Birth Control Movement, 1918–1942" (PhD diss., University of Massachusetts Amherst, 1991), 11.

Bibliography

ARCHIVES

Mary Ware Dennett Papers, Schlesinger Library, Harvard Radcliffe Institute, Cambridge, MA (MWD Papers)

Margaret Sanger Papers, Sophia Smith Library, Smith College Special Collections, Northampton, MA

Margaret Sanger Papers, Library of Congress, Washington, DC (MS LOC)

Schlesinger-Rockefeller Oral History Project Interview with Grant Sanger, MD, by Ellen Chesler, August 1976

Sharon Spaulding / Dennett Family Archives, Alstead, NH & Sandy, UT

Marie Stopes Papers, British Library, London, UK

American Birth Control League Papers, Harvard Houghton Library, Cambridge, MA

Juliet Barrett Rublee Papers, Rauner Special Collections, Dartmouth College, Hanover, NH

Robert Latou Dickinson Papers, Harvard Countway Library, Boston, MA

Massachusetts Historical Society, Boston, MA

Framingham History Center, Framingham, MA

PERIODICAL COLLECTIONS

The New York Times

The Washington Post

Time

The Sun

Variety

Fortune

The Crisis

The New York Amsterdam News

The American Mercury

The Birth Control Review

The Birth Control Herald

The Birth Control News

The Woman Rebel

Library of Congress, Chronicling America: Historic American Newspapers site

The Margaret Sanger Papers Project Newsletter

The Guttmacher Institute Fact Sheets

BOOKS

Allen, Frederick Lewis. *Only Yesterday: An Informal History of the 1920s*. New York: John Wiley & Sons, 1997 reprint of 1931 Harper & Row edition.

Baker, Jean. *Margaret Sanger: A Life of Passion*. New York: Hill and Wang, 2011.

Baker, S. Josephine. *Fighting for Life*. New York: The Macmillan Company, 1939.

Beisel, Nicola Kay. *Imperiled Innocents: Anthony Comstock and Family Reproduction in Victorian America*. Princeton: Princeton University Press, 1997.

Berg, Allison. *Mothering the Race: Women's Narratives of Reproduction, 1890–1930*. Urbana: University of Illinois Press, 2001.

Besant, Annie. *Marriage, as it was, as it is, and as it should be: A Plea for Reform*. 2nd ed. London: Freethought Publishing Company, 1882.

Black, Edwin. *War Against the Weak: Eugenics and America's Campaign to Create a Master Race*. New York: Four Walls Eight Windows, 2003.

Blanchard, Mary Warner. *Oscar Wilde's America: Counterculture in the Gilded Age*. Hartford: Yale University Press, 1998.

Boyd, Mary, and Marguerite Tracy. *Painless Childbirth: A General Survey of All Painless Methods with Special Stress on "Twilight Sleep" and Its Extension to America*. New York: Frederick A. Stokes, 1915.

Boyer, Paul S. *Purity in Print: Book Censorship in America from the Gilded Age to the Computer Age*. Series: Print Culture History in Modern America. Madison: University of Wisconsin Press, 2002.

Brodie, Janet Farrell. *Contraception and Abortion in 19th-Century America*. Ithaca, NY: Cornell University Press, 1994.

Brown, Dorothy M. *Setting a Course: American Women in the 1920s*. Boston: Twayne Publishers, 1987.

Brownlow, Kevin. *Behind the Mask of Innocence: Sex, Violence, Prejudice, Crime: Films of Social Conscience in the Silent Era*. New York: Knopf, 1990.

Bruinius, Harry. *Better for All the World: The Secret History of Forced Sterilization and America's Quest for Racial Purity*. New York: Vintage, 2007.

Burns, Gene. *The Moral Veto: Framing Contraception, Abortion, and Cultural Pluralism in the United States*. Cambridge, UK: Cambridge University Press, 2005.

Capo, Beth Widmaier. *Textual Contraception: Birth Control and Modern American Fiction*. Columbus: Ohio State University Press, 2021.

Carter, Julian B. *The Heart of Whiteness: Normal Sexuality and Race in America, 1880–1940*. Durham, NC: Duke University Press, 2007.

Catte, Elizabeth. *Pure America: Eugenics and the Making of Modern Virginia*. Cleveland: Belt Publishing, 2021.

Chen, Constance. *"The Sex Side of Life": Mary Ware Dennett's Pioneering Battle for Birth Control and Sex Education*. New York: The New Press, 1996.

Chesler, Ellen. *Woman of Valor: Margaret Sanger and the Birth Control Movement in America.* New York: Simon & Schuster, 1992.

Chopin, Kate. *The Awakening.* Chicago: Herbert S. Stone & Co., 1899.

Cleghorn, Elinor. *Unwell Women: Misdiagnosis and Myth in a Man-Made World.* New York: Dutton, 2021.

Comstock, Anthony. *Frauds Exposed or How the People Are Deceived and Robbed, and Youth Corrupted.* New York: J. H. Brown, 1880.

———. *Traps for the Young.* New York: Funk & Wagnalls, 1883.

Connelly, Matthew. *Fatal Misconception: The Struggle to Control World Population.* Cambridge, MA: The Belknap Press of Harvard University Press, 2008.

Cooper, James F. *Technique of Contraception: The Principles and Practice of Anti-Conceptional Methods.* New York: Day-Nichols, 1928.

Cott, Nancy. *The Grounding of Modern Feminism.* New Haven: Yale University Press, 1987.

Craig, Layne Parish. *When Sex Changed: Birth Control Politics and Literature between the World Wars.* New Brunswick, NJ: Rutgers University Press, 2013.

Critchlow, Donald T., ed. *The Politics of Abortion and Birth Control in Historical Perspective.* University Park, PA: Pennsylvania State University Press, 1996.

Critchlow, Donald T. *Intended Consequences: Birth Control, Abortion, and the Federal Government in Modern America.* New York: Oxford University Press, 2001.

Cuddy, Lois A., and Claire M. Roche, eds. *Evolution and Eugenics in American Literature and Culture, 1880–1940.* Lewisburg, PA: Bucknell University Press, 2003.

Degler, Carl. *At Odds: Women and the Family in America from the Revolution to the Present.* New York: Oxford University Press, 1980.

Davis, Angela Y. *Women, Race & Class.* New York: Random House, 1981.

———. *Blues Legacies and Black Feminism: Gertrude "Ma" Rainey, Bessie Smith, and Billie Holiday.* New York: Pantheon Books, 1998.

De Grazia, Edward. *Girls Lean Back Everywhere: The Law of Obscenity and the Assault on Genius.* New York: Random House, 1992.

D'Emilio, John, and Estelle B. Freedman. *Intimate Matters: A History of Sexuality in America.* New York: Harper & Row, 1988.

Dennett, Mary Ware. *Birth Control Laws: Shall We Keep Them, Change Them, or Abolish Them.* New York: Frederick H. Hitchcock, 1926.

———. *Who's Obscene?* New York: The Vanguard Press, 1930.

———. *The Sex Education of Children: A Book for Parents.* New York: The Vanguard Press, 1931.

Doak, Melissa, and Kristy Horaz, eds. *Why Did Congressional Lobbying Efforts Fail to Eliminate Contraception from Obscenity Laws, 1916–1937?* Binghamton, NY: State University of New York at Binghamton, 1999.

Doak, Melissa, and Rachel Brugger, eds. *How Did the Debate Between Margaret*

Sanger and Mary Ware Dennett Shape the Movement to Legalize Birth Control,
1915–1924? Binghamton, NY: State University of New York at Binghamton, 2000.

Drucker, Donna. *Contraception: A Concise History.* Cambridge, MA: MIT Press,
2020.

Du Bois, W. E. B. *Darkwater: Voices from Within the Veil.* New York: Harcourt &
Brace, 1920.

Eastman, Max. *Love and Revolution: My Journey Through an Epoch.* New York:
Random House, 1964.

Ehrenreich, Barbara, and Deirdre English. *Witches, Midwives & Nurses,* 2nd ed.
New York: Feminist Press, 2010.

Ellis, Havelock. *Studies in the Psychology of Sex,* vols. 1 & 2. New York: Random
House, 1936.

——. *The Task of Social Hygiene.* London: Constable, 1927.

Engelman, Peter C. *A History of the Birth Control Movement in America.* Series:
Healing Society: Disease, Medicine, and History. Santa Barbara, CA: Praeger,
2011.

English, Daylanne K. *Unnatural Selections: Eugenics in American Modernism
and the Harlem Renaissance.* Chapel Hill: University of North Carolina Press,
2004.

Faderman, Lillian. *Woman: The American History of an Idea.* New Haven: Yale
University Press, 2022.

Falk, Candace. *Love, Anarchy, & Emma Goldman: A Biography.* New York: Holt,
Rinehart and Winston, 1984.

Fisher, Michelle Millar, and Amber Winick, eds. *Designing Motherhood: Things
That Make and Break Our Births.* Cambridge, MA: The MIT Press, 2021.

Flexner, Eleanor. *Century of Struggle: The Woman's Rights Movement in the
United States.* Cambridge, MA: The Belknap Press of Harvard University,
1975.

Frank, Gillian, Bethany Moreton, and Heather R. White, eds. *Devotions and
Desires: Histories of Sexuality and Religion in the Twentieth-Century United
States.* Chapel Hill: University of North Carolina Press, 2018.

Fuller, Wayne E. *Morality and the Mail in Nineteenth-Century America.* Urbana:
University of Illinois Press, 2003.

Furgerson, Jessica L. *The Battle for Birth Control: Exploring the Lasting
Consequences of the Movement's Early Rhetoric.* Lanham, MD: Lexington
Books, 2022.

Garrow, David J. *Liberty & Sexuality: The Right to Privacy and the Making of* Roe
v. Wade. New York: Macmillan, 1994.

Gary, Brett. *Dirty Works: Obscenity on Trial in America's First Sexual Revolution.*
Stanford, CA: Stanford University Press, 2021.

Gilman, Charlotte Perkins. *Women and Economics: A Study of the Economic*

Relation Between Men and Women as a Factor in Social Evolution. Boston: Small, Maynard & Co., 1898.

Goldman, Emma. *Living My Life,* vol. 2. New York: Dover, 1970.

Gordon, Linda. *The Moral Property of Women: A History of Birth Control Politics in America.* Urbana: University of Illinois Press, 2007. Paperback edition, substantially revised and updated from *Woman's Body, Woman's Right,* 1974.

Hajo, Cathy Moran. *Birth Control on Main Street: Organizing Clinics in the United States, 1916–1939.* Urbana: University of Illinois Press, 2010.

Hamlin, Kimberly A. *From Eve to Evolution: Darwin, Science, and Women's Rights in Gilded Age America.* Chicago: University of Chicago Press, 2014.

Haney, Robert W. *Comstockery in America: Patterns of Censorship and Control.* New York: Beacon Press, 1960.

Hartman, Mary S., and Lois Banner, eds. *Clio's Consciousness Raised: New Perspectives on the History of Women.* New York: Octagon Books/FSG, 1976.

Hellerstein, Erna O., ed. *Victorian Women: A Documentary Account of Women's Lives in 19th Century England, France, and the United States.* Palo Alto: Stanford University Press, 1981.

Himes, Norman E. *The Medical History of Contraception.* New York: Schocken Books, 1936.

Horowitz, Helen Lefkowitz. *Rereading Sex: Battles over Sexual Knowledge and Suppression in Nineteenth-Century America.* New York: Vintage, 2003.

Hurston, Zora Neale. *Their Eyes Were Watching God.* New York: Perennial Classics, 1999.

Johnson, John W. *Griswold v. Connecticut: Birth Control and the Constitutional Right of Privacy.* Lawrence: University Press of Kansas, 2005.

Johnson, Joan. *Funding Feminism: Monied Women, Philanthropy, and the Women's Movement, 1870–1967.* Chapel Hill: University of North Carolina Press, 2017.

Kennedy, David M. *Birth Control in America: The Career of Margaret Sanger.* New Haven: Yale University Press, 1970.

Kline, Wendy. *Building a Better Race: Gender, Sexuality, and Eugenics from the Turn of the Century to the Baby Boom.* Berkeley: University of California Press, 2005.

Knowlton, Charles. *Fruits of Philosophy: A Treatise on the Population Question.* Edited by Norman E. Himes. Mount Vernon: Peter Pauper Press, 1937.

Konikow, Antoinette. *Voluntary Motherhood: A Study of the Physiology and Hygiene of Prevention of Conception.* 1923: no copyright information printed in book. https://archive.org/details/23KonikowVoluntarymotherhood/page /n3/mode/1up (accessed June 23, 2023).

Larsen, Nella. *Quicksand and Passing.* New Brunswick, NJ: Rutgers University Press, 1986.

Latz, Leo J. *The Rhythm of Sterility and Fertility in Women*. Chicago: Latz Foundation, 1950 edition.

Leaming, Barbara. *Katharine Hepburn*. New York: Crown, 1995.

Leavitt, Judith Walzer. *Brought to Bed: Childbearing in America, 1750 to 1950*, 30th anniversary edition. New York: Oxford University Press, 1986 and 2016.

Lepore, Jill. *The Secret History of Wonder Woman*. New York: Vintage, 2015.

Levinovitz, Alan. *Natural: How Faith in Nature's Goodness Leads to Harmful Fads, Unjust Laws, and Flawed Science*. New York: Beacon Press, 2020.

Lewis, David Levering. *W. E. B. Du Bois: A Biography 1868–1963*. New York: Holt, 2009.

Lord, Alexandra M. *Condom Nation: The U.S. Government's Sex Education Campaign from World War I to the Internet*. Baltimore: Johns Hopkins University Press, 2010.

Lovett, Laura L. *Conceiving the Future: Pronatalism, Reproduction, and the Family in the United States, 1890–1938*. Chapel Hill: University of North Carolina Press, 2007.

Ludovici, Anthony M. *The Night-Hoers, or The Case Against Birth-Control and an Alternative*. London: Herbert Jenkins Ltd, 1928.

Luhan, Mabel Dodge. *Movers and Shakers*. Albuquerque: University of New Mexico Press, 1936.

MacKinnon, Janice R., and Stephen R. *Agnes Smedley: The Life and Times of an American Radical*. Berkeley: University of California Press, 1987.

MacNamara, Trent. *Birth Control and American Modernity: A History of Popular Ideas*. New York: Cambridge University Press, 2018.

Maierhofer, Waltraud, and Beth Widmaier Capo, eds. *Reproductive Rights Issues in Popular Media: International Perspectives*. Jefferson, NC: McFarland & Co., 2017.

McCann, Carole R. *Birth Control Politics in the United States, 1916–1945*. Ithaca, NY: Cornell University Press, 1994.

———, ed. *What Perspectives Did African American Advocates Bring to the Birth Control Movement and How Did Those Perspectives Shape the History of the Harlem Branch Birth Control Clinic?* Binghamton, NY: State University of New York at Binghamton, 2006.

McCarthy, Mary. *The Group*. New York: Signet, 1963.

McFarland, Gerald. *Inside Greenwich Village: A New York City Neighborhood, 1898–1918*. Amherst: University of Massachusetts Press, 2001.

McKenzie, James F., Robert R. Pinger, and Jerome E. Kotecki. *An Introduction to Community Health*, 6th ed. Sudbury, MA: Jones and Bartlett Publishers, 2007.

Melody, M. E., and Linda M. Peterson. *Teaching America about Sex: Marriage Guides and Sex Manuals from the Late Victorians to Dr. Ruth*. New York: New York University Press, 1999.

Moran, Jeffrey P. *Teaching Sex: The Shaping of Adolescence in the 20th Century.* Cambridge, MA: Harvard University Press, 2000.

Okrent, Daniel. *The Guarded Gate: Bigotry, Eugenics, and the Law That Kept Two Generations of Jews, Italians, and Other European Immigrants Out of America.* New York: Scribner, 2019.

O'Neill, William L. *Divorce in the Progressive Era.* New Haven: Yale University Press, 1967.

Owen, Robert Dale. *Moral Physiology; or a Brief and Plain Treatise on the Population Question.* London: J. Watson, 1842.

Parry, Manon. *Broadcasting Birth Control: Mass Media and Family Planning.* New Brunswick, NJ: Rutgers University Press, 2013.

Peiss, Kathy, and Christina Simmons with Robert A. Padgug, eds. *Passion and Power: Sexuality in History.* Philadelphia: Temple University Press, 1989.

Plath, Sylvia. *The Bell Jar.* New York: Harper Perennial, 2005.

Reed, James. *The Birth Control Movement and American Society: From Private Vice to Public Virtue.* Princeton, NJ: Princeton University Press, 1978.

Reverby, Susan M., and David Rosner, eds. *Health Care in America: Essays in Social History.* Philadelphia: Temple University Press, 1979.

Richardson, Angelique. *Love and Eugenics in the Late Nineteenth Century: Rational Reproduction and the New Woman.* New York: Oxford University Press, 2003.

Riddle, John M. *Eve's Herbs: A History of Contraception and Abortion in the West.* Cambridge, MA: Harvard University Press, 1997.

Roberts, Dorothy. *Killing the Black Body: Race, Reproduction, and the Meaning of Liberty.* New York: Pantheon Books, 1997.

Robinson, Victor. *Pioneers of Birth Control in England and America.* New York: Voluntary Parenthood League, 1919.

Robinson, William J. *Practical Prevenception, or The Technique of Birth Control.* Hoboken: American Biological Society, 1929.

Robinson, Paul A. *The Modernization of Sex: Havelock Ellis, Alfred Kinsey, William Masters and Virginia Johnson.* Ithaca: Cornell University Press, 1989.

Rosen, Robyn L. *Reproductive Health, Reproductive Rights: Reformers and the Politics of Maternal Welfare, 1917–1940.* Columbus: The Ohio State University Press, 2003.

Rose, June. *Marie Stopes and the Sexual Revolution.* London: Faber & Faber, 1992.

Sanger, Margaret H. *The Case for Birth Control: A Supplementary Brief and Statement of Facts.* New York: privately printed, 1917.

——. *Woman and the New Race.* New York: Brentano's, 1920.

——. *The Pivot of Civilization.* New York: Brentano's, 1922.

——. *Happiness in Marriage.* New York: Brentano's, 1926.

——. *Motherhood in Bondage*. New York: Brentano's, 1928.

——. *My Fight for Birth Control*. New York: Farrar & Rinehart, 1931.

——. *Margaret Sanger: An Autobiography*. New York: W. W. Norton & Company, 1938.

——. *The Selected Papers of Margaret Sanger*, vol. 1: *The Woman Rebel, 1900–1928*. Edited by Esther Katz, with assistant editors Cathy Moran Hajo and Peter C. Engelman. Urbana: University of Illinois Press, 2003.

——. *The Selected Papers of Margaret Sanger*, vol. 2: *Birth Control Comes of Age, 1928–1939*. Edited by Esther Katz, with assistant editors Cathy Moran Hajo and Peter C. Engelman. Urbana: University of Illinois Press, 2007.

Schoen, Johanna. *Choice and Coercion: Birth Control, Sterilization, and Abortion in Public Health and Welfare*. Chapel Hill: University of North Carolina Press, 2005.

Schwarz, Judith. *Radical Feminists of Heterodoxy: Greenwich Village 1912–1940*. Norwich, VT: New Victoria Publishers, 1986.

Scutts, Joanna. *Hotbed: Bohemian Greenwich Village and the Secret Club that Sparked Modern Feminism*. New York: Seal Press, 2022.

Sibley, Katherine A. S., ed. *A Companion to Warren G. Harding, Calvin Coolidge, and Herbert Hoover*. Hoboken, NJ: John Wiley & Sons, 2014.

Smith-Rosenberg, Carroll. *Disorderly Conduct: Visions of Gender in Victorian America*. New York: Knopf, 1985.

Sohn, Amy. *The Man Who Hated Women: Sex, Censorship, and Civil Liberties in the Gilded Age*. New York: Farrar, Straus & Giroux, 2021.

Stansell, Christine. *American Moderns: Bohemian New York and the Creation of a New Century*. Princeton: Princeton University Press, 2009.

Stern, Scott W. *The Trials of Nina McCall: Sex, Surveillance, and the Decades-Long Government Plan to Imprison "Promiscuous" Women*. New York: Beacon Press, 2018.

Stopes, Marie Carmichael. *Married Love or Love in Marriage*. New York: The Critic and Guide Company, 1918.

Tobin, Kathleen A. *The American Religious Debate Over Birth Control, 1907–1937*. Jefferson, NC: McFarland & Co., 2001.

Tone, Andrea. *Devices and Desires: A History of Contraceptives in America*. New York: Hill and Wang, 2001.

Ward, Martha C. *Poor Women, Powerful Men: America's Great Experiment in Family Planning*. Boulder, CO: Westview Press, 1986.

Welke, Barbara Young. *Law and the Borders of Belonging in the Long Nineteenth Century United States*. New York: Cambridge University Press, 2010.

Werbel, Amy B. *Lust on Trial: Censorship and the Rise of American Obscenity in the Age of Anthony Comstock*. New York: Columbia University Press, 2018.

Wheeler, Leigh Ann. *Against Obscenity: Reform and the Politics of Womanhood in America, 1873–1935*. Baltimore: Johns Hopkins University Press, 2004.

Wilson, Aimee Armande. *Conceived in Modernism: The Aesthetics and Politics of Birth Control*. New York: Bloomsbury Academic, 2016.

Wolf, Jacqueline H. *Deliver Me from Pain: Anesthesia and Birth in America*. Baltimore: Johns Hopkins University Press, 2012.

Woolf, Virginia. *Mrs. Dalloway*. New York: Harcourt, Brace & World, 1925.

——. *Orlando: A Biography*. New York: Mariner Books, 1973.

DISSERTATIONS

Hollister, Susan E. "Rare Species Identified: A Discussion of the Life and Work of Hartley Dennett." MA thesis, typescript found in Dennett Family Papers, Utah.

Ishikawa, Chiaki. "From Respectable to Pleasurable: Companionate Marriage in African American Novels, 1919–1937." PhD dissertation. Columbus: University of Ohio, 2013.

Lederer, Lynn. "'The Dynamic Side of Life'—The Emergence of Mary Coffin Ware Dennett as a Radical Sex Educator." PhD dissertation. New Brunswick, NJ: Rutgers, 2011.

Lindenbaum, Tamar. "Patient's Orders: Twilight Sleep and the Female Medical Consumer in the Turn-of-the-Century United States, 1880–1920." Senior thesis. New York: Barnard College, 2018.

Minarich, Megan Lynn. "Hollywood's Reproduction Code: Regulating Contraception and Abortion in American Cinema, 1915–1952." PhD dissertation. Nashville: Vanderbilt University, 2014.

Rodrique, Jessie. "The Afro-American Community and the Birth Control Movement, 1918–1942." PhD dissertation. Amherst: University of Massachussetts Amherst, 1991.

Sarch, Amy C. "Dirty Discourse: Birth Control Advertising in the 1920s and 1930s." PhD dissertation. Philadelphia: University of Pennsylvania, 1994.

ARTICLES, PAMPHLETS, LEGAL DOCUMENTS & POETRY

ACOG/The Board of Directors of the American College of Obstetricians and Gynecologists. "ACOG Statement on 'Personhood' Measures." The American College of Obstetricians and Gynecologists Position Statements, November 9, 2022. https://www.acog.org/clinical-information/policy-and -position-statements/position-statements/2022/acog-statement-on-personhood -measures (accessed April 30, 2024).

An Act for the Suppression of Trade in, and Circulation of, Obscene Literature and Articles of Immoral Use. US Law. Ch. 258 § 17 Stat 598 (1873). Featured in "A Century of Lawmaking for a New Nation: U.S. Congressional Documents and Debates 1774–1875." May 1, 2003. https://memory.loc.gov/cgi-bin /ampage?collId=llsl&fileName=017/llsl017.db&recNum=639 (accessed April 30, 2024).

Adams, Mildred. "Crusader." *Delineator* 123, no. 3 (September 1933): 15, 46–49.

Aizenman, Nurith. "Remember That Time When Wonder Woman Was a U.N. Ambassador?" NPR, June 1, 2017, https://www.npr.org/sections/goatsandsoda/2017 /06/01/531106299/remember-that-time-when-wonder-woman-was-a-u-n -ambassador (accessed June 30, 2023).

Alperti, Cliff. "Viña Delmar and Uptown New York (1932)—World Wide's Bad Girl." *Immortal Ephemera,* January 4, 2016. https://immortalephemera .com/64040/uptown-new-york-1932-vina-delmar/ (accessed June 29, 2023).

Andrade-Rocha, Fernando Tadeu. "On the Origins of the Semen Analysis: A Close Relationship with the History of the Reproductive Medicine." *Journal of Human Reproductive Sciences* 2018. https://www.ncbi.nlm.nih.gov/pmc /articles/PMC5799927/ (accessed June 16, 2023).

Aspinwall, Cary. "'They railroad them': The States Using 'Fetal Personhood' Laws to Criminalize Mothers." *The Guardian,* July 25, 2023. https://www .theguardian.com/world/2023/jul/25/states-using-fetal-personhood-laws-to -criminalize-mothers (accessed April 30, 2024).

Barry, Ellen. "Chloroform in Childbirth? Yes, Please, the Queen Said." *New York Times,* May 6, 2019, https://www.nytimes.com/2019/05/06/world/europe/uk -royal-births-labor.html (accessed June 23, 2023).

Berkman, Joyce. "The Question of Margaret Sanger." *History Compass* 9, no. 6 (June 2011): 474–84.

Birth Control Review Editors. "Birth Control—What It Is, How It Works, What It Will Do; Proceedings of the First American Birth Control Conference Held at the Hotel Plaza, New York, November 11, 12, 1921." *Birth Control Review.* https://babel.hathitrust.org/cgi/pt?id=hvd.hwikw8&view=1up&seq=5 (accessed April 30, 2024).

Black, Edwin. "Hitler's Debt to America." *The Guardian,* February 5, 2004. https:// www.theguardian.com/uk/2004/feb/06/race.usa (accessed June 30, 2023).

Brecht, Bertolt. "The Ballade of Paragraph 218." Museum of Contraception and Abortion. https://muvs.org/en/topics/literary-quotes/bertolt-brecht-the-ballade -of-paragraph-218-1929-en/ (accessed June 23, 2023).

Bruenig, Elizabeth. "Sex Is Serious." *Boston Review,* January 12, 2015. https:// www.bostonreview.net/articles/feminists-christians-sex-ethics-affirmative -consent-elizabeth-stoker-bruenig/ (accessed June 29, 2023).

Burge, Ryan. "Is Catholic Teaching on Birth Control Driving People from the Pews?" *National Catholic Reporter,* January 13, 2023. https://www.ncronline .org/opinion/catholic-teaching-birth-control-driving-people-pews (accessed April 30, 2024).

Capo, Beth Widmaier. "Inserting the Diaphragm In(to) Modern American Fiction: Mary McCarthy, Philip Roth, and the Literature of Contraception." *The Journal of American Culture* 26, no. 1 (March 2003): 111–23.

Craig, John M. "The Sex Side of Life: The Obscenity Case of Mary Ware Dennett." *Frontiers: A Journal of Women Studies* 15, no. 3 (1995): 145–66.

Cummins-Vaile Bill, Washington: Government Printing Office, recorded April 8 and May 9, 1924. https://babel.hathitrust.org/cgi/pt?id=umn.31951d02092034u&view=1up&seq=1 (accessed June 27, 2023).

Dawson, D. A., D. J. Meny, and J. C. Ridley. "Fertility Control in the United States Before the Contraceptive Revolution." *Family Planning Perspective* 12, no. 2 (March–April 1980): 76–86.

Degler, Carl N. "What Ought to Be and What Was." *American Historical Review* 79, no. 5 (December 1974): 1467–90.

DenHoed, Andrea. "The Forgotten Lessons of the American Eugenics Movement." *The New Yorker*, April 27, 2018. https://www.newyorker.com/books/page-turner/the-forgotten-lessons-of-the-american-eugenics-movement (accessed June 26, 2023).

Dennett, Mary Ware. "The Sex Side of Life: An Explanation for Young People," 6th printing. Privately printed in 1919. https://www.gutenberg.org/files/31732/31732-h/31732-h.htm (accessed June 16, 2023).

——. "Testimony in Favor of the Cummins-Vaile Bill." April 8, 1924. Reproduced by Speaking While Female. https://speakingwhilefemale.co/reproductive-dennett/ (accessed June 27, 2023).

DeWolf, Rebecca. "The Fight for Women's Right to Hold Public Office." Gender on the Ballot, November 2, 2021. https://www.genderontheballot.org/the-fight-for-womens-right-to-hold-public-office/ (accessed April 18, 2024).

Eastman, Max. "Is the Truth Obscene?" New York: The Free Speech League, 1915.

Engelman, Peter C. "The Rivalry Between Margaret Sanger and Mary Ware Dennett." ProQuest, undated. https://pq-static-content.proquest.com/collateral/media2/documents/casestudy-histvault-engelman.pdf (accessed April 18, 2024).

Eschner, Kat. "It Didn't Take Very Long for Anesthesia to Change Childbirth." *Smithsonian*, December 27, 2017. https://www.smithsonianmag.com/smart-news/it-didnt-take-very-long-anesthesia-change-childbirth-180967636/ (accessed June 23, 2023).

Farley, Audrey Clare. "Eugenics, Racism, and the Forced Sterilization of Heiress Ann Cooper Hewitt." *Salon*, April 20, 2021. https://www.salon.com/2021/04/20/eugenics-racism-and-the-forced-sterilization-of-heiress-ann-cooper-hewitt/ (accessed June 26, 2023).

Feldman, Ellen. "A Brief Literary History of Birth Control." *Literary Hub*, March 23, 2017. https://lithub.com/a-brief-literary-history-of-birth-control/ (accessed April 18, 2024).

Felix, Mabel, Laurie Sobel, and Alina Salganicoff. "The Right to Contraception." KFF, October 26, 2023. https://www.kff.org/womens-health-policy/issue-brief

/the-right-to-contraception-state-and-federal-actions-misinformation-and
-the-courts/#:~:text=13%20States%20Have%20Legal%20Protections,
Contraception%20as%20of%20October%202023&text=Although%20a%20
number%20of%20the,instituted%20them%20before%20June%202022
(accessed January 6, 2024).

Finkbiner, Ann. "Labor Dispute." *New York Times*, October 31, 1999. https://www
.nytimes.com/1999/10/31/books/labor-dispute.html (accessed June 23, 2023).

Flamiano, Dolores. "The Birth of a Notion: Media Coverage of Contraception,
1915–1917." *Journalism & Mass Communication Quarterly*, 75, no. 3
(September 1998), 560–71.

——. "'The Sex Side of Life' in the News: Mary Ware Dennett's Obscenity Case,
1929–1930." *Journalism History* 25, no. 2 (Summer 1999), 64–74.

Frazier, Ian. "When W. E. B. Du Bois Made a Laughingstock of a White
Supremacist." *The New Yorker*, August 19, 2019. https://www.newyorker.com
/magazine/2019/08/26/when-w-e-b-du-bois-made-a-laughingstock-of-a-white
-supremacist (accessed June 26, 2023).

Freedman, Estelle B. "Separatism as Strategy: Female Institution Building and
American Feminism, 1870–1930." *Toward a New Feminism for the Eighties* 5,
no. 3 (Autumn 1979): 512–29.

——. "Sexuality in Nineteenth-Century America: Behavior, Ideology, and
Politics." *Reviews in American History* 10, no. 4 (December 1982): 196–215.

Gandy, Imani. "How False Narratives of Margaret Sanger Are Being Used to
Shame Black Women. *Rewire*, August 20, 2015. https://rewire.news/article
/2015/08/20/false-narratives-margaret-sanger-used-shame-black-women
/ (accessed April 18, 2024).

Gjelten, Tom. "Fifty Years Ago, The Pope Called Birth Control 'Intrinsically
Wrong.'" NPR, July 3, 2018. https://www.npr.org/2018/07/03/620105604/50
-years-ago-the-pope-called-birth-control-intrinsically-wrong (accessed April 30,
2024).

Gold, Rachel Benson. "Lessons from Before Roe: Will the Past Be Prologue?"
Guttmacher Policy Review 6, no. 1 (March 2003). https://www.guttmacher.org
/gpr/2003/03/lessons-roe-will-past-be-prologue (accessed June 29, 2023).

Gordon, Linda. "The Politics of Birth Control, 1920–1949: The Impact of
Professionals." *International Journal of Health Services* 5, no. 2 (1975): 253–77.

——. "Who Is Frightened of Reproductive Freedom for Women and Why? Some
Historical Answers." *Frontiers: A Journal of Women Studies* 9, no. 1 (1986):
22–26.

Gower, Karla K., and Vanessa Murphree. " 'Making Birth Control Respectable':
The Birth Control Review, 1917–1928." *American Journalism* 30, no. 2 (2013):
210–34.

Hart, Jamie. "Who Should Have the Children? Discussions of Birth Control

Among African-American Intellectuals, 1920–1939." *The Journal of Negro History* 79, no. 1 (Winter 1994): 71–84.

"Head of American Red Cross Tells the Women to Keep Cool." *New Britain Daily Herald*, April 22, 1914, 4. https://chroniclingamerica.loc.gov/lccn/sn82014519/1914-04-22/ed-1/seq-4/ (accessed July 12, 2023).

Heck, Constance. "Pioneers Against Prudery: Mary Ware Dennett and Margaret Sanger are interviewed by Constance Heck." *Food & Health Review* 1, no. 2 (July–August 1929): 20–24.

History.com Editors. "This Day in History: Abigail Adams Urges Husband to 'Remember the Ladies.'" HISTORY/A&E Television Networks, October 22, 2009. https://www.history.com/this-day-in-history/abigail-adams-urges-husband-to-remember-the-ladies (accessed April 21, 2022).

———. "Women's Suffrage." HISTORY/A&E Television Networks, October 29, 2009. https://www.history.com/topics/womens-history/the-fight-for-womens-suffrage (accessed April 21, 2022).

Hod, Itay. "Anti-Abortion Activist Tells Shocked Joy Reid Birth Control Should Be Illegal." Yahoo, January 28, 2017. https://sg.news.yahoo.com/anti-abortion-activist-tells-shocked-joy-reid-birth-201104008.html (accessed April 29, 2024).

Hodgman, Madeline. "On the Island of Dr. Morrow." The College of Physicians of Philadelphia, December 5, 2016. http://histmed.collegeofphysicians.org/on-the-island-of-dr-morrow/ (accessed June 23, 2023).

Holmes, Frederick. "Medicine in the First World War: Venereal Disease." The University of Kansas School of Medicine, undated. https://www.kumc.edu/school-of-medicine/academics/departments/history-and-philosophy-of-medicine/archives/wwi/essays/medicine/venereal-disease.html#:~:text=That%20is%2C%20from%201917%20and,disease%2C%20thus%2C%2011%25 (accessed June 23, 2023).

Holz, Rose. "Nurse Gordon on Trial: Those Early Days of the Birth Control Clinic Movement." *Journal of Social History* 39, no. 1 (Autumn 2005): 112–40.

Hopkins, Mary Alden. "Birth Control and Public Morals: An Interview with Anthony Comstock." *Harper's Weekly*, May 22, 1915, 490.

Horowitz, Helen Lefkowitz. "Victoria Woodhull, Anthony Comstock, and Conflict over Sex in the United States in the 1870s." *The Journal of American History* 87, no. 2 (September 2000): 403–434.

The Immigration Act of 1924 (The Johnson-Reed Act). Office of the Historian, U.S. State Department. https://history.state.gov/milestones/1921-1936/immigration-act (accessed June 26, 2023).

Jabour, Anya. "Why We Should Recognize Dr. Katharine Bement Davis Alongside Dr. Alfred Kinsey as a Pioneering Sex Researcher." *Nursing Clio*, September 16, 2021. https://nursingclio.org/2021/09/16/why-we-should

-recognize-dr-katharine-bement-davis-alongside-dr-alfred-kinsey-as-a
-pioneering-sex-researcher/ (accessed April 18, 2024).

——. "Abortion Opponents Are Gunning for Contraception, Too." *Washington Post*, March 25, 2022. https://www.washingtonpost.com/outlook/2022/03/25 /abortion-opponents-are-gunning-contraception-too/ (accessed June 28, 2023).

Jensen, Joan M. "The Evolution of Margaret Sanger's 'Family Limitation' Pamphlet, 1914–1921." *Signs* 6, no. 3 (1981): 548–67.

Kaelber, Lutz. "Mississippi." Segment of presentation about eugenic sterilizations in comparative perspective at the 2012 Social Science History Association. https://www.uvm.edu/~lkaelber/eugenics/MS/MS.html#:~:text=Mississippi %20was%20the%20twenty%2Dsixth%20state%20to%20pass%20a%20 sterilization%20law.&text=In%20the%20sterilization%20law%20that,91 (accessed April 30, 2024).

Kelly, Amita. "Fact Check: Was Planned Parenthood Started to 'Control' the Black Population?" NPR, August 14, 2015. https://www.npr.org/sections /itsallpolitics/2015/08/14/432080520/fact-check-was-planned-parenthood -started-to-control-the-black-population (accessed May 1, 2024).

Kirchwey, Freda. "Alice Paul Pulls the Strings." *The Nation*, March 2, 1921, 332–33.

Klein, Christopher. "The Strike that Shook America." History.com, September 3, 2012; updated November 26, 2019. https://www.history.com/news/the-strike -that-shook-america (accessed June 21, 2023).

Krogh, D. M. Ferd. "Physiology and Hygiene." *Mind and Body* 20 (March 1913– February 1914): 248.

Laskow, Sarah. "In 1914, Feminists Fought for the Right to Forget Childbirth." *Atlas Obscura*, February 23, 2017. https://www.atlasobscura.com/articles /twilight-sleep-childbirth-1910s-feminists (accessed June 23, 2023).

Leavitt, Judith Walzer. "Birthing and Anesthesia: The Debate Over Twilight Sleep." *Signs* 6. no. 1 (Autumn 1980): 147–64.

Lepore, Jill. "Fixed." *The New Yorker*, March 22, 2010. https://www.newyorker .com/magazine/2010/03/29/fixed (accessed June 20, 2023).

——. "Birthright." *The New Yorker*, November 6, 2011. https://www.newyorker .com/magazine/2011/11/14/birthright-jill-lepore (accessed June 23, 2023).

——. "The United States' Unamendable Constitution." *The New Yorker*, October 26, 2022. https://www.newyorker.com/culture/annals-of-inquiry/the -united-states-unamendable-constitution (accessed June 30, 2023).

Letterie, Gerard, and Dov Fox. "The Irony of Pro-Life Efforts to Grant Embryos Legal Personhood." Bill of Health, the blog of the Petrie-Flom Center at Harvard Law School, May 15, 2023. https://blog.petrieflom.law .harvard.edu/2023/05/15/the-irony-of-pro-life-efforts-to-grant-embryos-legal -personhood/ (accessed April 30, 2024).

Lindsey, Treva B. "What Did the Suffragists Really Think About Abortion?"

Smithsonian, May 26, 2022. https://www.smithsonianmag.com/history/what
-did-the-suffragists-really-think-about-abortion-180980124/ (accessed June 23,
2023).

Lord, A. M. "Models of Masculinity: Sex Education, the United States Public
Health Service, and the YMCA, 1919–1924)." *Journal of the History of
Medicine and Allied Sciences* 58, no. 2 (April 2003): 123–52.

Luker, Kristin. "Sex, Social Hygiene, and the State: The Double-Edged Sword of
Social Reform." *Theory and Society* 27, no. 5 (October 1998): 601–634.

Lurkins, Nancy. "'You are the Race, You are the Seeded Earth': Intellectual
Rhetoric, American Fiction, and Birth Control in the Black Community."
Historia (2008): 47–64.

Luterman, Sara. "31 States Have Laws that Allow Forced Sterilization, New
Report Shows." *19th*, February 4, 2022. https://19thnews.org/2022/02/forced
-sterilization-guardianship-reproductive-justice/ (accessed June 30, 2023).

McDonnell, Eleanor Kinsella. "Keeping the Stork in his Place." *Pictorial
Review* (Midwinter 1919). https://prod-cdn.atria.nl/wp-content/uploads
/2018/09/14103242/keeping-the-stork-in-his-place-eleanor-kinsella
-mcdonnell.pdf (accessed June 23, 2023).

McGarry, Molly. "Spectral Sexualities: Nineteenth-Century Spiritualism, Moral
Panics, and the Making of U.S. Obscenity Law." *Journal of Women's History*
12:2 (Summer 2000): 8–29.

McNearney, Allison. "How Mae West's Play 'Sex' Scandalized Broadway—
and Landed Her in Jail." *The Daily Beast*, October 15, 2021. https://www
.thedailybeast.com/how-mae-wests-play-sex-scandalized-broadwayand-landed
-her-in-jail (accessed June 28, 2023).

Millard, Ruth. "Birth Control Fight Opened by Margaret Sanger in 1914." *New
York World-Telegram*, March 28, 1931, 14.

Miller, Arthur. "Before Air-Conditioning." *The New Yorker*, June 14, 1998. https://
www.newyorker.com/magazine/1998/06/22/before-air-conditioning (accessed
June 26, 2023)

Mohan, Megha. "Kitty Marion: The Actress Who Became a 'Terrorist.'" BBC,
May 26, 2018. https://www.bbc.com/news/stories-44210012 (accessed May 1,
2024).

Moseley, George B., III. "The U.S. Health Care Non-System, 1908–2008." *AMA
Journal of Ethics* (May 2008). https://journalofethics.ama-assn.org/article/us
-health-care-non-system-1908-2008/2008-05 (accessed June 16, 2023).

Murphree, Vanessa, and Karla K. Gower. "Mission Accomplished: Margaret
Sanger and the National Committee on Federal Legislation for Birth Control,
1929–1937." *American Journalism* 25, no. 2 (2008): 7–32.

National Women's Law Center. "Don't Be Fooled: Birth Control Is Already at
Risk." National Women's Law Center resources, June 17, 2022. https://nwlc

.org/resource/dont-be-fooled-birth-control-is-already-at-risk/ (accessed April 29, 2024).

Nichols, Dudley. "Sex and the Law." *The Nation*, May 8, 1929, 552–54.

Norton, Mary Beth. "The Constitutional Status of Women in 1787." *Minnesota Journal of Law & Inequality* 6, no. 1 (June 1988). https://scholarship.law.umn.edu/cgi/viewcontent.cgi?article=1558&context=lawineq (accessed April 21, 2022).

O'Neill, William L. "Divorce in the Progressive Era." *American Quarterly* 17, no. 2 (Summer, 1965): 203–217.

Orwell, George. "St. Andrew's Day, 1935." The Orwell Foundation. https://www.orwellfoundation.com/the-orwell-foundation/orwell/poetry/st-andrews-day-1935/ (accessed June 30, 2023).

Pavard, Bibia. "The Right to Know? The Politics of Information about Contraception in France (1950s–80s)." *Medical History* 63, no. 2 (April 2019): 173–88.

Platoni, Kara. "The Sex Scholar." *Stanford Magazine* (March/April 2010). https://stanfordmag.org/contents/the-sex-scholar (accessed April 21, 2022).

Pollitt, Katha. "Abortion in American History." *The Atlantic* (May 1997). https://www.theatlantic.com/magazine/archive/1997/05/abortion-in-american-history/376851/ (accessed April 21, 2022).

Pringle, Henry. "What Do the Women of America Think? Birth Control." *Ladies' Home Journal* (March 1938), 114.

Ray, J. M., and F. G. Gosling. "American Physicians and Birth Control, 1936–1947." *Journal of Social History* 18, no. 3 (1985): 399–411.

Reynolds, Michele. "Abortion Is Killing the Black Community." On the Record, News from the Ohio Senate, October 18, 2023. https://ohiosenate.gov/news/on-the-record/abortion-is-killing-the-black-community (accessed April 30, 2024).

Rinkunas, Susan. "Republican Men Are Openly Questioning Our Right to Use Birth Control." *Jezebel,* February 23, 2022. https://jezebel.com/republicans-question-birth-control-supreme-court-case-1848577898 (accessed April 21, 2022).

Robeznieks, Andis. "Why Stopping Scope Creep Is About Protecting Patients." *American Medical Association*, September 7, 2022. https://www.ama-assn.org/print/pdf/node/91596 (accessed June 30, 2023).

Robinson, Victor. "A Rational Sex Primer." *Medical Review of Reviews* 24 (1918): 65–68.

Romm, Cari. "Before There Were Home Pregnancy Tests." *The Atlantic*, June 17, 2015. theatlantic.com/health/archive/2015/06/history-home-pregnancy-test/396077/ (accessed June 20, 2023).

Rooney, Kathleen. "Alice Duer Miller's Evergreen Question in 'Are Women

People?'" *Los Angeles Review of Books*, August 17, 2020. https://lareviewofbooks
.org/article/alice-duer-millers-evergreen-question-in-are-women-people
/ (accessed April 22, 2022).

Roosevelt, Theodore. "Remarks Before the Mothers' Congress, March 13, 1905."
The American Presidency Project, UC Santa Barbara. https://www.presidency
.ucsb.edu/documents/remarks-before-the-mothers-congress (accessed June 23,
2023).

Rorty, James. "What's Stopping Birth Control?" *New Republic*, February 3, 1932,
313–14.

Rosen, Robyn L. "Federal Expansion, Fertility Control, and Physicians in the
United States: The Politics of Maternal Welfare in the Interwar Years." *Journal
of Women's History* 10, no. 3 (Autumn 1998): 53–73.

Salidsbury, J. H. "The Twilight Sleep in Obstetrics." *JAMA*, October 17, 1914.
https://jamanetwork.com/journals/jama/article-abstract/437619 (accessed
June 23, 2023).

Sanger, Alexander. "Eugenics, Race, and Margaret Sanger Revisited." *Hypatia* 22,
no. 2 (2007): 210–17.

Sanger, Margaret. *Family Limitation*, 6th ed. Privately published, 1917.

Satell, Greg. "What Successful Movements Have in Common." *Harvard Business
Review*, November 30, 2016. https://hbr.org/2016/11/what-successful-movements
-have-in-common (accessed April 30, 2024).

Saydschoev, Safar. "History of Medicine Book of the Week: *Tokology* (1883)."
Indiana University School of Medicine, June 5, 2020. https://medicine
.iu.edu/blogs/medical-library/history-of-medicine-book-of-the-week–tokology
(accessed April 21, 2022).

Schuessler, Jennifer. "The Fight Over Abortion History." *New York Times*, May 4,
2022. https://www.nytimes.com/2022/05/04/arts/roe-v-wade-abortion-history
.html?referringSource=articleShare (accessed June 16, 2023).

Shah, Iqbal, and Annie Portela. "Birth Spacing—Report from a WHO Technical
Consultation." WHO Policy Brief based on birth spacing consultation held
June 13–15, 2005. https://apps.who.int/iris/bitstream/handle/10665/73710
/RHR_policybrief_birthspacing_eng.pdf (accessed June 30, 2023).

Shah, Neel. "I'm an OB/GYN who attended thousands of deliveries before
wondering why Americans give birth in bed." *The Conversation*, January 8,
2020. https://theconversation.com/im-an-ob-gyn-who-attended-thousands
-of-deliveries-before-wondering-why-americans-give-birth-in-bed-127894
(accessed June 23, 2023).

Shorto, Russell. "Contra-Contraception." *New York Times Magazine*, May 7,
2006. https://www.nytimes.com/2006/05/07/magazine/07contraception.html
(accessed April 20, 2024).

Silberman, Marsha. "The Perfect Storm: Late Nineteenth-Century Chicago Sex

Radicals: Moses Harman, Ida Craddock, Alice Stockham and the Comstock Obscenity Laws." *Journal of the Illinois State Historical Society* 102, nos. 3–4 (Fall–Winter, 2009): 324–67.

Skowronski, G. A. "Pain Relief in Childbirth: Changing Historical and Feminist Perspectives." *Anaesth Intensive Care* (July 2015). https://journals.sagepub .com/doi/pdf/10.1177/0310057X150430S106 (accessed June 23, 2023)

Smith, Helena Huntington. "They Were Eleven." *The New Yorker*, June 28, 1930. https://www.newyorker.com/magazine/1930/07/05/they-were-eleven (accessed June 28, 2023).

Souter, Vivienne, Elizabeth Nethery, Mary Lou Kopas, Hannah Wurz, Kristin Sitcov, and Aaron B. Caughey. "Comparison of Midwifery and Obstetric Care in Low-Risk Hospital Births." *Obstetrics & Gynecology* 134, no. 5 (November 2019): 1056–65.

Steinem, Gloria. "Margaret Sanger." *Time*, international ed., 51, no. 14 (April 13, 1998). https://content.time.com/time/subscriber/article/0,33009,988152,00 .html (accessed April 20, 2024).

Stenham, Polly. "Brutal! Vulgar! Dirty! Mae West and the Gay Comedy that Shocked 1920s America." *The Guardian*, July 5, 2017. https://www .theguardian.com/stage/2017/jul/05/polly-stenham-mae-west-gay-pride-the -drag-national-theatre (accessed June 28, 2023).

Stolberg, Sheryl Gay. "A Year After Dobbs, Advocates Push in the States for a Right to Birth Control." *New York Times*, June 17, 2023. https://www .nytimes.com/2023/06/17/us/politics/birth-control-dobbs-clarence-thomas .html?searchResultPosition=2 (accessed June 21, 2023).

Stone, Hannah. "The BC Raid." *Eugenics*, August 1929, 24.

Strong, Bryan. "Ideas of the Early Sex Education Movement in America, 1890–1920." *History of Education Quarterly* 12, no. 2 (Summer 1972): 136.

Stuart, Tessa. "Inside the MAGA Plan to Attack Birth Control, Surveil Women and Ban the Abortion Pill." *Rolling Stone*, December 22, 2023. https://www .rollingstone.com/politics/politics-features/maga-plan-attack-birth-control -surveil-women-ban-abortion-pill-1234934807/ (accessed April 29, 2024).

Szreter, Simon, and Kate Fisher. "'We Weren't the Sort that Wanted Intimacy Every Night': Birth Control and Abstinence in England, c. 1931–60." *History of the Family* 15, no. 2 (June 2010): 139–60.

Talbot, Margaret. "The Pill's Difficult Birth." *The New Yorker*, November 11, 2014. https://www.newyorker.com/culture/cultural-comment/pills-difficult -birth (accessed April 21, 2022).

Tatum, Polly A., ed. "Divorce History: How the Divorce Process Changed for the Better." The Law Office of Polly A. Tatum: Mediation Advantage, August 8, 2019. https://www.lawofficeofpollytatum.com/blog/divorce-history-how-the -divorce-process-changed-for-the-better/ (accessed April 22, 2022).

Theobald, Brianna. "A 1970 Law Led to the Mass Sterilization of Native American Women. That History Still Matters." *Time*, November 27, 2019. https://time .com/5737080/native-american-sterilization-history/ (accessed June 30, 2023).

Theroux, Rosemary, and Joellen W. Hawkins. "If Margaret Sanger Could See Us Now." *Journal of Obstetric, Gynecologic, and Neonatal Nursing* 37, no. 3 (May–June 2008): 353.

Thévenon, Olivier, and Anne H. Gauthier. "Family Policies in Developed Countries: a 'Fertility Booster' with Side-Effects." *Community, Work & Family* 14, no. 2 (2011): 197–216.

Thompson, Lauren MacIvor. "The Politics of Female Pain: Women's Citizenship, Twilight Sleep, and the Early Birth Control Movement." *Medical Humanities* 45 (2019): 67–74.

Tone, Andrea. "Black Market Birth Control: Contraceptive Entrepreneurship and Criminality in the Gilded Age." *Journal of American History* 87, no. 2 (September 2000): 435–59.

——. "Making Room for Rubbers: Gender, Technology, and Birth Control Before the Pill." *History and Technology* 18, no. 1 (2002): 51–76.

Tushnet, Eve. "'An Image of God': The Catholic Struggle Against Eugenics and Its Lessons for Today." *Patheos*, November 30, 2019. https://www.patheos .com/blogs/evetushnet/2019/11/an-image-of-god-the-catholic-struggle-against -eugenics-and-its-lessons-for-today.html (accessed June 26, 2023).

United States Second Circuit Court of Appeals. United States v. Dennett (1930). https://scholar.google.com/scholar_case?q=United+States+v.+Dennett,+39 +N.Y.+F+2d.+564+(1930).&hl=en&as_sdt=806&case=13482364592557808 136&scilh=0 (accessed May 1, 2024).

United States District Court. Extract from the Judgment United States District Court Southern District of New York, John Woolsey, U.S. District Judge, Libelant, versus One Obscene Book Entitled *Married Love* (1931). https://law.justia.com /cases/federal/district-courts/F2/48/821/1569043/ (accessed June 29, 2023).

Van De Walle, Etienne, and Virginie de Luca. "Birth Prevention in the American and French Fertility Transitions: Contrasts in Knowledge and Practice." *Population & Development Review* 32, no. 3 (September 2006): 529–55.

Walters, Lynne Masel. "Birth Control as Obscenity: Margaret Sanger and 'The Woman Rebel.'" Paper Presented at the Annual Meeting of The Association for Education in Journalism, August 1978.

Watkins, Claire Vaye. "The Classic Novel That Saw Pleasure as a Path to Freedom," *New York Times*, February 5, 2020. https://www.nytimes.com/2020/02/05 /books/review/kate-chopin-the-awakening.html (accessed April 22, 2022).

Weinrib, Laura. "The Sex Side of Civil Liberties: United States v. Dennett and the Changing Face of Free Speech." *Law and History Review* 30, no. 2 (May 2012), University of Chicago Public Law Working Paper No. 385.

Wharton, Don. "Birth Control: The Case for the State." *The Atlantic* (October 1939). https://www.theatlantic.com/magazine/archive/1939/10/birth-control-the-case-for-the-state/308924/ (accessed June 30, 2023).

Wheeler, Leigh Ann. "Rescuing Sex from Prudery and Prurience: American Women's Use of Sex Education as an Antidote to Obscenity, 1925–1932." *Journal of Women's History* 12, no. 3 (Autumn 2000): 173–95.

Wilson, Blake. "Art as Protest: Angelina Weld Grimke's *Rachel.*" *Boundary Stones* (WETA), April 2, 2019. https://boundarystones.weta.org/2019/04/02/art-protest-angelina-weld-grimk%C3%A9s-rachel (accessed June 29, 2023).

Wilson, Aimee Armande. "Modernism, Monsters, and Margaret Sanger." MFS: Modern Fiction Studies 59, no. 2 (2013): 440–60.

Wilson, Philip K. "Confronting 'Hereditary' Disease: Eugenic Attempts to Eliminate Tuberculosis in Progressive Era America." *Journal of Medical Humanities* 27 (2006): 19–37.

Winny, Annalies, and Rachel Bervell. "How Can We Solve the Black Maternal Health Crisis?" Johns Hopkins Bloomberg School of Public Health, May 12, 2023. https://publichealth.jhu.edu/2023/solving-the-black-maternal-health-crisis#:~:text=Black%20birthing%20people%20are%20also,birth%20and%20low%20birth%20weight (accessed April 30, 2024).

Wypijewski, JoAnn. "Reproductive Rights and the Long Hand of Slave Breeding." *The Nation*, March 21, 2012. https://www.thenation.com/article/archive/reproductive-rights-and-long-hand-slave-breeding/ (accessed April 29, 2024).

Younge, Gary. "The View from Middletown: A Typical US City that Never Did Exist." *The Guardian*, October 11, 2016. https://www.theguardian.com/membership/2016/oct/18/view-from-middletown-us-muncie-america (accessed June 29, 2023).

RADIO, FILM & DIGITAL COLLECTIONS

"Berenice Abbott." MoMa profile. https://www.moma.org/artists/41 (accessed June 28, 2023).

Abrash, Barbara, Esther Katz, Terese Svoboda, and Steve Bull. *Margaret Sanger: A Public Nuisance.* New York: Women Make Movies, 1992.

Coe, Tyler Mahan. "The Pill: Why Was Loretta Lynn Banned?" *Cocaine & Rhinestones*, October 31, 2017. https://cocaineandrhinestones.com/loretta-lynn-pill-ban (accessed May 1, 2024).

Designing Motherhood: Things That Make and Break Our Births. The MassArt Art Museum: June 11–December 18, 2022.

"History of Birth Control." Online exhibit: Case Western Reserve College of Arts and Sciences, Dittrick Medical History Center. https://artsci.case.edu/dittrick/online-exhibits/history-of-birth-control/, accessed June 20, 2023.

Joyce, James. The James Joyce Digital Archive. Edited by Danis Rose and John O'Hanlon. Produced 2018. https://jjda.ie/ (accessed May 1, 2024).

"Letter against the Comstock Act." Committee on Post Office and Post Roads Petitions and Memorials, 1808–1942. History, Art & Archives of the U.S. House of Representatives. https://history.house.gov/Records-and-Research /Listing/c_019/ (accessed June 20, 2023).

No More Children (1929) film booklet. Cliff Broughton Productions. https:// archive.org/details/NoMoreChildren1929FilmBooklet/page/n31/mode/2up (accessed July 5, 2023).

"New York City: The Harlem Renaissance and Beyond." Smithsonian American Art Museum. https://americanexperience.si.edu/wp-content/uploads/2014/07 /New-York-City_The-Harlem-Renaissance-and-Beyond.pdf (accessed June 30, 2023).

"The New York Foundling Hospital." National Orphan Train Complex, Concordia, KS. https://orphantraindepot.org/history/the-new-york-foundling-hospital/ (accessed April 30, 2024).

"Outcome for the Socialist Party." Part of the online exhibition 1912: Competing Visions for America, Ohio State University. https://ehistory.osu.edu /exhibitions/1912/content/debs_outcome (accessed April 22, 2022).

Paskin, Willa, and Katie Shepherd. "The 'Sex' Scandal that Made Mae West." Decoder Ring (Slate), August 16, 2022. https://slate.com/podcasts/decoder -ring/2022/08/the-sex-scandals-of-mae-west (accessed June 28, 2023).

"Suffrage Parade in New York City, ca. 1912." Record of the Office of War Information, National Archives at College Park, College Park, MD. https:// www.docsteach.org/documents/document/suffragette-parade-nyc (accessed April 30, 2024).

"The Two 1912 New York Suffrage Parades," Suffragette City 100. https:// suffragettecity100.com/57 (accessed December 18, 23).

"William Morris and His Legacy." National Portrait Gallery, for the exhibition Anarchy & Beauty: William Morris and His Legacy, 1860–1960, 2014–2015. https://www.npg.org.uk/whatson/anarchy-beauty-william-morris-and-his -legacy-1860-1960/home/explore (accessed April 21, 2022).

Index